A New Star-Rating System & Other Exciting News from Frommer's!

In our continuing effort to publish the savviest, most up-to-date, and most appealing travel guides available, we've added some great new features.

Frommer's guides now include a new **star-rating system.** Every hotel, restaurant, and attraction is rated from 0 to 3 stars to help you set priorities and organize your time.

We've also added **seven brand-new features** that point you to the great deals, in-the-know advice, and unique experiences that separate travelers from tourists. Throughout the guide, look for:

Finds   Special finds—those places only insiders know about

Fun Fact   Fun facts—details that make travelers more informed and their trips more fun

Kids   Best bets for kids—advice for the whole family

Moments Special moments—those experiences that memories are made of

Overrated Places or experiences not worth your time or money

Tips   Insider tips—some great ways to save time and money

Value   Great values—where to get the best deals

We've also added a **"What's New"** section in every guide—a timely crash course in what's hot and what's not in every destination we cover.

Here's what the critics say about Frommer's:

"Amazingly easy to use. Very portable, very complete."

—Booklist

"Detailed, accurate, and easy-to-read information for all price ranges."
—Glamour Magazine

"Hotel information is close to encyclopedic."

—Des Moines Sunday Register

"Frommer's Guides have a way of giving you a real feel for a place."
—Knight Ridder Newspapers

Other Great Guides for Your Trip:

Frommer's Washington State
Seattle & Portland For Dummies
Frommer's Vancouver & Victoria

Seattle

2003

by Karl Samson

with Jane Aukshunas

Wiley Publishing, Inc.

About the Authors

Karl Samson and **Jane Aukshunas,** a husband-and-wife travel-writing team, make their home in the Northwest. Together they also cover the rest of Washington for Frommer's. In addition, Karl is the author of *Frommer's Arizona.*

Published by:

Wiley Publishing, Inc.

909 Third Ave.
New York, NY 10022

ISBN 0-7645-6736-5
ISSN 1045-9308

Editor: Alexis Lipsitz Flippin
Production Editor: Donna Wright
Cartographer: Elizabeth Puhl
Photo Editor: Richard Fox
Production by Wiley Indianapolis Composition Services

Front cover photo: Man holding geoducks in Pike Place Market.
Back cover photo: Seattle skyline, with Mount Rainier in the distance.

For information on our other products and services or to obtain technical support, please contact our Customer Care Department within the U.S. at 800-762-2974, outside the U.S. at 317-572-3993 or fax 317-572-4002.

Wiley also publishes its books in a variety of electronic formats. Some content that appears in print may not be available in electronic formats.

Manufactured in the United States of America

5   4   3   2   1

Contents

6   Where to Dine in Seattle   76

7   Exploring Seattle   109

8   Strolling Around Seattle   142

9   Seattle Shopping   154

10   Seattle After Dark   167

List of Maps

An Invitation to the Reader

In researching this book, we discovered many wonderful places—hotels, restaurants, shops, and more. We're sure you'll find others. Please tell us about them, so we can share the information with your fellow travelers in upcoming editions. If you were disappointed with a recommendation, we'd love to know that, too. Please write to:

Frommer's Seattle 2003
Wiley Publishing, Inc. • 909 Third Ave. • New York, NY 10022

An Additional Note

Please be advised that travel information is subject to change at any time—and this is especially true of prices. We therefore suggest that you write or call ahead for confirmation when making your travel plans. The authors, editors, and publisher cannot be held responsible for the experiences of readers while traveling. Your safety is important to us, however, so we encourage you to stay alert and be aware of your surroundings. Keep a close eye on cameras, purses, and wallets, all favorite targets of thieves and pickpockets.

New! Frommer's Star Ratings & Icons

Every hotel, restaurant, and attraction listing in this guide has been ranked for quality, value, service, amenities, and special features using a star-rating scale. In country, state, and regional guides, we also rate towns and regions to help you narrow down your choices and budget your time accordingly. Hotels and restaurants in the Very Expensive and Expensive categories are rated on a scale of one (highly recommended) to three stars (exceptional). Those in the Moderate and Inexpensive categories rate from zero (recommended) to two stars (very highly recommended). Attractions, towns, and regions are rated according to the following scale: zero stars (recommended), one star (highly recommended), two stars (very highly recommended), and three stars (must-see).

In addition to the rating system, we also use seven icons to highlight insider information, useful tips, special bargains, hidden gems, memorable experiences, kid-friendly venues, places to avoid, and other useful information:

Finds   *Fun Fact*   *Kids*   *Moments*   *Overrated*   *Tips*   *Value*

The following abbreviations are used for credit cards:

AE	American Express	DISC	Discover	V	Visa
DC	Diners Club	MC	MasterCard		

FROMMERS.COM

Now that you have the guidebook to a great trip, visit our website at **www.frommers.com** for travel information on nearly 2,500 destinations. With features updated regularly, we give you instant access to the most current trip-planning information available. At Frommers.com, you'll also find the best prices on airfares, accommodations, and car rentals—and you can even book travel online through our travel booking partners. At Frommers.com, you'll also find the following:

- Online updates to our most popular guidebooks
- Vacation sweepstakes and contest giveaways
- Newsletter highlighting the hottest travel trends
- Online travel message boards with featured travel discussions

What's New in Seattle

The only thing constant in the world of travel is change, and Seattle is no exception. Although the slowing of the economy in 2002 temporarily put a halt to the boom times in Seattle, the city continues to be a vibrant vacation destination. Highlighted below are some of the most significant new developments in the city this past year.

ORIENTATION   If you're flying in to **Sea-Tac International Airport** (www.seatac.org/seatac), be prepared for a total mess. The central terminal is in the midst of a major expansion that won't be completed until 2004, Concourse A is closed for a remodel (but is scheduled to reopen sometime in 2003), and one of the loops on the airport's Satellite Transit System (in-airport trains between the main terminal and the north and south satellite terminals) will likely be closed for remodeling during your visit. In other words, leave lots of time for getting around the airport. Of course, you were already planning on extra time in the airport due to new security measures, right? Oh, yes, and if you're looking for a shuttle van or taxi, be sure to head to the third floor of the parking garage. If you're looking for a Metro bus, you'll find them outside the baggage claim area.

ACCOMMODATIONS   The rooms in the **Sorrento Hotel,** 900 Madison St. (© 800/426-1265 or 206/622-6400; www.hotelsorrento. com), one of Seattle's oldest luxury hotels, have undergone a total makeover that has once again made it one of the finest accommodations in the city. The **Sheraton Seattle Hotel and Towers,** 1400 Sixth Ave. (© 800/325-3535; www.sheraton.com/seattle), has also been undergoing an extensive room remodeling that, among other things, has added Dale Chihuly prints to all of the guest rooms.

Looking for a new, economically priced, well-located hotel? Try the **Holiday Inn Downtown Seattle,** 211 Dexter Ave. N. (© 800/465-4329 or 206/728-8123; www.holiday-inn.com/seattlewa), near the Space Needle. This place even has its own restaurant and espresso cart. On the other side of the Space Needle from the Holiday Inn, in the Lower Queen Anne neighborhood, you'll find the **Mediterranean Inn,** 425 Queen Anne Ave. N. (© 866/425-4700 or 206/428-4700; www.mediterranean-inn.com), a new apartment hotel designed for longer stays but still a good choice if you are only in town for a few nights.

In the University District, style-conscious travelers will want to book a room at the new **Watertown,** 4242 Roosevelt Way NE (© 866/944-4242 or 206/826-4242; www.watertown seattle.com), an economical hotel with loads of contemporary styling.

DINING   It's been a tough year for high-end restaurants in Seattle. Two venerable hotel restaurants—**Fuller's** and **The Painted Table**—that had long been reliable stalwarts of the Seattle restaurant scene bit the dust. Several other high-end restaurants had to rethink their pricing in order to stay afloat as the big spenders of the '90s started keeping closer tabs on their credit cards. Some of our favorite upscale restaurants that have wallet-friendly prix-fixe menus include **Cascadia, Campagne, Café Campagne, Chez Shea,** and **Kaspar's.**

We've added lots of new and newly discovered restaurants to this edition of *Frommer's Seattle.* If you're looking for a hot new restaurant in town, try **Restaurant Zoë,** 2137 Second Ave. (© **206/256-2060**), a Belltown spot serving contemporary American cuisine. Other great Belltown restaurants for foodies include **Cascadia,** 2328 First Ave. (© **206/448-8884;** www.cascadiarestaurant.com); and **Brasa,** 2107 Third Ave. (© **206/728-4220;** www.brasa.com). We suspect it's because of all the rain and gray skies, but for whatever reason, Seattle is obsessed with the cuisines of sunnier climes.

For south-of-the-border fare, check out some of the following Mexican restaurants that we've added to this edition. **El Puerco Lloron,** 1501 Western Ave. (© **206/624-0541**), in Pike Place Market, may not be fancy, but the food sure is great and the prices can't be beat. At **El Camino,** 607 N. 35th St. (© **206/632-7303**), in the Fremont neighborhood, you can get not only superb contemporary Mexican food but great margaritas, too. Over in the University District, check out **Agua Verde Café,** 1303 NE Boat St. (© **206/545-8570**), where the tasty tacos are made with nontraditional ingredients. This inexpensive waterfront restaurant also rents sea kayaks.

If you're into grazing, be sure to check out the **House of Hong,** 409 Eighth Ave. (© **206/622-7997;** www.houseofhong.com), an International District restaurant that serves the best dim sum in Seattle. For a very different sort of grazing, head to **Tango Tapas Restaurant & Lounge,** 1100

Pike St. (© **206/583-0382;** www.bandoleone.net), where you can get delicious little dishes from throughout the Latin world.

SIGHTSEEING The **Seattle Aquarium,** which is still planning for a big new facility in the next few years, has added an interesting new exhibit called "Life on the Edge," which focuses on the tide pools of Washington's Pacific coast and Puget Sound regions.

At Pike Place Market, be sure to search out the new **giant squid sculpture.** This life-size copper sculpture hangs from the ceiling of the atrium in the Pike Place Market Economy building. To find this space, turn left at Rachel the brass pig and continue up the hallway away from the crowds by the flying fish.

On the waterfront, the word is out: The Russians are coming, the Russians are coming! That's right, the *Russian Cobra,* Pier 48, 101 Alaskan Way (© **206/223-1767**), a Russian submarine, is now docked just south of the Washington State Ferries Colman Dock ferry terminal.

Even if you've never eaten *lutefisk* and don't have a clue what *lefse* is, you should check out the **Nordic Heritage Museum,** 3014 NW 67th St. (© **206/789-5707;** www.nordicmuseum.com), in Seattle's Ballard neighborhood, which was settled by Scandinavians. This small museum has been mounting fascinating art exhibits of late.

Gardeners won't want to miss **Kubota Garden,** Renton Avenue S. and 55th Avenue S. (© **206/725-5060**), a large Japanese garden in south Seattle. This garden was one man's life's work and is now a city park.

For all you fans of Dale Chihuly and art glass in general, Tacoma's new **Museum of Glass,** 1801 Dock St. (© **253/396-1768;** www.museumof glass.org), opened in July 2002. Although Tacoma isn't usually thought of as a major tourist destination, this museum, which is dedicated exclusively to art glass, is changing the way the public thinks about Seattle's ugly stepsister.

If dolls are your passion, be sure to take a drive to Bellevue, across Lake Washington from Seattle, to visit the **Rosalie Whyel Museum of Doll Art,** 1116 108th Ave. NE (© **425/455-1116;** www.dollart.com).

Seattle may not be London, but it does have double-decker buses. Two different companies—**Gray Line of Seattle** (© **800/426-7532** or 206/626-5208; www.graylineofseattle.com) and **Double Decker Tours of Seattle** (© **800/403-0024**)—now offer tours of the city in double-decker buses, some of which have open-air upper decks. Don't worry; if it starts to rain, you can always duck downstairs to the lower deck.

By the time you read this, the **Seattle Seahawks** (© **888/NFL-HAWK** or 206/682-2800; www.seahawks.com) football team should be happily ensconced in the new Seahawks Stadium adjacent to Safeco Field. The roof of this behemoth doesn't roll back, but, then, who ever heard of calling off a football game on account of rain?

NIGHTLIFE Opera fans, take note. The **Seattle Opera,** world renowned for its stagings of Wagner's *The Ring of the Nibelungen,* is not performing in the Seattle Opera House this season. The opera house is undergoing a major renovation, and until the renovation is completed in 2003, the Seattle Opera will be performing at the Mercer Arts Arena, which is adjacent to the Seattle Opera House.

EXCURSIONS Look for many more great excursions from Seattle in this edition, including coverage of Olympic National Park and the Victorian seaport town of Port Townsend, also on the Olympic Peninsula. There's expanded coverage of Seattle's nearby wine country as well. The Kirkland art gallery district and Snohomish, the antiques capital of the Northwest, have also been added to chapter 11, "Side Trips from Seattle."

The San Juan Islands Up at the north end of San Juan Island, you'll find the new **Westcott Bay Reserve** (© **360/370-5050**), a sculpture park that includes more than 45 works of art. The sculptures are set in grassy fields and along the shores of a small pond. In Friday Harbor, be sure to check out **Vinny's,** 165 West St. (© **360/378-1934**), a great new Italian restaurant with a good view. On Orcas Island, in the tiny community of Olga, the **Olga Store,** Olga Road (© **360/376-5862**), which until recently was a little general store but is now a great little cafe and eclectic gift shop, should not be missed. Also on Orcas Island, the **West Sound Cafe** (© **360/376-4440**), another old general store turned into a cafe, is a good spot for breakfast or lunch.

1

The Best of Seattle

Imagine yourself sitting in a park on the Seattle waterfront, a double tall latte and an almond croissant close at hand. The snowy peaks of the Olympic Mountains are shimmering on the far side of Puget Sound, and the ferryboats are coming and going across Elliott Bay. It's a summer day, and the sun is shining. (Hey, as long as we're dreaming, why not dream big?) It just doesn't get much better than this, unless of course you swap the latte for a microbrew and catch a 9:30 summer sunset. No wonder people love this town so much.

OK, so the waterfront is as touristy as San Francisco's Fisherman's Wharf, but what a view! Seattle is a city of views, and the must-see vista is, of course, the panorama from the top of the Space Needle. With the 21st century in full swing, this image of the future looks decidedly mid-20th-century modern, but still, it's hard to resist an expensive elevator ride in any city. And you can even take a monorail straight out of *The Jetsons* to get there (and pass right through the Frank Gehry–designed Experience Music Project en route).

EMP, as the Experience Music Project has come to be known, is one of Seattle's latest architectural oddities. Its swooping, multicolored, metal-skinned bulk rises from the foot of the Space Needle, proof that real 21st-century architecture looks nothing like the vision of the future people dreamed of when the Space Needle was built for the 1962 Seattle World's Fair. EMP is the brainchild of Microsoft cofounder Paul Allen, who built this rock 'n' roll cathedral to house his vast collection of Northwest rock memorabilia.

Paul Allen's money has also been hard at work changing the architectural face of the south end of downtown Seattle, where, in March 2000, the Kingdome stadium came crashing down, imploded to make way for a new, state-of-the-art football stadium home for Allen's Seattle Seahawks. At press time, the new stadium was being readied to kick off the Seahawks' 2002–2003 football season. Together with the Seattle Mariners' Safeco Field, the stadium has created a massive sports arena district at the south end of downtown Seattle.

Allen has also developed much of the land around the old Kingdome site into office space, renovating the old Union Station building and adding an unusual glass-walled "waterfall building" that, when it rains, appears to have a waterfall cascading down its windows.

Paul Allen projects aside, Seattle has become one of the nation's most talked-about and popular cities, and life here has undergone dramatic changes in recent years. An influx of urban residents has brought a new vibrancy to the downtown area, and as the city has grown wealthier and more sophisticated, it has built itself not just a spanking-new football stadium and a retractable-roof baseball stadium (Safeco Field), but also chic condominiums, a new symphony hall, glittering new hotels, and countless upscale restaurants and shops. Still in the works are a controversial light-rail system and an extension of Seattle's monorail—although both transportation projects have repeatedly stalled and may end up being sidetracked completely. A new aquarium and a large waterfront sculpture park are a couple of years away.

It's clear that Seattle has not grown complacent. Sure, it's become a congested city, with traffic problems rivaling those of L.A. And yes, the weather really is lousy for most of the year. But Seattleites manage to overcome these minor inconveniences, in large part by spilling out into the streets and parks whenever the sun shines. To visit Seattle in the summer is to witness an exodus; follow the lead of the locals and head for the great outdoors. Should you brave a visit in the rainy season, don't despair: There are compensations for such misfortune, including a roof on Pike Place Market and an espresso bar on every block.

WATER, WATER EVERYWHERE . . . & FORESTS & MOUNTAINS, TOO

Though the times may be a-changing for Seattle, one thing has stayed the same—the beautiful and wild landscape that surrounds the city. The sparkling waters of Elliott Bay, Lake Union, and Lake Washington wrap around this city of shimmering skyscrapers, and forests of evergreens crowd the city limits. Everywhere you look, another breathtaking vista unfolds. With endless boating opportunities and beaches and mountains within a few hours' drive, Seattle is ideally situated for the outdoor pursuits that are so important to the fabric of life in the Northwest.

Few other cities in the United States are as immersed in the outdoor aesthetic as Seattle. The Cascade Range lies less than 50 miles to the east of downtown Seattle, and across Puget Sound stand the Olympic Mountains. In the spring, summer, and fall, the forests and mountains attract hikers, mountain bikers, anglers, and campers, and in winter the ski areas of Snoqualmie Pass and Stephens Pass attract downhill and cross-country skiers.

Though impressive mountains line both the city's eastern and western horizons, a glance to the southeast on a sunny day will reveal the city's most treasured sight—Mount Rainier, a 14,410-foot-tall dormant volcano that looms large, so unexpected that it demands your attention. When "the

Mountain is out," as they say here in Seattle, Seattleites head for the hills.

However, as important as "the Mountain" is to Seattle, it is water that truly defines the city's character. To the west lies Elliott Bay, an arm of Puget Sound; to the east is Lake Washington; and right in the middle of the city is Lake Union. With so much water all around, Seattle has become a city of boaters, who take to the water in everything from regally appointed yachts to slender sea kayaks. Consequently, the opening day of boating season has become one of Seattle's most popular annual festivals.

A CITY DRIVEN BY CAFFEINE

Despite Seattle's affinity for its nearby natural environment, this city is best known as the coffee capital of America. To understand Seattle's coffee addiction, it is necessary to study the city's geography and climate. Seattle lies at almost 50° north latitude, which means that winter days are short. The sun comes up around 7:30am, goes down as early as 4:30pm, and is frequently hidden behind leaden skies. A strong stimulant is almost a necessity to get people out of bed through the gray days of winter. Seattleites love to argue over which espresso bar or cafe in town serves the best coffee (and the answer isn't always Starbucks, despite its massive expansion across the country from its humble beginnings in Pike Place Market).

Seattle's popularity and rapid growth, however, have not been

Site Seeing: The Best Seattle Websites

If you're surfing the Web in search of information on Seattle, the following sites are great places to start.

- **http://seattle.citysearch.com**: CitySearch includes listings and reviews for dining, nightlife, shopping, and more by neighborhood and date (with a handy interactive calendar). In addition to places and events, you can also check the weather or get driving directions.
- **www.seeseattle.org**: Here at the official Seattle–King County Convention and Visitors Bureau website, you can take a photo tour of the Emerald City, check a calendar of events, learn more about attractions (from museums, to theaters, to shopping, to sports), and download coupons good for discounts at area attractions and on lodgings.
- **www.seattletimes.com**: A solid virtual version of Seattle's print stalwart, the *Seattle Times*, offers many of the paper's stories online. There's also an entertainment section with information on movies, theater, and concerts around town.

entirely smooth. The streets and highways have been unable to handle the increased traffic load, and commuting has become almost as nightmarish as it is in California, from whence so many of the city's recent transplants fled (ironically, partly due to the traffic congestion). With roads growing ever more crowded and the cost of living continuing to rise, Seattle may not be the Emerald City it once was, but it remains a metropolis in a singularly spectacular setting and a superb summertime vacation destination.

1 Frommer's Favorite Seattle Experiences

- **Taking in the Sunset from the Waterfront.** On a clear summer day, the setting sun silhouettes the Olympic Mountains on the far side of Puget Sound and makes the view from the Seattle waterfront truly memorable. Try the rooftop park at the Bell Street Pier, Myrtle Edwards Park at the north end of the waterfront, or the lounge at the Edgewater Hotel.
- **Riding a Ferry Across Puget Sound.** Sure you can spend $13 to $27 for a narrated tour of the Seattle waterfront, but for a fraction of that, you can take a ferry to Bremerton or Bainbridge Island and see not just Elliott Bay but plenty more of Puget Sound. Keep an eye out for porpoises, orcas, and bald eagles.
- **Eating Your Way Through Pike Place Market.** Breakfast at Le Panier, espresso at the original Starbucks, lunch at Café Campagne, a martini at the Pink Door, dinner at Chez Shea, Celtic music at Kells, and a nightcap at Il Bistro—that's how you could spend a day at Pike Place. Between stops on this rigorous itinerary, you can people-watch, listen to street musicians, and shop for everything from fresh salmon to tropical fruits to magic tricks to art glass to live parrots.
- **Relaxing over a Latte.** If the rain and gray skies start to get to you, there is no better pick-me-up

- **www.seattleweekly.com**: *Seattle Weekly* is Seattle's main arts-and-entertainment weekly and provides detailed information on what's happening in film, music, theater, and the arts. The weekly also features an extensive dining guide and database of restaurant reviews.
- **www.seatac.org/seatac**: At the Seattle–Tacoma International Airport's website, you'll find maps of individual terminals to help you find your way around. Parking and transportation news also comes in handy. Here you can also keep tabs on any construction projects underway at the airport. A large list of links will point you to everything from freeway traffic updates to local lodging.
- **www.wsdot.wa.gov/ferries**: This is the official website for Washington State Ferries, which are an essential part of any visit to Seattle. This site offers route destinations, schedule and fare information, a calendar of events, and an online ferry reservation service for ferries to Sidney, British Columbia (near Victoria), as well as a section of things to do at various stops along the ferry routes.

(short of a ticket to the tropics) than a frothy latte in a cozy cafe. Grab a magazine and just hang out until the rain stops (maybe sometime in July).

- **Wandering Around Fremont.** This quirky neighborhood considers itself the center of the universe, but it's really a little bit left of center. Retro clothing and vintage furniture stores, cafes, a couple of brewpubs, a great flea market, and the city's best public art make this the most eccentric neighborhood in Seattle.
- **Attending a Show at the Fifth Avenue Theatre.** This historic theater was designed to resemble the imperial throne room in Beijing's Forbidden City. Can you say ornate? Nothing else in Seattle compares, including the show onstage.
- **Going to the Spring Flower and Garden Show.** Each spring, gardening madness descends on the Washington State Convention and Trade Center in the form of one of the largest flower-and-garden shows in the country, with more than 5 acres of garden displays and hundreds of vendors.
- **Catching Concerts at Bumbershoot.** It isn't often that you can agonize about picking one great music performance over another, but that's just what you have to do at the annual Labor Day music and arts extravaganza known as Bumbershoot. Whether your tastes run to Grieg or grunge, salsa or swing, you'll have plenty of choices.
- **Riding the Monorail.** Though the ride is short, covering a distance that could easily be walked in half an hour, the monorail provides a different perspective on the city. The retro-futurist transport, built for the Seattle World's Fair in 1962, ends at the foot of the Space Needle and even passes right through the Experience Music Project.
- **Spending an Afternoon at Volunteer Park.** Whether the day is sunny or gray, this park on Capitol Hill is a great spot to spend an afternoon. You can relax in the

grass, study Chinese snuff bottles in the Seattle Asian Art Museum, marvel at the orchids in the park's conservatory, or simply enjoy the great view of the city from the top of the park's water tower.

- **Enjoying a Day at the Zoo.** The cages are almost completely gone from this big zoo, replaced by spacious animal habitats that give the residents the feeling of being back at home in the wild. Zebras gallop, brown bears romp, river otters cavort, elephants stomp, and orangutans swing. The levels of activity here make it clear that the animals are happy with their surroundings.
- **Strolling Through the Arboretum in Spring.** Winters in Seattle may not be long, but they do lack color. So, when spring hits, the sudden bursts of brightness it brings are reverently appreciated. There's no better place in the city to enjoy the spring floral displays than the Washington Park Arboretum.
- **Walking, Jogging, Biking, or Skating a Seattle Path.** There are several paved trails around the city

that are ideal for pursuing any of these sports. The trail around Green Lake is the all-time favorite, but the Burke-Gilman/Sammamish River Trail, the trail along the western shore of Lake Washington, the trail along Alki Beach, and the trail through Myrtle Edwards Park at the north end of the Seattle waterfront are equally good choices.
- **Sea Kayaking on Lake Union.** Lake Union is a very urban body of water, but it has a great view of the Seattle skyline, and you can paddle right up to several waterfront restaurants. For more natural surroundings, kayak over to the marshes at the north end of the Washington Park Arboretum.
- **Exploring a Waterfront Park.** Seattle abounds in waterfront parks where you can gaze out at distant shores, wiggle your toes in the sand, or walk through a remnant patch of old-growth forest. Some of our favorites include Discovery Park, Seward Park, Lincoln Park, and Golden Gardens Park.

2 Best Hotel Bets

See chapter 5, "Where to Stay in Seattle," for complete reviews of all these accommodations.

- **Best Historic Hotel:** Built in 1924, the **Four Seasons Olympic Hotel,** 411 University St. (© 800/ 223-8772 or 206/621-1700; www.fourseasons.com/seattle), is styled after Italian Renaissance palaces and is by far the most impressive of Seattle's handful of historic hotels. The grand lobby is unrivaled. See p. 58.
- **Best for Business Travelers:** If your company has sent you to Seattle to close a big deal, insist on the best. Stay at the **Elliott Grand**

Hyatt Seattle, 721 Pine St. (© 800/233-1234 or 206/774-1234; http://grandseattle.hyatt.com), and you can avail yourself of all kinds of high-tech amenities. If you're here on Microsoft business, head for **The Woodmark Hotel on Lake Washington,** 1200 Carillon Point, Kirkland (© 800/822-3700 or 425/822-3700; www.thewoodmark.com). Not only are rooms set up for taking care of business, but most have water views. See pages 55 and 74.
- **Best for a Romantic Getaway:** Though Seattle has quite a few hotels that do well for a romantic weekend, the **Inn at the Market,**

86 Pine St. (© **800/446-4484** or 206/443-3600; www.innatthe market.com), with its Elliott Bay views, European atmosphere, and proximity to many excellent (and very romantic) restaurants, is sure to set the stage for lasting memories. See p. 64.

- **Best Trendy Hotel:** The **W Seattle,** 1112 Fourth Ave. (© **877/W-HOTELS** or 206/264-6000; www. whotels.com/seattle), one of a chain of ultrahip hotels that have become popular with the dot-com generation, has brought to Seattle a high-end hipness that also emphasizes service. Dressing entirely in black is de rigueur. See p. 60.

- **Best for Families:** Located just across the street from Lake Union, the **Silver Cloud Inns Seattle–Lake Union,** 1150 Fairview Ave. N. (© **800/330-5812** or 206/447-9500; www.scinns.com), is far enough from downtown to be affordable and yet has a great location overlooking the lake and not far from Seattle Center. There are indoor and outdoor pools, and several restaurants right across the street. See p. 69.

- **Best Moderately Priced Hotel:** The **Best Western University Tower Hotel,** 4507 Brooklyn Ave. NE (© **800/WESTERN** or 206/634-2000; www.university towerhotel.com), is surprisingly reasonably priced for what you get, which is one of the most stylish contemporary accommodations in Seattle. Ask for a room on an upper floor, and you'll also get good views. See p. 72.

- **Best Budget Hotel:** Located a 5-minute drive from Seattle Center, the **Howard Johnson Express Inn,** 2500 Aurora Ave. N. (© **877/284-1900** or 206/284-1900; www.hojo.com), may not be the newest budget hotel in town, but it certainly has the best views. Set high on the northern slopes of Queen Anne Hill, the motel has a great view of Lake Union. See p. 68.

- **Best B&B:** Set in the Capitol Hill neighborhood, **The Gaslight Inn,** 1727 15th Ave. (© **206/325-3654;** www.gaslight-inn.com), is a lovingly restored and maintained Craftsman bungalow filled with original Stickley furniture. Lots of public spaces, very tasteful decor, and a swimming pool in the backyard all add up to unexpected luxury for a Seattle B&B. See p. 71.

- **Best Service:** The **Alexis Hotel,** 1007 First Ave. (© **800/426-7033** or 206/624-4844; www. alexishotel.com), a downtown boutique hotel, is small enough to offer that personal touch. See p. 55.

- **Best Location:** Located on a pier right on the Seattle waterfront, **The Edgewater,** Pier 67, 2411 Alaskan Way (© **800/624-0670** or 206/728-7000; www.edgewater hotel.com), is only 5 blocks from Pike Place Market and the Seattle Aquarium and 3 blocks from the restaurants of Belltown. The Waterfront Streetcar, which goes to Pioneer Square and the International District, stops right in front of the hotel; and ferries to Victoria, British Columbia, leave from the adjacent pier. See p. 54.

- **Best Health Club:** So, you're on the road again, but you don't want to give up your circuit training. Don't worry; bring your gymwear and book a room at the **Bellevue Club Hotel,** 11200 SE Sixth St., Bellevue (© **800/579-1110** or 425/454-4424; www.bellevue club.com), where you'll have access to a huge private health club complete with an indoor Olympic-size pool. See p. 74.

- **Best Hotel Pool:** Most hotels in the city center stick their swimming pool (if they have one at all) down in the basement or on some hidden-away terrace, but at the **Sheraton Seattle Hotel and Towers,** 1400 Sixth Ave. (© **800/325-3535** or 206/621-9000; www.sheraton.com/seattle), you can do laps up on the top floor with the lights of the city twinkling all around you. See p. 60.
- **Best Views:** If you're not back in your room by sunset at the **Westin Seattle,** 1900 Fifth Ave. (© **800/WESTIN-1** or 206/728-1000; www.westin.com/seattle), you may not turn into a pumpkin, but you will miss a spectacular light show. Because it is the tallest hotel in the city, the Westin boasts fabulous views from its upper floors, especially those facing northwest. See p. 61.

- **Best Room Decor:** If you plan to spend a lot of time in your room, then a room at the **Bellevue Club Hotel,** 11200 SE Sixth St., Bellevue (© **800/579-1110** or 425/454-4424; www.bellevueclub.com), is the place to be. The rooms here are plush enough to please the most demanding of hedonists. See p. 74.
- **Best for Pets:** If you'll be traveling to Seattle with your pooch and don't mind shelling out big bucks for a top-end hotel, then the **Alexis Hotel,** 1007 First Ave. (© **800/426-7033** or 206/624-4844; www.alexishotel.com), is the place for you. For an additional $25, they offer a special "Pet Amenities" package that includes dog treats, distilled water and water bowl, and morning and afternoon walks. See p. 55.

3 Best Dining Bets

See chapter 6, "Where to Dine in Seattle," for complete reviews of all the restaurants mentioned below.

- **Best Spot for a Romantic Dinner:** At **Chez Shea,** Corner Market Building, 94 Pike St., Suite 34 (© **206/467-9990**), in a quiet corner of Pike Place Market, candlelit tables, subdued lighting, views of ferries crossing the bay, and superb meals add up to the perfect combination for a romantic dinner. See p. 90.
- **Best Waterfront Dining:** Palisade, Elliott Bay Marina, 2601 W. Marina Place (© **206/285-1000**), has a 180° view that takes in Elliott Bay, downtown Seattle, and West Seattle. Never mind that it also has great food and some of the most memorable decor of any Seattle restaurant, with a saltwater tide pool pond in the middle of the dining room and beautiful koa

wood details everywhere. See p. 95.
- **Best View:** There's no question here. **SkyCity at the Needle,** Seattle Center, 400 Broad St. (© **800/937-9582** or 206/905-2100), has the best views in Seattle—360° worth of them. Sure it's expensive, but there's no place in town with views to rival these. See p. 94.
- **Best Outdoor Dining with a View:** Located across Elliott Bay from downtown Seattle, **Salty's on Alki Beach,** 1936 Harbor Ave. SW (© **206/937-1600**), has a gorgeous view of the Seattle skyline. You can even get here by water taxi. See p. 103.
- **Best Wine List: Canlis,** 2576 Aurora Ave. N. (© **206/283-3313**), has been around for almost 50 years, so the folks here have had plenty of time to develop

an extensive and well-thought-out wine list. See p. 94.

- **Best Value:** While Wild Ginger usually gets all the accolades for its Pan-Asian cuisine, Belltown's little **Noodle Ranch,** 2228 Second Ave. (© **206/728-0463**), is every bit as good, despite a more limited menu. See p. 89.

- **Best for Kids:** Located on the south shore of Lake Union, **Cucina! Cucina!,** Chandler's Cove, 901 Fairview Ave. N. (© **206/447-2782**), is Seattle's most popular family restaurant because of all the things they do here to make dining out fun for kids. Adults like it, too. See p. 99.

- **Best Service: Canlis,** 2576 Aurora Ave. N. (© **206/283-3313**), is a Seattle tradition, the perfect place to close a big deal or celebrate a very special occasion. When you want to be pampered, the professional staff at Canlis will do just that. See p. 94.

- **Best French:** Tucked into a quiet courtyard in a secluded corner of Pike Place Market, **Campagne,** Inn at the Market, 86 Pine St. (© **206/728-2800**), is a casually elegant little restaurant that makes the most of fresh market produce, meats, and fish. You can even enjoy views of Elliott Bay with your country French meal. See p. 89.

- **Best Northwest Cuisine:** Chef Thierry Rautureau at **Rover's,** 2808 E. Madison St. (© **206/325-7442**), combines his love of local ingredients with his classic French training to produce his own distinctive take on Northwest cuisine. See p. 100.

- **Best Seafood:** Chef Tom Douglas seems to be able to do no wrong, and at **Etta's Seafood,** 2020 Western Ave. (© **206/443-6000**), he focuses his culinary talents on more than just his famed crab cakes. See p. 90.

- **Best Place to Slurp Down Raw Oysters:** The Northwest produces an astonishing variety of oysters, and locals are almost as obsessive about their bivalves as they are about coffee and beer. For the best selection, head to **Elliott's,** Pier 56, Alaskan Way (© **206/623-4340**). See p. 80.

- **Best Steaks: Metropolitan Grill,** 820 Second Ave. (© **206/624-3287**), in downtown Seattle, serves corn-fed, aged beef grilled over mesquite charcoal. Steaks just don't get any better than this. See p. 81.

- **Best Burger:** We all have our own ideas of what constitutes the perfect burger, and here in Seattle there are plenty of worthy contenders. We split our vote between the burgers at **Two Bells Tavern,** 2313 Fourth Ave. (© **206/441-3050**), and those at the **74th Street Ale House,** 7401 Greenwood Ave. N. (© **206/784-2955**). See pages 89 and 103.

- **Best Desserts:** The **Dahlia Lounge,** 2001 Fourth Ave. (© **206/682-4142**), has long been one of the best restaurants in Seattle, and while the food is reliably tasty, the triple coconut cream pie is absolutely divine. The rest of the desserts are pretty good, too. See p. 86.

- **Best Late-Night Dining: Palace Kitchen,** 2030 Fifth Ave. (© **206/448-2001**), is an urbane palace of food, where chef Tom Douglas serves tasty specialties from the grill and rotisserie until 1am. The bar here is also a happening place. See p. 88.

- **Best Espresso: Torrefazione,** 320 Occidental Ave. S. (© **206/624-5847**), 622 Olive Way (© **206/624-1429**), and a couple of other locations, serves its brew in hand-painted Italian crockery, and offers delectable pastries to accompany your espresso. See p. 105.

2

Planning Your Trip to Seattle

Seattle is one of the West Coast's most popular vacation destinations, and as its popularity has grown, so too has the need for pre-visit planning. Try to make your hotel and car reservations as far in advance as possible—not only will you save money, but you'll also be more likely to find rooms available in the most highly recommended hotels. Summer is the peak tourist season in Seattle, and from June through September downtown hotels are often fully booked for days or even weeks at a time. Consequently, reservations—for hotel rooms, rental cars, or a table at a restaurant—are imperative. If you plan to visit during the city's annual Seafair summer festival in late July and early August, when every hotel in town can be booked, reservations are especially important.

Oh, yeah, and about that rain. Seattle's rainy weather may be infamous, but Seattleites have ways of dealing with the dreary days. They either put on their rain gear and head outdoors just as if the sun were shining, or they retreat to the city's hundreds of excellent restaurants and cafes, its dozens of theaters and performance halls, its outstanding museums, its many movie theaters, and its excellent bookstores. They rarely let the weather stand in the way of having a good time, and neither should you.

Although summer is the best time to visit, Seattle offers year-round diversions and entertainment, and because it is still a seasonal destination, hotel rooms here are a real bargain during the rainy months between October and April.

1 Visitor Information

If you still have questions about Seattle after reading this book, contact the **Seattle–King County Convention and Visitors Bureau,** 520 Pike St., Suite 1300, Seattle, WA 98101 (© **206/461-5840;** www.seeseattle. org), which operates a visitor information center inside the Washington State Convention and Trade Center, 800 Convention Place, Galleria Level.

For information on other parts of Washington, contact the **Washington State Tourism Office,** P.O. Box 42500, Olympia, WA 98504 (© **800/ 544-1800** or 360/725-5052; www. experiencewashington.com).

2 Money

ATMS

ATMs are linked to a national network that most likely includes your bank at home. **Cirrus** (© **800/ 424-7787;** www.mastercard.com) and **PLUS** (© **800/843-7587;** www.visa. com) are the two most popular networks; check the back of your ATM card to see which network your bank belongs to. Use the 800 numbers to locate ATMs in your destination. Other ATM networks found in the Seattle area are Accel, The Exchange, and Interlink. Expect to pay $1.50 or $2 each time you withdraw money from an ATM, in addition to what your home bank charges.

TRAVELER'S CHECKS

ATMs have made **traveler's checks** all but obsolete. But if you still prefer the security of traveler's checks to carrying cash (and you don't mind showing identification every time you want to cash one), you can get them at almost any bank, paying a service charge that usually ranges from 1% to 7%. You can also get **American Express** traveler's checks online at www.americanexpress.com or over the phone by calling ✆ **800/221-7282;** by using this number, Amex gold and platinum cardholders are exempt from the 1% fee. AAA members can obtain checks without a fee at most AAA offices. If you opt for traveler's checks, be sure to keep a record of the serial numbers, separate from the checks, of course, so you can claim a refund in an emergency.

CREDIT CARDS

Credit cards are invaluable when you travel. They are a safe way to carry money, they provide a convenient record of all your expenses, and they're accepted practically everywhere.

At most banks, you can get a cash advance with your credit card at the ATM if you know your PIN (personal identification number), but this should only be used as an emergency measure, since interest begins mounting immediately on cash advances—you'll pay dearly for the privilege.

WHAT TO DO IF YOUR WALLET GETS STOLEN

Be sure to block charges against your account the minute you discover a card has been lost or stolen. Then be sure to file a police report.

Almost every credit card company has an emergency 800-number to call if your card is stolen. They may be able to wire you a cash advance off your credit card immediately, and in many places, they can deliver an emergency credit card in a day or two. The issuing bank's 800-number is usually on the back of your credit card—though of course, if your card has been stolen, that won't help you unless you recorded the number elsewhere.

Visa's U.S. assistance number is ✆ **800/336-8472.** American Express cardholders and traveler's check holders should call ✆ **800/221-7282.** MasterCard holders should call ✆ **800/307-7309.** Otherwise, call the toll-free number directory at ✆ **800/ 555-1212.**

Odds are that if your wallet is gone, the police won't be able to recover it for you. However, it's still worth informing the authorities. Your credit card company or insurer may require a police report number or record of the theft.

If you choose to carry traveler's checks, be sure to keep a record of their serial numbers separate from your checks. You'll get a refund faster if you know the numbers.

If you need emergency cash over the weekend when all banks and American Express offices are closed, you can have money wired to you from **Western Union** (✆ **800/325-6000;** www.westernunion.com/). You simply present valid ID to pick up the cash at the Western Union office. However, you can pick up a money transfer even if you don't have valid identification, as long as you can answer a test question provided by the sender. Be sure to let the sender know in advance that you don't have an ID. If you need to use a test question instead of ID, the sender must take cash to his or her local Western Union office, rather than transfer the money over the phone or online.

3 When to Go

THE WEATHER

Let's face it, Seattle's weather has a bad reputation. As they say out here, "The rain in Spain stays mainly in Seattle." I wish I could tell you that it isn't so, but I can't. It rains in Seattle—and rains and rains and rains. However, when December 31 rolls around each year, a funny thing happens: They total up the year's precipitation, and Seattle almost always comes out behind such cities as Washington, D.C., Boston, New York, and Atlanta. So, it isn't the *amount* of rain here that's the problem—it's the number of rainy or cloudy days, which far outnumber those of any of those rainy Eastern cities.

Most of Seattle's rain falls between October and April, so if you visit in the summer, you might not see a drop the entire time. But just in case, you should bring a rain jacket or at least an umbrella whenever you come. Also, no matter what time of year you plan to visit Seattle, be sure to bring at least

a sweater or light jacket. Summer nights can be quite cool, and daytime temperatures rarely climb above the low 80s. Winters are not as cold as they are in the East, but snow does fall in Seattle.

Because of the pronounced seasonality of the weather here, people spend as much time outdoors during the summer as they can, and accordingly, summer is when the city stages all its big festivals. Because it stays light until 10pm in the middle of summer, it's difficult to get Seattleites indoors to theater or music performances. But when the weather turns wet, Seattleites head for the theaters and performance halls in droves.

To make things perfectly clear, here's an annual weather chart:

Seattle's Average Temperature & Days of Rain

	Jan	Feb	Mar	Apr	May	June	July	Aug	Sept	Oct	Nov	Dec
Temp. (°F)	46	50	53	58	65	69	75	74	69	60	52	47
Temp. (°C)	8	10	11	15	18	21	24	23	21	16	11	8
Rain (days)	19	16	17	14	10	9	5	7	9	14	18	20

SEATTLE CALENDAR OF EVENTS

Seattleites will hold a festival at the drop of a rain hat, and summers here seem to revolve around the city's myriad celebrations. To find out what special events will be taking place while you're in town, check the "Ticket" arts-and-entertainment section of the Friday *Seattle Times* or pick up a copy of *Seattle Weekly*. Remember, festivals here take place rain or shine. For more specific dates than those listed here, take a look at the calendar of events on the **Seattle–King County Convention and Visitors Bureau website** (www.seeseattle.org), which is updated as dates become available.

In addition to festivals listed here, a series of nearly a dozen cultural community festivals is held each year at Seattle Center. Called **Festál,** this series celebrates the city's cultural diversity. In the past there have been Vietnamese, African, Japanese, Filipino, Brazilian, and Tibetan festivals. For more information, contact **Seattle Center** (© 206/684-7200; www.seattlecenter.com).

January

Seattle International Boat Show (© 206/634-0911; www.seattleboatshow.com), Stadium Exhibition Center. At one of the biggest national shows, more than 1,500 boats of every style and size are displayed. Mid-January.

February

Chinatown/International District Lunar New Year Celebration, International District. Each year's date depends on the lunar calendar (it may fall in January some years). In 2003, Chinese New Year falls on February 1. Call © 206/382-1197 for information.

Northwest Flower & Garden Show (© 800/229-6311 or 206/789-5333; www.gardenshow.com), Washington State Convention and Trade Center. This massive show for avid gardeners has astonishing floral displays. Early to mid-February.

April

Skagit Valley Tulip Festival (© 877/875-2448 or 360/428-5959; www.tulipfestival.org), Skagit Valley. View a rainbow of blooming tulip fields 60 miles north of Seattle. Second and third week of April.

Cherry Blossom and Japanese Cultural Festival (© 206/684-7200; www.seattlecenter.com), Seattle Center. Traditional Japanese spring festival. Mid- to late April.

May

Opening Day of Boating Season, Lake Union and Lake Washington. A parade of boats and much fanfare take place as Seattle boaters bring out everything from kayaks to yachts. For information call © 206/325-1000. First Saturday in May.

Seattle Maritime Festival (© 206/728-3000 or 206/443-3830; www.portseattle.org/portandyou/events/default.htm). Tugboat races are the highlight of this annual Port of Seattle event. Festivities are centered on the Bell Street Pier (Pier 66) on the Seattle waterfront. Early May.

Seattle International Film Festival (© 206/324-9997 for information or 206/324-9996 to buy tickets; www.seattlefilm.com), at theaters around town. At this highly regarded film festival, new foreign and independent films are screened over several weeks. Mid-May to mid-June.

Northwest Folklife Festival (© 206/684-7300; www.nwfolklife.org). This is the largest folk festival in the country, with dozens of national and regional folk musicians performing on numerous stages. In addition, you'll find crafts vendors from all over the Northwest, lots of good food, and dancing. The festival is held at the Seattle Center, and admission is by suggested $5 donation. Memorial Day weekend.

Pike Place Market Festival (© 206/587-0351), Pike Place Market. A celebration of the market, with lots of free entertainment. Memorial Day weekend.

Seattle International Children's Festival (© 206/684-7346; www.seattleinternational.org), Seattle Center. Hungarian gypsy musicians, a Chinese martial arts ballet, Yoruba drummers from Nigeria—these are just some of the acts that you might see at this festival that celebrates world cultures through the performing arts. Mid- to late May.

June

Fremont Fair (© 206/633-4409; www.fremontfair.com), Fremont neighborhood. A celebration of the summer solstice with a wacky parade, naked bicyclists, food, arts and crafts, and entertainment in one of Seattle's favorite neighborhoods. Third weekend in June.

Out to Lunch (© 206/623-0340; www.downtownseattle.com). Free lunchtime music concerts in plazas and parks throughout downtown. Mid-June through early September.

July

Fourth of Jul-Ivar's fireworks (© 206/587-6500; www.ivars.net), Myrtle Edwards Park, north end of Seattle waterfront. Fireworks over Elliott Bay. July 4.

Washington Mutual Family Fourth at Lake Union (© 206/281-7788), Lake Union. Seattle's other main Fourth of July fireworks display. July 4.

Lake Union Wooden Boat Festival (© 206/382-2628; www.cwb.org), Center for Wooden Boats on Lake Union. Featured are wooden boats, both old and new, from all over the Northwest. Races, demonstrations, food, and entertainment. July 4th weekend.

Chinatown/International District Summer Festival (© 206/382-1197), International District. Features the music, dancing, arts, and food of Seattle's Asian district. Second weekend in July.

Bite of Seattle, Seattle Center (© 206/232-2982; www.biteof seattle.com). Sample bites from Seattle restaurants, or take in a wine-tasting exhibit. Third weekend in July.

Seafair (© 206/728-0123; www. seafair.com). This is the biggest Seattle event of the year, with daily festivities—parades, hydroplane boat races, an air show with the navy's Blue Angels, a Torchlight Parade, ethnic festivals, sporting events, and open house on naval ships. Events take place all over Seattle. Early July to early August.

Bellevue Art Museum Fair (© 425/519-0770; www.bellevue art.org), Bellevue Square shopping mall, Bellevue. This is the largest arts and fine crafts fair in the Northwest. Last weekend in July.

August

Chief Seattle Days (© 360/598-3311), at Suquamish tribal headquarters. Celebration of Northwest Native American culture across Puget Sound from Seattle. Third weekend in August.

September

Bumbershoot, the Seattle Arts Festival (© 206/281-8111; www. bumbershoot.org). Seattle's second most popular festival derives its peculiar name from a British term for an umbrella—an obvious reference to the rainy weather. Lots of rock music and other events pack Seattle's youthful set into Seattle Center and other venues. You'll find plenty of arts and crafts on display too. Labor Day weekend.

Seattle Fringe Festival (© 206/342-9172; www.seattlefringe.org), var-ious venues. Avant-garde, experimental, and otherwise uncategorizable theater performances from a variety of companies. Late September.

October

Salmon Days Festival (© 425/392-0661). This festival in Issaquah, 15 miles east of Seattle, celebrates the annual return of salmon that spawn within the city limits. First full weekend in October.

Elliott's Oyster New Year (© 206/623-4340), Elliott's Oyster House, Seattle. Summer months are not the best for oysters, but as the cooler weather returns, so does the bounty of oysters. To celebrate this occasion, oyster lovers slurp down more than two dozen different types here at Elliott's on Pier 56. Late October or early November.

November

Seattle Marathon (© 206/729-3660; www.seattlemarathon.org), around the city. What with all the hills, you have to be crazy to want to run a marathon in Seattle, but plenty of people show up in running shoes every year. First Sunday after Thanksgiving.

December

Seattle Christmas Ships (© 206/623-1445), various locations. Boats decked out with imaginative Christmas lights parade past various waterfront locations. **Argosy Cruises** (© 800/642-7816 or 206/623-1445; www.argosycruises. com) offers tours; see chapter 7, "Exploring Seattle," for more details. Throughout December.

AT&T New Year's at the Needle, Seattle Center. The Space Needle ushers in the new year by bursting into light when midnight strikes. Call © 206/443-2100 for information. December 31.

4 Insurance, Health & Safety

TRAVEL INSURANCE AT A GLANCE

Check your existing insurance policies before you buy travel insurance to cover trip cancellation, lost luggage, medical expenses, or car-rental insurance. You're likely to have partial or complete coverage. But if you need some, ask your travel agent about a comprehensive package. The cost of travel insurance varies widely, depending on the cost and length of your trip, your age and overall health, and the type of trip you're taking. Insurance for extreme sports or adventure travel, for example, will cost more than coverage for a cruise. Some insurers provide packages for specialty vacations, such as skiing or backpacking. More dangerous activities may be excluded from basic policies.

For information, contact one of the following popular insurers:

- **Access America** (© 800/284-8300); www.accessamerica.com)
- **Travel Guard International** (© 800/826-1300; www.travel guard.com)
- **Travel Insured International** (© 800/243-3174; www.travel insured.com)
- **Travelex Insurance Services** (© 800/228-9792; www.travelex-insurance.com)

TRIP-CANCELLATION INSURANCE (TCI)

There are three major types of trip-cancellation insurance—one, in the event that you pre-pay a cruise or tour that gets cancelled, and you can't get your money back; a second when you or someone in your family gets sick or dies, and you can't travel (but beware that you may not be covered for a pre-existing condition); and a third, when bad weather makes travel impossible. Some insurers provide coverage for events like jury duty; natural disasters close to home, like floods or fire; even the loss of a job. A few have added provisions for cancellations due to terrorist activities. Always check the fine print before signing on, and don't buy trip-cancellation insurance from the tour operator that may be responsible for the cancellation; buy it only from a reputable travel insurance agency. Don't overbuy. You won't be reimbursed for more than the cost of your trip.

MEDICAL INSURANCE

Most health insurance policies cover you if you get sick away from home—but check, particularly if you're insured by an HMO.

Some credit cards (American Express and certain gold and platinum Visas and MasterCards, for example) offer automatic flight insurance against death or dismemberment in case of an airplane crash if you charged the cost of your ticket.

Also, check to see if your medical insurance covers you for emergency medical evacuation: If you have to buy a one-way same-day ticket home and forfeit your nonrefundable round-trip ticket, you may be out big bucks.

If you require additional insurance, try one of the following companies:

- **MEDEX International,** P.O. Box 5375, Timonium, MD 21094-5375 (© **888/MEDEX-00** or 410/453-6300; fax 410/453-6301; www.medexassist.com)
- **Travel Assistance International** (© **800/821-2828;** www.travel assistance.com), 9200 Keystone Crossing, Suite 300, Indianapolis, IN 46240 (for general information on services, call the company's Worldwide Assistance Services, Inc., at © **800/777-8710**).

LOST-LUGGAGE INSURANCE

On domestic flights, checked baggage is covered up to $2,500 per ticketed passenger. If you plan to check items more valuable than the standard liability, you may purchase "excess valuation" coverage from the airline, up to $5,000. Be sure to take any valuables or irreplaceable items with you in your carry-on luggage. If you file a lost luggage claim, be prepared to answer detailed questions about the contents of your baggage, and be sure to file a claim immediately, as most airlines enforce a 21-day deadline. Before you leave home, compile an inventory of all packed items and a rough estimate of the total value to ensure you're properly compensated if your luggage is lost. You will only be reimbursed for what you lost, no more. If you arrive at a destination without your bags, ask the airline to forward them to your hotel or to your next destination; they will usually comply. If your bag is delayed or lost, the airline may reimburse you for reasonable expenses, such as a toothbrush or a set of clothes, but the airline is under no legal obligation to do so.

Lost luggage may also be covered by your homeowner's or renter's policy. Many platinum and gold credit cards cover you as well. If you choose to purchase additional lost-luggage insurance, be sure not to buy more than you need. Buy in advance from the insurer or a trusted agent (prices will be much higher at the airport).

CAR-RENTAL INSURANCE (LOSS/DAMAGE WAIVER OR COLLISION DAMAGE WAIVER)

If you hold a private auto insurance policy, you probably are covered in the U.S., but not abroad, for loss or damage to the car, and liability in case a passenger is injured. The credit card you used to rent the car also may provide some coverage.

Car-rental insurance probably does not cover liability if you caused the accident. Check your own auto insurance policy, the rental company policy, and your credit-card coverage for the extent of coverage: Is your destination covered? Are other drivers covered? How much liability is covered if a passenger is injured? (If you rely on your credit card for coverage, you may want to bring a second credit card with you, as damages may be charged to your card and you may find yourself stranded with no money.)

Car-rental insurance costs about $20 a day.

WHAT TO DO IF YOU GET SICK AWAY FROM HOME

If you worry about getting sick away from home, consider purchasing **medical travel insurance** and carry your ID card in your purse or wallet. In most cases, your existing health plan will provide the coverage you need. See the section on insurance earlier in this chapter for more information.

If you suffer from a chronic illness, consult your doctor before your departure. For conditions like

---

Tips **Quick ID**

Tie a colorful ribbon or piece of yarn around your luggage handle, or slap a distinctive sticker on the side of your bag. This makes it less likely that someone will mistakenly appropriate it. And if your luggage gets lost, it will be easier to find.

epilepsy, diabetes, or heart problems, wear a **Medic Alert Identification Tag** (© 888/633-4298; www.medical ert.org), which will immediately alert doctors to your condition and give them access to your records through Medic Alert's 24-hour hot line.

Pack **prescription medications** in your carry-on luggage, and carry prescription medications in their original containers. Also bring along copies of your prescriptions in case you lose your pills or run out.

And don't forget **sunglasses** and an extra pair of **contact lenses** or **prescription glasses.**

If you get sick, consider asking your hotel concierge to recommend a **local doctor**—even his or her own. You can also try the **emergency room** at a local hospital; many have walk-in clinics for emergency cases that are not life-threatening. You may not get immediate attention, but you won't pay the high price of an emergency room visit (usually a minimum of $300 just for signing your name).

5 Tips for Travelers with Special Needs

FOR TRAVELERS WITH DISABILITIES

The greatest difficulty of a visit to Seattle for anyone who is restricted to a wheelchair is dealing with the city's many steep hills, which rival those of San Francisco. One solution for dealing with downtown hills is to use the elevator at the Pike Place Market to get between the waterfront and First Avenue. There's also a public elevator at the west end of Lenora Street (just north of Pike Place Market). This elevator connects the waterfront with the Belltown neighborhood. Also, by staying at the Edgewater hotel, right on the waterfront, you'll have easy access to all of the city's waterfront attractions and can use the Waterfront Streetcar to get between the Pike Place Market and Pioneer Square area. Also keep in mind that the downtown bus tunnel, which connects the International District to Westlake Center shopping mall and is wheelchair accessible, can make traveling across downtown somewhat less strenuous.

When making airline reservations, always mention your disability. Airline policies differ regarding wheelchairs and Seeing Eye dogs.

Most hotels now offer wheelchair-accessible accommodations, and some of the larger and more expensive hotels also offer TDD telephones and other amenities for the hearing and sight impaired.

Many of the major car-rental companies now offer hand-controlled cars for drivers with disabilities. Avis can provide such a vehicle at any of its airport locations in the United States with 72-hour advance notice; Hertz requires between 24 and 48 hours of advance reservation at most of its locations. **Wheelchair Getaways** (© 800/ 642-2042; www.wheelchair-getaways. com) rents specialized vans with wheelchair lifts and other features for travelers with disabilities in about 45 cities across the United States.

If you plan to visit Mount Rainier or Olympic National Park, you can avail yourself of the **Golden Access Passport.** This lifetime pass is issued free to any U.S. citizen or permanent resident who has been medically certified as disabled or blind (you will need to show proof of disability). The pass permits free entry into national parks and monuments and can be obtained through the visitor center at either Mount Rainer or Olympic National Park.

Amtrak's (© 800/872-7245; www. amtrak.com) services for disabled passengers include wheelchair assistance and special seats with 24 hours' notice. Passengers with disabilities are also entitled to a discount of 15% off the lowest available rail fare at the time of booking. Documentation from a doctor or an ID card proving your disability is required. Amtrak also provides wheelchair-accessible sleeping accommodations on long-distance trains, and service animals are permitted and travel free of charge. Amtrak publishes a handbook called *Access Amtrak,* which tells you all you need to know about traveling on Amtrak when you have a disability; call ✆ **877/268-7252** to order it and allow 7 to 10 days for delivery. Amtrak's TDD number is ✆ **800/ 523-6590.**

On **Greyhound** (✆ **800/229-9424;** www.greyhound.com) buses, a companion may be able to accompany a person with a disability at no charge (you must inform Greyhound in advance; they'll ask for proof of disability and will want to confirm that the companion is truly necessary and capable of helping the disabled passenger). Call ✆ **800/752-4841** at least 24 hours in advance to discuss other special needs. Greyhound's TDD number is ✆ **800/345-3109.**

AGENCIES/OPERATORS

Travelers with disabilities might also want to consider joining a tour that caters specifically to them.

- **Accessible Journeys** (✆ **800/ TINGLES** or 610/521-0339; www.accessiblejourneys.com), for slow walkers and wheelchair travelers, offers excursions to the Northwest.
- **Wilderness Inquiry** (✆ **800/ 728-0719** or 612/676-9400; www.wildernessinquiry.org) offers trips to the San Juan Islands for persons of all abilities.

ORGANIZATIONS

- **The Society for Accessible Travel and Hospitality** (✆ **212/447-7284;** fax 212/725-8253; www. sath.org) offers a wealth of travel resources for all types of disabilities and informed recommendations on destinations, access guides, travel agents, tour operators, vehicle rentals, and companion services. Annual membership costs $45 for adults; $30 for seniors and students.
- **The American Foundation for the Blind** (✆ **800/232-5463;** www.afb.org) provides information on travel with Seeing Eye dogs.
- **The Moss Rehab Hospital** (✆ **215/456-9603;** www.moss resourcenet.org) provides friendly, helpful phone assistance through its **Travel Information Service.**

FOR GAY & LESBIAN TRAVELERS

Seattle is one of the most gay-friendly cities in the country, with a large gay and lesbian community centered around the Capitol Hill neighborhood. In Capitol Hill you'll find numerous bars, nightclubs, stores, and bed-and-breakfast inns catering to the gay community. Broadway Avenue, Capitol Hill's main drag, is also the site of the annual Gay Pride March, held each year in late June.

The *Seattle Gay News* (✆ **206/ 324-4297;** www.sgn.org) is the community's newspaper, available at bookstores and gay bars and nightclubs.

Beyond the Closet, 518 E. Pike St. (✆ **206/322-4609**); and **Bailey Coy Books,** 414 Broadway Ave. E. (✆ **206/323-8842**), are the gay community's two main bookstores and are good sources of information on what's going on within the community.

The **Lesbian Resource Center,** 2214 S. Jackson St. (✆ **206/322-DYKE;** www.lrc.net), is a community resource center that provides housing and job information, therapy, and business referrals.

The **Gaslight Inn** and **Bacon Mansion** are two gay-friendly bed-and-breakfasts in the Capitol Hill area; see chapter 5, "Where to Stay in

Seattle," for full reviews. For information on gay and lesbian bars and nightclubs, see "The Gay & Lesbian Scene" in chapter 10, "Seattle After Dark."

If you want help planning your trip, the **International Gay & Lesbian Travel Association (IGLTA;** © **800/ 448-8550** or 954/776-2626; www. iglta.org) can link you with the appropriate gay-friendly service organization or tour specialist. With around 1,200 members, it offers quarterly newsletters, marketing mailings, and a membership directory that's updated quarterly. Members are kept informed of gay and gay-friendly hoteliers, tour operators, and airline and cruise-line representatives. **GayWired Travel Services (www.gaywired.com)** is another great trip-planning resource; click on "Travel Services."

Out and About (© **800/929-2268** or 415/644-8044; www.outandabout. com) offers a monthly newsletter packed with good information on the global gay and lesbian scene. Its website features links to gay and lesbian tour operators and other gay-themed travel links, plus extensive travel information for subscribers only.

SENIOR TRAVEL

Don't be shy about asking for discounts, but always carry some kind of identification, such as a driver's license, that shows your date of birth, especially if you've kept your youthful glow. In Seattle, most attractions, some theaters and concert halls, tour companies, and the Washington State Ferries all offer senior-citizen discounts. These can add up to substantial savings, but you have to remember to ask.

Discounts abound for seniors, beginning with the 10%-off-your-airfare deal that most airlines offer to anyone age 62 or older. In addition, a number of airlines have clubs you can join and coupon books you can buy that may or may not increase your savings beyond that base 10% discount, depending on how often you travel, where you're going, and how long you're going to stay. Always ask an airline whether it has a club for seniors or sells coupon books, either of which often qualifies "mature" travelers for discounted tickets.

Both **Amtrak** (© **800/872-7245;** www.amtrak.com) and **Greyhound** (© **800/752-4841;** www.greyhound. com) offer discounts to persons over 62.

Many hotels offer senior discounts. **Choice Hotels** (Clarion Hotels, Quality Inns, Comfort Inns, and Sleep Inns), for example, give 20% to 30% off their published rates to anyone over 60 depending on availability, provided you book your room through their nationwide toll-free reservations numbers (not directly with the hotels or through a travel agent).

If you aren't a member of the **AARP,** 601 E St. NW, Washington, DC 20049 (© **800/424-3410;** www. aarp.org), you should consider joining. This association provides discounts on many lodgings, car rentals, airfares, and attractions, although you can sometimes get a similar discount simply by showing your ID.

If you plan to visit either Mount Rainier National Park or Olympic National Park while in the Seattle area, you can save on park admissions by getting a **Golden Age Passport,** available for $10 to U.S. citizens and permanent residents age 62 and older. This federal government pass allows lifetime entrance privileges. You can apply in person for this passport at a national park or other location where it's honored, as long as you can show reasonable proof of age.

For more information, check out www.nps.gov/fees_passes.htm or call © **888-go-parks.**

AGENCIES/OPERATORS

- **Grand Circle Travel** (© **800/ 221-2610** or 617/350-7500; www.gct.com) offers package deals for the 50-plus market, mostly of the tour-bus variety, with free trips thrown in for those who organize groups of 10 or more.
- **Elderhostel** (© **877/426-8056;** www.elderhostel.org) arranges study programs for those ages 55 and over (and a spouse or companion of any age) in the U.S. and in more than 80 countries around the world. Most courses last 5 to 7 days in the U.S. (2 to 4 weeks abroad), and many include airfare, accommodations in university dormitories or modest inns, meals, and tuition.

PUBLICATIONS

- **The Mature Traveler,** a monthly newsletter on senior travel, is a valuable resource. It's available by subscription for $29.95 a year (© **800/460-6676;** www.the maturetraveler.com).
- **The Book of Deals,** a collection of more than 1,000 senior discounts on airlines, lodging, tours, and attractions around the country, comes free with the newsletter subscription but is available by itself for $9.90.

FOR FAMILIES

The family vacation is a rite of passage for many households, one that in a split second can devolve into a *National Lampoon* farce. But as any veteran family vacationer will assure you, a family trip can be among the most pleasurable and rewarding times of your life.

Many of the city's hotels allow kids to stay free in their parents' room. Some budget hotels also allow children to eat for free in the hotel's dining room. Keep in mind that most downtown hotels cater almost exclusively to business travelers and don't offer the sort of amenities that appeal to families—a swimming pool, game room, or inexpensive restaurant. For information on hotels that are good for families, see the "Family-Friendly Hotels" box in chapter 5.

At mealtimes, many of the larger restaurants, especially along the waterfront, offer children's menus. You'll also find plenty of variety and low prices at the many food vendors' stalls at the Pike Place Market. There's also a food court in Westlake Center shopping mall. For information on restaurants that cater to families, see the "Family-Friendly Restaurants" box in chapter 6, "Where to Dine in Seattle."

For information on family attractions in Seattle, see the "Especially for Kids" section of chapter 7.

Frommer's Family Vacations in the National Parks (Wiley Publishing) has tips for enjoying your trip to Olympic National Park.

Note: If you plan to travel on to Canada during your Seattle vacation, be sure to bring your children's birth certificates with you.

NEWSLETTERS

The *Family Travel Times,* a bimonthly newsletter published by FTT Marketing, is an excellent resource for family travel. It includes information about hotel deals for families. To subscribe or get information, contact them at © **888/822-4388** or 212/477-5524; www.familytraveltimes.com. For $39 per year, you get six issues of the newsletter and discounts on other publications and back issues.

Family Travel Forum (© **212/ 665-6124;** www.familytravelforum. com) is another helpful source of information and travel discounts for families planning trips. You can receive a newsletter in the mail and/or access information online to read tips on traveling with children, staff-written travel articles, and members' firsthand accounts of experiences in various destinations. Each issue of the newsletter focuses on a specific theme, from traveling with teens to intergenerational travel. A comprehensive annual membership is $48, or you can subscribe monthly for $3.95.

6 Getting There

BY PLANE
THE MAJOR AIRLINES

The **Seattle–Tacoma International Airport** (© **800/544-1965** or 206/431-4444; www.seatac.org/seatac) is served by about 30 airlines. The major carriers include: **Air Canada** (© 800/247-2262; www.aircanada.ca), **Alaska Airlines** (© 800/426-0333; www.alaskaair.com), **America West** (© 800/235-9292; www.americawest.com), **American Airlines** (© 800/433-7300; www.aa.com), **Continental** (© 800/525-0280; www.continental.com), **Delta** (© 800/221-1212; www.delta.com), **Frontier** (© 800/432-1359; www.frontierairlines.com), **Horizon Air** (© 800/547-9308; www.horizonair.com), **Jet-Blue Airways** (© 800/JETBLUE; www.jetblue.com), **Northwest/KLM** (© 800/225-2525; www.nwa.com), **Shuttle by United** (© 800/748-8853; www.ual.com), **Southwest** (© 800/435-9792; www.iflyswa.com), **United** (© 800/241-6522; www.united.com), and **US Airways** (© 800/428-4322; www.usairways.com).

For information on flights to the United States from other countries, see "Getting to the United States" in chapter 3, "For International Visitors."

Seaplane service between Seattle and the San Juan Islands and Victoria, British Columbia, is offered by **Kenmore Air** (© **800/543-9595** or 425/486-1257; www.kenmoreair.com), which has its Seattle terminals at the south end of Lake Union and at the north end of Lake Washington.

There is also helicopter service to Seattle's Boeing Field from Victoria and Vancouver, British Columbia, on **Helijet Airways** (© **800/665-4354;** www.helijet.com). The flights take about 35 minutes from Victoria and 80 minutes from Vancouver (depending on the connection, as you must connect in Victoria for the flight to Seattle). Ballpark round-trip airfares are about $238 ($298 Canadian) between Victoria and Seattle and about $384 ($616 Canadian) between Vancouver and Seattle.

FLY FOR LESS: TIPS ON GETTING THE BEST AIRFARES

If you happen to be flying from another city on the West Coast or elsewhere in the West, check first with Frontier Airlines, Shuttle by United, Alaska Airlines, Horizon Airlines, or Southwest. These airlines often have the best fares between Western cities.

Check your newspaper for advertised sales or call the airlines directly and ask if any promotional rates or special fares are available. You'll almost never see a sale during the peak summer vacation months of July and August, or during the Thanksgiving or Christmas seasons; but in periods of low-volume travel, you should pay no more than $400 for a cross-country flight.

Note, however, that the lowest-priced fares are often nonrefundable, require advance purchase of 1 to 3 weeks and a certain length of stay, and carry penalties for changing dates of travel. So, when you're quoted a fare, make sure you know exactly what the restrictions are before you commit. If you already hold a ticket when a sale breaks, it may even pay to exchange your ticket, which usually incurs a $50 to $75 charge.

If your schedule is flexible, ask if you can secure a cheaper fare by staying an extra day, staying over Saturday night, or flying midweek. (Many airlines won't volunteer this information, so be aggressive and ask the reservations agent lots of questions.)

Consolidators, also known as bucket shops, are a good place to find low fares. Consolidators buy seats in bulk from the airlines and then sell them back to the public at prices below even the airlines' discounted rates. Their small boxed ads usually run in the Sunday travel section of newspapers at the bottom of the page. Before you pay, however, ask for a confirmation number from the consolidator and then call the airline itself to confirm your seat. Also be aware that bucket shop tickets are usually nonrefundable or rigged with stiff cancellation penalties, often as high as 50% to 75% of the ticket price. And when an airline runs a special deal, you won't always do better with a consolidator.

For discount and last-minute bookings, contact **Air 4 Less** (© **800/FLY-FACTS;** www.air4less.com), which can often get you tickets at significantly less than full fare. Other reliable consolidators include **1-800-FLY-CHEAP** (www.1800flycheap.com); **TFI Tours International** (© **800/745-8000** or 212/736-1140; www.lowestprice.com), which serves as a clearinghouse for unused seats; or "rebators" such as **Travel Avenue** (© **800/333-3335;** www.travelavenue.com), which rebate part of their commissions to you.

Council Travel (© **800/226-8624;** www.counciltravel.com) and **STA Travel** (© **800/781-4040;** www.statravel.com) cater especially to young travelers, but their bargain basement prices are available to people of all ages.

BY CAR

Seattle is 1,190 miles from Los Angeles, 175 miles from Portland, 835 miles from Salt Lake City, 810 miles from San Francisco, 285 miles from Spokane, and 110 miles from Vancouver, British Columbia.

I-5 is the main north–south artery through Seattle, running south to Portland and north to the Canadian border. I-405 is Seattle's east-side bypass and accesses the cities of Bellevue, Redmond, and Kirkland on the east side of Lake Washington. I-90, which ends at I-5, connects Seattle to Spokane in the eastern part of Washington. Wash. 520 connects I-405 with Seattle just north of downtown and also ends at I-5. Wash. 99, the Alaskan Way Viaduct, is another major north–south highway through downtown Seattle; it passes through the waterfront section of the city. Currently, there is heated debate over the fate of the Alaskan Way Viaduct, which was damaged in an earthquake a few years ago. One suggestion is to tear it down entirely, which would certainly make the waterfront a much pleasanter place.

One of the most important benefits of belonging to the **American Automobile Association (AAA)** (© **800/222-4357;** www.aaa.com) is that it supplies members with emergency road service and towing services if you have car trouble during your trip. You also get maps and detailed Trip-Tiks that give precise directions to a destination, including up-to-date information about areas of construction. In Seattle, AAA is located at 330 Sixth Ave. N. (© **206/448-5353**).

See "Getting Around" in chapter 4 for details on driving, parking, and car rentals in Seattle.

BY FERRY

Seattle is served by **Washington State Ferries** (© **800/84-FERRY** or 888/808-7977 within Washington state, or 206/464-6400; www.wsdot.wa.gov/ferries), the most extensive ferry system in the United States. Car ferries travel

Tips   What You Can Carry On—and What You Can't

The Transportation Security Administration (TSA), the government agency that now handles all aspects of airport security, has devised new restrictions for carry-on baggage, not only to expedite the screening process but to prevent potential weapons from passing through airport security. Passengers are now limited to bringing just one carry-on bag and one personal item onto the aircraft (previous regulations allowed two carry-on bags and one personal item, like a briefcase or a purse). For more information, go to the TSA's website, www.tsa.gov. The agency has released an updated list of items passengers are not allowed to carry onto an aircraft:

Not permitted: knives and box cutters, corkscrews, straight razors, metal scissors, golf clubs, baseball bats, pool cues, hockey sticks, ski poles, ice picks.

Permitted: nail clippers, nail files, tweezers, eyelash curlers, safety razors (including disposable razors), syringes (with documented proof of medical need), walking canes and umbrellas (must be inspected first).

The airline you fly may have **additional restrictions** on items you can and cannot carry on board. Call ahead to avoid problems.

between downtown Seattle and both Bainbridge Island and Bremerton (on the Kitsap Peninsula) from Pier 52, Colman dock. Passenger-only ferries to Bremerton and to Vashon Island use the adjacent Pier 50. Car ferries also connect Fauntleroy (in west Seattle) with both Vashon Island and the Kitsap Peninsula at Southworth; Tahlequah (at the south end of Vashon Island) with Point Defiance in Tacoma; Edmonds with Kingston (on the Kitsap Peninsula); Mukilteo with Whidbey Island; Whidbey Island at Keystone with Port Townsend; and Anacortes with the San Juan Islands and Sidney, British Columbia (on Vancouver Island near Victoria). See "Getting Around," in chapter 4, for fare information.

If you are traveling between Victoria, British Columbia, and Seattle, several options are available from **Victoria Clipper,** Pier 69, 2701 Alaskan Way (© **800/888-2535,** 206/448-5000, or 250/382-8100 in Victoria; www.victoriaclipper.com).

Throughout the year, a ferry taking either 2 or 3 hours makes the trip ($59–$125 round-trip for adults). The lower fare is for advance-purchase tickets. Some scheduled trips also stop in the San Juan Islands.

BY TRAIN

Amtrak (© **800/872-7245;** www.amtrak.com) service runs from Vancouver, B.C., to Seattle and from Portland and as far south as Eugene, Oregon, on the *Cascades* (a high-speed, European-style Talgo train). The train takes about 4 hours from Vancouver to Seattle and 3½ to 4 hours from Portland to Seattle. One-way fares from Vancouver to Seattle are usually between $23 and $34, and fares between Portland and Seattle are usually between $23 and $36. Booking earlier will get you a less expensive ticket. There is also Amtrak service to Seattle from San Diego, Los Angeles, San Francisco, and Portland on the *Coast Starlight,* and from Spokane and points east on the *Empire Builder.* Amtrak also operates a bus between Vancouver and Seattle.

Like the airlines, Amtrak offers several discounted fares; although they're not all based on advance purchase, you have more discount options by reserving early. The discount fares can be used only on certain days and hours of the day; be sure to find out exactly what restrictions apply. Tickets for children ages 2 to 15 cost half the price of a regular coach fare when the children are accompanied by a fare-paying adult. Amtrak's website features a bargain fares service, Rail SALE, which allows you to purchase tickets for one-way designated coach seats at great discounts. This program is only available on **www.amtrak.com** when you charge your tickets by credit card.

Also inquire about money-saving packages that include hotel accommodations, car rentals, tours, and so on with your train fare. Call © **800/ 321-8684** for details.

BY BUS

The **Greyhound bus station,** 811 Stewart St. (© **800/229-9424** or 206/628-5526; www.greyhound.com), is located a few blocks northeast of downtown Seattle. **Greyhound** bus service provides connections to almost any city in the continental United States. Several budget chain motels are located only a few blocks from the bus station. It's a bit farther to the Hosteling International–Seattle hostel, yet walkable if you don't have much luggage. Otherwise, you can grab a free ride on a Metro bus.

7 Package Tours

Before you start your search for the lowest airfare, you may want to consider booking your flight as part of a travel package such as an escorted tour or a package tour. What you lose in adventure, you'll gain in time and money saved when you book accommodations, and maybe even food and entertainment, along with your flight.

PACKAGE TOURS FOR INDEPENDENT TRAVELERS

Package tours are not the same thing as escorted tours. Package tours are simply a way to buy the airfare, accommodations, and other elements of your trip (such as car rentals, airport transfers, and sometimes even activities) at the same time and often at discounted prices—kind of like one-stop shopping. Packages are sold in bulk to tour operators—who resell them to the public at a cost that drastically undercuts standard rates.

Package tours do have their advantages—chiefly in that you almost always save money. But among the disadvantages are limited choices, such as where you stay (the hotels may be unremarkable and are usually located more for the packager's convenience than for yours), or a fixed itinerary that doesn't allow for an extra day of shopping. Some packages offer a better class of hotels than others. Some offer the same hotels for lower prices than their competitors. Some offer flights on scheduled airlines while others book charters. In some packages, your choices of travel days may be limited. Some packages let you choose between escorted vacations and independent vacations; others allow you to add on a few guided excursions or escorted day trips (also at prices lower than if you booked them yourself) without booking an entirely escorted tour.

RECOMMENDED PACKAGE TOUR OPERATORS

One good source of package deals is the airlines themselves. Most major airlines offer air/land packages, including **American Airlines Vacations** (📞 800/321-2121; http://aav1. aavacations.com), **Delta Vacations** (📞 800/221-6666; www.delta vacations.com), **US Airways Vacations** (📞 800/455-0123 or 800/ 422-3861; www.usairwaysvacations. com), **Continental Airlines Vacations** (📞 800/301-3800; www.cool vacations.com), and **United Vacations** (📞 888/854-3899; www.united vacations.com).

Online Vacation Mall (📞 800/ 839-9851; www.onlinevacationmall. com) allows you to search for and book packages offered by a number of tour operators and airlines. The **United States Tour Operators Association's** website (www.ustoa.com) has a search engine that allows you to look for operators that offer packages to a specific destination. Travel packages are also listed in the travel section of your local Sunday newspaper.

8 Planning Your Trip Online

Internet users today can tap into the same travel-planning databases that were once accessible only to travel agents—and do it at the same speed. Sites such as **Frommers.com, Travelocity.com, Expedia.com,** and **Orbitz.com** (see below) allow consumers to comparison-shop for airfares, access special bargains, book flights, and reserve hotel rooms and rental cars.

Last-minute specials, such as weekend deals or Internet-only fares, are offered by airlines to fill empty seats. Most of these are announced on Tuesday or Wednesday and must be purchased online. They are only valid for travel that weekend, but some can be booked weeks or months in advance. Sign up for weekly e-mail alerts at airline websites or check mega-sites that compile comprehensive lists of last-minute specials, such as **Smarter Living** (http://smarter living.com) or **WebFlyer** (www. webflyer.com).

Some sites, such as Expedia.com, will send you **e-mail notification** when a cheap fare becomes available to your favorite destination. Some will also tell you when fares to a particular destination are lowest.

The list of travel-planning websites below is selective, not comprehensive. New sites are popping up all the time,

offering consumers even more tools for plotting out the perfect vacation.

- **Travelocity** (www.travelocity.com or www.frommers.travelocity. com) and **Expedia** (www.expedia. com) are among the most popular sites, each offering an excellent range of options. Travelers search by destination, dates, and cost.

- **Orbitz** (www.orbitz.com) is a popular site launched by United, Delta, Northwest, American, and Continental airlines. With this site, you're granted access to the largest database of low rates, airline tickets, rental cars, hotels, vacation packages, and other travel products. You get, among other offerings, available fares from more than 450 airlines.

- **Priceline** (www.priceline.com) lets you "name your price" for airline tickets, hotel rooms, and rental cars. For airline tickets, you can't say what time you want to fly—you have to accept any flight between 6am and 10pm on the dates you've selected, and you may have to make one or more stopovers. Tickets are nonrefundable, and no frequent-flier miles are awarded.

9 Tips on Accommodations

As a major metropolitan area, Seattle has a wide range of accommodations, from downtown high-rise business hotels to B&Bs in historic neighborhoods to freeway off-ramp chain motels.

TIPS FOR SAVING ON YOUR HOTEL ROOM

The **rack rate** is the maximum rate that a hotel charges for a room. It's the rate you'd get if you walked in off the street and asked for a room for the night. Hardly anybody pays these prices, however, and there are many ways around them.

- **Don't be afraid to bargain.** Most rack rates include commissions of 10% to 25% for travel agents, which some hotels may be willing to reduce if you make your own reservations and haggle a bit. Always ask whether a room less expensive than the first one quoted is available, or whether any special rates apply to you. You may qualify for corporate, student, military, senior citizen, or other discounts. Be sure to mention membership in AAA, AARP, frequent-flier programs, or trade unions, which may entitle you to special deals as well. Find out the hotel policy on children—do kids stay free in the room or is there a special rate?

- **Rely on a qualified professional.** Certain hotels give travel agents discounts in exchange for steering business their way, so if you're shy about bargaining, an agent may be better equipped to negotiate discounts for you.

- **Dial direct.** When booking a room in a chain hotel, compare the rates offered by the hotel's local line with that of the toll-free number. Also check with an agent and online. A hotel makes nothing on a room that stays empty, so the local hotel reservation desk may be willing to offer a special rate unavailable elsewhere.

- **Remember the law of supply and demand.** Business hotels in downtown locations are busiest during the week, so you can expect big discounts over the weekend. Avoid high-season stays whenever you can: Planning your vacation just a week before or after official peak season can mean big savings.

- **Avoid excess charges.** When you book a room, ask whether the hotel charges for parking. Many hotels charge a fee just for dialing out on the phone in your room. Find out whether your hotel imposes a surcharge on local and long-distance calls. A pay phone, however inconvenient, may save you money, although many calling cards charge a fee or delete minutes when you use them on pay phones. And don't be tempted by the minibar: Most hotels charge through the nose for water, soda, and snacks. Finally, ask about local taxes and service charges, which can increase the cost of a room by 25% or more.

- **Consider a suite.** If you are traveling with your family or another couple, you can pack more people into a suite (which usually comes with a sofa bed), and thereby reduce your per-person rate. Remember that some places charge for extra guests.

3

For International Visitors

Although American trends have spread across Europe and other parts of the world to the extent that America may seem like familiar territory before your arrival, there are still many peculiarities and uniquely American situations that any foreign visitor will encounter.

1 Preparing for Your Trip

ENTRY REQUIREMENTS

Immigration law is a hot political issue in the United States these days, and the following requirements may have changed somewhat by the time you plan your trip. Check at any U.S. embassy or consulate for current information and requirements. You can also go to the **U.S. State Department** website at **www.state.gov**.

VISAS The U.S. State Department has a **Visa Waiver Program** allowing citizens of certain countries to enter the United States without a visa for stays of up to 90 days. At press time, these countries included Andorra, Australia, Austria, Belgium, Brunei, Denmark, Finland, France, Germany, Iceland, Ireland, Italy, Japan, Liechtenstein, Luxembourg, Monaco, the Netherlands, New Zealand, Norway, Portugal, San Marino, Singapore, Slovenia, Spain, Sweden, Switzerland, the United Kingdom, and Uruguay. Citizens of these countries need only a valid passport and a round-trip air or cruise ticket in their possession upon arrival. If they first enter the United States, they may also visit Mexico, Canada, Bermuda, and/or the Caribbean islands and return to the United States without a visa. Canadian citizens may enter the United States without a visa; they need only proof of residence.

Citizens of all other countries must have (1) a valid passport that expires at least 6 months later than the scheduled end of their visit to the United States, and (2) a tourist visa, which can be obtained without charge from any U.S. consulate.

To get a visa, the traveler must submit a completed application form (either in person or by mail) with a 1½-inch-square photo, and must demonstrate binding ties to a residence abroad. Usually you can get a visa at once or within 24 hours, but it may take longer during the summer rush from June through August. If you cannot go in person, contact the nearest U.S. embassy or consulate for directions on applying by mail. Your travel agent or airline office may also be able to supply you with visa applications and instructions. The U.S. consulate or embassy that issues your visa determines whether you will be issued a multiple- or single-entry visa and any restrictions on the length of your stay.

British subjects can get up-to-date passport and visa information by calling the **U.S. Embassy Visa Information Line** (© 09061/500-590) or the **London Passport Service** (© 0990/210-410).

MEDICAL REQUIREMENTS

Unless you're arriving from an area known to be suffering from an epidemic (particularly cholera or yellow fever), inoculations or vaccinations are not required for entry into the United States. If you have a disease that requires treatment with narcotics or syringe-administered medications, carry a valid signed prescription from your physician to allay any suspicions that you may be smuggling narcotics (a serious offense that carries severe penalties in the United States).

DRIVER'S LICENSES Foreign driver's licenses are usually recognized in the United States, although you may want to get an international driver's license if your home license is not written in English.

CUSTOMS REQUIREMENTS Every visitor over 21 years of age may bring in, free of duty, the following: (1) 1 liter of beer, wine, or hard liquor; (2) 200 cigarettes, 50 cigars (but not from Cuba; an additional 100 cigars may be brought in under your gift exemption), or 4.4 pounds (2kg) of smoking tobacco; and (3) $100 worth of gifts. These exemptions are offered to travelers who spend at least 72 hours in the United States and who have not claimed them within the preceding 6 months. Meat (with the exception of some canned meat products) is prohibited, as are most fruits, vegetables, and plants (including seeds, tropical plants, and the like). Foreign tourists may bring in or take out up to $10,000 in U.S. or foreign currency with no formalities; larger sums must be declared to U.S. Customs on entering or leaving, which includes filing form CM 4790. For specific information regarding U.S. Customs, call your nearest U.S. embassy or consulate, or contact the **U.S. Customs** office at ℂ **202/927-1770** or www.customs.ustreas.gov.

INSURANCE
Although it's not required of travelers, health insurance is highly recommended. Unlike many European countries, the United States does not usually offer free or low-cost medical care to its citizens or visitors. Doctors and hospitals are expensive, and in most cases require advance payment or proof of coverage before they render their services. Other policies can cover everything from the loss or theft of your baggage to trip cancellation to the guarantee of bail in case you're arrested. Good policies also cover the costs of an accident, repatriation, or death. See "Insurance, Health & Safety" in chapter 2, "Planning Your Trip to Seattle," for more information. In Europe, packages such as **Europ Assistance** are sold by automobile clubs and travel agencies at attractive rates. **Worldwide Assistance Services** (ℂ **800/821-2828**; www.worldwideassistance.com) is the agent for Europ Assistance in the United States.

Although lack of health insurance may prevent you from being admitted to a hospital in nonemergencies, don't worry about being left on a street corner to die: The American way is to fix you now and bill you later.

MONEY
The U.S. monetary system has a decimal base: one American **dollar** ($1) = 100 **cents** (100¢). Bills commonly come in $1 (a "buck"), $5, $10, $20, $50, and $100 denominations (the last two are not welcome when paying for small purchases or taxi fares). Common coins include the penny (1¢), nickel (5¢), dime (10¢), and quarter (25¢). You may come across a 50¢ or $1 coin as well.

CURRENCY EXCHANGE The foreign-exchange bureaus so common in many countries are rare in the United States, even at airports, and nonexistent outside major cities. Try to avoid having to change foreign money or traveler's checks not denominated in U.S. dollars at a small-town bank or even a branch bank in a big city. In fact, leave any currency other than

---

Tips **In Case of Emergency**
Be sure to keep copies of all your travel papers separate from your wallet or purse, and leave copies with someone at home should you need them faxed in an emergency.

U.S. dollars at home—it could prove more nuisance to you than it's worth.

TRAVELER'S CHECKS   Traveler's checks *denominated in U.S. dollars* are readily accepted at most hotels, motels, restaurants, and large stores, but might not be accepted at small stores or for small purchases. The best place to change traveler's checks is at a bank. Do not bring traveler's checks denominated in other currencies. The three most widely recognized traveler's checks are **Visa, American Express,** and **Thomas Cook.**

CREDIT CARDS & ATMS   Credit cards are the most widely used form of payment in the United States. Among the most commonly accepted are **Visa** (BarclayCard in Britain), **MasterCard** (EuroCard in Europe, Access in Britain, Chargex in Canada), **American Express, Diners Club, Discover,** and **Carte Blanche.** You must have a credit or charge card to rent a car. There are, however, a handful of stores and restaurants, and even a few guest ranches and bed-and-breakfast inns, that do not take credit cards, so be sure to ask in advance. Most businesses display a sticker near their entrance to let you know which cards they accept. (*Note:* Often businesses require a minimum purchase price, usually around $10, to use a credit card.)

It is strongly recommended that you bring at least one major credit card. Hotels, car-rental companies, and airlines usually require a credit-card imprint as a deposit against expenses, and in an emergency a credit card can be priceless.

You'll find automated teller machines (ATMs) on just about every block in larger cities. Some ATMs allow you to draw U.S. currency against your bank and credit cards. Check with your bank before leaving home, and remember that you need your personal identification number (PIN) to do so. Most accept Visa, MasterCard, and American Express, as well as ATM cards from other U.S. banks. Expect to be charged from $1 to $2 per transaction, however. One way around these fees is to ask for cash back at grocery stores, which generally accept ATM cards and don't charge usage fees. Of course, you'll have to purchase something first.

SAFETY

While tourist areas are generally safe, U.S. urban areas tend to be less safe than those in Europe or Japan. You should always stay alert. It is wise to ask your hotel's front desk staff if you're in doubt about which neighborhoods are safe. Avoid deserted areas, especially at night, and don't go into public parks at night unless there's a concert or similar occasion that will attract a crowd.

Avoid carrying valuables with you on the street, and don't display expensive cameras or electronic equipment. If you're using a map, consult it inconspicuously. Hold onto your pocketbook, and place your billfold in an inside pocket. In public places, keep your possessions in sight.

Remember also that hotels are open to the public, and in a large hotel, security may not be able to screen everyone entering. Always lock your room door—don't assume that once inside your hotel you are automatically safe.

DRIVING SAFETY Safety while driving is particularly important. Ask your rental agency about personal safety or request a brochure of traveler safety tips when you pick up your car. Get written directions or a map with the route marked in red from the agency to show you how to get to your destination. If possible, arrive and depart during daylight hours.

Recently more and more crime has involved cars and drivers. If you drive off a highway into a questionable neighborhood, try to leave the area as quickly as possible. If you have an accident, even on the highway, stay in your car with the doors locked until you assess the situation or until the police arrive. If you are bumped from behind on the street or are involved in a minor accident with no injuries, and the situation appears to be suspicious, motion to the other driver to follow you to the nearest police precinct, gas station, or open store. Never get out of your car in such situations.

Park in well-lit, well-traveled areas if possible. Always keep your car doors locked, whether the vehicle is attended or unattended. Look around you before you get out of your car and never leave any packages or valuables in sight. If someone attempts to rob you or steal your car, do *not* try to resist the thief/carjacker—then report the incident to the police department immediately by calling ✆ **911.**

Also, make sure you have enough gasoline in your tank to reach your intended destination so that you're not forced to look for a service station in an unfamiliar and possibly unsafe neighborhood—especially at night.

2 Getting to the United States

BY PLANE

For an extensive listing of airlines that fly into Seattle, see "Getting There" in chapter 2, "Planning Your Trip to Seattle."

A number of U.S. airlines offer service from Europe to the United States. If they do not have direct flights from Europe to Seattle, they can book you straight through on a connecting flight.

You can make reservations by calling the following numbers in Great Britain: **American** (✆ 0208/572-5555 in London and 08457/789-789 outside London; www.aa.com), **British Airways** (✆ 0845/773-3377; www.britishairways.com), **Continental** (✆ 0800/776-464; www. continental.com), **Delta** (✆ 0800/414-767; www.delta.com), **Northwest/KLM** (✆ 012/93-502710; www.nwa.com), **United** (✆ 0845/8444-777; www.united.com), and **US Airways** (✆ 4420/7484-2100; www.usairways.com).

International carriers that fly from Europe to Los Angeles and San Francisco include **Aer Lingus** (✆ 0818/365-000 in Ireland; www.aerlingus.com) and **British Airways** (✆ 0845/773-3377; www.britishairways.com), which also flies direct to Seattle from London.

From New Zealand and Australia, there are flights to Los Angeles on **Qantas** (✆ 13 13 13 in Australia; www.qantas.com.au) and **Air New Zealand** (✆ 0800/737-000 in Auckland; www.airnewzealand.co.nz). From there, you can continue on to Seattle on a regional airline such as **Alaska Airlines** (✆ 800/252-7522; www.alaskaair.com) or **Southwest** (✆ 800/435-9792; www.southwest.com).

From Toronto, there are flights to Seattle on **Air Canada** (✆ 800/247-2262; www.aircanada.ca), **American Airlines** (✆ 800/433-7300; www.aa.com), **Northwest** (✆ 800/225-2525; www.nwa.com), and **United** (✆ 800/241-6522; www.united.com).

From Vancouver, B.C., there are flights to Seattle on **Air Canada, Horizon Airlines** (© 800/547-9308; www.horizonair.com), **United Express,** and **Alaska Airlines** (© 800/252-7522; www.alaskaair.com).

Operated by the European Travel Network, **www.discount-tickets.com** is a great online source for regular and discounted airfares.

For more money-saving airline advice, see the "Getting There" section of chapter 2.

AIRLINE DISCOUNTS Travelers from overseas can take advantage of the advance-purchase excursion (APEX) fares offered by the major U.S. and European carriers. For more money-saving airline advice, see "Getting There," in chapter 2.

BY TRAIN

Amtrak (© 800/872-7245; www.amtrak.com) offers service from Vancouver, B.C., to Seattle, a trip that takes about 4 hours. From Portland to Seattle takes about the same length of time. One-way fares from Vancouver to Seattle are usually between $23 and $34, and fares between Portland and Seattle are usually between $23 and $36. Booking earlier will get you a less expensive ticket. Amtrak also operates service between Vancouver and Eugene, Oregon, and runs bus service between Vancouver and Seattle.

Like the airlines, Amtrak offers several discounted fares; although they're not all based on advance purchase, you have more discount options by reserving early.

BY FERRY

If you are traveling between Victoria, B.C., and Seattle, several options are available from **Victoria Clipper,** Pier 69, 2701 Alaskan Way (© **800/888-2535,** 206/448-5000, or 250/382-8100 in Victoria; www.victoriaclipper.com). Throughout the year, a ferry taking either 2 or 3 hours makes the trip ($59–$125 round-trip for adults).

IMMIGRATION & CUSTOMS CLEARANCE

The visitor arriving by air, no matter what the port of entry, should cultivate patience before setting foot on U.S. soil. Getting through Immigration Control might take as long as 2 hours on some days, especially summer weekends. Add the time it takes to clear Customs, and you'll see that you should make a very generous allowance for delay in planning connections between international and domestic flights—an average of 2 to 3 hours at least.

In contrast, travelers arriving by car, by ferry, or by rail from Canada will find border-crossing formalities somewhat more streamlined, though not nearly as easy as they were before the September 11, 2001, terrorist attacks. Air travelers from Canada, Bermuda, and some places in the Caribbean can sometimes go through Customs and Immigration at the point of departure, which is much quicker.

3 Getting Around the United States

For specific information on traveling to and around Seattle, see "Getting There" in chapter 2, and "Getting Around" in chapter 4.

BY PLANE Some large airlines (for example, United and Delta) offer travelers on their transatlantic or transpacific flights special discount tickets under the name **Visit USA,** allowing mostly one-way travel from one U.S. destination to another at very low prices. These discount tickets are not on sale in the United States and must be purchased abroad in conjunction with your international ticket. This system is the best, easiest, and fastest way to see the United States at low cost. You should get information well in advance from your travel agent or the office of the airline concerned, since the conditions attached to these discount tickets can be changed without advance notice.

If you are arriving by air, allow lots of time to make connections between international and domestic flights—an average of 2 to 3 hours at least.

BY CAR   The United States is a car culture through and through. Driving is the most cost-effective, convenient, and comfortable way to travel here. The interstate highway system connects cities and towns all over the country, and in addition to these high-speed, limited-access roadways, there's an extensive network of federal, state, and local highways and roads. Driving will give you a lot of flexibility in making, and altering, your itinerary and in allowing you to see some off-the-beaten-path destinations that cannot be reached easily by public transportation. You'll also have easy access to inexpensive motels at interstate highway off-ramps.

BY TRAIN   International visitors can also buy a **USA Railpass,** good for 15 or 30 days of unlimited travel on **Amtrak** (© **800/USA-RAIL;** www.amtrak.com). These passes are available through many foreign travel agents and are valid in specific regions of the United States. At press time, a 15-day Far West costs $190 off-peak, $325 peak; a 30-day pass costs $250 off-peak, $405 peak. (With a foreign passport, you can also buy passes at staffed Amtrak offices in the United States, including locations in San Francisco, Los Angeles, Chicago, New York, Miami, Boston, and Washington, D.C.) Reservations are generally required and should be made for each part of your trip as early as possible. Amtrak also offers an **Air/Rail Travel Plan** that allows you to travel by both train and plane; for information, call © **800/437-3441.**

BY BUS   Although bus travel is often the most economical form of public transit for short hops between U.S. cities, it can also be slow and uncomfortable—certainly not an option for everyone (particularly when Amtrak, which is far more luxurious, offers similar rates). **Greyhound/Trailways** (© **800/229-9424** or 402/330-8552; www.greyhound.com), the sole nationwide bus line, offers an unlimited-travel **Ameripass/Discovery Pass** for 7 days at $199 to $219, 15 days at $299 to $339, 30 days at $389 to $449, and 60 days at $549 to $629. Passes valid for other lengths of time are also available. Passes must be purchased at a Greyhound terminal. Special rates are available for senior citizens and students.

 FAST FACTS: For the International Traveler

Automobile Organizations   Auto clubs can supply maps, suggested routes, guidebooks, accident and bail-bond insurance, and emergency road service. The **American Automobile Association (AAA)** is the major auto club in the United States. If you belong to an auto club in your home country, inquire about AAA reciprocity before you leave. You may be able to join AAA even if you're not a member of a reciprocal club; to inquire, call **AAA** (© **800/222-4357**). AAA is actually an organization of regional auto clubs; so look under "AAA Automobile Club" in the White Pages of the telephone directory. AAA has a nationwide **emergency road service** telephone number (© **800/AAA-HELP**).

Business Hours See "Fast Facts: Seattle," in chapter 4.

Climate See "When to Go," in chapter 2.

Currency See "Money" under "Preparing for Your Trip," earlier in this chapter.

Currency Exchange You'll find currency-exchange services in major international airports. There's a **Travelex/Thomas Cook** kiosk (© **206/248-0401**) at Sea-Tac International Airport in the North Esplanade, Concourse D. There's another Travelex/Thomas Cook office in downtown Seattle at Westlake Center shopping center, 400 Pine St. (© **206/682-4525**).

Drinking Laws The legal age for purchase and consumption of alcoholic beverages is 21; proof of age is required and often requested at bars, nightclubs, and restaurants, so it's always a good idea to bring ID when you go out.

Do not carry open containers of alcohol in your car or any public area that isn't zoned for alcohol consumption. The police can fine you on the spot. And nothing will ruin your trip faster than getting a citation for DUI ("driving under the influence"), so don't even think about driving while intoxicated.

See also the "Liquor Laws" entry in the "Fast Facts" at the end of chapter 4.

Electricity Like Canada, the United States uses 110 to 120 volts AC (60 cycles), compared to 220 to 240 volts AC (50 cycles) in most of Europe, Australia, and New Zealand. If your small appliances use 220 to 240 volts, you'll need a 110-volt transformer and a plug adapter with two flat parallel pins to operate them here. Downward converters that change 220 to 240 volts to 110 to 120 volts are difficult to find in the United States, so bring one with you.

Embassies & Consulates All embassies are located in Washington, D.C. Some consulates are located in major U.S. cities, and most nations have a mission to the United Nations in New York City. If your country isn't listed below, call **directory information** in Washington, D.C. (© **202/555-1212**), for the number of your national embassy.

The embassy of **Australia** is at 1601 Massachusetts Ave. NW, Washington, D.C. 20036 (© **202/797-3000**; www.austemb.org). There is no consulate in Seattle; the nearest is at 625 Market St., Suite 200, San Francisco, CA 94105-3304 (© **415/536-1970**).

The embassy of **Canada** is at 501 Pennsylvania Ave. NW, Washington, D.C. 20001 (© **202/682-1740**; www.canadianembassy.org). There is a consulate in Seattle at 412 Plaza 600 Building, Sixth Avenue and Stewart Street, Seattle, WA 98101-1286 (© **206/443-1777**).

The embassy of **Ireland** is at 2234 Massachusetts Ave. NW, Washington, D.C. 20008 (© **202/462-3939**; www.irelandemb.org). There is no consulate in Seattle; the nearest is at 44 Montgomery St., Suite 3830, San Francisco, CA 94104 (© **415/392-4214**).

The embassy of **New Zealand** is at 37 Observatory Circle NW, Washington, D.C. 20008 (© **202/328-4800**; www.nzemb.org). There is also a consulate in Seattle at 10649 N. Beach Rd., Bow, WA 98232 (© **360/766-6791**).

The embassy of the **United Kingdom** is at 3100 Massachusetts Ave. NW, Washington, D.C. 20008 (✆ **202/588-7850;** www.britainusa.com). There is a consulate in Seattle at 900 Fourth Ave., Suite 3100, Seattle, WA 98164 (✆ **206/622-9255**).

Emergencies Dial ✆ **911** to report a fire, call the police, or get an ambulance. This is a free call (no coins are required at a public telephone).

If you encounter problems, check the local telephone directory to find an office of the **Traveler's Aid Society,** a nationwide nonprofit social-service organization geared to helping travelers in difficult straits. The society's services might include reuniting families separated while traveling, providing food and/or shelter to people stranded without cash, or even emotional counseling. If you're in trouble, seek it out.

Gasoline (Petrol) Petrol is known as gasoline (or simply "gas") in the United States, and petrol stations are known as both gas stations and service stations. Gasoline costs less here than it does in Europe, and taxes are already included in the printed price. One U.S. gallon equals 3.8 liters or .85 Imperial gallons.

Holidays Banks, government offices, post offices, and many stores, restaurants, and museums are closed on the following legal national holidays: January 1 (New Year's Day), the third Monday in January (Martin Luther King Jr. Day), the third Monday in February (Presidents' Day, Washington's Birthday), the last Monday in May (Memorial Day), July 4 (Independence Day), the first Monday in September (Labor Day), the second Monday in October (Columbus Day), November 11 (Veterans' Day/Armistice Day), the fourth Thursday in November (Thanksgiving Day), and December 25 (Christmas). Also, the Tuesday following the first Monday in November is Election Day and is a federal government holiday in presidential-election years (held every 4 years, and next in 2004).

Internet Access Checking the Yellow Pages under Internet Access may turn up a few cybercafes. Many copy shops (Kinko's is one large national chain) also provide Internet access. If you are traveling with your laptop computer, note that many hotels, especially those frequented by business travelers, have telephones with dataports and dual phone lines in guest rooms.

Legal Aid The foreign tourist will probably never become involved with the American legal system. If you are pulled over for a minor infraction (for example, of the highway code, such as speeding), never attempt to pay the fine directly to a police officer; this could be construed as attempted bribery, a much more serious crime. Pay fines by mail or directly into the hands of the clerk of the court. If accused of a more serious offense, say and do nothing before consulting a lawyer. The burden is on the state to prove a person's guilt beyond a reasonable doubt, and everyone has the right to remain silent, whether he or she is suspected of a crime or actually arrested. Once arrested, a person can make one telephone call to a party of his or her choice. Call your embassy or consulate.

Mail Mailboxes are blue with a red-and-white stripe and carry the inscription U.S. MAIL. Outside of major urban areas, such mailboxes can be difficult to locate. Look in front of supermarkets and at other large shopping centers. If your mail is addressed to a U.S. destination, don't forget to add the five-digit postal code (or ZIP code), after the two-letter abbreviation of the state to which the mail is addressed.

At press time, domestic postage rates were 23¢ for a postcard and 37¢ for a letter. International mail rates vary. For example, a 1-ounce first-class letter to England costs 80¢, or 60¢ to Canada and Mexico; a first-class postcard to England costs 70¢, or 50¢ to Canada and Mexico.

Medical Emergencies To call an ambulance, dial ⓒ **911** from any phone. No coins are needed.

Newspapers & Magazines National newspapers include the *New York Times*, *USA Today*, and the *Wall Street Journal*. National newsweeklies include *Newsweek*, *Time*, and *U.S. News & World Report*. In large cities, most newsstands offer a small selection of the most popular foreign periodicals and newspapers, such as *The Economist*, *Le Monde*, and *Der Spiegel*. For information on local publications, see the "Fast Facts" section of chapter 4, "Getting to Know Seattle."

Restrooms You won't find public toilets on the streets in most U.S. cities, but they can be found in hotel lobbies, bars, restaurants, museums, department stores, shopping malls, railway and bus stations, and service stations. Note, however, that restaurants and bars in resorts or heavily visited areas may reserve their restrooms for the use of their patrons. Some establishments display a notice that toilets are for the use of patrons only. You can ignore this sign or, better yet, avoid arguments by paying for a cup of coffee or a soft drink, which will qualify you as a patron. Large hotels and fast-food restaurants are probably the best bet for good, clean facilities.

Safety See section 1 of this chapter.

Taxes The United States does not have a value-added tax (VAT) or other indirect tax at a national level. Every state, and each county and city in it, is allowed to levy its own local tax on purchases. Taxes are already included in the prices of certain services, such as public transportation, cab fares, telephone calls, and gasoline.

In Seattle, the sales tax rate is 8.8%. Also, you'll pay 28.5% to 29.61% in taxes and concession fees when you rent a car at Seattle–Tacoma Airport. You'll save 10% to 11.11% by renting somewhere other than the airport. Hotel room taxes range from around 10% to 16%. Travelers on a budget should keep both car-rental and hotel-room taxes in mind when planning a trip.

Telephone & Fax The telephone system in the United States is run by private corporations, so rates, especially for long-distance service and operator-assisted calls, can vary widely. Generally, hotel surcharges on long-distance and local calls are astronomical, so you're usually better off using a **public pay telephone,** which you'll find clearly marked in most public buildings and private establishments as well as on the street. Convenience grocery stores and gas stations almost always have them. Many supermarkets and convenience stores sell **prepaid calling cards** in denominations up to $50; these cards can be the least expensive way to call home. Many public phones at airports now accept American Express, MasterCard, and Visa credit cards. **Local calls** made from public pay phones in most locales cost either 35¢ or 50¢. Pay phones do not accept pennies, and few take anything larger than a quarter.

Most long-distance and international calls can be dialed directly from any phone. **For calls within the United States and to Canada,** dial 1 followed by the area code and the seven-digit number. **For other international calls,** dial 011 followed by the country code, city code, and telephone number of the person you are calling.

Calls to area codes **800, 888, 877,** and **866** are toll-free. However, calls to numbers in area codes **700** and **900** (chat lines, bulletin boards, "dating" services, and so on) can be very expensive—usually 95¢ to $3 or more per minute.

For **reversed-charge** or **collect calls,** and for **person-to-person calls,** dial 0 (zero, not the letter *O*) followed by the area code and number you want; an operator then comes on the line, and you should specify that you are calling collect, or person-to-person, or both. If your operator-assisted call is international, ask for the overseas operator.

For **local directory assistance** ("information"), dial 411; for long-distance information, dial 1 and then the appropriate area code and 555-1212.

Most hotels have **fax machines** available for guest use (be sure to ask about the charge to use it). A less expensive way to send and receive faxes may be at stores such as Kinko's (see "Internet Access," above) or Mail Boxes Etc., a national chain of packing service shops (look in the Yellow Pages under "Packing Services").

There are two kinds of telephone directories in the United States. The **White Pages** lists private households and business subscribers in alphabetical order. The inside front cover lists emergency numbers for police, fire, ambulance, the Coast Guard, poison-control center, crime-victims hot line, and so on. The first few pages tell you how to make long-distance and international calls, complete with country codes and area codes. Government numbers are usually printed on blue paper within the White Pages. Printed on yellow paper, the **Yellow Pages** lists all local services, businesses, industries, and houses of worship according to category, with an index at the front or back. (Drugstores/pharmacies and restaurants are also listed by geographic location.) The Yellow Pages includes city plans or detailed area maps, postal ZIP codes, and public transportation routes.

Time The United States is divided into six time zones. From east to west, they are Eastern Standard Time (EST), Central Standard Time (CST), Mountain Standard Time (MST), Pacific Standard Time (PST), Alaska Standard Time (AST), and Hawaii-Aleutian Standard Time (HST). Seattle is on Pacific Standard Time.

Tipping Tipping is so ingrained in the American way of life that the annual income tax of tip-earning service personnel is based on how much they *should* have received in light of their employers' gross revenues.

In hotels, tip **bellhops** at least $1 per bag ($2–$3 if you have a lot of luggage), and tip the **housecleaning** or **chamber staff** $1 to $2 per day (more if you've left a disaster area to clean up, or if you're traveling with kids and/or pets). Tip the **doorman** or **concierge** only if he or she has provided you with some specific service (for example, calling a cab for you or obtaining difficult-to-get theater tickets). Tip the **valet-parking attendant** $1 every time you get your car.

In restaurants, bars, and nightclubs, tip **service staff** 15% to 20% of the check, tip **bartenders** 10% to 15%, tip **checkroom attendants** $1 per garment, and tip **valet-parking attendants** $1 per vehicle. Tip the **doorman** only if he has provided you with some specific service (such as calling a cab for you). Tipping is not expected in cafeterias and fast-food restaurants.

Tip **cab drivers** 15% of the fare.

As for other service personnel, tip **skycaps** (luggage carriers) at airports at least $1 per bag ($2 to $3 if you have a lot of luggage) and tip **hairdressers** and **barbers** 15% to 20%.

4

Getting to Know Seattle

Because it is surrounded on three sides by water, built on six hills, and divided into numerous neighborhoods, Seattle can be a very confusing city. While most of its top attractions are located downtown, there are places of interest in other areas, too, including eclectic neighborhoods and attractive parks. In other words, the city's charms aren't all right in your face. This chapter, which includes information on the city's layout, its neighborhoods, and the basics of how to get around, should help you get out and explore so you can get to know the real Seattle.

1 Orientation

ARRIVING

BY PLANE

Seattle–Tacoma International Airport (© 800/544-1965 or 206/431-4444; www.seatac.org/seatac), most commonly referred to simply as Sea-Tac, is located about 14 miles south of Seattle.

Inside the arrivals terminal, you'll find **Visitor Information Desks** (© 206/433-5218) in the baggage-claim area across from carousels no. 1 and no. 8. They are open daily from 9am to 5pm. However, these desks cannot make hotel reservations for you.

Also at the airport, you'll find a **Travelex** currency exchange desk (© 206/248-0401) and branches of all the major car-rental companies (for further details see "Getting Around," later in this chapter).

GETTING INTO THE CITY BY CAR   There are two main exits from the airport: From the loading/unloading area, take the first exit if you're staying near the airport. Take the second exit (Wash. 518) if you're headed to downtown Seattle. Driving east on Wash. 518 will connect you to I-5, where you'll then follow the signs for Seattle. Generally, allow 30 minutes for the drive between the airport and downtown—45 minutes to an hour during rush hour.

During rush hour, it's sometimes quicker to take Wash. 518 west to Wash. 509 north to Wash. 99 to Wash. 519 (which becomes the Alaskan Way Viaduct along the Seattle waterfront).

GETTING INTO THE CITY BY TAXI, SHUTTLE, OR BUS   A **taxi** into downtown Seattle will cost you about $32. There are usually plenty of taxis around, but if not, call **Yellow Cab** (© 206/622-6500) or **Farwest Taxi** (© 206/622-1717). The flag-drop charge is $1.80; after that, it's $1.80 per mile.

Gray Line Airport Express (© 800/544-0739 or 206/626-6088; www.gray lineofseattle.com) provides service between the airport and downtown Seattle daily from about 5am to 11pm and is your best bet for getting to downtown. These shuttle vans pick up from two booths outside the baggage claim area—one outside Door 24 and one outside Door 8. Shuttles operate every 20 minutes and stop at the following hotels: Madison Renaissance, Crowne Plaza, Four Seasons

Olympic, Seattle Hilton, Sheraton Seattle, Westin, and Warwick. Fares are $8.50 one-way and $14 round-trip. Connector service to the above hotels is also provided from numerous other downtown hotels, as well as from the Amtrak station, the Washington State Ferries ferry terminal (Pier 52), and the Greyhound station. Connector service is free from some downtown hotels, but from other locations, it costs $2.50 one-way or $5 round-trip; call for details. The biggest drawback of this shuttle service is that you may have to stop at several hotels before getting dropped off, and it could take you 45 minutes to get from the airport to your hotel. However, if you're traveling by yourself or with one other person, this is your most economical choice other than the public bus.

Shuttle Express (© 800/487-7433 in Washington, or 425/981-7000; www. shuttleexpress.com) provides 24-hour service between Sea-Tac and the Seattle, North Seattle, and Bellevue areas. The rate to downtown Seattle is $21 for 1 to 3 adults and $25 for 4 adults. You need to make a reservation to get to the airport, but to leave the airport, simply call when you arrive. Push 48 on one of the Traveler's Information Center courtesy phones outside the baggage-claim area. If there are three or more of you traveling together, this is going to be your cheapest alternative for getting into town unless you take a public bus.

Metro Transit (© 800/542-7876 in Washington, or 206/553-3000; http:// transit.metrokc.gov) operates two buses between the airport and downtown. These buses leave from near Door 6 (close to baggage carousel 1) of the baggage claim area. It's a good idea to call for the current schedule when you arrive in town. Bus 194 operates (to Third Ave. and Union St. or the bus tunnel's Convention Place Station, depending on the time of day) every 30 minutes weekdays from 4:55am to 8:33pm, weekends from about 6:20am to about 7:20pm. Bus 174 operates (to Second Ave. and Union St.) about every 25 to 30 minutes from 4:47am to 2:43am (5:45am–2:47am Sat and 6:49am–2:46pm Sun). Bus trips take 40 to 50 minutes depending on conditions. The fare is $1.25 during off-peak hours and $2 during peak hours.

BY TRAIN OR BUS

Amtrak (© 800/872-7245 or 206/382-4125; www.amtrak.com) trains stop at King Street Station, which is located at 303 S. Jackson St., within a few blocks of the historic Pioneer Square neighborhood and adjacent to the south entrance of the downtown bus tunnel. Any bus running north through the tunnel will take you to within a few blocks of most downtown hotels. The Waterfront Streetcar also stops within a block of King Street Station and can take you to the Hotel Edgewater.

The **Greyhound bus station,** 811 Stewart St. (© 800/229-9424 or 206/628-5526; www.greyhound.com), is located a few blocks northeast of downtown Seattle not far from Lake Union and Seattle Center. Several budget chain motels are located only a few blocks from the bus station. It's a bit farther to the Hostelling International–Seattle hostel, yet walkable if you don't have much luggage. Otherwise, you can grab a free ride on a Metro bus.

BY CAR

See section 6, "Getting There," at the end of chapter 2; and section 2, "Getting Around," later in this chapter.

VISITOR INFORMATION

Visitor information on Seattle and the surrounding area is available by contacting the **Seattle–King County Convention & Visitors Bureau Visitor Information Center,** Washington State Convention & Trade Center, 800

Convention Place, Galleria Level, at the corner of Eighth Avenue and Pike Street (© **206/461-5840;** www.seeseattle.org). To find it, walk up Union Street until it goes into a tunnel under the Convention Center. You'll see the information center on your left. Alternatively, you can enter the building from Pike Street.

CITY LAYOUT

Although downtown Seattle is fairly compact and can easily be navigated on foot, finding your way by car can be frustrating. The Seattle area has been experiencing phenomenal growth for more than a decade, and this has created traffic-congestion problems. Here are some guidelines to help you find your way around.

MAIN ARTERIES & STREETS   Three interstate highways serve Seattle. Seattle's main artery is I-5, which runs through the middle of the city. Take the James Street exit west if you're heading for the Pioneer Square area, take the Seneca Street exit for Pike Place Market, or take the Olive Way exit for Capitol Hill. I-405 is the city's north-south bypass and travels up the east shore of Lake Washington through Bellevue and Kirkland (Seattle's high-tech corridor). I-90 comes in from the east, crossing one of the city's two floating bridges, and ends at the south end of downtown.

Downtown is roughly defined as extending from the stadium district just south of the Pioneer Square neighborhood on the south, to Denny Way on the north, and from Elliott Bay on the west to I-5 on the east. Within this area, most avenues are numbered, whereas streets have names. Exceptions to this rule are the first two roads parallel to the waterfront (Alaskan Way and Western Avenue) and avenues east of Ninth Avenue.

Many downtown streets and avenues are one-way. Spring, Pike, and Marion streets are all one-way eastbound, while Seneca, Pine, and Madison streets are all one-way westbound. Second and Fifth avenues are both one-way southbound, while Fourth and Sixth avenues are one-way northbound. First Avenue and Third Avenue are both two-way streets.

To get from downtown to Capitol Hill, take Pike Street or Olive Way. Madison Street, Yesler Way, or South Jackson Street will get you over to Lake Washington on the east side of Seattle. If you are heading north across town, Westlake Avenue will take you to the Fremont neighborhood, and Eastlake Avenue will take you to the University District. These two roads diverge at the south end of Lake Union. To get to the arboretum from downtown, take Madison Street.

FINDING AN ADDRESS   After you become familiar with the streets and neighborhoods of Seattle, there is really only one important thing to remember: Pay attention to the compass point of an address. Most downtown streets have no directional designation attached to them, but when you cross I-5 going east,

---

Remembering Seattle's Streets

Locals use an irreverent little mnemonic device for remembering the names of Seattle's downtown streets, and since most visitors spend much of their time downtown, this phrase could be useful to you as well. It goes like this: "Jesus Christ made Seattle under protest." This stands for all the downtown east-west streets between Yesler Way and Olive Way/Stewart Street—Jefferson, James, Cherry, Columbia, Marion, Madison, Spring, Seneca, University, Union, Pike, Pine.

most streets and avenues are designated "East." South of Yesler Way, which runs through Pioneer Square, streets are designated "South." West of Queen Anne Avenue, streets are designated "West." The University District is designated "NE" (Northeast), and the Ballard neighborhood, "NW" (Northwest). So if you're looking for an address on First Avenue South, head south of Yesler Way.

Another helpful hint is that odd-numbered addresses are likely to be on the west and south sides of streets, whereas even-numbered addresses will be on the east and north. Also, in the downtown area, address numbers increase by 100 with each block as you move away from Yesler Way going north or south and as you go east from the waterfront.

STREET MAPS   If the streets of Seattle seem totally unfathomable to you, rest assured that even longtime residents sometimes have a hard time finding their way around. Don't be afraid to ask directions. You can obtain a free map of the city from one of the two Seattle–King County Convention & Visitors Bureau Visitor Information Centers (see above).

You can buy a decent map of Seattle in most convenience stores and gas stations around the area or, for a greater selection, stop in at **Metsker Maps,** 702 First Ave. (© **206/623-8747;** www.metskers.com).

If you're a member of AAA, you can get free maps of Seattle and Washington state, either at an AAA office near you or at the Seattle office, 330 Sixth Ave. N. (© **206/448-5353**).

NEIGHBORHOODS IN BRIEF

DOWNTOWN This is Seattle's main business district and can roughly be defined as the area from Pioneer Square in the south, to around Pike Place Market in the north, and from First Avenue to Eighth Avenue. It's characterized by steep streets, high-rise office buildings, luxury hotels, and a high density of retail shops (primarily national chains). This is also where you'll find the Seattle Art Museum and Benaroya Hall, which is home to the Seattle Symphony. Because hotels in this area are convenient to both Pioneer Square and Pike Place Market, this is a good neighborhood in which to stay. Unfortunately, the hotels here are the most expensive in the city.

FIRST HILL Because it is home to several large hospitals, this hilly neighborhood just east of downtown and across I-5 is known as Pill Hill by Seattleites. First Hill is home to the Frye Art Museum and a couple of good hotels.

THE WATERFRONT The Seattle waterfront, which stretches along Alaskan Way from roughly Washington Street in the south to Broad Street and Myrtle Edwards Park in the north, is the most touristy neighborhood in Seattle. In recent years, however, Seattleites have been reclaiming the waterfront as a new residential area, and the north end of Alaskan Way is now lined with water-view condos. In addition to the many tacky gift shops, greasy fish-and-chips windows, and tour-boat docks, the waterfront also has the city's only waterfront hotel (the Edgewater), the Seattle Aquarium, and a few excellent seafood restaurants.

PIONEER SQUARE The Pioneer Square Historic District, known for its restored 1890s buildings, is centered around the corner of First Avenue and Yesler Way. The tree-lined streets and cobblestone plazas make this one of the prettiest downtown neighborhoods. Pioneer

Square (which refers to the neighborhood, not a specific square) is full of antiques shops, art galleries, restaurants, bars, and nightclubs. Because of the number of bars in this neighborhood, late nights are not a good time to wander here—plus, the number of street people in this area is off-putting to many visitors.

THE INTERNATIONAL DISTRICT Known to locals as the I.D., this is the most distinctive of Seattle's neighborhoods and is home to a large Asian population. Here you'll find the Wing Luke Asian Museum, Hing Hay Park (with an ornate pagoda), Uwajimaya (an Asian supermarket), and many other small shops and restaurants. The International District begins around Fifth Avenue South and South Jackson Street. This neighborhood is interesting for a stroll, but there really isn't a lot to do here.

BELLTOWN Located in the blocks north of **Pike Place Market** between Western and Fourth avenues, this area once held mostly warehouses, but over the past decade it has become gentrified. Today Belltown is ground zero for upscale Seattle restaurants. Keeping the restaurants in business are the residents of the neighborhood's many new high-rise condominiums. Belltown's many nightclubs attract crowds of the young and the hip—which, in turn, attract a lot of nighttime panhandlers.

QUEEN ANNE HILL Queen Anne is located just northwest of **Seattle Center** and offers great views of the city. This affluent neighborhood, one of the most prestigious in Seattle proper, is where you'll find some of Seattle's oldest homes. Today the neighborhood is divided into the Upper Queen Anne and Lower Queen Anne neighborhoods. Upper Queen Anne has a very peaceful neighborhood feel and abounds in moderately priced restaurants. Lower Queen Anne, adjacent to the theaters and Opera House at Seattle Center, is something of a theater district and has a more urban character.

CAPITOL HILL To the northeast of downtown, centered along Broadway near Volunteer Park, Capitol Hill is Seattle's main gay community and is also a popular youth-culture shopping district. Broadway sidewalks are always crowded, and it is nearly impossible to find a parking place in the neighborhood. Although there are lots of inexpensive restaurants in the area, few are really worth recommending. This is also the city's main hangout for runaways and street kids, many of whom have become involved in the city's infamous heroin scene. Despite the youthful orientation, Capitol Hill is also where you'll find many of the city's bed-and-breakfast inns. These inns are housed in some of the neighborhood's impressive old homes and mansions.

MADISON PARK One of Seattle's more affluent neighborhoods, Madison Park fronts the western shore of Lake Washington, northeast of downtown. The University of Washington Arboretum, which includes the Japanese Gardens, is the centerpiece of the neighborhood. There are several excellent restaurants here, at the end of East Madison Street.

UNIVERSITY DISTRICT As the name implies, this neighborhood in the northeast section of the city surrounds the University of Washington. The "U" District, as it's known to locals, provides all the amenities of a college neighborhood: cheap ethnic restaurants, bars, pubs, espresso bars, and music stores. The neighborhood has several good hotels that offer substantial savings

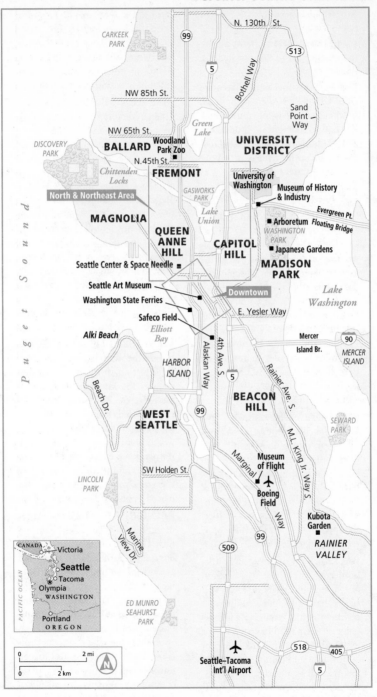

N. 130th St.

CARKEEK PARK

99

5

513

Bothell Way

NW 85th St.

Sand Point Way

DISCOVERY PARK

NW 65th St.

Green Lake

BALLARD

Woodland Park Zoo

N.45th St.

FREMONT

Chittenden Locks

North & Northeast Area

GASWORKS PARK

UNIVERSITY DISTRICT

University of Washington

Museum of History & Industry

Evergreen Pt.

MAGNOLIA

Lake Union

Arboretum

Floating Bridge

WASHINGTON PARK

QUEEN ANNE HILL

CAPITOL HILL

Japanese Gardens

MADISON PARK

Seattle Center & Space Needle

Seattle Art Museum

Downtown

Lake Washington

Washington State Ferries

Safeco Field

E. Yesler Way

Alki Beach

Elliott Bay

Mercer Island Br.

90

MERCER ISLAND

Puget Sound

HARBOR ISLAND

Alaskan Way

4th Ave. S.

5

99

BEACON HILL

Rainier Ave. S.

M.L. King Jr. Way S

SEWARD PARK

Beach Dr.

WEST SEATTLE

SW Holden St.

LINCOLN PARK

Marginal Way

Museum of Flight

Boeing Field

Kubota Garden

RAINIER VALLEY

Marine View Dr.

509

99

CANADA

Victoria

Seattle

Tacoma

Olympia

WASHINGTON

PACIFIC OCEAN

Portland

OREGON

ED MUNRO SEAHURST PARK

Seattle–Tacoma Int'l Airport

518

405

5

0   2 mi

0   2 km

over comparable downtown Seattle hotels.

WALLINGFORD This neighborhood is another of Seattle's up-and-comers. Located just west of the University District and adjacent to Lake Union, it's filled with small, inexpensive-but-good restaurants. You'll find interesting little shops and an old school that has been renovated and is now filled with boutiques and restaurants.

FREMONT Located north of the Lake Washington Ship Canal between Wallingford and Ballard, Fremont is home to Seattle's best-loved piece of public art—*Waiting for the Interurban*—as well as the famous Fremont Troll sculpture. This is Seattle's wackiest neighborhood and is filled with eclectic shops and ethnic restaurants. During the summer, there's a Sunday flea market, and outdoor movies are screened on Saturday nights. If you have time to visit only one neighborhood outside of downtown, make it Fremont.

MAGNOLIA This affluent residential neighborhood lies to the west of Queen Anne Hill. Magnolia's few cafes, restaurants, and bars are frequented primarily by area residents, but it's also home to Palisade, one of Seattle's best waterfront restaurants. The west side of Magnolia borders the sprawling Discovery Park, Seattle's largest green space.

BALLARD In northwest Seattle, bordering the Lake Washington Ship Canal and Puget Sound, you'll find Ballard, a former Scandinavian community that retains visible remnants of its past. Now known for its busy nightlife, Ballard is one of Seattle's up-and-coming neighborhoods and is undergoing a pronounced change in character. You'll find art galleries and a few interesting boutiques and shops along the tree-shaded streets of the neighborhood's old commercial center. It's definitely worth a stroll here to see what's happening. The neighborhood's Nordic Heritage Museum often has interesting art exhibits.

THE EASTSIDE Home to Bill Gates, Microsoft, countless high-tech spinoff companies, and seemingly endless suburbs, the Eastside lies across Lake Washington from Seattle proper and is comprised of the fast-growing cities of **Kirkland, Bellevue, Redmond, Bothell,** and a few other smaller communities. As the presence of Bill Gates's media-hyped mansion attests, there are some pretty wealthy neighborhoods here; but wealth doesn't necessarily equal respect, and the Eastside is still much derided by Seattle citizens, who perceive it as an uncultured bedroom community.

WEST SEATTLE West Seattle, across the wasteland of the port facility from downtown Seattle, is not just the site of the ferry terminal for ferries to Vashon Island and the Kitsap Peninsula. It's also the site of Seattle's favorite beach (Alki), which is as close to a Southern California beach experience as you can get in the Northwest. Here too is the waterfront restaurant with the best view of Seattle: Salty's on Alki.

BAINBRIDGE ISLAND Seattle's most exurban bedroom community. Though it is only a 35-minute ferry ride, Bainbridge feels worlds away from the inner-city asphalt to the east. Green, green, green is the best way to characterize this rural residential island. Downtown Bainbridge Island (formerly known as Winslow), the island's main commercial area, has the feel of an upscale San Francisco Bay Area community. When you hear about Seattle's quality of life, this is what people are talking about.

2 Getting Around

BY PUBLIC TRANSPORTATION

BY BUS   The best thing about Seattle's **Metro** bus system (① 800/542-7876 in Washington, or 206/553-3000; http://transit.metrokc.gov) is that as long as you stay within the downtown area, you can ride for free between 6am and 7pm. The Ride Free Area is between Alaskan Way (the waterfront) in the west, Sixth Avenue and I-5 in the east, Battery Street in the north, and South Jackson Street in the south. Within this area are Pioneer Square, the waterfront attractions, Pike Place Market, the Seattle Art Museum, and almost all of the city's major hotels. Three blocks from South Jackson Street is Safeco Field (where the Mariners play), and 6 blocks from Battery Street is Seattle Center. Keeping this in mind, you can see a lot of Seattle without having to spend a dime on transportation.

The Ride Free Area also encompasses the Metro Tunnel, which allows buses to drive underneath downtown Seattle, thus avoiding traffic congestion. The tunnel extends from the International District in the south to the Convention Center in the north, with three stops in between. Commissioned artworks decorate each of the stations, making a trip through the tunnel more than just a way of getting from point A to point B. It's open Monday through Friday from 5am to 7pm and Saturday from 10am to 6pm (closed Sun and holidays). When the Bus Tunnel is closed, buses operate on surface streets. Because the tunnel is within the Ride Free Area, there is no charge for riding through it, unless you are traveling to or from outside of the Ride Free Area.

If you travel outside the Ride Free Area, fares range from $1.25 to $2, depending on the distance and time of day. (The higher fares are incurred during commuter hours.) Keep in mind when traveling out of the Ride Free Area that you pay when you get off the bus. When traveling into the Ride Free Area, you pay when you get on the bus. Exact change is required; dollar bills are accepted.

BY WATERFRONT STREETCAR   In addition to the bus system, **Metro** (① 800/542-7876 in Washington, or 206/553-3000; http://transit.metrokc.gov) also operates old-fashioned streetcars that follow a route along the waterfront from Pier 70 to Pioneer Square and then east to the corner of Fourth Avenue South and South Main Street, which is on the edge of the International District. These streetcars are more tourist attraction than commuter transportation and actually are much more useful to visitors than are most of the city's buses. Tourist sites along

---

Value Discount Passes

On Saturday, Sunday, and holidays, you can purchase an All Day Pass for $2.50; it's available on any Metro bus or the Waterfront Streetcar, and it's good for anywhere outside the Ride Free Area. For other days of the week, you can purchase a Visitor Pass for $5. These passes can be used on buses, the water taxi, and the Waterfront Streetcar. However, these latter passes can only be purchased online (**http://www.cpostores.com/metro_ online/**), over the phone (① **206/624-7277**), through the mail (King County Metro Transit Division, Pass Sales Office, 201 S. Jackson St., MS KSC-TR-0108, Seattle, WA 98104-3856), or at a Metro Transit Customer Service Office. These are located in the Metro Tunnel on the mezzanine level at Westlake Station (open Mon–Fri 9am–5:30pm), or at King Street Center, 201 S. Jackson St. (open Mon–Fri 8am–5pm).

the streetcar route include Pioneer Square, the Seattle Aquarium, IMAXDome Film Experience, and Pike Place Market. In the summer, streetcars operate Monday through Friday from 6:46am to 11:28pm, departing every 20 to 30 minutes; on Saturday, Sunday, and holidays they operate from 8:46am to 11:58pm (shorter hours in other months). One-way fare is $1.25 in off-peak hours and $1.50 in peak hours (50¢ for youth ages 5–17); exact change is required. If you plan to transfer to a Metro bus, you can get a transfer good for 90 minutes. Streetcars are wheelchair accessible.

BY MONORAIL   If you are planning a visit to Seattle Center, there is no better way to get there from downtown than on the **Seattle Monorail** (© 206/ **905-2620;** www.seattlemonorail.com), which leaves from Westlake Center shopping mall (Fifth Ave. and Pine St.). The elevated trains cover the 1¼ miles in 2 minutes and pass right through the middle of the Experience Music Project as they arrive and depart from Seattle Center. The monorail operates Monday through Friday from 7:30am to 11pm, Saturday and Sunday from 9am to 11pm. Departures are every 10 minutes. The one-way fare is $1.25 for adults and 50¢ for seniors and children ages 5 to 12.

BY WATER TAXI   As long as funding continues to be found, a water taxi operates between the downtown Seattle waterfront (Pier 54) and Seacrest Park in West Seattle, providing access to West Seattle's popular Alki Beach and adjacent paved path. For a schedule of service, check with the Metro (© **206/205-3866;** http://transit.metrokc.gov). The one-way fare is $2 (free for children under age 5). Also free with a valid bus transfer or all-day pass.

BY FERRY   Washington State Ferries (© **800/84-FERRY** or 888/808-7977 within Washington state, or 206/464-6400; www.wsdot.wa.gov/ferries/) is the most extensive ferry system in the United States, and while these ferries won't help you get around Seattle itself, they do offer scenic options for getting out of town (and cheap cruises, too). From downtown Seattle, car ferries sail to Bremerton (60-min. crossing) and Bainbridge Island (35-min. crossing), and passenger-only ferries sail for Bremerton (30-min. crossing) and Vashon Island (25-min. crossing). From West Seattle, car ferries go to Vashon Island (15-min. crossing) and Southworth (35-min. crossing), which is on the Kitsap Peninsula. One-way fares between Seattle and Bainbridge Island or Bremerton, or between Edmonds and Kingston via car ferry are $9 ($11.25 from mid-May to mid-Oct) for a car and driver, $5.10 for adult car passengers or walk-ons, $2.50 for seniors, and $3.60 for children ages 5 to 18. Car passengers and walk-ons only pay fares on westbound car ferries. One-way fares between Fauntleroy (West Seattle) and Vashon Island or between Southworth and Vashon Island are $11.75 ($14.75 from mid-May to mid-Oct) for a car and driver, $3.20 for car passengers or walk-ons, $1.60 for seniors, and $2.40 for children ages 5 to 18.

BY CAR

Before you venture into downtown Seattle in a car, keep in mind that traffic congestion is bad, parking is limited (and expensive), and streets are almost all one-way. You'll avoid a lot of frustration and aggravation by leaving your car in your hotel's parking garage or by not bringing a car into downtown at all.

Depending on what your plans are for your visit, you might not need a car at all. If you plan to spend your time in downtown Seattle, a car is a liability. The city center is well serviced by public transportation, with free public buses in the downtown area, the monorail from downtown to Seattle Center, and the

Waterfront Streetcar connecting Pike Place Market and Pioneer Square by way of the waterfront. You can even take the ferries over to Bainbridge Island or Bremerton for an excursion out of the city. Most Seattle neighborhoods of interest to visitors are also well served by public buses. However, if your plans include any excursions out of the city, say to Mount Rainier or the Olympic Peninsula, you'll definitely need a car.

CAR RENTALS   Car-rental rates vary as widely and as wildly as airfares, so it pays to do some comparison-shopping. In Seattle, daily rates for a compact car might run anywhere from around $30 to $70, with weekly rates running between $150 and $350 (although the average is around $250). Rates are, of course, highest in the summer and lowest in the winter, but you'll almost always get lower rates the farther ahead you reserve. Be sure to budget for the 18.5% car-rental tax (and, if you rent at the airport, an additional 10% to 11.11% airport concession fee, for a whopping total of 28.5% to 29.61%!).

All the major car-rental agencies have offices in Seattle and at or near Seattle–Tacoma International Airport. Companies with a desk and cars inside the terminal include **Alamo** (② 800/327-9633 or 206/433-0182; www.goalamo.com), **Avis** (② 800/331-1212 or 206/448-1700; www.avis.com), **Budget** (② 800/527-0700 or 206/682-2277; https://rent.drivebudget.com), **Hertz** (② 800/654-3131 or 206/248-1300; www.hertz.com), and **National** (② 800/227-7368 or 206/433-5500; www.nationalcar.com). Companies with desks inside the terminal but cars parked off the airport premises include **Dollar** (② 800/800-4000 or 206/433-6768; www.dollar.com), **Enterprise** (② 800/736-8222 or 206/382-1051; www.enterprise.com), and **Thrifty** (② 800/367-2277 or 206/625-1133; www.thrifty.com).

PARKING   On-street parking in downtown Seattle is expensive, extremely limited, and, worst of all, rarely available near your destination. Most downtown parking lots (either above or below ground) charge from $12 to $20 per day, though many lots offer early-bird specials that allow you to park all day for around $8 if you park before a certain time in the morning (usually around 9am). With a purchase of $20 or more, many downtown merchants offer CityPark tokens that can be used for $1 off parking fees in many downtown lots (mostly in the main shopping district around Sixth and Pine). Look for the CityPark signs.

You'll also save money by parking near the Space Needle, where parking lots charge $3 to $6 per day. The parking lot at Fifth Avenue North and North Republican Street, on the east side of Seattle Center, charges only $5 for all-day parking if you show up with three or more people in your car. The Pike Place Market parking garage, accessed from Western Avenue under the sky bridge, offers free parking if you park for less than an hour (just enough time to run in and grab a quick bite). If you don't mind a bit of a walk, try the parking lot off Jackson Street between Eighth and Ninth avenues in the International District. This lot charges only $5 to park all day on weekdays. Also in the International District, the Lower Queen Anne neighborhood, and a few streets south of Seattle Center, you'll find free 2-hour on-street parking.

DRIVING RULES   A right turn at a red light is permitted after coming to a full stop. A left turn at a red light is permissible from a one-way street onto another one-way street.

If you park your car on a sloping street, be sure to turn your wheels to the curb—you may be ticketed if you don't. When parking on the street, be sure to check the time limit on your parking meter. Some allow only as little as

Value   Driving a Bargain in Seattle

For the best deal on a rental car, make your reservation at least a week in advance. It also pays to call several times over a period of a few weeks just to check prices. You're likely to be quoted different rates every time you call, since rates fluctuate based on demand and availability. Remember the old Wall Street adage: Buy low!

Always ask about special weekend rates, promotional rates, or discounts for which you might be eligible (AAA, AARP, corporate, Entertainment Book). Also make sure you clarify whether there is a charge for mileage. And don't forget to mention that you're a frequent flier: You might be able to get miles for your car rental.

If you have your own car insurance, you may have collision coverage. If you do not hold your own policy, your credit card may provide collision coverage, allowing you to decline the collision-damage waiver, which can add a bundle to the cost of a rental. (Gold and platinum cards usually offer this perk, but check with your card issuer before relying on it. Note that while many cards provide collision coverage, they do not provide liability coverage.)

If there's any way you can arrange to pick up your car somewhere other than the airport, you can save the 10% to 11.11% airport concession fee.

It's always smart to decline the gasoline plans offered by rental agencies and simply plan on returning your rental car with a full tank of gas. The prices the rental companies charge you to fill your tank when you don't do it yourself are usually a rip-off.

15 minutes of parking, while others are good for up to 4 hours. Also be sure to check whether or not you can park in a parking space during rush hour.

Stoplights in the Pioneer Square area are particularly hard to see, so be alert at all intersections.

BY TAXI

If you decide not to use the public-transit system, call **Yellow Cab** (© 206/622-6500) or **Farwest Taxi** (© 206/622-1717). Taxis can be difficult to hail on the street in Seattle, so it's best to call or wait at the taxi stands at major hotels. The flag-drop charge is $1.80; after that, it's $1.80 per mile. A maximum of four passengers can share a cab; the third and fourth passengers will each incur an extra charge of 50¢.

ON FOOT

Seattle is a surprisingly compact city. You can easily walk from Pioneer Square to Pike Place Market and take in most of downtown. Remember, though, that the city is also very hilly. When you head in from the waterfront, you will be climbing a very steep hill. If you get tired while strolling downtown, remember that between 6am and 7pm, you can always catch a bus for free as long as you plan to stay within the Ride Free Area. Cross the street only at corners and only with the lights in your favor. Jaywalking, especially in the downtown area, is a ticketable offense.

FAST FACTS: Seattle

AAA The **American Automobile Association** (☏ 800/222-4357; www.aaa.com) has a local Seattle office at 330 Sixth Ave. N. (☏ 206/448-5353).

Airport See "Getting There" in chapter 2, and "Arriving" in section 1 of this chapter.

American Express In Seattle, the Amex office is in the Plaza 600 building at 600 Stewart St. (☏ 206/441-8622). The office is open Monday through Friday from 8:30am to 5:30pm. For card member services, phone ☏ 800/528-4800. Call ☏ 800/AXP-TRIP or go to **www.americanexpress.com** for other locations or general information.

Area Code The area code in Seattle is **206**; it's **425** for the Eastside (including Kirkland and Bellevue), and **253** for south King County (near the airport).

Business Hours The following are general hours; specific establishments may vary. Banks are open Monday through Friday from 9am to 5pm (some also on Sat 9am–noon). Stores are open Monday through Saturday from 10am to 6pm and Sunday from noon to 5pm (malls usually stay open until 9pm Mon–Sat). Bars generally open around 11am, but are legally allowed to be open Monday through Saturday from 6am to 1am and Sunday from 10am to 1am.

Car Rentals See section 2, "Getting Around," earlier in this chapter.

Climate See section 3, "When to Go," in chapter 2.

Dentist Contact the **Dental Referral Service** (☏ 800/577-7322).

Doctor To find a physician, check at your hotel for a referral, or contact **Swedish Medical Center** (☏ 206/386-6000; www.swedish.org).

Emergencies For police, fire, or medical emergencies, phone ☏ **911.**

Hospitals Hospitals convenient to downtown include **Swedish Medical Center,** 747 Broadway (☏ 206/386-6000); and **Virginia Mason Hospital and Clinic,** 925 Seneca St. (☏ 206/583-6433 for emergencies, or 206/624-1144 for information).

Information See "Visitor Information" in section 1 of this chapter.

Internet Access First, ask at your hotel to see if it provides Internet access. If not, **Kinko's,** 1335 Second Ave. (☏ 206/292-9255) and other locations, is an alternative.

Liquor Laws The legal minimum drinking age in Washington state is 21. Aside from on-premise sales of cocktails in bars and restaurants, hard liquor can only be purchased in liquor stores. Beer and wine are available in convenience stores and grocery stores. Brewpubs tend to sell only beer and wine, but some also have licenses to sell hard liquor.

Newspapers & Magazines The *Seattle Post-Intelligencer* and *Seattle Times* are Seattle's two daily newspapers. *Seattle Weekly* is the city's free arts-and-entertainment weekly.

Pharmacies Conveniently located downtown pharmacies include **Rite Aid,** 319 Pike St. (☏ 206/223-0512), and also at 1300 Madison St. (☏ 206/322-9316). Alternatively, call Rite Aid (☏ 800/748-3243) for the location nearest you. For 24-hour service, try **Bartell Drug Store,** 600 First Ave. N. (© **206/284-1353**).

Photographic Needs **Cameras West,** 1908 Fourth Ave. (© **206/622-0066**), is the largest-volume camera and video dealer in the Northwest. Best of all, it's right downtown and also offers 1-hour film processing. It's open Monday through Friday from 9:30am to 6pm, and on Saturday from 10am to 5pm.

Police For police emergencies, phone © **911.**

Restrooms There are public restrooms in Pike Place Market, Westlake Center, Pacific Place, Seattle Center, and the Washington State Convention & Trade Center. You'll also find restrooms in most hotel lobbies and coffee bars in downtown Seattle.

Safety Although Seattle is a relatively safe city, it has its share of crime. The most questionable neighborhood you're likely to visit is the Pioneer Square area, which is home to more than a dozen bars and nightclubs. By day, this area is quite safe (though it has a large contingent of street people), but late at night, when the bars are closing, stay aware of your surroundings and keep an eye out for suspicious characters and activities. Also take extra precautions with your wallet or purse when you're in the crush of people at Pike Place Market. Whenever possible, try to park your car in a garage, instead of on the street, at night. If you must park on the street, make sure there are no valuables in view and nothing that even looks like it might contain something of worth. We once had our car broken into because we left a shopping bag full of trash on the back seat.

Smoking Although many of the restaurants listed in this book are smoke-free establishments, there are also many Seattle restaurants that do allow smoking. At most high-end restaurants, the smoking area is usually in the bar/lounge, and although many restaurants have separate bar menus, most will serve you off the regular menu even if you are eating in the bar. There are very few smoke-free bars in Seattle.

Taxes In Seattle you'll pay an 8.8% sales tax, and in restaurants, you'll also pay an additional 0.5% food-and-beverage tax on top of the sales tax. The hotel-room tax in the Seattle metro area ranges from around 10% to 16%. On rental cars, you'll pay not only an 18.5% car-rental tax, but also, if you rent at the airport, an additional 10% to 11.11% airport concession fee, for a whopping total of 28.5% to 29.61%!

Taxis See section 2, "Getting Around," earlier in this chapter.

Time Seattle is on Pacific Standard Time (PST), making it 3 hours behind the East Coast.

Transit Info For 24-hour information on Seattle's Metro bus system, call © **206/553-3000.** For information on the Washington State Ferries, call © **800/84-FERRY** or 888/808-7977 in Washington, or 206/464-6400.

Weather Currently, Seattle has no phone number for weather information. Check the *Seattle Times* or *Seattle Post-Intelligencer* newspapers for forecasts. If you want to know how to pack before you arrive, go to **www.wrh.noaa.gov/seattle, www.cnn.com/weather,** or **www.weather.com.**

Where to Stay in Seattle

Seattle is close on the heels of San Francisco as a West Coast summer-in-the-city destination, so its hotels stay pretty much booked solid for July and August. If you aren't on an expense account, you may be faced with sticker shock when you see what these places are charging. But if you're willing to head out a bit from downtown, you'll find prices a little easier to swallow.

As the city has grown more affluent in recent years, the hotel scene has also become more sophisticated. San Francisco's hip aesthetics have spilled over into Seattle, and as a result you'll find chic, postmodern hotels around town, as well as several historic hotels and lots of characterless convention hotels. This all adds up to plenty of options for the traveler planning a trip to Seattle.

Seattle's largest concentrations of hotels are located downtown and near the airport, with a few good hotels in the University District and also over in the suburbs of Bellevue and Kirkland (on the east side of Lake Washington). If you don't mind high prices, downtown hotels are the most convenient, but if your budget won't allow for a first-class business hotel, try to stay near the Space Needle, in the Lower Queen Anne neighborhood, or in the University District where prices are more reasonable.

Be sure to make reservations as far in advance as possible, especially if you plan a visit during Seafair or another major festival. See the "Seattle Calendar of Events" on p. 14 for the dates of major festivals.

In the following listings, price categories are based on rates for a double room in high season (most hotels charge the same for a single or double room). Keep in mind that the rates listed do not include taxes, which add up to around 16% in Seattle.

For comparison purposes, we list what hotels call "rack rates" or walk-in rates—but you should never have to pay these highly inflated prices. Various discounts and specials are often available, so make it a point to ask if any are being offered during your stay (and be sure to check the hotel's website for Internet specials). At inexpensive chain motels, discounted rates are almost always available for AAA members and senior citizens.

Room rates can be considerably lower from October through April (the rainy season), and downtown hotels often offer substantially reduced prices on weekends throughout the year (while budget hotels often charge more on weekends).

A few hotels include breakfast in their rates; others offer complimentary breakfast only on certain deluxe floors. Most Seattle hotels offer nonsmoking rooms, while most bed-and-breakfast inns are exclusively nonsmoking establishments. Most hotels, but few inns, also offer wheelchair-accessible rooms.

HELPING HANDS

If you're having a hard time finding a room in your price range, consider using the services of **Pacific Northwest Journeys** (© **800/935-9730** or 206/935-9730; www.pnwjourneys.com). This company specializes in itinerary planning, but also offers a reservation service. The charge is $45 per reservation; however, you can usually make that up in savings on just a 2-night stay. If you're going to be in town for longer than that, you'll definitely save money. Last-minute reservations are often possible, too. A phone and e-mail consultation service is also available for people who have already done a lot of planning but who want a little more assistance with their itinerary.

Every year from November through March, more than two dozen Seattle hotels offer deep-cut discounts on their rooms through the **Seattle Hotel Hotline**'s (© **800/535-7071** or 206/461-5882) Seattle Super Saver Package. Room rates under this plan are generally 50% of what they would be in the summer months. Any time of year, you can call this hot line for help with making hotel reservations.

Seattle is a city of diverse neighborhoods, and in many of those neighborhoods, you'll discover fine B&Bs. Often less expensive than downtown hotels, these B&Bs provide an opportunity to see what life in Seattle is like for the locals. We've listed some of our favorites in the pages that follow, but to find out about other good B&Bs in Seattle, contact the **Seattle Bed & Breakfast Association** (© **800/348-5630** or 206/547-1020; www.seattle bandbs.com). Alternatively, you can contact **A Pacific Reservation Service** (© **800/684-2932** or 206/439-7677; www.seattlebedandbreakfast.com), which represents dozens of accommodations, mostly bed-and-breakfast homes, in the Seattle area. A wide range of rates is available.

1 The Waterfront

The city's most touristy neighborhood, the waterfront also has the city's finest views and is home to several worthwhile attractions and activities. Seattle's only actual waterfront hotel is here (The Edgewater; see below), and it should be the top choice of anyone wanting to spend a Seattle vacation in the thick of things.

EXPENSIVE

The Edgewater ★★ *Value*   Located on a pier at the north end of the waterfront, the Edgewater is Seattle's only hotel situated directly on the bay. It's designed to resemble a deluxe mountain or fishing lodge. In fact, it's difficult to believe that the crowded streets of downtown Seattle are only steps away. The views out the windows are among the best in the city, and sunsets are memorable. On a clear day you can see the Olympic Mountains rising across Puget Sound. Pull up a seat between the lobby's river-stone fireplace and the wall of glass that looks out on busy Elliott Bay, and you'll see why this is one of our favorite Seattle hotels. The hotel's restaurant and lounge also serve up those same views. The mountain-lodge theme continues in the rooms, which feature rustic lodgepole pine furniture and fireplaces. The least expensive rooms here overlook the parking lot (and city), so it's worth it to spring for a water-view room. The rooms with balconies may be a bit smaller than other rooms but are our top choice. Beatles fans can even stay in the same suite the Fab Four had when they visited (and fished out the window) back in 1964.

Pier 67, 2411 Alaskan Way, Seattle, WA 98121. © **800/624-0670** or 206/728-7000. Fax 206/441-4119. www.edgewaterhotel.com. 236 units. $159–$329 double; $379–$1,500 suite. AE, DC, DISC, MC, V. Valet parking $18. **Amenities:** Restaurant (Pacific Rim/international); lounge; exercise room and access to nearby health club; courtesy bikes; concierge; business center; room service; laundry service; dry cleaning. *In room:* A/C, TV, dataport, coffeemaker, hair dryer, iron.

INEXPENSIVE

Hostelling International—Seattle   This conveniently located hostel, housed in the former Longshoreman's Hall, which was built in 1915, is only a block off the waterfront and is popular with young European and Japanese travelers. The hostel is located between Pike Place Market and Pioneer Square, only 2 blocks away from the waterfront, which makes it very convenient for exploring downtown Seattle. A kitchen and luggage-storage facility make this a solid budget alternative. Some of the hostel's rooms even have views of Puget Sound. To find the hostel, walk down Post Alley, which runs through and under Pike Place Market, to the corner of Union Street.

84 Union St., Seattle, WA 98101. (© 888/622-5443 or 206/622-5443. Fax 206/682-2179. www.hiseattle.org. 199 beds. $19– $21 per person for members in dorms; $50 double in private room; $76 for up to 4 people in family room. AE, MC, V. Parking in area garages $12–$16. **Amenities:** Coin-op laundry. *In room:* No phone.

2 Downtown & First Hill

Downtown Seattle is the heart of the city's business community and home to numerous business hotels. Although these properties are among the most conveniently located Seattle hotels, they are also the most expensive choices and are designed primarily for business travelers on expense accounts, not vacationers. Many of these hotels do offer discounted weekend and winter rates, however. The area has plenty of good restaurants, but they tend to fall into one of two categories—cheap lunch spots and expense-account dinner places.

VERY EXPENSIVE

Alexis Hotel ★★   Listed in the National Register of Historic Places, this century-old building is a sparkling gem in an enviable location halfway between Pike Place Market and Pioneer Square and only 3 blocks from the waterfront, the Seattle Art Museum, and Benaroya Hall. In the middle of the lobby is a massive Dale Chihuly chandelier, and throughout the hotel there's an extensive art collection. The pleasant mix of contemporary and antique furnishings, and cheerful and personalized service give the Alexis a very special atmosphere. In the guest rooms, classic styling with a European flavor prevails. Almost half of the rooms here are suites, including very comfortable fireplace suites with whirlpool baths. In the John Lennon Suite, you'll find serigraphs by Lennon, and in the Miles Davis suite are artworks by the famous jazz musician. The spa suites are the real winners, offering whirlpool tubs in exceedingly luxurious bathrooms. The hotel also has complimentary evening wine tastings, and, for an additional $25, you can get all kinds of special treats for your dog.

1007 First Ave. (at Madison St.), Seattle, WA 98104. (© 800/426-7033 or 206/624-4844. Fax 206/621-9009. www.alexishotel.com. 109 units. $295–$315 double; $415–$595 suite. AE, DC, DISC, MC, V. Valet parking $23. Pets accepted with $25 fee per stay. **Amenities:** Restaurant (New American); lounge; exercise room and access to nearby health club; Aveda day spa; steam room; concierge; 24-hr. room service; massage; babysitting; laundry/dry cleaning; concierge-level rooms. *In room:* A/C, TV, fax, dataport, minibar, hair dryer, iron.

Elliott Grand Hyatt Seattle ★★★   If you are accustomed to staying in only the very finest hotels, book your room here. Luxury and technology merge at this downtown hotel, which is also the most up-to-the-minute, business-savvy hotel in Seattle. A Willem de Kooning sculpture outside the hotel's front door and a spacious lobby full of regionally inspired glass art set the tone the moment you arrive. However, unless you spring for something pricier than the basic "deluxe guest room," you're going to be a bit cramped. The least expensive

Accommodations: The Waterfront, Downtown, First Hill, Belltown, Pike Place Market, Pioneer Square & the International District

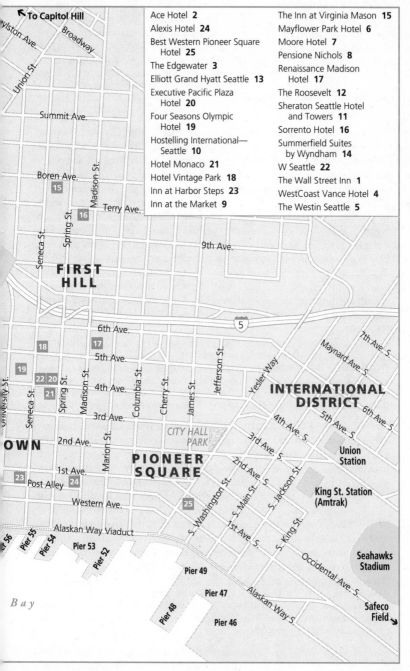

Ace Hotel **2**
Alexis Hotel **24**
Best Western Pioneer Square Hotel **25**
The Edgewater **3**
Elliott Grand Hyatt Seattle **13**
Executive Pacific Plaza Hotel **20**
Four Seasons Olympic Hotel **19**
Hostelling International—Seattle **10**
Hotel Monaco **21**
Hotel Vintage Park **18**
Inn at Harbor Steps **23**
Inn at the Market **9**

The Inn at Virginia Mason **15**
Mayflower Park Hotel **6**
Moore Hotel **7**
Pensione Nichols **8**
Renaissance Madison Hotel **17**
The Roosevelt **12**
Sheraton Seattle Hotel and Towers **11**
Sorrento Hotel **16**
Summerfield Suites by Wyndham **14**
W Seattle **22**
The Wall Street Inn **1**
WestCoast Vance Hotel **4**
The Westin Seattle **5**

rooms here are definitely designed for solo travelers. But all the rooms and suites are equipped with three phone lines, complimentary high-speed Internet access, two dataports, and an in-room safe large enough for your laptop. The health club is well outfitted, but there is no swimming pool, which means that families might want to opt for the Four Seasons instead. The large, multilevel dining room provides a number of different ambiences for different meals.

721 Pine St., Seattle, WA 98101. ✆ 800/233-1234 or 206/774-1234. Fax 206/774-6311. http://grandseattle. hyatt.com. 425 units. $129–$255 double; $1,250–$3,000 suite. AE, DC, DISC, MC, V. Valet parking $28; self-parking $22. **Amenities:** Restaurant (New American); lounge; health club with Jacuzzi, sauna, and steam room; concierge; business center; 24-hr. room service; massage; laundry/dry cleaning. *In room:* A/C, TV, dataport, fridge, coffeemaker, hair dryer, iron, safe.

Four Seasons Olympic Hotel ★★★   If nothing but classically elegant surroundings will do, then head straight for the Four Seasons Olympic Hotel, an Italian Renaissance palace. Without a doubt, this hotel has the grandest lobby in Seattle. Gilt-and-crystal chandeliers hang from the arched ceiling, and ornate moldings grace the glowing hand-burnished oak walls and pillars. Although many of the guest rooms tend to be rather small (with either two twin beds or one king), all are very elegant. If you crave extra space, opt for one of the suites, of which there are more than 200 (however, be aware that the executive suites aren't much bigger than the hotel's deluxe rooms). For plush surroundings, excellent service, and great amenities, this hotel can't be beat. (Although the Four Seasons doesn't have a full-fledged children's program, it does offer amenities such as kids' menus, kids' robes, baby supplies, and the like.)

In keeping with the overall character of the hotel, the **Georgian** is the most elegant restaurant in Seattle—with prices to match; its menu combines creative Northwest and Continental cuisines (see chapter 6, "Where to Dine in Seattle," for a full review).

411 University St., Seattle, WA 98101. ✆ 800/223-8772, 800/821-8106 (in Washington state), 800/ 268-6282 (in Canada), or 206/621-1700. Fax 206/682-9633. www.fourseasons.com/seattle. 450 units. $355–$385 double; $405–$1,850 suite. AE, DC, MC, V. Valet parking $26. Pets accepted. **Amenities:** 3 restaurants (Continental/Northwest, seafood); 2 lounges; health club with indoor pool, exercise machines, Jacuzzi, and saunas; spa; concierge; downtown courtesy shuttle; business center; shopping arcade; 24-hr. room service; massage; babysitting; laundry/dry cleaning. *In room:* A/C, TV, dataport, minibar, coffeemaker, hair dryer, iron.

Hotel Monaco ★★   Housed in a building that was once a telephone company switching center, the Monaco is one of downtown Seattle's hippest business hotels, attracting a young and affluent clientele. If you appreciate cutting-edge style, you'll go for the eclectic over-the-top retro-contemporary design here, which includes reproductions of ancient Greek murals in the lobby. In the guest rooms, you'll find wild color schemes, with bold striped wallpaper, and stereos with CD players. For a view of Mount Rainier, ask for rooms 1019, 1119, or 1219. Missing your pet at home? Call the front desk, and a staff member will send up a pet goldfish for the night. **Sazerac,** the hotel's restaurant, is as boldly designed as the rest of the hotel and serves New American cuisine. At the adjacent bar, be sure to order the restaurant's namesake cocktail.

1101 Fourth Ave., Seattle, WA 98101. ✆ 800/945-2240 or 206/621-1770. Fax 206/621-1779. www.monaco-seattle.com. 189 units. $315–$395 double; $395–$940 suite. AE, DC, DISC, MC, V. Valet parking $24. Pets accepted. **Amenities:** Restaurant (New American); lounge; exercise room and access to nearby health club; concierge; business center; 24-hr. room service; massage; babysitting; dry cleaning. *In room:* A/C, TV, fax, dataport, minibar, coffeemaker, hair dryer, iron.

Hotel Vintage Park ★★   Small, classically elegant, and exceedingly romantic, the Vintage Park is a must for both lovers and wine lovers. The guest rooms, all of which are named for a Washington winery, are perfect for romantic getaways, and each evening in the library-like lobby, the hotel hosts a complimentary wine tasting featuring Washington vintages. Later on in the evening, port is available. Throughout the hotel are numerous references to grapes and wine—even the minibars are stocked with Washington wines. Rooms vary quite a bit here, but when you see the plush draperies framing the beds and the neo-Victorian furnishings in the deluxe rooms, you'll likely want to spend your days luxuriating amid the sumptuous surrounds. Deluxe rooms have the best views (including views of Mount Rainier), and although the bathrooms are small, they do have attractive granite counters. Standard rooms, though smaller and less luxuriously appointed, are still very comfortable, and surprisingly, the bathrooms are larger than those in the deluxe rooms. Dogs also get the royal treatment here, sampling grape-shaped dog treats during the evening wine tastings.

1100 Fifth Ave., Seattle, WA 98101. © 800/624-4433 or 206/624-8000. Fax 206/623-0568. www.hotel vintagepark.com. 126 units. $285–$315 double; $525 suite. AE, DC, DISC, MC, V. Valet parking $24. Pets accepted. **Amenities:** Restaurant (Italian); lounge; access to nearby health club; concierge; 24-hr. room service; massage; laundry/dry cleaning. *In room:* A/C, TV, fax, dataport, minibar, hair dryer, iron.

Renaissance Madison Hotel ★★   Despite its large size, the Madison is quieter and less hectic than most convention hotels, and its rooftop restaurant and swimming pool with a view make it a good choice for leisure travelers as well as the corporate crowd. The biggest drawback is that the hotel is a bit of a walk from the waterfront (and it's all uphill coming back). Most rooms are larger than average, and many have views of either Puget Sound or the Cascade Range. For the best views, ask for a room on the west side of the hotel. Happily, you'll find plenty of counter space in the bathrooms. **Prego,** the hotel's Italian restaurant, is up on the 28th floor and has eye-catching views of Seattle. Still, the rooftop indoor pool with a view is by far the best reason to stay here.

515 Madison St., Seattle, WA 98104. © 800/278-4159 or 206/583-0300. Fax 206/624-8125. www.renais sancehotels.com. 553 units. $250–$300 double; $750–$2,000 suite. AE, DC, DISC, MC, V. Valet parking $21; self-parking $19. **Amenities:** 2 restaurants (Italian, Continental); 2 lounges; indoor rooftop pool; exercise room; Jacuzzi; concierge; business center; 24-hr. room service; dry cleaning; concierge-level rooms. *In room:* A/C, TV, dataport, minibar, hair dryer, iron.

Sorrento Hotel ★   With its wrought-iron gates, palm trees in the entrance courtyard, and plush seating in the octagonal lobby, the Sorrento, which first opened its doors in 1909, has a classic elegance and old-world atmosphere. All the rooms have just undergone a complete renovation, so they are once again the equal of the luxurious lobby and are among the finest guest rooms in the city. No two rooms are alike, and most are set up for business travelers. Although more than half the units are suites, many provide little more space than you get in a standard room. The hotel does boast commanding views of downtown Seattle from its setting high on First Hill, yet downtown is only a few (steep) blocks away (but there's complimentary limousine service if you don't feel like walking). Ask for a room on the west side of the hotel; you'll have a view of the city and Puget Sound. The hotel's dining room is a dark, clubby place, and in the lounge, which has live jazz piano, you can get light meals, afternoon tea, and cocktails. In the summer, cafe tables are set up in the hotel's courtyard.

900 Madison St., Seattle, WA 99104-1297. © 800/426-1265 or 206/622-6400. Fax 206/343-6155. www.hotelsorrento.com. 76 units. $270–$295 double; $340–$2,500 suite. AE, DC, DISC, MC, V. Valet parking $24. Pets accepted ($50 deposit). **Amenities:** Restaurant (Northwest/Mediterranean); lounge; exercise room and access to nearby health club; concierge; business center; salon; room service; massage; laundry/dry cleaning. *In room:* A/C, TV, fax, dataport, minibar, coffeemaker, hair dryer, iron.

W Seattle ★★ The W hotel chain has won plenty of national attention and devoted fans for its oh-so-hip accommodations, and here in the land of dot.coms and espresso, the W is a natural. The lobby has the look and feel of a stage set, with dramatic lighting and sleek furniture, and in the evenings it's transformed into a trendy lounge scene. Not only are the rooms beautifully designed and filled with plush amenities, but they also tend to be larger than those at other W hotels. If you can spring for an additional $50 per night, the -09 or -02 "Cool Corner" rooms are worth requesting. Guest rooms are full of great perks such as Aveda bath products, goose-down comforters, and CD players (there's a CD library from which you can borrow disks).

1112 Fourth Ave., Seattle, WA 98101. ✆ **877/W-HOTELS** or 206/264-6000. Fax 206/264-6100. www.whotels. com/seattle. 426 units. $199–$390 double; from $599 suite. AE, DC, DISC, MC, V. Valet parking $25. Pets accepted. **Amenities:** Restaurant (New American); lounge; exercise room and access to nearby health club; concierge; business center; 24-hr. room service; laundry/dry cleaning. *In room:* A/C, TV, dataport, minibar, coffeemaker, hair dryer, iron, safe.

EXPENSIVE

Inn at Harbor Steps ★★ Situated on the lower floors of a modern apartment building across the street from the Seattle Art Museum, this inn offers an excellent location that's convenient to all of downtown Seattle's major attractions. The guest rooms, which overlook a courtyard garden, are so spacious that they feel like apartments, and styling leans decidedly toward the Martha Stewart aesthetic. Every room has a gas fireplace, and the largest rooms have whirlpool tubs. The only real drawback here is the lack of views. In the same building as the hotel, the **Wolfgang Puck Cafe** features contemporary food and decor, plus water views.

1221 First Ave., Seattle, WA 98101. ✆ **888/728-8910** or 206/748-0973. Fax 206/748-0533. www.foursisters. com. 25 units. $175–$230 double. Rates include full breakfast. AE, DC, MC, V. Parking $15. **Amenities:** Restaurant (New American); lounge; indoor pool; health club with Jacuzzi, sauna, basketball court; concierge; room service; massage; babysitting; dry cleaning. *In room:* A/C, TV, dataport, fridge, coffeemaker, hair dryer, iron.

Mayflower Park Hotel ★★ If your favorite recreational activities include shopping or sipping martinis, the Mayflower Park is for you. Built in 1927, this historic hotel is connected to the upscale Westlake Center shopping plaza and is within a block of both Nordstrom and the Bon Marché. Most rooms here are furnished with an eclectic blend of contemporary Italian and traditional European pieces. Some rooms still have small, old-fashioned bathrooms, but all have been recently renovated and are now up to modern hotel standards. The smallest guest rooms are cramped, but these standard rooms have also been renovated in the past 2 years; if you crave space, ask for one of the larger corner rooms or a suite. There are also rooms with two bathrooms (popular with women traveling together). Martini drinkers will want to spend time at the hotel's **Oliver's Lounge,** which serves the best martinis in Seattle and has free hors d'oeuvres in the evening. The hotel's **Andaluca** restaurant is a plush, contemporary spot serving a highly creative cuisine (see chapter 6, "Where to Dine in Seattle," for a full review).

405 Olive Way, Seattle, WA 98101. ✆ **800/426-5100,** 206/382-6990, or 206/623-8700. Fax 206/382-6997. www.mayflowerpark.com. 171 units. $119–$200 double; $129–$365 suite. AE, DC, DISC, MC, V. Valet parking $21. **Amenities:** Restaurant (Mediterranean/Northwest); lounge; small state-of-the-art exercise room; concierge; 24-hr. room service; laundry/dry cleaning. *In room:* A/C, TV, dataport, coffeemaker, hair dryer, iron.

Sheraton Seattle Hotel and Towers ★★★ At 35 stories, this is one of the two largest hotels in Seattle. Because it's so large, it does a brisk convention business, and you'll almost always find the building buzzing with activity. But don't let the crowds put you off. There's a reason so many people want to stay here—the hotel does things right and captures much of the essence of Seattle in its many features. It has a 35th-floor exercise room and swimming pool with great views of the city. The rooms were in the process of being renovated at press time, so be sure to ask for one of the newly spiffed-up rooms. You get decent views from the higher floors, and all rooms are fairly spacious. For even more space, book one of the king rooms, which are designed for business travelers.

1400 Sixth Ave., Seattle, WA 98101. © 800/325-3535 or 206/621-9000. Fax 206/621-8441. www.sheraton. com/seattle. 840 units. $169–$385 double; $250–$5,000 suite. AE, DC, DISC, MC, V. Valet parking $24; self-parking $22. **Amenities:** 3 restaurants (American, oyster bar, pizza); 2 lounges; indoor pool; health club; Jacuzzi; sauna; concierge; business center; 24-hr. room service; massage; babysitting; laundry service; dry cleaning; concierge-level rooms. In room: A/C, TV, dataport, minibar, coffeemaker, hair dryer, iron, safe.

The Westin Seattle ★★★   With its distinctive cylindrical towers, the 47-story Westin is the tallest hotel in Seattle, and consequently provides the best views of any hotel in the city. From rooms on the upper floors of the north tower's northwest side, you'll get breathtaking views of the Space Needle, Puget Sound, and the Olympic Mountains. Views from lower floors can be good, too, if you are higher than the buildings in the surrounding blocks. Couple those great views with the Westin's plush "heavenly beds," and you'll be sleeping on clouds both literally and figuratively. There are also two excellent restaurants. Although the pool here doesn't have the great views that the Sheraton's pool has, keep in mind that few downtown hotels have pools at all—which makes the Westin a good choice for families. With great beds and unusual curved walls of glass looking out to those views, guest rooms here are some of the nicest in town.

1900 Fifth Ave., Seattle, WA 98101. © 800/WESTIN-1 or 206/728-1000. Fax 206/728-2007. www.westin. com/seattle. 891 units. $169–$345 double; from $419 suite. AE, DC, DISC, MC, V. Valet parking $24; self-parking $21. Small pets accepted ($50 deposit). **Amenities:** 3 restaurants (Euro-Asian, Japanese, American); lounge; large indoor pool; 2 exercise rooms; Jacuzzi; concierge; business center; 24-hr. room service; laundry/dry cleaning. In room: A/C, TV, dataport, minibar, coffeemaker, hair dryer, iron.

MODERATE

Executive Pacific Plaza Hotel ★ *Value*   There aren't too many reasonably priced choices left in downtown Seattle, but this hotel, built in 1928, offers recently renovated, moderately priced rooms and a prime location—halfway between Pike Place Market and Pioneer Square, and just about the same distance from the waterfront. Despite the tasteful new decor, the rooms are still small (verging on tiny) and sometimes quite cramped. Also, be aware that the hotel has no air-conditioning, and west-facing rooms can get warm in the summer. Bathrooms, although very small, were completely upgraded during the recent renovation. Currently, the room rates here are only slightly higher than at motels near the Space Needle, which makes this place a great deal.

400 Spring St., Seattle, WA 98104. © 800/426-1165 or 206/623-3900. Fax 206/623-2059. www.pacificplaza hotel.com. 160 units. $114–$144 double. Rates include continental breakfast. AE, DC, DISC, MC, V. Parking $14. **Amenities:** Restaurant (American); concierge; dry cleaning. In room: TV, dataport, coffeemaker, hair dryer, iron.

The Inn at Virginia Mason ★   You may think we've sent you to a hospital rather than a hotel when you first arrive at this older hotel on Pill Hill—but don't have a heart attack. This is definitely a hotel, though it is adjacent to the Virginia Mason Hospital. Regardless of the fact that most guests are here because of the hospital, the hotel is a good choice for vacationers as well. Rates are economical, the location is quiet, and you're close to downtown. There's a rooftop sun deck and a shady little courtyard just off the lobby. Although the carpets and furniture here are in need of replacement, the rooms are still serviceable. Because this is an old building, room sizes vary, but most have large closets, modern bathrooms, and wingback chairs. Deluxe rooms and suites can be quite large, and some have whirlpool baths and fireplaces. The hotel also keeps good company: The Sorrento Hotel, a great place to stop in for a drink, is only a block away.

1006 Spring St., Seattle, WA 98104. ⓒ 800/283-6453 or 206/583-6453. Fax 206/223-7545. 79 units. $120–$175 double; $165–$245 suite. DC, DISC, MC, V. Parking $11. **Amenities:** Restaurant (American); access to nearby health club; room service; laundry/dry cleaning. *In room:* TV.

The Roosevelt, A WestCoast Hotel ⭐ With a small lobby decorated to resemble a library in an old mansion (complete with bookshelves around the fireplace and a grand piano off to one side), the Roosevelt is a vintage 1929 hotel with plenty of class. Be forewarned, though, that the rooms tend to be quite small, and rates can be high for what you get, unless you're visiting in the rainy season or can get some sort of discounted deal. The smallest rooms, known here as studios, have one double bed and a tiny bathroom with a shower only (no tub) and are very cramped. For more space, you'll have to opt for a queen or king room. Most units have small bathrooms with little counter space. The largest rooms verge on being suites and have double whirlpool tubs. The hotel's restaurant, which is more than 80 years old, specializes in grilling meat and fish over applewood. In the bar, a wild array of "objets d'junk" hangs from the ceiling.

1531 Seventh Ave., Seattle, WA 98101. ⓒ 800/324-4000 or 206/621-1200. Fax 206/233-0335. www.roosevelt hotel.com. 151 units. $130–$220 double. AE, DC, DISC, MC, V. Valet parking $18. **Amenities:** Restaurant (American); lounge; exercise room; concierge; room service; massage; dry cleaning. *In room:* A/C, TV, dataport, coffeemaker, hair dryer, iron.

Summerfield Suites by Wyndham ⭐ *Value* Located just a block uphill from the Washington State Convention and Trade Center, this hotel caters primarily to business travelers who need a bit of extra room for getting work done while in town. At the same time, the hotel is about equidistant between the waterfront and the hip Capitol Hill shopping and nightlife district, which makes it a good choice if you're just here for fun. The suites are well laid out and have full kitchens, so you can save on restaurant bills (maybe do some shopping at Pike Place Market). Many rooms have good views that take in the Space Needle, but be aware that a good number of them also get traffic noise from both the freeway and Pike Street. The pool, though tiny, is on a pleasant terrace in an attractively landscaped courtyard area. Local restaurants will deliver meals to your room.

1011 Pike St., Seattle, WA 98101. ⓒ 800/833-4353 or 206/682-8282. Fax 206/682-5315. www.wyndham.com. 193 units. $79–$179 double. Rates include continental breakfast. AE, DC, DISC, MC, V. Valet parking $18. **Amenities:** Small outdoor pool; exercise room; Jacuzzi; concierge; downtown courtesy shuttle; coin-op laundry; dry cleaning. *In room:* A/C, TV, dataport, coffeemaker, hair dryer, iron.

WestCoast Vance Hotel ⭐ *Value* Built in the 1920s by lumber baron Joseph Vance, this hotel has a very elegant little lobby with wood paneling, marble floors, Oriental carpets, and ornate plasterwork moldings. Accommodations vary in size and style, and some are absolutely tiny (bathrooms are also uniformly small); corner rooms compensate with lots of windows and decent views. Furniture is in keeping with the style of the lobby and for the most part is fairly upscale, and rooms have been recently renovated. If you're here on business or don't care about exercise facilities (there's neither a pool nor an exercise room), this hotel offers good value and a convenient location for a downtown business hotel. With the convention center only a couple of blocks away, this hotel also does puts up a lot of convention-goers.

620 Stewart St., Seattle, WA 98101. (C) **800/325-4000** or 206/441-4200. Fax 206/441-8612. www.west coasthotels.com/vance. 165 units. $99–$149 double. AE, DC, DISC, MC, V. Parking $18. **Amenities:** Restaurant (nuevo Latino); lounge; access to nearby health club; concierge; room service; dry cleaning. *In room:* A/C, TV, dataport, coffeemaker, hair dryer, iron.

3 Belltown

Belltown, which extends north from Pike Place Market, has for several years now been Seattle's fastest-growing urban neighborhood, sprouting dozens of restaurants and several good hotels. If your Seattle travel plans include lots of eating out at hip restaurants, then Belltown is the place to stay.

MODERATE

The Wall Street Inn ★ (*Value* Located in the heart of Belltown, upstairs from El Gaucho (Seattle's most stylish steak house), this B&B was once a sailors' union boardinghouse. Today, the rooms, though not fancy, are bright and modern, and a few still have kitchenettes. The inn has a comfortable living room with leather couches and a fireplace, and a small deck with a barbecue. Cookies, coffee, and tea are set out in the afternoon. Although Belltown is Seattle's most self-consciously hip neighborhood, this is a traditionally styled, comfortable, and conveniently located base from which to explore the city. Best of all, there are loads of great restaurants within a few blocks.

2507 First Ave., Seattle, WA 98121. (C) **800/624-1117** or 206/448-0125. Fax 206/448-2406. www.wallstreet inn.com. 20 units. $119–$179 double. Rates include deluxe continental breakfast. AE, DC, DISC, MC, V. Parking $6–$10. **Amenities:** Access to nearby health club; concierge; business center; massage; coin-op laundry. *In room:* TV, dataport, fridge, coffeemaker, hair dryer, iron.

INEXPENSIVE

Ace Hotel Belltown is Seattle's trendiest neighborhood, and the Ace, in the heart of Belltown, is the city's hippest economy hotel, sort of a B&B (without the breakfast) for young scene-makers. White-on-white and stainless steel are the hallmarks of the minimalist decor, and brick walls and wood floors have been painted white—even the TVs are white. Wall decorations are minimal, except in those rooms with 1970s photo murals of the great outdoors. Platform beds and blankets salvaged from foreign hotels add to the chic feel, as do the tiny stainless steel sinks and shelves in the rooms with shared bathrooms. Basically, aside from the eight large rooms with private bathrooms, this place is a step above a hostel; it's aimed at the 20- and 30-something crowd out to make the scene in Seattle. Be aware, however, that the walls here are paper-thin and the people who stay here tend to keep late hours. Don't plan on going to sleep early.

2423 First Ave., Seattle, WA 98121. (C) **206/448-4721.** Fax 206/374-0745. www.theacehotel.com. 34 units, 15 with shared bathroom. $65 single with shared bathroom; $85 double with shared bathroom; $130–$175 deluxe with private bathroom. AE, DC, DISC, MC, V. Parking $15. Pets accepted. *In room:* TV, dataport, coffeemaker.

Moore Hotel If you've ever traveled through Europe on a tight budget, you'll know what to expect from this place. No, it's nothing fancy, and the rooms aren't in the best shape. But you just won't find too many acceptable downtown-area hotels in this price range, so it's fine for young travelers and other low-maintenance types who don't demand perfection from cheap accommodations. You certainly can't beat the Belltown location. Trendy restaurants and nightclubs line First and Second avenues starting about a block from the hotel, and Pike Place Market is only 2 blocks away. The lobby, with its marble, tiles, and decorative moldings, is in much better shape than the rooms. There's a hip restaurant/lounge on the premises, as well as an adjacent theater that stages rock concerts. Ask for a room with a view of the sound.

1926 Second Ave., Seattle, WA 98101. ℂ 800/421-5508 or 206/448-4851. Fax 206/728-5668. www.moore hotel.com. 140 units, 45 with shared bathroom. $45 double with shared bathroom; $59–$74 double with private bathroom. MC, V. Parking $12. **Amenities:** Restaurant (American); lounge. *In room:* TV.

4 Pike Place Market

Pike Place Market is one of Seattle's top attractions and is a fascinating place to explore. In addition to all the small shops, produce stalls, and fishmongers, the market has lots of great restaurants and a couple of lodging options. If you aren't going to stay on the waterfront, this area makes an excellent alternative.

EXPENSIVE

Inn at the Market ★★ For romance, convenience, and the chance to immerse yourself in the Seattle aesthetic, it's hard to beat this small, European-style hotel located right in Pike Place Market. A rooftop deck overlooking the harbor provides a tranquil spot to soak up the sun on summer afternoons and further adds to this hotel's distinctive sense of place. Don't look for a grand entrance or large sign here; there's only a small plaque on the wall to indicate that the building in fact houses a tasteful and understated luxury hotel. To make the most of a stay here, be sure to ask for one of the water-view rooms, which have wide bay windows that overlook Puget Sound. But even if you don't get a water-view room, you'll still find spacious accommodations and large bathrooms. The decor is tastefully elegant and gives the feel of an upscale European beach resort. If you need more room than a standard hotel room offers, consider the bilevel town-house suites. **Campagne,** the hotel's formal main dining room, serves excellent southern French fare, while **Café Campagne** offers country-style French food amid casual surroundings (see chapter 6 for full reviews of both restaurants).

86 Pine St., Seattle, WA 98101. ℂ 800/446-4484 or 206/443-3600. www.innatthemarket.com. 70 units. $190–$310 double; $335–$380 suite. AE, DISC, MC, V. Parking $17. **Amenities:** 3 restaurants (country French, juice bar); access to nearby health club; concierge; courtesy downtown shuttle; room service; dry cleaning. *In room:* A/C, TV, dataport, minibar, fridge, coffeemaker, hair dryer, iron, safe.

MODERATE

Pensione Nichols It's never easy finding an economical downtown-area lodging with character, but that's exactly what you'll discover at this European-style B&B, located in the heart of Pike Place Market. It's a popular choice with younger travelers and families. The budget-priced units with shared bathroom are all on the third floor of the building, and though most of the eclectically furnished rooms don't have windows, they do have skylights. However, most guests spend their time in the comfortable lounging area, with huge windows overlooking Elliott Bay. If you want to splurge, the two suites are quite large and have private bathrooms and windows with water views. Be prepared to climb a lot of stairs.

1923 First Ave., Seattle, WA 98101. ℂ 800/440-7125 or 206/441-7125. www.seattle-bed-breakfast.com. 12 units, 10 with shared bathroom. $110 double with shared bathroom; $195 suite with private bathroom. 2-night minimum on summer weekends. Rates include breakfast. AE, DC, DISC, MC, V. Parking $10. Pets accepted. *In room:* No phone.

5 Pioneer Square & the International District

The historic Pioneer Square area is Seattle's main nightlife district and can be a pretty rowdy place on a Saturday night. By day, however, the area's many art galleries and antiques stores attract a very different clientele. Still, even in the daylight, be prepared to encounter a lot of street people. Warnings aside, this is one of the prettiest corners of Seattle and the only downtown neighborhood with historic flavor. The International District lies but a few blocks away from Pioneer Square—again, a good place to explore by day but less appealing at night. There is only one recommendable hotel in the area.

EXPENSIVE

Best Western Pioneer Square Hotel ⋆   This hotel is located right in the heart of the Pioneer Square historic district, Seattle's main nightlife neighborhood. As such, things get especially raucous on weekend nights, and this hotel is only recommended for urban dwellers accustomed to dealing with street people and noise. However, if you're in town to party (or to attend a Mariners or Seahawks game), there's no more convenient location in the city. This economical hotel is also convenient to the Waterfront Trolley and the Washington State Ferries terminal. However, take care on the streets around here late at night. Guest rooms are, for the most part, fairly small (some are positively cramped) but are furnished in an attractive classic style.

77 Yesler Way, Seattle, WA 98104. ⓒ 800/800-5514 or 206/340-1234. Fax 206/467-0707. www.pioneer square.com. 75 units. July–Sept $129–$189 double, $229–$299 suite; Oct–June $109–$169 double, $189–$249 suite. Rates include continental breakfast. AE, DC, DISC, MC, V. Parking $18. **Amenities:** Access to nearby health club; concierge; business center; room service; laundry service; dry cleaning. *In room:* A/C, TV, dataport, coffeemaker, hair dryer.

6 Queen Anne & Seattle Center

The Queen Anne neighborhood is divided into an Upper Queen Anne and a Lower Queen Anne. The upper neighborhood is an upscale residential area with an attractive shopping district. The hotels listed here are in the lower neighborhood, which conveniently flanks Seattle Center. The neighborhood also offers lots of inexpensive restaurants for the budget-minded.

MODERATE

Comfort Suites Downtown/Seattle Center ⋆ *Kids*   Although it's none too easy to find this place (call and get specific directions for the approach you'll be taking), the bargain rates and spacious new rooms make the Comfort Suites worth searching out. Since it's located only 3 blocks from the Seattle Center, you could feasibly leave your car parked at the hotel for most of your stay and walk or use public transit to get around. If you've brought the family, the suites are a good deal, and the proximity to Seattle Center will help moms and dads keep the kids entertained. Ask for a room away from the busy highway that runs past the hotel.

601 Roy St., Seattle, WA 98109. ⓒ 800/517-4000 or 206/282-2600. Fax 206/282-1112. www.comfortsuites. com. 158 units. $99–$129 double; $104–$179 suite. Rates include continental breakfast. AE, DISC, MC, V. Free parking. **Amenities:** Exercise room; downtown courtesy shuttle; coin-op laundry. *In room:* A/C, TV, dataport, fridge, coffeemaker, hair dryer, iron, free local calls.

Holiday Inn Downtown Seattle ⋆   With a restaurant serving Asian and Northwest fare and an espresso cart in the lobby, this new Holiday Inn 3 blocks from the Space Needle is far superior to the older budget chain motels in this neighborhood. Sure, room rates are a little bit higher than at the older places, but the rooms are far more comfortable, and if you can get a discounted room rate, the price can end up being comparable to those at the older places nearby.

Accommodations: Seattle Center, Lake Union, Capitol Hill & the "U" District

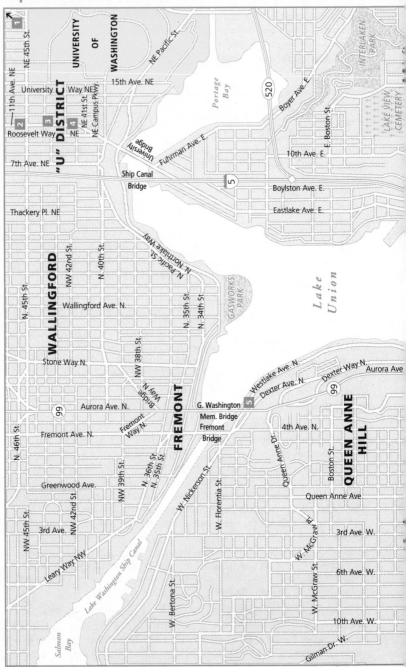

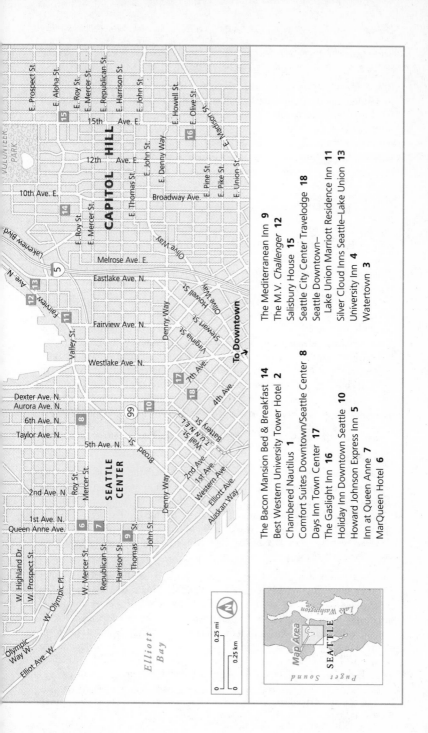

The Bacon Mansion Bed & Breakfast **14**
Best Western University Tower Hotel **2**
Chambered Nautilus **1**
Comfort Suites Downtown/Seattle Center **8**
Days Inn Town Center **17**
The Gaslight Inn **16**
Holiday Inn Downtown Seattle **10**
Howard Johnson Express Inn **5**
Inn at Queen Anne **7**
MarQueen Hotel **6**

The Mediterranean Inn **9**
The M.V. *Challenger* **12**
Salisbury House **15**
Seattle City Center Travelodge **18**
Seattle Downtown—
   Lake Union Marriott Residence Inn **11**
Silver Cloud Inns Seattle–Lake Union **13**
University Inn **4**
Watertown **3**

211 Dester Ave. N., Seattle, WA 98109. ☎ 800/465-4329 or 206/728-8123. Fax 206/441-9794. www.holiday inn.com/seattlewa. 198 units. $109–$139 double; $129–$159 suite. AE, DC, DISC, MC, V. Free parking. **Amenities:** Restaurant (Asian/Northwest); lounge; exercise room; business center; room service; laundry service; dry cleaning. *In room:* A/C, TV, dataport, fridge, coffeemaker, hair dryer, iron.

Inn at Queen Anne   Located in the Lower Queen Anne neighborhood close to Seattle Center and numerous restaurants and espresso bars, this inn is housed in a converted older apartment building. Though the rooms here aren't as nice as those at the nearby MarQueen, they're comfortable enough, albeit sometimes a bit cramped and not entirely modern. The convenient location and economical rates are the big pluses here. A pleasant garden surrounds the hotel.

505 First Ave. N., Seattle, WA 98109. ☎ 800/952-5043 or 206/282-7357. Fax 206/217-9719. www.innatqueen anne.com. 68 units. May–Sept $99–$109 double, $119–$159 suite; Oct–Apr $89 double, $109–$139 suite. Rates include continental breakfast. AE, DC, DISC, MC, V. Parking $10. **Amenities:** Coin-op laundry; laundry service; dry cleaning. *In room:* TV, kitchenette, fridge, free local calls.

MarQueen Hotel ★ *Kids* *Finds*   Located in the up-and-coming Lower Queen Anne neighborhood, this hotel is in a renovated 1918 brick building. Seattle Center, with its many performance venues and museums, is only 3 blocks away, and from there you can take the monorail into downtown. Although the hotel is geared toward business travelers (with lots of high-tech amenities), it's a good choice for vacationers as well. Guest rooms are spacious, though a bit oddly laid out due to the hotel's previous incarnation as an apartment building. Many rooms have separate little seating areas and full kitchens, which makes this a good choice for families (especially considering the proximity to Seattle Center's kid-oriented attractions). Lots of dark wood trim and hardwood floors give rooms here a genuinely old-fashioned feel. There's an excellent espresso bar in the hotel building and numerous good restaurants nearby.

600 Queen Anne Ave. N., Seattle, WA 98109. ☎ 888/445-3076 or 206/282-7407. Fax 206/283-1499. www. marqueen.com. 56 units. $130–$175 double; $195–$275 suite. AE, DC, DISC, MC, V. Valet parking $15. **Amenities:** 2 restaurants (Northwest/Eclectic, espresso bar); access to nearby health club; concierge; room service; laundry service; dry cleaning. *In room:* A/C, TV, dataport, kitchen, minibar, fridge, coffeemaker, hair dryer, iron.

INEXPENSIVE

Days Inn Town Center   Conveniently located near the Seattle Center and within walking distance (or a free bus ride) of the rest of downtown Seattle, this three-story chain hotel offers large, clean accommodations. It has a combination restaurant and bar on the premises if you don't feel like going out.

2205 Seventh Ave., Seattle, WA 98121. ☎ 800/DAYS-INN or 206/448-3434. Fax 206/441-6976. www.daysinn towncenter.com. 91 units. $79–$139 double. AE, DC, DISC, MC, V. Free parking. **Amenities:** Restaurant (American); lounge. *In room:* A/C, TV.

Howard Johnson Express Inn ★ *Value*   Located on the eastern slopes of Queen Anne Hill, overlooking Lake Union and the distant Cascade Range, this older motel is just a short drive (or bus ride) from Seattle Center and is just across the Aurora Bridge from Fremont, which has lots of inexpensive restaurants. The best guest rooms, which can usually be had for around $80 to $85 in the summer, have balconies overlooking Lake Union. Right next door to the motel you'll find Canlis, one of Seattle's top restaurants—even if you can't afford to eat here, you can still have a drink at the bar and soak up the atmosphere.

2500 Aurora Ave. N., Seattle, WA 98109. ☎ 877/284-1900 or 206/284-1900. Fax 206/283-5298. www. hojo.com. 94 units. $55–$84 double. Rates include continental breakfast. AE, DC, DISC, MC, V. **Amenities:** Seasonal outdoor pool. *In room:* A/C, TV, coffeemaker.

The Mediterranean Inn ✦ Don't be fooled by the name; this is not a bed-and-breakfast-type inn. But this recently constructed apartment hotel in the Lower Queen Anne neighborhood just a couple of blocks from Seattle Center is an ideal choice for longer stays in the city. Because the hotel is so new and because it was designed with travelers in mind, the rooms are much more comfortable than those at the nearby Inn at Queen Anne. Although all the rooms here are studio apartments, some have beds that roll back toward the wall to form a couch. We prefer the more standard rooms. A Starbucks is just off the lobby.

425 Queen Anne Ave. N., Seattle, WA 98109. © **866/425-4700** or 206/428-4700. Fax 206/428-4699. www.mediterranean-inn.com. 180 units. $89–$109 double (from $450 weekly). AE, DISC, MC, V. Parking $10. **Amenities:** Exercise room; business center; coin-op laundry. *In room:* A/C, TV, dataport, kitchenette, fridge, coffeemaker, hair dryer, iron.

Seattle City Center Travelodge This conveniently located downtown motel can be a bit overpriced for what you get, but the location, midway between the Westlake Center shopping mall and Seattle Center, makes it a fairly convenient choice if you don't mind doing a bit of walking (alternatively, from here you can ride the bus for free within downtown Seattle). The rooms are up to motel standards (and include free local calls—a nice perk), and some even have balconies and views of the Space Needle.

2213 Eighth Ave., Seattle, WA 98121. © **800/578-7878** or 206/624-6300. Fax 206/233-0185. www.travelodge. com. 73 units. $76–$189 double. Rates include continental breakfast. AE, DC, DISC, MC, V. Free parking. **Amenities:** Tour desk. *In room:* A/C, TV, coffeemaker, safe.

7 Lake Union

Located less than a mile from downtown and lined with houseboats, marinas, and waterfront restaurants, Lake Union has a quintessentially Seattle character. Floatplanes use the lake as a runway, and you can rent a kayak, canoe, or rowboat from several places around the lake. If you are happiest when you're close to the water but want to avoid the crowds of the Seattle waterfront, this area is an excellent alternative.

EXPENSIVE

Silver Cloud Inns Seattle–Lake Union ✦✦ *Kids* √Value Located across the street from Lake Union, this moderately priced hotel offers good views (some of which take in the Space Needle). The rooms are big and filled with lots of amenities, which makes them convenient for long stays and family vacations. The two swimming pools (one indoors and one outdoors) should also appeal to kids. Although the hotel doesn't have a restaurant of its own, there are plenty of waterfront restaurants within walking distance. Floatplane tours also leave from right across the street. This is a good value for such a great location.

1150 Fairview Ave. N., Seattle, WA 98109. © **800/330-5812** or 206/447-9500. Fax 206/812-4900. www.sc inns.com. 184 units. June–Sept $155–$230 double; Oct–May $89–$215 double. Rates include continental breakfast. AE, DC, DISC, MC, V. Free parking. **Amenities:** Indoor pool and an outdoor pool; exercise room and access to nearby health club; 2 Jacuzzis; courtesy local shuttle; business center; laundry service; dry cleaning. *In room:* A/C, TV, dataport, fridge, coffeemaker, hair dryer, iron, free local calls.

MODERATE

The M.V. *Challenger* *Finds* If you love ships and the sea and want a taste of Seattle's water-oriented lifestyle, consider stowing away aboard the M.V. *Challenger,* a restored and fully operational 1944 tugboat. If, however, you need lots of space, this place is definitely not for you. Guest rooms are as tiny as you would expect berths to be on any small boat. But nautical types will consider a stay here a memorable experience—and you just can't beat the marina location (at the south end of Lake Union) and waterside views. You're a bit of a hike (or a short bus ride) from downtown, but you'll find plenty of waterfront restaurants within walking distance. This is a great place for a weekend getaway or romantic vacation. There are also two berths on a second, much more modern boat.

Yale St. Landing, 1001 Fairview Ave. N., Ste. 1600, Seattle, WA 98109-4416. ✆ **800/288-7521** or 206/340-1201. Fax 206/332-0303. www.tugboatchallenger.com. 10 units, 3 with shared bathroom. $85–$200 double. Rates include full breakfast. AE, DC, DISC, MC, V. Free parking. Pets accepted. *In room:* No phone.

Seattle Downtown–Lake Union Marriott Residence Inn ★★ A bit removed from downtown Seattle but across the street from Lake Union, this Marriott Residence Inn is within a couple of blocks of several waterfront restaurants, making a stay here a quintessential Seattle experience. A seven-story atrium floods the hotel's plant-filled lobby court with light, while the sound of a waterfall soothes traffic-weary nerves. All accommodations here are suites, so you get quite a bit more space for your money than you do at downtown hotels. You'll also have use of a full kitchen, complete with dishes, so you can prepare your own meals if you like, though breakfasts are provided. The suites here, though generally quite spacious, don't have much character. They do, however, have phones and televisions in the bedrooms and living rooms. The hotel has no restaurant of its own, but several restaurants are right across the street, and one of these provides the hotel's room service. Amenities include Wednesday-night guest receptions and a grocery-shopping service.

800 Fairview Ave. N., Seattle, WA 98109. ✆ **800/331-3131** or 206/624-6000. Fax 206/223-8160. www.residenceinn.com/sealu/. 234 units. $159–$199 1-bedroom suite, $289–$329 2-bedroom suite. Rates include expanded continental breakfast. AE, DC, DISC, MC, V. Parking $12. Pets accepted with $10 fee per day. **Amenities:** Indoor lap pool and children's pool; exercise room; Jacuzzi; sauna/steam room; concierge; downtown courtesy shuttle; room service; laundry/dry cleaning. *In room:* A/C, TV, dataport, kitchen, coffeemaker, hair dryer, iron.

8 Capitol Hill & East Seattle

Located a mile or so uphill and to the east of downtown Seattle, Capitol Hill is a neighborhood with a split personality. It's a hangout for the 20-something crowd and has a vibrant gay scene, yet it's also home to numerous large restored homes, many of which have been converted into bed-and-breakfast inns. If you prefer B&Bs to corporate hotels, this is the best neighborhood in which to base yourself. Although Capitol Hill is a bit of a walk from downtown, the neighborhood has good public bus connections to the city center.

MODERATE

The Bacon Mansion Bed & Breakfast ★ As the name implies, this is a big place (a 9,000-sq.-ft. Tudor built in 1909, to be precise) and has all the accouterments of a mansion—a crystal chandelier, a grand piano, a huge dining-room table, and a library. Located on a shady stretch of Broadway 2 blocks beyond Capitol Hill's busy commercial area, the inn combines a quiet residential feel with proximity to a hip shopping and dining scene. Decor includes a mix of antiques and period reproductions, with an abundance of floral prints. Although you may catch a glimpse of the Space Needle from the Capitol Suite, other rooms lack views. Two of the rooms are located in the old carriage house.

959 Broadway E., Seattle, WA 98102. ✆ **800/240-1864** or 206/329-1864. Fax 206/860-9025. www.baconmansion.com. 11 units, 2 with shared bathroom. $84–$104 double with shared bathroom; $104–$184 double with private bathroom. Rates include expanded continental breakfast. AE, DISC, MC, V. **Amenities:** Concierge. *In room:* TV, dataport, hair dryer.

The Gaslight Inn ★   Anyone enamored of Craftsman bungalows and the Arts and Crafts movement of the early 20th century should enjoy a stay in this 1906 home. Throughout the inn are numerous pieces of Stickley furniture, and everywhere you turn, oak trim frames doors and windows. The common rooms are spacious and attractively decorated with a combination of Western and Northwestern flair, and throughout the inn's two houses are lots of art-glass pieces. A library filled with interesting books and magazines makes a comfortable spot for a bit of free time, or, if it's cold out, take a seat by the fireplace. In summer, guests can swim in the backyard pool or lounge on the deck. Guest rooms continue the design themes of the common areas with lots of oak furnishings and heavy, peeled-log beds in some rooms. An annex next door has a studio and six suites with kitchens, dining areas, and separate bedrooms and living rooms. One of these suites, done in a contemporary style with an art-glass chandelier, has a fireplace and an outstanding view of the city. The innkeepers here can provide a wealth of information about the surrounding Capitol Hill neighborhood, which is the center of Seattle's gay scene.

1727 15th Ave., Seattle, WA 98122. ✆ **206/325-3654.** Fax 206/328-4803. www.gaslight-inn.com. 15 units, 3 with shared bathroom. $78–$148 double; $128 studio; $148–$178 suite. Rates include continental breakfast. AE, MC, V. Off-street parking for suites. **Amenities:** Small outdoor pool; access to nearby health club; concierge. *In room:* TV, dataport, hair dryer, iron.

Salisbury House   Located on tree-lined 16th Avenue East, this grand old house has a wide wraparound porch from which you can enjoy one of Seattle's prettiest residential streets. Inside there's plenty to admire as well. Two living rooms (one with a wood-burning fireplace) and a second-floor sun porch provide great spots for relaxing and meeting other guests. On sunny summer days, breakfast may even be served in the small formal garden in the backyard. Guest rooms all have queen-size beds with down comforters, and one has a fireplace and a whirlpool tub. One of the other rooms has an old claw-foot tub in the bathroom. Breakfasts here are deliciously filling and might include fresh fruit, juice, quiche, fresh-baked muffins or bread, and oatmeal pancakes.

750 16th Ave. E., Seattle, WA 98112. ✆ **206/328-8682.** Fax 206/720-1019. www.salisburyhouse.com. 5 units. $95–$159 double. Rates include full breakfast. AE, MC, V. *In room:* Hair dryer, iron.

⟨Kids⟩ Family-Friendly Hotels

Comfort Suites Downtown/Seattle Center (p. 65)   The suites make this a good family choice, and the location near the Seattle Center will make the kids happy.

MarQueen Hotel (p. 68)   Located within a few blocks of Seattle Center and its many attractions, this converted apartment building provides a convenient location for families, and spacious suites with kitchenettes.

Seattle Marriott Sea-Tac Airport (p. 73)   With a huge jungly atrium containing a swimming pool and whirlpool spas, kids can play Tarzan and never leave the hotel. A small game room will keep the young ones occupied if need be.

Silver Cloud Inns Seattle–Lake Union (p. 69)   Located right across the street from Lake Union and with a good family restaurant (Cucina! Cucina!) a short walk away, this modern hotel is a good choice for families. It also has two swimming pools and big rooms.

9 North Seattle (The University District)

Located 10 to 15 minutes north of downtown Seattle, the University District (more commonly known as the "U" District) appeals primarily to younger travelers, but it does offer less expensive accommodations than downtown and is still fairly convenient to Seattle's major attractions. Also nearby are the Burke Museum, Henry Art Gallery, Museum of History and Industry, Woodland Park Zoo, and, of course, University of Washington. As you would expect in a university neighborhood, there are lots of cheap restaurants, making this an all-round good choice for anyone on a budget.

MODERATE

Best Western University Tower Hotel ★★ *Value*   Despite the location away from downtown, this is one of Seattle's handful of hip hotels, and the modern Art Deco decor will surround you in retro style. Best of all, it's considerably cheaper than comparable downtown hotels, and if you need to be near the university, this is definitely the top choice in the neighborhood. You'll even get views of downtown Seattle, distant mountains, and various lakes and waterways. Every room here is a large corner unit, which means plenty of space to spread out and plenty of views from the higher floors. Small bathrooms are the biggest drawback.

4507 Brooklyn Ave. NE, Seattle, WA 98105. © **800/WESTERN** or 206/634-2000. Fax 206/547-6029. www.universitytowerhotel.com. 155 units. June–Sept $129–$169 double; Oct–May $119–$139 double. Rates include continental breakfast. AE, DC, DISC, MC, V. Free parking. **Amenities:** Restaurant (espresso bar); exercise room and access to nearby health club. *In room:* A/C, TV, dataport, coffeemaker, hair dryer, iron.

Chambered Nautilus Bed and Breakfast Inn ★   Located on an apartment-lined street in the University District, this Georgian Colonial inn sits high above the street atop an ivy-covered embankment, out of view of the street. The shady forest surrounding it gives it a very secluded feel (you'll hardly realize you're in the middle of the city). The antiques-filled inn, which dates from 1915, has a homey feel, and innkeepers Joyce Schulte and Steve Poole make sure guests are comfortable and well fed. Four of the rooms have porches, and some have mountain views (third-floor rooms have the best views). Be advised that this inn is not recommended for anyone who has trouble climbing stairs. Four suites, designed for long-term stays, are located in an adjacent house.

5005 22nd Ave. NE, Seattle, WA 98105. © **800/545-8459** or 206/522-2536. Fax 206/528-0898. www.chamberednautilus.com. 10 units. $99–$144 double; $134–$144 suite. Rates include full breakfast. AE, MC, V. *In room:* TV, dataport, hair dryer, iron.

University Inn ★   Located within easy walking distance of the university, this renovated 1960s hotel offers surprisingly attractive rooms, many of which have views of Lake Union. Although the standard rooms have showers but no tubs in the bathrooms, they make up for this shortcoming with small balconies. The deluxe rooms are more spacious, and those on the west side of the hotel offer glimpses of Lake Union (the best views are in winter). For even more room and the best views, opt for one of the junior suites, which have large windows, microwaves, small refrigerators, and coffeemakers (ask for room 331, which has a view of Mount Rainier).

4140 Roosevelt Way NE, Seattle, WA 98105. © **800/733-3855** or 206/632-5055. Fax 206/547-4937. www.universityinnseattle.com. 102 units. $102–$149 double. Rates include continental breakfast. AE, DC, DISC, MC, V. Free parking. Pets accepted ($10 fee per day). **Amenities:** Restaurant (American); small outdoor pool; access to nearby health club; Jacuzzi; courtesy shuttle; coin-op laundry; dry cleaning. *In room:* A/C, TV, dataport, safe, free local calls.

Watertown ★★   Billing itself a "unique urban hotel," the Watertown is Seattle's latest entry in the hip hotel market. Located as it is only blocks from the University of Washington, it is definitely well-placed for a young and hip clientele. It's also beautifully designed, with many a bow to the Bauhaus. If you're into contemporary styling, you'll love this hotel, even if you aren't in town on university business. Platform beds, desks with frosted-glass tops, ergonomic desk chairs, and huge full-length mirrors are just a few of the interesting features in the guest rooms. To streamline the look of the rooms, there are lots of built-ins, and the coffeemakers are so well hidden that many guests never find them. Bathrooms are large and have granite countertops. When you see the frosted-glass portal on the bathroom door, you might even imagine you're on a cruise ship.

4242 Roosevelt Way NE, Seattle, WA 98105. ✆ 866/944-4242 or 206/826-4242. Fax 206/315-4242. www. watertownseattle.com. 100 units. $129–$155 double; $149–$189 suite. Rates include continental breakfast. AE, DC, DISC, MC, V. Free parking. **Amenities:** Exercise room; complimentary use of bikes; courtesy shuttle; coin-op laundry. *In room:* A/C, TV, dataport (and high-speed Internet access), fridge, coffeemaker, hair dryer, iron, safe, free local calls.

10 Near Sea-Tac Airport

The airport is 20 to 30 minutes south of downtown Seattle. Other than convenience, there's little to recommend this area as a place to stay.

EXPENSIVE

Seattle Marriott Sea-Tac Airport ★★ *Kids*   With a steamy atrium garden in which you'll find plenty of tropical plants, a swimming pool, and two whirlpool tubs, this resortlike hotel is an excellent choice if you're visiting during the rainy season. There are even waterfalls and totem poles for that Northwest outdoorsy feeling; and best of all, it's always sunny and warm in here (which is more than you can say for the real Northwest outdoors). In the lobby, a huge stone fireplace conjures up images of a remote mountain lodge and helps you forget that this is really an airport hotel. With its stone pillars, rough-hewn beams, and deer-antler chandeliers, the hotel's restaurant perpetuates the lodge feel. Guest rooms don't have the same lodge feel as the public areas, but they're comfortable enough. Ask for one of the rooms with a view of Mount Rainier.

3201 S. 176th St., Seattle, WA 98188. ✆ 800/643-5479 or 206/241-2000. Fax 206/248-0789. www. marriott.com. 459 units. $129–$150 double ($79–$150 on weekends); $225–$450 suite. AE, DC, DISC, MC, V. Parking $12. Pets accepted. **Amenities:** Restaurant (American); lounge; indoor atrium pool; exercise room; Jacuzzi; sauna; concierge; car-rental desk; airport shuttle; business center; room service; massage; laundry/dry cleaning; concierge-level rooms. *In room:* A/C, TV, dataport, coffeemaker, hair dryer, iron.

MODERATE

WestCoast Sea-Tac Hotel ★   Located almost directly across from the airport's main entrance, this modern hotel provides comfortable accommodations designed for business travelers. Guest rooms are generally quite large (if you need space, this is the place). In superior king rooms, you also get evening turndown service, coffee and the morning newspaper, terry-cloth robes, and an honor bar. The hotel backs onto a small lake, but only a few rooms have lake views.

18220 International Blvd., Seattle, WA 98188. ✆ 800/325-4000 or 206/246-5535. Fax 206/246-9733. www.westcoasthotels.com/seatac. 146 units. $99–$135 double. AE, DC, DISC, MC, V. Valet parking $13.95; free self-parking. Pets accepted. **Amenities:** Restaurant (American); lounge; outdoor pool; exercise room; Jacuzzi; sauna; courtesy airport shuttle; room service; laundry/dry cleaning. *In room:* A/C, TV, dataport, coffeemaker, hair dryer, iron.

11 The Eastside

The Eastside (a reference to this area's location on the east side of Lake Washington) is Seattle's main high-tech suburb and is comprised of the cities of Bellevue, Kirkland, Issaquah, and Redmond. Should you be out this way on business, you may find that an Eastside hotel is more convenient than one in downtown Seattle. Surprisingly, two of the most luxurious hotels in the entire Seattle area are here on this side of Lake Washington. If it isn't rush hour, you can usually get from the Eastside to downtown in about 20 minutes via the famous floating I-90 and Wash. 520 bridges. During rush hour, however, it can take much longer.

VERY EXPENSIVE

Bellevue Club Hotel ★★★   In its gardens, architecture, and interior design, this hotel epitomizes contemporary Northwest style. Beautifully landscaped gardens surround the entrance, and works of contemporary art can be found throughout the public areas. The "club" in this hotel's name refers to a state-of-the-art health club that has everything from an indoor running track and three pools to indoor squash and outdoor tennis courts (there's also a full-service spa), but even if you aren't into aerobic workouts, this hotel has much to offer. You won't find more elegant rooms anywhere in the Seattle area. Accommodations are extremely plush, with the high-ceiling garden rooms among our favorites. These have a floor-to-ceiling wall of glass, massive draperies, and a private patio facing onto a beautiful garden. Luxurious European fabrics are everywhere, giving rooms a romantic feel. Bathrooms are resplendent in granite and glass, and most have whirlpool tubs. The same elegant contemporary design seen in the lobby is found in the hotel's **Polaris Restaurant.**

11200 SE Sixth St., Bellevue, WA 98004. © 800/579-1110 or 425/454-4424. Fax 425/688-3101. www.belle vueclub.com. 67 units. $250–$310 double ($125–$230 weekends); $550–$1,450 suite ($325–$895 weekends). AE, DC, DISC, MC, V. Parking $5. **Amenities:** 2 restaurants (Northwest); lounge; espresso bar; 2 indoor pools and an outdoor pool; expansive health club with Jacuzzi, saunas, steam rooms, 11 tennis courts, racquetball courts, squash courts, and aerobics studios; children's programs; game room; concierge; business center; 24-hr. room service; massage; babysitting; laundry/dry cleaning; executive-level rooms. In room: A/C, TV, fax, dataport, minibar, hair dryer, iron, safe.

EXPENSIVE

Best Western Bellevue Inn ★   The Bellevue Inn is one of the few hotels in the Seattle area that captures the feel of the Northwest in its design and landscaping. The sprawling two-story hotel is roofed with cedar-shake shingles, and the grounds are lushly planted with rhododendrons, ferns, azaleas, and fir trees. Guest rooms here are quite sophisticated and upscale, with elegant Country French furnishings and decor. Bathrooms have plenty of counter space.

11211 Main St., Bellevue, WA 98004. © 800/421-8193 or 425/455-5240. Fax 206/455-0654. www.best western.com/bellevueinnbellevuewa. 181 units. Mar–Oct $159–$189 double; Nov–Feb $139–$169 double. AE, DC, DISC, MC, V. Free parking. **Amenities:** Restaurant (American); lounge; pool; exercise room; laundry/ dry cleaning. In room: A/C, TV, dataport, fridge, coffeemaker, hair dryer, iron.

The Woodmark Hotel on Lake Washington ★★   Despite all the lakes and bays in the area, Seattle has a surprising dearth of waterfront hotels. Although Kirkland's Woodmark Hotel is 20 minutes from downtown Seattle (on a good day), it is the metro area's premier waterfront lodging. Surrounded by a luxury residential community, the Woodmark has the feel of a beach resort and looks out over the very same waters that Bill Gates views from his nearby Xanadu.

There are plenty of lake-view rooms here, and you'll pay a premium for them. For less expensive lodging, try the creek-view rooms, which offer a pleasant view of an attractively landscaped little stream. Floor-to-ceiling windows that open are a nice feature on sunny summer days, and, for techies, there is high-speed Internet access. The hotel's dining room is pricey, but several less-expensive restaurants are in the same complex of buildings. For cocktails and afternoon tea, there's the cozy **Library Bar,** which often has live piano music in the evenings. In addition, complimentary late-night snacks and drinks are available.

1200 Carillon Point, Kirkland, WA 98033. ✆ **800/822-3700** or 425/822-3700. Fax 425/822-3699. www.the woodmark.com. 100 units. $205–$275 double; $320–$1,800 suite. AE, DISC, MC, V. Valet parking $12; self-parking $10. Pets accepted ($100 deposit). **Amenities:** Restaurant (New American); lounge; exercise room; full-service spa; concierge; car-rental desk; business center; salon; 24-hr. room service; massage; laundry service; dry cleaning. In room: A/C, TV, dataport, minibar, coffeemaker, hair dryer, iron, safe.

INEXPENSIVE

Extended StayAmerica–Bellevue ✪   Located just off I-405 near downtown Bellevue, this modern off-ramp motel caters primarily to long-term guests. To this end, the rooms are all large, have kitchenettes, and offer free local calls. If you're only staying for a few days, you'll have to pay around $85, but if you stay for a week, rates drop to around $60 per day. This is about the most expensive of the Seattle area's Extended StayAmerica hotels, so if you don't mind staying in a different less-upscale suburb, you can find even lower rates.

11400 Main St., Bellevue, WA 98009. ✆ **800/EXT-STAY** or 425/453-8186. Fax 425/453-8178. www.extended stay.com. 148 units. $84–$99 double ($400–$470 weekly). AE, DC, DISC, MC, V. Free parking. **Amenities:** Coin-op laundry. In room: A/C, TV, dataport, kitchenette, fridge, coffeemaker.

6

Where to Dine in Seattle

With its abundant fresh seafood, Northwest berries, rain-fed mushrooms, and other market-fresh produce, Seattle has become something of a culinary capital. Although the dot-com crash winnowed out some of the city's higher-end restaurants, many that remain have lowered their prices considerably from their highs of a few years ago, often offering relatively inexpensive prix fixe dinners in order to keep their tables filled. This means great deals are to be had at restaurants that just a few years ago were prohibitively expensive.

Nowhere in the city is this more apparent than in the **Belltown** neighborhood, just north of Pike Place Market along First, Second, and Third avenues. The abundant cash of the high-tech boom times saw the opening of loads of high-style (and high-priced) restaurants in Belltown. Small fortunes were spent on interior decor so that beautiful people could have beautiful surroundings in which to see and be seen. All this translated into high food prices. With the crash of the economy, many of these places are now offering three-course prix fixe meals for under $30. However, if you're determined to drop a bundle on dinner here, you still can.

The culinary offerings in most of the Belltown restaurants constitute a style that is not exactly comfort food and not exactly Northwest cuisine, but rather something in between—call it **American Regional,** sort of a California cuisine redux. One constant is the emphasis on fresh Northwest ingredients, and Belltown's proximity to Pike Place Market makes this easy. And the financially challenged need not despair. Despite the many high-priced restaurants, you can still get a cheap meal in hip Belltown. These lesser stars in the Belltown firmament serve everything from African to Vietnamese fare, and while the atmosphere may not be, er, swanky, all have a dash of style. In slower economic times, these places have been doing booming business.

One Seattle dining trend that has not changed is the city's near obsession with **seafood.** You may be aware that wild salmon in the Northwest are rapidly disappearing from the region's rivers, but this doesn't bar nearly every menu in the city from featuring salmon. Much of it is now hatchery fish, or fish imported from Canada or Alaska. Along with the salmon, there are dozens of varieties of regional oysters available. Dungeness crabs, another Northwest specialty, may not be as large as king crabs, but they're quite a bit heftier than the blue crabs of the eastern United States. You may also run across such unfamiliar shellfish as razor clams and geoducks (pronounced "gooey dux"). The former is shaped like a straight razor and can be chewy if not prepared properly, and the latter is a bivalve of prodigious proportions (as heavy as 12 lb.) so highly prized in Asia that it rarely ever shows up on Seattle menus.

With so much water all around, you would be remiss if you didn't eat at a **waterfront restaurant** while you're in Seattle. You'll find restaurants on the shores of virtually every body of water in the area. Views take in not only water, but also everything from marinas to Mount Rainier, the Space Needle to the Olympic Mountains. We have listed waterfront restaurants in appropriate neighborhood categories below.

1 Restaurants by Cuisine

AFRICAN
Afrikando ✦ (Belltown, $$, p. 86)

AMERICAN
Alki Homestead Restaurant ✦ (West Seattle, $, p. 103)
Belltown Pub and Cafe ✦ (Belltown, $, p. 88)
Icon Grill ✦ (Belltown, $$, p. 87)
Maggie Bluffs Marina Grill ✦ (Queen Anne & Seattle Center, $, p. 95)
Merchants Cafe (Pioneer Square & the International District, $, p. 93)
Red Mill Burgers ✦ (North Seattle, $, p. 102)
74th St. Ale House ✦ (North Seattle, $, p. 103)
Two Bells Tavern ✦ (Belltown, $, p. 89)
Virginia Inn ✦ (Belltown, $, p. 89)

AMERICAN REGIONAL
Bluwater Bistro ✦ (Lake Union, $$, p. 98)
The 5 Spot ✦ (Queen Anne & Seattle Center, $, p. 95)
Matt's in the Market ✦✦ (Pike Place Market, $$, p. 91)
Palace Kitchen ✦✦ (Belltown, $$, p. 88)

BAKERIES & PASTRY SHOPS
Boulangerie ✦ (North Seattle, $, p. 107)
Cow Chips (Pioneer Square & the International District, $, p. 106)
Dahlia Bakery (Belltown, $, p. 107)
Dilettante Chocolates ✦✦ (Capitol Hill & East Seattle, $, p. 107)
Grand Central Baking Company ✦ (Pioneer Square & the International District, $, p. 106)
Le Panier (Pike Place Market, $, p. 106)
Macrina ✦✦ (Belltown, $, p. 107)
North Hill Bakery (Capitol Hill & East Seattle, $, p. 107)
Three Girls Bakery (Pike Place Market, $, p. 106)

BARBECUE
Pecos Pit BBQ (Pioneer Square & the International District, $, p. 93)

CAFES, COFFEE BARS & TEA SHOPS
Ancient Grounds (Downtown, $, p. 105)
Bauhaus Coffee & Books ✦ (Capitol Hill & East Seattle, $, p. 106)
Blue Willow Tea Company (Capitol Hill & East Seattle, $, p. 106)
Café Allegro (North Seattle, $, p. 106)
Caffe Ladro Espresso Bar & Bakery ✦✦ (The Seattle Center & Queen Anne Areas, $, p. 105)
Caffe Vita, (The Seattle Center & Queen Anne Areas, $, p. 105)
The Crumpet Shop ✦ (Pike Place Market, $, p. 106)
El Diablo Coffee Co. (The Seattle Center & Queen Anne Areas, $, p. 105)
Still Life in Fremont Coffeehouse ✦ (North Seattle, $, p. 106)
Teahouse Kuan Yin (North Seattle, $, p. 106)

Torrefazione ★★ (Pioneer Square
& the International District, $,
p. 105)

Uptown Espresso (The Seattle
Center & Queen Anne Areas,
$, p. 105)

Zeitgeist Art/Coffee ★ (Pioneer
Square & the International
District, $, p. 105)

CHINESE

Hing Loon ★ (Pioneer Square &
the International District, $,
p. 92)

House of Hong ★ (Pioneer Square
& the International District, $,
p. 93)

CONTINENTAL

The Georgian ★★ (Downtown &
First Hill, $$$$, p. 80)

FRENCH

Café Campagne ★★ (Pike Place
Market, $$, p. 90)

Campagne ★★ (Pike Place Market,
$$$, p. 89)

Le Pichet ★ (Pike Place Market,
$$, p. 91)

Virginia Inn ★ (Belltown, $,
p. 89)

HIMALAYAN

Himalayan Sherpa Restaurant ★
(North Seattle, $, p. 102)

INTERNATIONAL

Beach Cafe ★★ (The Eastside, $$,
p. 104)

Marco's Supperclub ★ (Belltown,
$$, p. 87)

Matt's in the Market ★★ (Pike
Place Market, $$, p. 91)

Shea's Lounge ★★ (Pike Place
Market, $$, p. 92)

ITALIAN

Assaggio ★★ (Belltown, $$, p. 86)

Bizarro Italian Café ★ (North
Seattle, $$, p. 101)

Cucina! Cucina! ★ (Lake Union,
$, p. 99)

Il Bistro ★ (Pike Place Market,
$$$, p. 90)

The Pink Door ★ (Pike Place
Market, $$, p. 91)

Salumi ★ (Pioneer Square & the
International District, $, p. 94)

Serafina ★★ (Lake Union, $$,
p. 99)

Trattoria Mitchelli ★ (Pioneer
Square & the International
District, $$, p. 92)

JAPANESE

Koraku (Pioneer Square & the
International District, $, p. 93)

Shiro's ★★ (Belltown, $$, p. 88)

LATE-NIGHT

Bluwater Bistro ★ (Lake Union,
$$, p. 98)

El Gaucho ★★ (Belltown, $$$$,
p. 85)

The 5 Spot ★ (Queen Anne &
Seattle Center, $, p. 95)

Flying Fish ★★ (Belltown, $$,
p. 87)

Hing Loon ★ (Pioneer Square &
the International District, $,
p. 92)

Palace Kitchen ★★ (Belltown, $$,
p. 88)

The Pink Door ★ (Pike Place
Market, $$, p. 91)

Shea's Lounge ★★ (Pike Place
Market, $$, p. 92)

Trattoria Mitchelli ★ (Pioneer
Square & the International
District, $$, p. 92)

LATIN AMERICAN

Fandango ★★ (Belltown, $$,
p. 87)

MEDITERRANEAN

Andaluca ★★ (Downtown & First
Hill, $$, p. 84)

Brasa ★★ (Belltown, $$$, p. 86)

Palace Kitchen ★★ (Belltown, $$,
p. 88)

Palomino ★★ (Downtown & First
Hill, $$, p. 84)

MEXICAN
Agua Verde ⚝ (North Seattle, $, p. 102)
El Camino ⚝⚝ (North Seattle, $$, p. 101)
El Puerco Lloron ⚝ (Pike Place Market, $, p. 92)

NORTHWEST
Andaluca ⚝⚝ (Downtown & First Hill, $$, p. 84)
Canlis ⚝⚝⚝ (Queen Anne & Seattle Center, $$$, p. 94)
Cascadia ⚝⚝⚝ (Belltown, $$$, p. 85)
Chez Shea ⚝⚝⚝ (Pike Place Market, $$$, p. 90)
Dahlia Lounge ⚝⚝ (Belltown, $$$, p. 86)
Flying Fish ⚝⚝ (Belltown, $$, p. 87)
The Georgian ⚝⚝ (Downtown & First Hill, $$$$, p. 80)
The Herbfarm ⚝⚝⚝ (The Eastside, $$$$, p. 220)
Kaspar's Restaurant & Wine Bar ⚝⚝ (Queen Anne & Seattle Center, $$$, p. 94)
Palisade ⚝⚝⚝ (Queen Anne & Seattle Center, $$$, p. 95)
Palomino ⚝⚝ (Downtown & First Hill, $$, p. 84)
Restaurant Zoë ⚝⚝ (Belltown, $$, p. 88)
Rover's ⚝⚝⚝ (Capitol Hill & East Seattle, $$$$, p. 100)
Shea's Lounge ⚝⚝ (Pike Place Market, $$, p. 92)
SkyCity at the Needle ⚝⚝ (Queen Anne & Seattle Center, $$$$, p. 94)
Yarrow Bay Grill ⚝⚝ (The Eastside, $$$, p. 104)

PAN-ASIAN
Dahlia Lounge ⚝⚝ (Belltown, $$$, p. 86)
Noodle Ranch ⚝ (Belltown, $, p. 89)
Wild Ginger Asian Restaurant & Satay Bar ⚝⚝ (Downtown & First Hill, $$, p. 85)

PAN-LATIN
Tango Tapas Restaurant & Lounge ⚝⚝ (Downtown & First Hill, $$, p. 84)

PIZZA
Pizzeria Pagliacci ⚝ (Queen Anne & Seattle Center, $, p. 98)

QUICK BITES
Briazz Cafe (Downtown, $, p. 107)
DeLaurenti ⚝⚝ (Pike Place Market, $$, p. 107)
La Tienda Cádiz (Capitol Hill & East Seattle, $, p. 108)
Michou (Pike Place Market, $, p. 107)
Piroshky, Piroshky (Pike Place Market, $, p. 108)
The Spanish Table (Pike Place Market, $, p. 108)
Three Girls Bakery (Pike Place Market, $, p. 108)
Westlake Center shopping mall food court (Downtown, $, p. 107)
World Class Chili ⚝ (Pike Place Market, $, p. 108)

SEAFOOD
Anthony's Pier 66 & Bell Street Diner ⚝⚝ (The Waterfront, $$, p. 80)
The Brooklyn Seafood, Steak, & Oyster House ⚝⚝ (Downtown & First Hill, $$$, p. 81)
Chinook's at Salmon Bay ⚝ (North Seattle, $$, p. 101)
Elliott's ⚝⚝ (The Waterfront, $$, p. 80)
Etta's Seafood ⚝⚝ (Pike Place Market, $$, p. 90)
Flying Fish ⚝⚝ (Belltown, $$, p. 87)
Ivar's Salmon House ⚝⚝ (Lake Union, $$, p. 98)
Kaspar's Restaurant & Wine Bar ⚝⚝ (Queen Anne & Seattle Center, $$$, p. 94)
McCormick and Schmick's ⚝⚝ (Downtown & First Hill, $$, p. 84)

McCormick & Schmick's
Harborside ⭐ (Lake Union,
$$, p. 98)

Ponti Seafood Grill ⭐⭐ (North
Seattle, $$$, p. 100)

Ray's Boathouse and Cafe ⭐⭐
(North Seattle, $$, p. 101)

Salty's on Alki Beach ⭐⭐ (West
Seattle, $$$, p. 103)

Third Floor Fish Cafe ⭐⭐ (The
Eastside, $$$, p. 103)

STEAK

El Gaucho ⭐⭐ (Belltown, $$$$,
p. 85)

Metropolitan Grill ⭐⭐ (Down-
town & First Hill, $$$, p. 81)

THAI

Siam on Broadway (Capitol Hill &
East Seattle, $, p. 100)

Siam on Lake Union ⭐ (Lake
Union, $, p. 99)

VEGETARIAN

Cafe Flora ⭐ (Capitol Hill & East
Seattle, $, p. 100)

2 The Waterfront

MODERATE

Anthony's Pier 66 & Bell Street Diner ⭐⭐ SEAFOOD   The Anthony's chain has several outposts around the Seattle area, but this complex is the most convenient and versatile. Anthony's not only has an upper-end, stylish seafood restaurant with good waterfront views, but it includes a moderately priced casual restaurant and a walk-up counter. The bold contemporary styling and abundance of art glass set this place apart from most of the waterfront restaurants. The upscale crowd heads upstairs for the likes of Asian-inspired seafood dishes, and the more cost-conscious stay downstairs at the Bell Street Diner where meals are much easier on the wallet (though far less creative). For the higher prices, you get better views, as long as you don't get stuck at the counter that overlooks the exhibition kitchen. In summer, the decks are the place to be.

2201 Alaskan Way. ✆ **206/448-6688.** www.anthonys.com. Reservations recommended. Pier 66 main courses $15–$28; Bell Street Diner main courses $8–$28. AE, MC, V. Pier 66 Sun–Thurs 5–10:30pm, Fri–Sat 5–11:30pm; Bell Street Diner Sun–Thurs 11:30am–10:30pm, Fri–Sat 11:30am–11:30pm.

Elliott's ⭐⭐ SEAFOOD   While most of its neighbors are content to coast along on tourist business, Elliott's actually aims to keep locals happy by serving some of the best seafood in Seattle. Maybe the quality of the food here is in inverse proportion to the view: Although the restaurant is right on the waterfront, the view isn't that great. If you're looking for superbly prepared fresh seafood, however, Elliott's is an excellent bet. The oyster bar can have as many as 20 varieties of oysters available, so this is definitely the place to get to know your Northwest oysters. Salmon and Dungeness crabs are usually prepared any of several different ways.

Pier 56, Alaskan Way. ✆ **206/623-4340.** Reservations recommended. Main courses $9–$17 at lunch, $16–$35 at dinner. AE, DC, DISC, MC, V. Sun–Thurs 11am–10pm, Fri–Sat 11am–11pm.

3 Downtown & First Hill

VERY EXPENSIVE

The Georgian ⭐⭐ NORTHWEST/CONTINENTAL   Nowhere in Seattle will you find a more rarefied atmosphere than at the Georgian, where you'll feel as though you're dining in an elegant palace. A recent makeover has left the restaurant lighter and brighter than in the past, but this is still by far the most traditionally formal restaurant in the city. The meals are serious haute cuisine, and the attentive service will likely have you convinced that yours is the only table in the restaurant. So, if you happen to be celebrating a special occasion and have an appreciation for such dishes as crisp veal sweetbreads or roast rabbit saddle with seared duck liver, you'd be hard-pressed to find a more memorable dining experience in Seattle. The wine list is well suited to both the food and the restaurant's ambience.

In the Four Seasons Olympic Hotel, 411 University St. © 206/621-1700. Reservations recommended. Main courses $18–$27. AE, DC, DISC, MC, V. Mon 6:30am–2:30pm, Tues–Thurs 6:30am–2:30pm and 5:30–10pm, Fri 6:30am–2:30pm and 5:30–10:30pm, Sat 7am–noon and 5:30–10:30pm, Sun 7am–noon (tea served daily 2–3:30pm).

EXPENSIVE

The Brooklyn Seafood, Steak, & Oyster House ★★ SEAFOOD   This classic seafood restaurant looks as if it's been here since the great Seattle fire and is housed in one of the city's oldest buildings. The specialty here is definitely oysters, with about 10 different types piled up at the oyster bar on any given night. If oysters on the half shell don't appeal to you, there are plenty of other tempting appetizers, ranging from cilantro-battered calamari to Dungeness crab cakes with wasabi aioli. For a classic Northwest dish, try the alder-planked king salmon (roasted on a slab of alder wood), or, for something a bit more unusual, try the grilled black tiger prawns with morel mushrooms and brandy cream sauce.

1212 Second Ave. © 206/224-7000. Reservations recommended. Main courses $10–$15 at lunch, $16–$35 at dinner. AE, DC, DISC, MC, V. Mon–Thurs 11am–3pm and 5–10pm, Fri 11am–3pm and 5–10:30pm, Sat 4:30–10:30pm, Sun 4–10pm (oyster bar open later every night).

Metropolitan Grill ★★ STEAK   Fronted by massive granite columns that make it look more like a bank than a restaurant, the Metropolitan Grill is a very traditional steakhouse that attracts a well-heeled clientele, primarily men in suits. When you walk in the front door, you're immediately confronted by a case full of meat, from filet mignon to triple-cut lamb chops (with the occasional giant lobster tail tossed in). Perfectly cooked 28-day-aged steaks are the primary attraction, and a baked potato and a pile of thick-cut onion rings complete the

---

(Kids) Family-Friendly Restaurants

Belltown Pub and Café (p. 88)   The best burgers in Seattle and a kid-friendly atmosphere make this Belltown spot a winner for families.

Cucina! Cucina! (p. 99)   Every day's a party at this lively Italian restaurant on Lake Union, and kids always get special treatment (pictures to color, puzzles to do, pizza dough to shape and then let the kitchen cook). Birthdays are even better!

Ivar's Salmon House (p. 98)   This restaurant is built to resemble a Northwest Coast Native American longhouse and is filled with artifacts that kids will find fascinating. If they get restless, they can go out to the floating patio and watch the boats passing by.

Maggie Bluffs Marina Grill (p. 95)   Located at a marina overlooking Elliott Bay and downtown Seattle, this economical place has food the kids will enjoy and provides crayons to keep them occupied while they wait. Before or after a meal, you can take a free boat ride across the marina to an observation deck atop the breakwater.

Dining: The Waterfront, Downtown, First Hill, Belltown, Pike Place Market, Pioneer Square & the International District

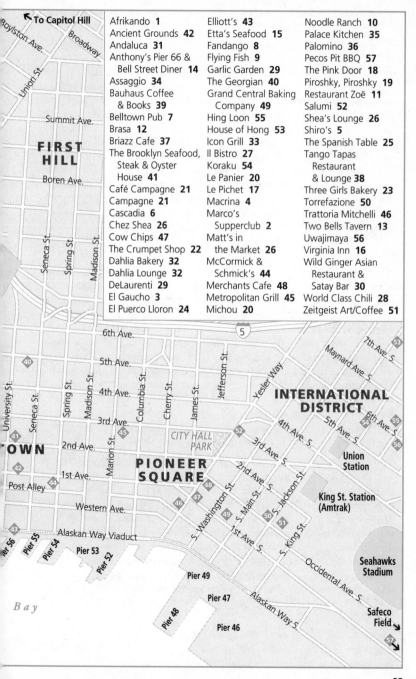

ultimate carnivorous dinner. Financial matters are a frequent topic of discussion here, and the bar even has a "Guess the Dow" contest. I hope you sold high, since it'll take some capital gains to finance a dinner for two here.

820 Second Ave. Ⓒ **206/624-3287.** www.themetropolitangrill.com. Reservations recommended. Main courses $9–$30 at lunch, $18–$42 at dinner. AE, DC, DISC, MC, V. Mon–Fri 11am–3pm and 4:30–11pm, Sat 4–11pm, Sun 4:30–10pm.

MODERATE

Andaluca ★★ NORTHWEST/MEDITERRANEAN Located in the Mayflower Park Hotel, this sumptuous restaurant mixes the traditional and the contemporary like no other place in town. To step through its doors is to enter a world of vibrant artistry, in both decor and cuisine. Specialties include such dishes as traditional Spanish *zarazuela* (shellfish stew) and beef tenderloin crusted with *cabrales* (Spanish blue cheese) and served with grilled pears. The menu is divided into small and large plates, so you'll find something to satisfy your appetite regardless of its size. Don't miss the Dungeness crab tower, made with avocado, palm hearts, and gazpacho salsa—it's a work of art. Keep in mind that you can assemble a meal of small plates here and get away with a lighter bill.

In the Mayflower Park Hotel, 407 Olive Way. Ⓒ **206/382-6999.** Reservations recommended. Main courses $17.50–$28, small plates $6–$9.25. AE, DC, DISC, MC, V. Mon–Thurs 6:30–11am, 11:30am–2:30pm, and 5–10pm; Fri– 6:30–11am, 11:30am–2:30pm, and 5–11pm; Sat 7am–noon and 5–11pm; Sun 7am–noon and 5–9pm.

McCormick & Schmick's ★★ SEAFOOD Force your way past the crowds of business suits at the bar and you'll find yourself in a classic fish house—complete with cafe curtains, polished brass, leaded glass, and wood paneling. Daily fresh sheets commonly list more than 30 seafood entrees and feature well-prepared seafood dishes such as grilled steelhead with artichokes and spinach, Dungeness crab and shrimp cakes with red-pepper aioli, and cedar-plank-roasted salmon with berry *beurre rouge.* There are also usually a half-dozen or more different varieties of oysters available. In late afternoons and late evenings, bar appetizers are only $1.95. If the restaurant is crowded and you can't get a table, consider sitting at the counter and watching the cooks perform amazing feats with fire.

1103 First Ave. Ⓒ **206/623-5500.** Reservations recommended. Main courses $7–$26. AE, DC, DISC, MC, V. Mon–Fri 11:30am–11pm, Sat 11:30am–11pm, Sun 4:30–9pm (bar menu served later).

Palomino ★★ NORTHWEST/MEDITERRANEAN Located on the upper level of the City Centre shopping center, only a block away from Nordstrom and Pacific Place, this large, casual restaurant may be part of a chain, but its many art-glass chandeliers give it a decidedly Seattle feel. Anything from the applewood-fired oven is a good bet, and the pizzas are particularly tasty, as are the juicy spit-roasted chickens. For dessert, you'd be remiss if you didn't order the tiramisu. The convenient location and somewhat moderate prices make this a good choice if you want to save your vacation money for shopping at Nordstrom.

1420 Fifth Ave. (in City Centre). Ⓒ **206/623-1300.** www.palominoseattle.com. Reservations recommended. Main courses $8.50–$28. AE, DC, DISC, MC, V. Mon 11:15am–3pm and 4–9pm, Tues–Thurs 11:15am–3pm and 4–9:30pm, Fri 11:15am–3pm and 5–10:30pm, Sat 11:15am–3pm and 3:30–10:30pm, Sun noon–3pm and 4–9pm.

Tango Tapas Restaurant & Lounge ★★ PAN-LATIN In Spain, the appetizer-size plates of food known as tapas are traditionally served with drinks in bars. Here at Tango, however, tapas are front and center, taking cues from both classic and creative Spanish and Latin cuisine. Many of the items on the menu are substantial enough to serve as an entree, but you'll be much happier if you order lots of different plates and share everything among your dinner companions. Don't miss the *berenjena novata* (eggplant served with a half-dozen different flavor-packed side dishes) or the *gambas picantes* (chipotle-pepper flavored tiger prawns with an unusual coconut-corn cake and a sauce made from pumpkin seeds and cilantro). On Monday nights, all wines by the bottle are half price, and Sunday through Thursday nights, half-price tapas are served in the bar between 5 and 7pm.

1100 Pike St. © 206/583-0382. www.bandoleone.net. Reservations recommended. Main courses $10–$16. MC, V. Sun–Wed 5:30–10:30pm, Thurs–Sat 5:30–11pm.

Wild Ginger Asian Restaurant & Satay Bar ★★ PAN-ASIAN This Pan-Asian restaurant has long been a Seattle favorite and is now located across the street from Benaroya Hall. Pull up a comfortable stool around the large satay grill and watch the cooks grill little skewers of anything from chicken to scallops to pork to prawns to lamb. Each skewer is served with a small cube of sticky rice and pickled cucumber. Order three or four satay sticks and you have a meal. If you prefer to sit at a table and have a more traditional dinner, Wild Ginger can accommodate you. Try the Panang beef curry (rib-eye steak in pungent curry sauce of cardamom, coconut milk, Thai basil, and peanuts).

1401 Third Ave. © 206/623-4450. Reservations recommended. Satay $2.75–$5.50; main courses $8.75–$23.75. AE, DC, DISC, MC, V. Mon–Thurs 11:30am–3pm and 5–11pm, Fri 11:30am–3pm and 5pm–midnight, Sat 11:30am–3pm and 4:30pm–midnight, Sun 4:30–11pm. Satay Bar until 1am nightly.

4 Belltown

VERY EXPENSIVE

Cascadia ★★★ NORTHWEST Chef Kerry Sear made a name for himself in Seattle at the Georgian, the opulent restaurant at the Four Seasons Olympic Hotel. Here, at his own restaurant, he celebrates all foods Northwestern in an elegant, understated space in Belltown. For the full Cascadia experience, indulge in one of Sear's Decidedly Northwest or Wild & Gathered seven-course tasting menus. The former menu is prepared exclusively with seasonal ingredients from around the Cascadia region, which stretches from British Columbia to Northern California. It is on this menu that you will find the exquisite soup in a can, a wild mushroom soup made with Oregon white truffles, and yes, it is indeed served in a can (with a label drawn by Sear himself). Because the menu changes with the seasons, you never know what you might find, but rest assured it will be memorable. Just to make the meal prices more palatable, the wine list includes 30 wines for under $30. Want the dining experience but can't afford the prices? Try the bar, which has a menu of 10 dishes for under $10.

2328 First Ave. © 206/448-8884. www.cascadiarestaurant.com. Reservations highly recommended. Main courses $17–$32; 3-course prix fixe dinner $25, 7-course prix fixe dinner $45–$65.

El Gaucho ★★ LATE-NIGHT/STEAK Conjuring up the ghosts of dinner clubs of the 1930s and 1940s, this high-end Belltown steakhouse looks like it could be a Fred Astaire film set. The pure theatrics make this place a must if you're in the mood to spend big bucks on a thick, juicy steak. Sure, you may get a better steak at one of the other high-end steakhouses in town, but you just can't duplicate the experience of dining at El Gaucho. Stage-set decor aside, the real stars of the show here are the 28-day dry-aged Angus beef steaks, definitely some of the best in town—but know that the perfect steak doesn't come cheap. All the classics are here, too, including Caesar salad tossed tableside, and chateaubriand carved before your eyes. Not a steak eater? How about venison chops, an ostrich filet, or Australian lobster tail? There's also a classy bar off to one side, a separate cigar lounge and, for after-dinner dancing, the affiliated **Pampas Room** nightclub.

2505 First Ave. ✆ 206/728-1337. www.elgaucho.com. Reservations recommended. Main courses $16–$90. AE, DC, MC, V. Mon–Sat 5pm–2am, Sun 5pm–midnight.

EXPENSIVE

Brasa ★★ MEDITERRANEAN   Chef Tamara Murphy, much lauded over the years by national food magazines, is one of Seattle's finest chefs, and here, at her attractive Belltown restaurant, she has exposed many a Seattleite to the joys of Mediterranean cuisine. Because Brasa is equally divided between lounge and dining room and serves dinner until midnight on weekends, it attracts a wide range of diners, from foodies out for an evening of haute cuisine and fine wine to revelers looking for a late-night bite. If you've got a few dinner companions, start with the Brasa tapas plate, which changes with the seasons. Stick to the wood-fired and grilled items and you won't go wrong.

2107 Third Ave. ✆ 206/728-4220. www.brasa.com. Reservations highly recommended. Main courses $18–$28. AE, DC, DISC, MC, V. Sun–Thurs 5–10:30pm, Fri–Sat 5pm–midnight.

Dahlia Lounge ★★ PAN-ASIAN/NORTHWEST   The neon chef holding a flapping fish may suggest that the Dahlia is little more than a roadside diner, but a glimpse at the stylish interior will likely have you thinking otherwise. One bite of any dish will convince you that this is one of Seattle's finest restaurants. Mouthwatering Dungeness crab cakes, a bow to Chef Tom Douglas's Maryland roots, are the house specialty and should not be missed. The menu, influenced by the far side of the Pacific Rim, changes regularly, with the lunch menu featuring many of the same offerings at slightly lower prices. For dessert, it takes a Herculean effort to resist the crème caramel. It's way too easy to fill up on the restaurant's breads, which are baked in the adjacent Dahlia Bakery.

2001 Fourth Ave. ✆ 206/682-4142. www.tomdouglas.com. Reservations highly recommended. Main courses $18–$34. AE, DC, DISC, MC, V. Mon–Thurs 11:30am–2pm and 5:30–10pm, Fri 11:30am–2pm and 5:30–11pm, Sat 5:30–11pm, Sun 5–10pm.

MODERATE

Afrikando ★ *Finds* AFRICAN   Trendy Belltown seems an unlikely place for a casual restaurant specializing in the flavors of West Africa, but that's exactly what you'll find here at the Seattle Center end of the neighborhood. We love Afrikando's hearty African home cooking. The bold and spicy flavors of hot climates merge with the influences of France in West Africa. Start your meal with the spicy and delicious halibut soup, which has a thick tomato base, and maybe split a plate of the *akra* fritters, made with black-eyed peas. Although the *thiebu djen,* a Senegalese fish dish, is hard to resist, we always go for the *mafe,* baked chicken topped with a homemade habañero sauce and accompanied by root vegetables smothered in peanut sauce. Be sure to try the strong Senegalese tea.

2904 First Ave. ✆ 206/374-9714. Reservations recommended for 4 or more. Main courses $9–$18. MC, V. Mon–Fri 11am–2:30pm and 5–10pm, Sat 5–10pm, Sun 4–9pm.

Assaggio ★★ ITALIAN   Assaggio has long been one of Seattle's favorite Italian restaurants. The large, casual restaurant has an old-world feel, with a high ceiling, arches, and Roman-style murals on the walls. However, what really makes this place is the excellent food. For a starter, you might try the grilled radicchio wrapped in pancetta (Italian bacon) and topped with a balsamic vinaigrette. Pastas come from all over Italy, but it's hard to beat the *pappardelle boscaiola* with pancetta and wild mushrooms in a wine cream sauce. Or go for an old standby like veal saltimbocca.

2010 Fourth Ave. ✆ **206/441-1399.** www.assaggioseattle.com. Reservations recommended. Main courses $13–$25. AE, DC, DISC, MC, V. Mon–Sat 5–10pm.

Fandango ★★ LATIN AMERICAN Fandango is another groundbreaking restaurant from celebrity chef Christine Keff, who also operates the ever-popular Flying Fish restaurant diagonally across the street. The focus here is on the sunny flavors of Latin America, and Fandango's menu is filled with combinations you aren't likely to have encountered this far north before. Fandango just might be the only place in the city where you can a get a *huitlacoche* quesadilla (made with a corn fungus that's considered a delicacy in Mexico). Whether you order the ceviche of the day, the Brazilian seafood stew, or the suckling pig, you'll enjoy some real taste treats. If you're lucky, you just might find grilled bananas on the dessert menu. Be sure to have a *mojito* cocktail while you're here.

2313 First Ave. ✆ **206/441-1188.** Reservations recommended. Main courses $12–$20. AE, DC, MC, V. Daily 5pm–midnight (until 2am in the bar).

Flying Fish ★★ LATE-NIGHT/NORTHWEST/SEAFOOD Chef Christine Keff has been on the Seattle restaurant scene for years now, and with Flying Fish, she hit on something the city really wanted. Not only does it offer the bold combinations of vibrant flavors demanded by the city's well-traveled palates, but the hip Belltown restaurant serves dinner past midnight every night, keeping late-night partiers from going hungry. Every dish here is a work of art, and with small plates, large plates, and platters for sharing, diners are encouraged to sample a wide variety of the kitchen's creations. The menu changes daily, but keep an eye out for the smoked rock shrimp spring rolls, which are positively sculptural. The festive desserts are almost a mini party on the plate. There's also a huge wine list.

2234 First Ave. ✆ **206/728-8595.** www.flyingfishseattle.com. Reservations recommended. Main courses $15–$20. AE, DC, MC, V. Daily 5pm–2am.

Icon Grill ★ AMERICAN With colorful art glass hanging from chandeliers, overflowing giant vases, and every inch of wall space covered with framed artwork, this place goes way overboard with its decor, but that's exactly what makes it so fun. Basically, it's an over-the-top rendition of a Victorian setting gone 21st century. The food is a mix of basic comfort food (including a molasses-glazed meatloaf that locals swear by) and more inventive dishes such as grilled pear salad, merlot-glazed lamb shank, and lamb tenderloin stuffed with prosciutto, arugula, and goat cheese. Unfortunately, the food can be unpredictable, so don't come here just for a culinary experience, but rather for a Seattle experience.

1933 Fifth Ave. ✆ **206/441-6330.** Reservations recommended. Main courses $13.50–$33. AE, MC, V. Mon–Fri 11:30am–2pm; Sun–Mon 5:30–9pm, Tues–Thurs 5:30–10pm, Fri–Sat 5:30–11pm.

Marco's Supperclub ★ *Finds* INTERNATIONAL This Belltown restaurant has a casual ambience that belies the high-quality meals turned out by its kitchen. The menu draws on cuisines from around the world, so even jaded gourmets may find something new here. Don't miss the unusual fried sage leaves appetizer, which comes with a variety of dipping sauces, or the mussels in a yellow coconut curry. Among the entrees, the Jamaican jerk chicken with sautéed greens and sweet potato purée is a standout. On the seasonal menu, you might encounter the likes of Tuscan bread salad, pan-seared halibut with Lebanese walnut-pepper sauce, or mushroom tamales. If you enjoy creative cookery at reasonable prices, check this place out.

2510 First Ave. ✆ **206/441-7801.** Reservations highly recommended. Main courses $14–$20. AE, MC, V. Sun–Thurs 5:30–10pm, Fri–Sat 5:30–11pm.

Palace Kitchen ★★ AMERICAN REGIONAL/LATE-NIGHT/MEDITER-RANEAN   This is the most casual of chef Tom Douglas's three Seattle establishments, with a bar that attracts nearly as many customers as the restaurant. The atmosphere is urban chic, with cement pillars, simple wood booths, and a few tables in the front window, which overlooks the monorail tracks. The menu is short and features a nightly selection of unusual cheeses and different preparations from the applewood grill. To begin a meal, we like the creamy goat cheese fondue. Entrees are usually simple and delicious and range from the Palace burger royale (a strong contender for best burger in Seattle) to Southern-influenced dishes such as barbecued beef brisket with beans and collard greens. For dessert, the coconut cream pie is an absolute must.

2030 Fifth Ave. ✆ **206/448-2001.** www.tomdouglas.com. Reservations only for parties of 6 or more. Main courses $11–$22. AE, DC, DISC, MC, V. Daily 5pm–1am.

Restaurant Zoë ★★ NORTHWEST   Belltown is packed with trendy, upscale restaurants where being seen is often more important than the food being served. This is definitely *not* one of those places, although the huge windows facing Second Avenue provide plenty of people-watching opportunities. The decor is subtly stylish and the waitstaff (dressed in black) lack the attitude that mars the experience at many other trendy restaurants. Chef/owner Scott Staples mines the bounties of the Northwest to prepare his seasonal fare, preparing such dishes as creamy celery-root soup made with white truffle oil and a few strips of house-made lox. Risottos here are reliably good and change with the seasons. Be sure to start your meal with the restaurant's signature Zoë cocktail, a citrusy concoction with an intriguing blue color. If you can, have dinner here on a Monday night, when all bottles of wine are half price.

2137 Second Ave. ✆ **206/256-2060.** Reservations highly recommended. Main courses $15.50–$23. AE, MC, V. Mon–Thurs 5–10pm, Fri–Sat 5–11pm.

Shiro's ★★ JAPANESE   If ogling all the fresh fish at Pike Place Market puts you in the mood for some sushi, here is where to head. Shiro's serves the best sushi in the city. It's fresh, flavorful, and perfectly prepared. Eat at the sushi bar and you'll be rubbing shoulders with locals and visiting Japanese businessmen, all of whom know that sushi maestro Shiro Kashiba has a way with raw fish. Be sure to order at least one of Shiro's special rolls, and, if you're feeling adventurous, try the sea urchin roe (you won't find it any fresher anywhere). For a sushi dessert, try the smoked eel drizzled with a sweet sauce.

2401 Second Ave. ✆ **206/443-9844.** Reservations recommended. Sushi $1.75–$12.50; main courses $18.50–$21.50. MC, V. Daily 5:30–9:45pm.

INEXPENSIVE

Belltown Pub and Cafe ★ *Kids* AMERICAN   Located in Belltown in what was once a sleeping-bag factory, this lively pub serves a surprisingly varied menu. Although you'll find everything from wasabi chicken salad to smoked salmon ravioli here, the bacon and cheddar burger is hard to pass up. It's definitely one of the best burgers in Seattle—thick, juicy, well flavored, and set on a large, chewy roll. Accompany your burger with a pint from one of the many microbrew taps. More sophisticated palates may prefer the likes of chicken Marsala with wine chosen from the fairly decent wine list. There are tables on the sidewalk in summer, and huge wooden booths for inclement weather. This place is family friendly, a rarity in trendy Belltown.

2322 First Ave. © **206/728-4311.** www.belltownpub.com. Reservations accepted. Main courses $8.25–$20. AE, MC, V. Sun–Thurs 11:30am–midnight, Fri–Sat 11:30am–1am.

Noodle Ranch ★ *(Finds)* PAN-ASIAN   This Belltown hole-in-the-wall serves Pan-Asian cuisine for the hip-yet-financially-challenged crowd. It's a lively, boisterous scene, and the food is packed with intense, and often unfamiliar, flavors. Don't miss the fish grilled in grape leaves with its nice presentation and knockout dipping sauce. In fact, all of the dipping sauces here are delicious. The Mekong grill—rice noodles with a rice wine vinegar and herb dressing topped with grilled pork, chicken, catfish, or tofu—is another dish not to be missed. You'll also find the likes of Laotian cucumber salad and Japanese-style eggplant. In fact, you'll find lots of vegetarian options. Although the place is frequently packed, you can usually get a seat without having to wait too long.

2228 Second Ave. © **206/728-0463.** Main courses $7–$11.25. AE, MC, V. Mon–Thurs 11am–10pm, Fri 11am–11pm, Sat noon–11pm.

Two Bells Tavern ★ AMERICAN   Looking for the best burger in Seattle? Give the patties here a try. You just might become a convert. Although this is little more than an old tavern and a local hangout for Belltown residents who can still remember the days before all the condos went up, the burgers are superb. They're thick, hand-formed patties served on chewy, crusty slabs of baguette. You can get your burger with grilled onions and bacon, with blue cheese, or a few other ways. Accompany your burger with a pint of local microbrewed ale and some mustardy cole slaw for the perfect burger-and-beer binge.

2313 Fourth Ave. © **206/441-3050.** Reservations not accepted. Main courses $6–$10. AE, MC, V. Mon–Thurs 11am–11pm, Fri–Sat 11am–midnight, Sun 11am–10pm.

Virginia Inn ★ AMERICAN/FRENCH   In business since 1903, this restaurant/bar near Pike Place Market is a cozy spot for lunch or a cheap dinner. This has long been a favorite hangout of Belltown residents and is as popular for its microbrews as it is for its food (the crab cakes are a perennial favorite). Big windows let lots of light into the small room, but if the sun is shining, most people try to get a seat on the sidewalk patio.

1937 First Ave. © **206/728-1937.** Reservations accepted only for parties of 5 or more. Main courses $6.50–$10.50. AE, MC, V. Daily 11:30am–10pm.

5 Pike Place Market

EXPENSIVE

Campagne ★★ COUNTRY FRENCH   With large windows that look out over the top of Pike Place Market to Elliott Bay, Campagne is an unpretentious, yet elegant, French restaurant. With such a prime location, it shouldn't be surprising that Campagne relies heavily on the wide variety of fresh ingredients that the market provides. The menu leans toward country French, with such dishes as paté de campagne or lamb loin and lamb sausage with a potato *galette* (potato cake). There are always several interesting salads as well. The three-course prix fixe dinner for $35 is an excellent deal.

Inn at the Market, 86 Pine St. ⓒ **206/728-2800**. Reservations recommended. Main courses $24–$37; 3-course prix fixe dinner $35. AE, DC, MC, V. Daily 5–10pm.

Chez Shea ⭐⭐⭐ NORTHWEST   Quiet, dark, and intimate, Chez Shea is one of the finest restaurants in Seattle, and with only a dozen candlelit tables and views across Puget Sound to the Olympic Mountains, it's an ideal setting for romance. The menu changes with the season, and ingredients come primarily from the market below. On a recent spring evening, dinner started with green onion pancakes served with an unusual Roquefort-and-radish mousse. This was then followed by a fragrant carrot soup. Among the five or so nightly entrees were halibut with lemon-grass-sesame vinaigrette, cilantro pesto, and pickled ginger; lamb shank braised with onion, fennel, tomatoes, and garlic; and scallops with saffron-orange beurre blanc. Though dessert is a la carte, you'll find it impossible to let it pass you by. The city may have equally fine restaurants, but none has quite the romantic atmosphere as Chez Shea.

Pike Place Market, Corner Market Building, 94 Pike St., Ste. 34. ⓒ **206/467-9990**. www.chezshea.com. Reservations highly recommended. Prix fixe 3-course dinner (available Tues–Thurs and Sun) $30, 4-course dinner $43. AE, MC, V. Tues–Sun 5–10:30pm.

Il Bistro ⭐ ITALIAN   What with the fishmongers and crowds of tourists, Pike Place Market might not seem like the place for a romantic candlelit dinner. But romantic dinners are what Il Bistro is all about. This restaurant takes Italian cooking very seriously, and in so doing also puts the Northwest's bountiful ingredients to good use. The menu includes such mouthwatering starters as calamari sautéed with fresh basil, garlic, vinegar, and tomatoes. Hundreds of loyal fans insist that Il Bistro's rack of lamb with wine sauce is the best in Seattle, and we'd have to agree. However, the pasta here can also be a genuine revelation. You'll find this basement trattoria down the cobblestone alley beside the market information kiosk.

93-A Pike St. and First Ave. (inside Pike Place Market). ⓒ **206/682-3049**. www.ilbistro.net. Reservations recommended. Pastas $13–$18; main courses $20–$38. AE, DC, DISC, MC, V. Daily 5:30–10pm; late-night menu until 1am; bar nightly until 2am.

MODERATE

Café Campagne ⭐⭐ *Finds* FRENCH   This cozy little cafe is an offshoot of the popular Campagne, a much more formal French restaurant, and though it's in the heart of the Pike Place Market neighborhood, it's a world away from the market madness. We like to duck in here for lunch and escape the shuffling crowds. What a relief—so civilized, so very French. The dark and cozy place has a hidden feel to it, and most people leave feeling like they've discovered some secret hideaway. The menu changes with the seasons, but a daily rotisserie special such as stuffed quail or leg of lamb marinated with garlic and anchovy is always offered Monday through Saturday—highly recommended. The cafe doubles as a wine bar and has a good selection of reasonably priced wines by the glass or by the bottle.

1600 Post Alley. ⓒ **206/728-2233**. Reservations accepted for dinner only. Main courses $15–$18; 3-course prix fixe menu $25. AE, DC, MC, V. Mon–Thurs 11am–10pm, Fri 11am–11pm, Sat 8–4am and 5:30–11pm, Sun 8am–4pm and 5–10pm.

Etta's Seafood ⭐⭐ SEAFOOD   Seattle chef Tom Douglas's strictly seafood (well, almost) restaurant, Etta's, is located smack in the middle of the Pike Place Market area and, of course, serves Douglas's signature crab cakes (crunchy on the outside, creamy on the inside), which are not to be missed (and if they're not on the menu, just ask). Don't ignore your side dishes, either; they can be exquisite and are usually enough to share around the table. In addition to the great seafood dishes, the menu always has a few other fine options, including several that date from Douglas's Café Sport days in the early 1980s. Stylish contemporary decor sets the mood, making this place as popular with locals as it is with tourists.

2020 Western Ave. ✆ **206/443-6000.** www.tomdouglas.com. Reservations recommended. Main courses $9.50–$26. AE, DC, DISC, MC, V. Mon–Thurs 11:30am–9:30pm, Fri 11:30am–10:30pm, Sat 9am–10:30pm, Sun 9am–9pm.

Le Pichet ★ FRENCH   Seattle seems to have a thing for French restaurants. They're all over the place in this city, with a surprising number clustered around Pike Place Market, and Le Pichet is one of our favorites. The name is French for "pitcher," and is a reference to the traditional ceramic pitchers used for serving inexpensive French wines. This should clue you in to the casual nature of the place, the sort of spot where you can drop by any time of day, grab a stool at the bar, and have a light meal. Almost everything is made fresh on the premises, and with lots of small plates and appetizers, it's fun and easy to piece together a light meal of shareable dishes. We like the warm salt cod purée with garlic and olive, and the country-style paté, which here is served with honey and walnuts.

1933 First Ave. ✆ **206/256-1499.** Reservations recommended. Main courses $15–$17. MC, V. Sun–Thurs 8am–midnight, Fri–Sat 8am–2am.

Matt's in the Market ★★ *Finds* AMERICAN REGIONAL/INTERNA-TIONAL   Quite possibly the smallest gourmet restaurant in Seattle, Matt's is a tiny cubbyhole of a place in the Corner Market Building, directly across the street from the market information booth at First and Pike. The restaurant has only a handful of tables and a few stools at the counter, and the kitchen takes up almost half the restaurant, giving the cooks little more than the space of a walk-in closet in which to work their culinary magic. The menu changes regularly, with an emphasis on fresh ingredients from the market stalls only steps away, and there's a good selection of reasonably priced wines. The menu pulls in whatever influences and styles happen to appeal to the chef at that moment, perhaps Moroccan, perhaps Southern. This is a real Pike Place Market experience. If you spot anything with smoked catfish on the menu, try it.

94 Pike St. ✆ **206/467-7909.** Dinner reservations accepted for first seating and highly recommended. Main courses $8–$9 at lunch, $15–$18 at dinner. MC, V. Mon 11:30–2:30pm, Tues–Sat 11:30am–2:30pm and 5:30–9:30pm.

The Pink Door ★ ITALIAN/LATE-NIGHT   Pike Place Market's better restaurants tend to be well hidden, and if we didn't tell you about this one, you'd probably never find it. There's no sign out front—only the pink door for which the restaurant is named (look for it between Stewart and Virginia sts.). On the other side of the door, stairs lead to a cellarlike space, which is almost always empty on summer days, when folks forsake it to dine on the deck with a view of Elliott Bay. What makes this place so popular is as much the fun atmosphere as the Italian food. You might encounter a tarot card reader or a magician, and most nights in the bar there's some sort of Felliniesque cabaret performer. Be sure to start your meal with the fragrant roasted garlic and ricotta-Gorgonzola spread or the locally made salami from Salumi, which is another of our favorite Seattle restaurants. From there, you might move on to an Italian classic such as lasagna or something made with fresh seafood from Pike Place Market.

1919 Post Alley. ✆ **206/443-3241.** Reservations recommended. Main courses $13.50–$19. AE, MC, V. Tues–Thurs 11:30am–midnight, Fri–Sat 11:30am–2am, Sun 4–11pm.

Shea's Lounge 🕏🕏 NORTHWEST/INTERNATIONAL/LATE-NIGHT
Convenient, casual, economical, romantic. What's not to like about this hidden
jewel in Pike Place Market? This is the lounge for the ever-popular Chez Shea,
and it's one of the most sophisticated little spaces in Seattle. Romantic lighting
and a view of the bay make it a popular spot with couples, and whether you just
want a cocktail and an appetizer or a full meal, you can get it here. The menu
features gourmet pizzas, combination appetizer plates, a few soups and salads,
and several nightly specials such as chicken stew with spicy chorizo sausage and
chipotle pepper or risotto cakes with spinach and roasted fennel. You can even
order dishes from the main restaurant's menu. The desserts are divinely decadent. This is a great spot for a light or late-night meal.

Pike Place Market, Corner Market Building, 94 Pike St., Ste. 34. ⓒ 206/467-9990. Reservations not
accepted. Main courses $13–$26. AE, MC, V. Tues–Thurs and Sun 4:30pm–midnight, Fri–Sat 4:30pm–2am.

INEXPENSIVE

El Puerco Lloron 🕏 MEXICAN   Located on one of the terraces of the Pike
Hill Climb, a stairway that leads up from the waterfront to Pike Place Market,
this Mexican fast-food place has a genuinely authentic feel in large part due to the
battered Mexican tables and chairs. And though the menu is limited, but the food
is as authentic as it gets. A little patio seating area is very popular in summer.

1501 Western Ave. ⓒ 206/624-0541. Main courses $5.25–$6.25. Mon–Thurs 11:30am–8pm, Fri–Sat
11:30am–8pm, Sun 11am–5pm.

6 Pioneer Square & the International District

In addition to the two International District restaurants listed below, you'll find
a large all-Asian food court at **Uwajimaya,** 600 Fifth Ave. S. (ⓒ **206/624-6248**),
a huge Asian supermarket. The food court's stalls serve the foods of different
Asian countries. It all smells great, and everything is inexpensive, which makes
this a great place for a quick meal. With the bus tunnel entrance right across the
street, Uwajimaya is easy to reach even from the north end of downtown.

MODERATE

Trattoria Mitchelli 🕏 ITALIAN/LATE-NIGHT   Located in the heart of
Pioneer Square, Trattoria Mitchelli serves good, basic Italian food in a cozy spot
with friendly, old-world atmosphere. A vintage wooden-topped lunch counter
in a room with classic hexagonal tile floors is a popular after-work and late-night
gathering spot, and the conversation is lively. You can't go wrong here with the
fettuccine con pollo, pizza from the wood-fired oven, or the pasta of the week
served with your choice of sauce. For a rich dessert, dig into a caramello, a
creamy caramel with toasted walnuts and whipped cream. If you're a night owl,
keep Mitchelli's in mind—full meals are served until 4am Thursday through
Saturday nights, catering to the starving hordes who pour out of the area's many
bars after last call.

84 Yesler Way. ⓒ 206/623-3883. Reservations accepted only for parties of 6 or more. Main courses $8–$15.
AE, DISC, MC, V. Mon–Wed 11:30am–11pm, Thurs–Fri 11:30am–4am, Sat 8am–4am, Sun 8am–11pm.

INEXPENSIVE

Hing Loon 🕏 CHINESE/LATE-NIGHT   Bright fluorescent lighting, big
Formica-top tables, zero atmosphere—this is the sort of place you'd pass by with-
out a thought if you were aimlessly searching for a restaurant in the International
District. With so many choices in a few square blocks, it's easy to be distracted by

fancy decor. But forget the rest and take a seat in Hing Loon. Seafood is the house specialty, and none is done better than the oysters with ginger and green onion served on a sizzling platter. You can't go wrong ordering chow mein or chow fun—but be prepared for a large helping. Pork dishes tend to be fatty.

628 S. Weller St. ✆ 206/682-2828. Main courses $3.50–$9.25. DC, MC, V. Sun–Thurs 10am–1am, Fri–Sat 10am–2am.

House of Hong ★ *Value* CHINESE   If you're in the International District anytime between 10am and 5pm and want to sample the best dim sum in Seattle, head for the House of Hong. It's located at the uphill end of the neighborhood in a big yellow building. All the little dumplings, pot stickers, and stuffed wontons that comprise the standards of dim sum are done to perfection here—not too greasy, not too starchy, with plenty of meat in the fillings. Keep an eye out for the whole fried shrimp, crunchy on the outside and moist and meaty on the inside. There's lots of variety to the dim sum offerings, so pace yourself and keep an eye out for whatever looks particularly appetizing. The House of Hong also has free parking.

409 Eighth Ave. ✆ 206/622-7997. Reservations not necessary. www.houseofhong.com. Dim sum $2–$5; main courses $6.50–$14. AE, DC, DISC, MC, V. Mon–Fri 10am–midnight, Sat 9:30am–midnight, Sun 9:30am–10pm.

Koraku *Finds* JAPANESE   Eating lunch at this little International District hole-in-the-wall is like ducking into a back-street cafe in Japan. Only slightly larger than a walk-in closet, Koraku feels as though it hasn't changed in half a century or more, which seems to be just fine with the regular patrons, most of whom will be speaking Japanese. The menu is limited to a handful of daily specials, of which the fried mackerel lunch is our favorite.

419 Sixth Ave. ✆ 206/624-1389. Main courses $4.50–$6.50. No credit cards. Mon–Tues and Thurs–Fri 11am–5pm.

Merchants Cafe AMERICAN   Merchants Cafe is Seattle's oldest restaurant and looks every bit of its 100-plus years. A well-scuffed tile floor surrounds the bar, which came around the Horn in the 1800s, and an old safe and gold scales are left over from the days when Seattle was the first, or last, taste of civilization for Yukon prospectors. At one time the restaurant's basement was a card room, and the upper floors were a brothel. In fact, this may be the original Skid Row saloon (Yesler Way was the original Skid Road down which logs were skidded to a sawmill). Straightforward sandwiches, salads, and soups are the mainstays of the menu.

109 Yesler Way. ✆ 206/624-1515. Main courses and sandwiches $6–$8. AE, MC, V. Mon 11am–3pm, Tues–Thurs 11am–9pm, Fri 11am–2am, Sat 10am–2am, Sun 10am–3pm.

Pecos Pit BBQ *Finds* BARBECUE   This barbecue joint, located in an industrial area south of Pioneer Square, looks like an old gas station with picnic tables out front, and the first thing you'll notice is the line of about 30 people standing at the walk-up window. The second thing you'll notice is that the bag they give you comes with five napkins and a spoon. Yep, this joint is both popular and a great place to ruin a good shirt, but those sandwiches sure are tasty. Unless you're a confirmed fire-eater, don't go beyond "mild" unless you want to feel your lips burning long after you've finished eating. Pecos Pit BBQ may be out of the way, but it's worth the drive.

2260 First Ave. S. ✆ 206/623-0629. Sandwiches $5.55. No credit cards. Mon–Fri 11am–3pm.

Salumi ★ *Finds* ITALIAN For many folks, salami is a guilty pleasure. We all know it's got way too much fat, but it tastes too good to resist. Now, raise the bar on salami, and you have the artisan-cured meats of this closet-size eatery near Pioneer Square. The owner makes all his own salami (as well as traditional Italian-cured beef tongue). Order up a meat plate with a side of cheese and some roasted red bell peppers, pour yourself a glass of wine from the big bottle on the table, and you have a perfect lunchtime repast in the classic Italian style. Did I mention the great breads and tapenades? Wow! If you're down in the Pioneer Square area at lunch, don't miss this place.

309 Third Ave. S. ✆ 206/621-8772. Reservations not accepted. Main courses $5.50–$14. MC, V. Tues–Fri 11am–4pm.

7 Queen Anne & Seattle Center

VERY EXPENSIVE

SkyCity at the Needle ★★ NORTHWEST Both the restaurant and the prices are sky-high at this revolving restaurant, located just below the observation deck at the top of Seattle's famous Space Needle. But because you don't have to pay extra for the elevator ride if you dine here, the high prices start to seem a little bit more in line with those at other Seattle splurge restaurants. OK, so maybe you'd get better food somewhere else, and maybe you can dine with a view at other Seattle restaurants, but you won't get as spectacular a panorama anywhere but here. The menu works hard at offering some distinctly Northwestern flavor combinations but still has plenty of familiar fare for those diners who aren't into culinary adventures. Simply prepared steaks and seafood make up the bulk of the menu, with a couple of vegetarian options as well. We recommend coming here for lunch. The prices are considerably more reasonable, and the views, encompassing the city skyline, Mount Rainier, and the Olympic Mountains, are unsurpassed.

Space Needle, 400 Broad St. ✆ 800/937-9582 or 206/905-2100. www.spaceneedle.com. Reservations highly recommended. Main courses $16.50–$25 at lunch, $20–$32 at dinner. Weekend brunch $34.50 adults, $21.50 children 5–12. AE, DC, DISC, MC, V. Mon–Fri 11am–2:45pm and 4:30–8:45pm, Sat 10am–2:45pm and 4:30–9:45pm, Sun 10am–2:45pm and 4:30–8:45pm.

EXPENSIVE

Canlis ★★★ NORTHWEST You'll definitely want to dress up for a meal here: This is the perfect place to close a big deal or celebrate a very special occasion. A Seattle institution, Canlis has been in business since 1950. A major remodeling a few years back gave the restaurant a stylish new look that mixes contemporary decor with Asian antiques, and Canlis continues to make improvements aimed at luring in Seattle's new movers and shakers. The Northwest cuisine, with Asian and Continental influences, keeps both traditionalists and more adventurous diners content. Steaks from the copper grill are perennial favorites here, as are the spicy Canlis prawns. To finish, why not go all the way and have the Grand Marnier soufflé? Canlis also has one of the best wine lists in Seattle.

2576 Aurora Ave. N. ✆ 206/283-3313. www.canlis.com. Reservations highly recommended. Main courses $22–$55; chef's tasting menu $100 with wines. AE, DC, DISC, MC, V. Mon–Sat 5:30pm–midnight. Valet parking $5.

Kaspar's Restaurant & Wine Bar ★★ NORTHWEST/SEAFOOD Located in the Lower Queen Anne neighborhood not far from Seattle Center, Kaspar's has long been a favorite with Seattleites, offering many dining options for various hungers and pocketbooks. Throughout the year, chef Kaspar Donier puts on interesting special dinners, such as wine-tasting dinners for connoisseurs and oenophiles. The last Friday of each month is an inexpensive jazz and jambalaya night. Any time of month, head to the wine bar for light meals, drinks, and desserts. The menu places an emphasis on seafood (don't miss the scallops) and draws on worldwide influences in such dishes as Vietnamese spring rolls with miso aioli, or duck confit and breast with wild huckleberry sauce. Kaspar's is also justly famous for its desserts. Perhaps best of all are the $25 three-course summer dinner specials.

19 W. Harrison St. ✆ 206/298-0123. www.kaspars.com. Reservations recommended. Main courses $16–$24; prix fixe dinners $25–$65. AE, MC, V. Tues–Thurs 4:30–10pm, Fri–Sat 5–11pm.

Palisade ★★★ NORTHWEST   With a panorama that sweeps from downtown to West Seattle and across the sound to the Olympic Mountains, Palisade has one of the best views of any Seattle waterfront restaurant. It also happens to have fine food and inventive interior design (incorporating a saltwater pond, complete with fish, sea anemones, and starfish, in the middle of the dining room). The extensive menu features dishes prepared on a searing grill, in a wood-fired oven, in a wood-fired rotisserie, and in an applewood broiler—it all adds up to many choices of flavorful seafoods and meats. Palisade also has an excellent and very popular Sunday brunch. The restaurant is not easy to find, but it's more than worth the search. Call for directions.

Elliott Bay Marina, 2601 W. Marina Place. ✆ 206/285-1000. Reservations recommended. Main courses $9–$16 at lunch, $17–$65 at dinner. AE, DC, DISC, MC, V. Mon–Thurs 11:30am–2pm and 5–9pm, Fri 11:30am–2pm and 5–10pm, Sat 4–10pm, Sun 10am–2pm and 4:30–9pm.

INEXPENSIVE

The 5 Spot ★ AMERICAN REGIONAL/LATE-NIGHT   The 5 Spot is one of Seattle's favorite diners. Every 3 months or so, the restaurant changes its menu to reflect a different regional U.S. cuisine. Maybe you'll find Brooklyn comfort food or Cuban-influenced Miami-style meals featured on the menu, but you can bet that whatever's featured will be filling and fun. The atmosphere here is pure kitsch—whenever the theme is "Florida," the restaurant is adorned with palm trees and flamingos and looks like the high school gym done up for prom night. This bustling diner is popular with all types, who appreciate the fact that you won't go broke eating here. To find The 5 Spot, look for the neon coffee pouring into the giant coffee cup sign at the top of Queen Anne Hill.

1502 Queen Anne Ave. N. ✆ 206/285-SPOT. www.chowfoods.com. Reservations accepted only for parties of 6–10. Main courses $7–$10.50 at lunch, $9–$18 at dinner. MC, V. Mon–Fri 8:30am–midnight, Sat–Sun (and holidays) 8:30am–3pm and 5–midnight.

Maggie Bluffs Marina Grill ★ *Kids* AMERICAN   It's never easy to find affordable waterfront dining in any city, and Seattle is no exception. However, if you're willing to drive a few miles from downtown Seattle, you can save quite a few bucks at this casual marina restaurant located at the foot of Magnolia Bluff (northwest of downtown Seattle). The menu is fairly simple, with burgers and fish and chips, but it includes a few dishes that display a bit more creativity. The restaurant overlooks a marina and, while the view is partially obstructed by a breakwater, you can still see Elliott Bay, West Seattle, downtown, and even the Space Needle. Crayons are on hand to keep the kids entertained. After a meal, walk out on Pier G and take a free shuttle boat a few yards through the marina to an observation deck atop the breakwater. The patio dining area is popular on sunny summer days.

Dining: Queen Anne/Seattle Center, Lake Union, Capitol Hill & North Seattle

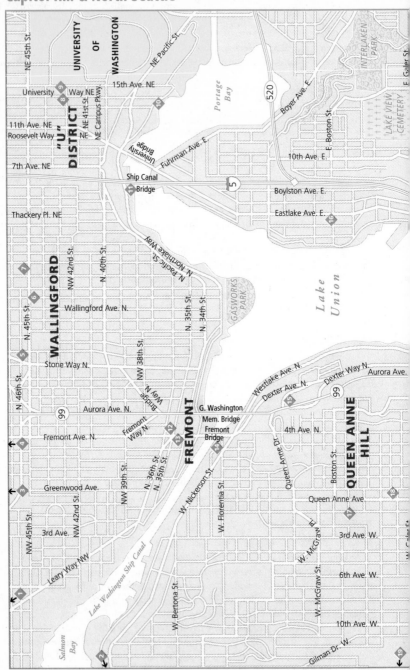

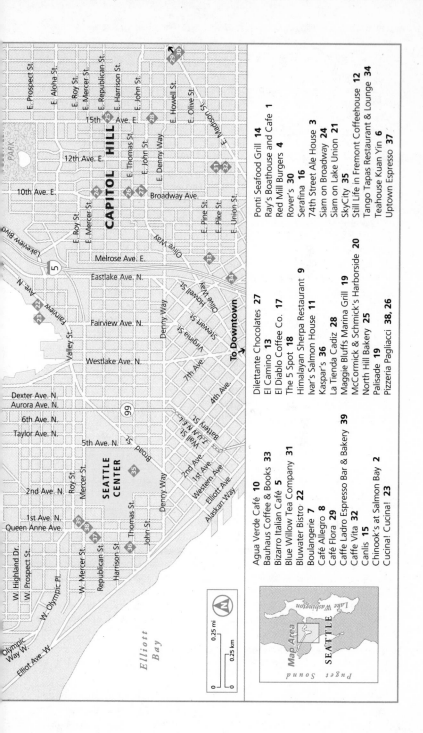

Agua Verde Café **10**
Bauhaus Coffee & Books **33**
Bizarro Italian Café **5**
Blue Willow Tea Company **31**
Bluwater Bistro **22**
Boulangerie **7**
Café Allegro **8**
Café Flora **29**
Caffe Ladro Espresso Bar & Bakery **39**
Caffe Vita **32**
Canlis **15**
Chinook's at Salmon Bay **2**
Cucina! Cucina! **23**

Dilettante Chocolates **27**
El Camino **13**
El Diablo Coffee Co. **17**
The 5 Spot **18**
Himalayan Sherpa Restaurant **9**
Ivar's Salmon House **11**
Kaspar's **36**
La Tienda Cadiz **28**
Maggie Bluffs Marina Grill **19**
McCormick & Schmick's Harborside **20**
North Hill Bakery **25**
Palisade **19**
Pizzeria Pagliacci **38**, **26**

Ponti Seafood Grill **14**
Ray's Boathouse and Cafe **1**
Red Mill Burgers **4**
Rover's **30**
Serafina **16**
74th Street Ale House **3**
Siam on Broadway **24**
Siam on Lake Union **21**
SkyCity **35**
Still Life in Fremont Coffeehouse **12**
Tango Tapas Restaurant & Lounge **34**
Teahouse Kuan Yin **6**
Uptown Espresso **37**

Elliott Bay Marina, 2601 W. Marina Place. © 206/283-8322. Reservations not accepted. Main courses $7–$11. AE, MC, V. Mon–Fri 11:30am–9pm, Sat–Sun 8am–9pm.

Pizzeria Pagliacci ✿ PIZZA   Pagliacci's pizza has repeatedly been voted the best in Seattle, and not just by us. There are now three Pagliaccis around town, so you're never very far from great pizza. Although you can order a traditional cheese pizza, there are much more interesting pies on the menu, such as pesto pizza or the sun-dried tomato primo. It's strictly counter service, but each of the bright restaurants has plenty of seats. For those in a hurry or who just want a snack, Pagliacci has pizza by the slice. You'll find another Pagliacci at 426 Broadway E. (© **206/324-0730**) in the Capitol Hill neighborhood.

550 Queen Anne Ave. N. © **206/285-1232** or 206/726-1717 for delivery. www.pagliacci.com. Reservations not accepted. Pizza $11.50–$20. AE, MC, V. Sun–Thurs 11am–11pm, Fri–Sat 11am–midnight.

8 Lake Union

MODERATE

Bluwater Bistro ✿ AMERICAN REGIONAL/LATE-NIGHT   Although this restaurant is located on the shore of Lake Union, its views are limited, which is probably why the Bluwater Bistro is more popular with locals than with tourists. However, you can watch seaplanes take off and land right in front of the restaurant. Best of all, the prices here are considerably lower than at most tourist-targeted waterfront restaurants around town. Good choices include the New York steak topped with blue cheese and, at lunch, the blackened mahimahi sandwich with Creole mayonnaise. You'll find this little bistro on the next pier north of Cucina! Cucina! This is also a popular watering hole for marina types who arrive by boat. A second Bluwater Bistro is near the Woodland Park Zoo at 7900 E. Green Lake Dr. N. (© **206/524-3985**).

1001 Fairview Ave. N. (on Lake Union). © **206/447-0769**. www.bluwaterbistro.com. Reservations accepted only for parties of 6 or more. Main courses $7.50–$12.75 at lunch, $14.75–$21 at dinner. AE, DC, MC, V. Daily 11:30am–1am.

Ivar's Salmon House ✿✿ *Kids* SEAFOOD   With a view of the Space Needle on the far side of Lake Union, flotillas of sea kayaks silently slipping by, sailboats racing across the lake, and powerboaters tying up at the dock out back, this restaurant on the north side of Lake Union is quintessential Seattle. Add to the scene an award-winning building designed to resemble a Northwest Coast Indian longhouse, and you have what just might be the very best place in town for a waterfront meal. OK, so maybe, just maybe, you can find better food at a few other waterfront places, but none has the unequivocally Seattle atmosphere you'll find at Ivar's Salmon House. This place is a magnet for weekend boaters who abandon their own galley fare in favor of Ivar's clam chowder and famous alder-smoked salmon. Lots of artifacts, including long dugout canoes and historic photographic portraits of Native American chiefs, make Ivar's a hit with both kids and adults. Bear in mind that this restaurant's popularity means that service can be slow; just relax and keep enjoying the views.

401 NE Northlake Way. © **206/632-0767**. www.ivars.net. Reservations recommended. Main courses $8–$15 at lunch, $15–$27 at dinner. AE, DC, DISC, MC, V. Mon–Thurs 11am–10pm, Fri–Sat 11am–11pm, Sun 10am–2pm and 3:30–10pm.

McCormick & Schmick's Harborside ✿ SEAFOOD   With its waterfront setting and views of the marinas on the west side of Lake Union, this restaurant has the best location of any of Seattle's McCormick & Schmick's restaurants.

The menu, which changes daily, includes seemingly endless choices of appetizers, sandwiches, salads, and creative entrees. Just be sure to order something with seafood, such as seared rare ahi with sticky rice and wasabi; Parmesan-crusted petrale sole; or seared catfish with caramelized onion ragout. Sure, there are meat dishes on the menu, but why bother (unless you only came here for the excellent view)? Bar specials for $1.95 are available in the late afternoon and late evening, and there are always plenty of varieties of oysters on the half shell.

1200 Westlake Ave. N. ☎ **206/270-9052.** www.mccormickandschmicks.com. Reservations recommended. Main courses $7–$24. AE, DC, DISC, MC, V. Mon–Fri 11:30am–11pm, Sat–Sun 11:30am–3pm (summer only) and 4–11pm.

Serafina ★★ COUNTRY ITALIAN   Located a bit off the beaten tourist track, Serafina is one of our favorite Seattle dining spots. It has a nice touch of sophistication, but overall, it's a relaxed, neighborhood sort of place. The rustic, romantic atmosphere underscores the earthy, country-style dishes served here. The antipasti Serafina is always a good choice for a starter and changes daily. It's also hard to resist ordering at least one of the bruschetta appetizers, which come with any of three different toppings. Among the pasta offerings, you might find a ragout made with duck, veal, and pork served over hand-cut fettuccine, or the ever-popular and delicious veal meatballs in a green olive-tomato sauce served over Italian *strangozzi* pasta. Be sure not to miss the *melanzane alla Serafina* (thinly sliced eggplant rolled with ricotta cheese, basil, and Parmesan and baked in tomato sauce). There's live music (mostly jazz and Latin) Thursday through Saturday nights.

2043 Eastlake Ave. E. ☎ **206/323-0807.** www.serafinaseattle.com. Reservations recommended. Pastas $12–$15; entrees $16–$25. MC, V. Mon–Thurs 11:30am–2pm and 4:30–10pm, Fri 11:30am–2:30pm and 4:30–11pm, Sat 5:30–11pm, Sun 5:30–10pm.

INEXPENSIVE

Cucina! Cucina! ★ *Kids* ITALIAN   Although it's part of a local restaurant chain, Cucina! Cucina! is a good bet not only for its waterfront view and reliable pizzas and pasta, but for its lively party atmosphere. Located at the south end of Lake Union, this restaurant is also a favorite of Seattle families because of all the special attention kids are given here. But just because families are welcome doesn't mean this place isn't fun for grown-ups, too. In summer, the deck is the place to be.

Chandler's Cove, 901 Fairview Ave. N. ☎ **206/447-2782.** www.cucinacucina.com. Call ahead to place name on wait list. Main courses $9–$18. AE, DC, DISC, MC, V. Sun–Thurs 11:30am–10pm, Fri–Sat 11:30am–10:30pm.

Siam on Lake Union ★ THAI   This large, casual restaurant, one of the best Thai restaurants in Seattle, may not be located right on the lake, but it's close enough to be convenient if you're staying at one of the hotels in Lake Union. The *tom yum* soups, made with either shrimp or chicken, are among the richest and creamiest we've ever had—also some of the spiciest. If you prefer your food less fiery, let your server know. Just remember that they mean it when they say *very hot.* The pad Thai (spicy fried noodles) is excellent, and the *nua phad bai graplau* (spicy meat and vegetables) is properly fragrant. This restaurant also has two other affiliated restaurants: Siam on Broadway, 616 Broadway E. (☎ **206/324-0892**); and Siam on Queen Anne, 101 John St. (☎ **206/285-9000**).

1880 Fairview Ave. E. ☎ **206/323-8101.** Reservations recommended on weekends. Main courses $7.25–$12. AE, DC, MC, V. Mon–Thurs 11:30am–10pm, Fri 11:30am–11pm, Sat 5–11pm, Sun 5–10pm.

9 Capitol Hill & East Seattle

Also worth trying in this area are **Siam on Broadway,** 616 Broadway E. (𝄞 **206/324-0892**), which is affiliated with Siam on Lake Union (see the listing just above); and **Pizzeria Pagliacci,** 426 Broadway E. (𝄞 **206/324-0730**), which is affiliated with the Pizzeria Pagliacci in the Lower Queen Anne neighborhood (see the review on p. 98).

VERY EXPENSIVE

Rover's ✿✿✿ NORTHWEST   Tucked away in a quaint clapboard house behind a chic little shopping center in the Madison Valley neighborhood east of downtown, this is one of Seattle's most acclaimed restaurants. Thierry Rautureau, Rover's much-celebrated and award-winning chef, received classical French training before falling in love with the Northwest and all the wonderful ingredients it has to offer an imaginative chef. Voilà! Northwest cuisine with a French accent.

The delicacies on the frequently changing menu are enough to send the most jaded of gastronomes into fits of indecision. Luckily, you can simply opt for one of the fixed-price dinners and leave the decision making to a professional—the chef. Culinary creations include scrambled eggs with lime crème fraîche and caviar, baby white asparagus with prosciutto and Perigord truffle mousseline, spice-infused pinot noir sorbet, and venison with wild mushrooms and peppercorn sauce. Vegetarians, take note: You won't often find a vegetarian feast that can compare with the ones served here.

2808 E. Madison St. 𝄞 **206/325-7442.** www.rovers-seattle.com. Reservations required. 5-course menu degustation $75 (vegetarian) and $90; chef's 8-course grand menu $120. AE, MC, V. Tues–Sat 5:30 to about 9:30pm.

INEXPENSIVE

Cafe Flora ✿ VEGETARIAN   Big, bright, and airy, this Madison Valley cafe will dispel any ideas you might have about vegetarian food being boring. This is meatless gourmet cooking and draws on influences from around the world—it's a vegetarian's dream come true. One of the house specialties is a portobello Wellington made with mushroom-pecan paté and sautéed leeks in a puff pastry. While the menu changes weekly, unusual pizzas (such as strawberries and brie or eggplant and pine nut) are always on the menu. On weekends, a casual brunch features interesting breakfast fare.

2901 E. Madison St. 𝄞 **206/325-9100.** www.cafeflora.com. Reservations accepted only for parties of 8 or more. Main courses $10–$17. MC, V. Tues–Fri 11:30am–10pm, Sat 9am–2pm and 5–10pm, Sun 9am–2pm and 5–9pm.

10 North Seattle (Including Fremont, Wallingford & the University District)

EXPENSIVE

Ponti Seafood Grill ✿✿ SEAFOOD   Situated at the south end of the Fremont Bridge overlooking the Lake Washington Ship Canal (not officially in north Seattle), Ponti is one of Seattle's most elegant and sophisticated restaurants. The menu here, which changes weekly, has an international flavor that roams the globe from Thailand to Italy, though it also offers some solidly Northwestern creations. Perennial favorites among the appetizers include Dungeness crab spring rolls with a peanut-lime dipping sauce, and the Cajun barbecued prawns. The weekly listing of fresh seafood might include the likes of grilled rare ahi with a coconut-rice cake or a simple penne pasta with grilled prawns. The lunch menu includes some of the same dishes served at dinner (though at sometimes half the price), which makes this restaurant a good bet for a gourmet midday meal on a tight budget. Before or after you dine here, take a walk around Fremont to check out the funky shops and eclectic public art.

3014 Third Ave. N. ✆ **206/284-3000.** Reservations recommended. Main courses $8–$14 at lunch, $17–$29 at dinner. AE, DC, DISC, MC, V. Mon–Thurs 11:30am–2:30pm and 5–9:30pm, Fri 11:30am–2:30pm and 5–10pm, Sat 5–10pm, Sun 5–9:30pm.

MODERATE

Bizarro Italian Café ✿ *Finds* ITALIAN   The name certainly sums up this very casual Italian restaurant where a party atmosphere reigns most nights. The tiny room is filled with mismatched thrift-store furnishings and strange things hanging from the walls and ceiling. Also around the restaurant are numerous paintings of the namesake "Bizarro," a character who looks a bit like a deranged cook. It's sort of like eating in someone's attic. The food, however, is good and cheap, and there are always lots of interesting specials on the blackboard. You'll find Bizarro at the west end of the Wallingford neighborhood just off Stone Way North.

1307 N. 46th St. ✆ **206/545-7327.** Reservations accepted before 6:30pm Fri–Sat and for 6 or more people Sun–Thurs. Main courses $14–$16. AE, DISC, MC, V. Daily 5–10pm (summer, Fri–Sat 5–11pm).

Chinook's at Salmon Bay ✿ SEAFOOD   Seattle's Fishermen's Terminal, the winter home of the large Alaska fishing fleet, is located just across the Lake Washington Ship Canal from the Ballard neighborhood. Overlooking all the moored commercial fishing boats, you'll find one of Seattle's favorite seafood restaurants, a big, casual, boisterous place with walls of windows looking out onto the marina. With a long menu featuring seafood fresh off the boats, this place tries to have a little something for everyone. However, our recommendation is to go for the alder-plank-roasted salmon with maybe some oyster stew to start things off.

The only real problem with this place is that it isn't very easy to reach. Take Elliott Avenue north from the downtown waterfront, continue north on 15th Avenue West, take the last exit before crossing the Ballard Bridge, and follow the signs to Fishermen's Terminal. Before or after a meal, stroll around the marina and have a look at all the fishing boats.

1900 W. Nickerson St. ✆ **206/283-4665.** Reservations not accepted. Main courses $7.50–$20. AE, DISC, MC, V. Mon–Thurs 11am–10pm, Fri 11am–11pm, Sat 7:30am–11pm, Sun 7:30am–10pm.

El Camino ✿✿ MEXICAN   Maybe it's the implied promise of sunshine and warm weather in every bite, but the Northwest seems to have an obsession with southwestern and Mexican food. If you, too, need a dose of spicy food, hit the road *(el camino)* in the Fremont neighborhood. As soon as you sit down, a little dish of spicy nuts will be placed at your table. A few of these crunchy gems later, and you'll need to order a margarita. The house margarita here is the best I've had north of Tucson. Start a meal with the unusual chile rellenos appetizer, made here without batter but decorated with guacamole cream sauce. The pork carnitas are superb—crunchy and tender at the same time. Don't miss them.

607 N. 35th St. ✆ **206/632-7303.** Reservations recommended. Main courses $12–$18. AE, MC, V. Sun–Thurs 5–10pm, Fri–Sat 5–11pm.

Ray's Boathouse and Cafe ✿✿ SEAFOOD   When Seattleites want to impress visiting friends and relatives, this restaurant often ranks right up there with the Space Needle, the ferries, and Pike Place Market. The view across Puget Sound to the Olympic Mountains is superb. You can watch the boat traffic coming and going from the Lake Washington Ship Canal, and bald eagles can often be seen fishing just offshore. Then there's Ray's dual personality—upstairs is a lively (and loud) cafe and lounge, while downstairs is a much more formal, sedate scene. The upstairs menu is more creative and less expensive than the one downstairs, but even upstairs you can order from the downstairs menu. The crab cakes are delicious and packed full of crab, and the black cod glazed with sake kasu, a typically Northwestern preparation, is well worth trying. Whatever your mood, Ray's has got you covered. No reservations are taken for dinner upstairs, and waiting times of up to an hour are not unusual (which is why the bar gets so lively).

6049 Seaview Ave. NW. © 206/789-3770. www.rays.com. Reservations recommended (not accepted for dinner in cafe). Main courses $18–$45 (Boathouse), $8.50–$16.25 (Cafe). AE, DC, DISC, MC, V. Boathouse daily 5–9:30pm. Cafe daily 11:30am–10pm.

INEXPENSIVE

Agua Verde Café ⭐ *Finds* MEXICAN   Set on the shore of Portage Bay, which lies between Lake Union and Lake Washington, this casual Mexican restaurant is very popular with college students from the adjacent University of Washington. Consequently, there's often a line out the door as customers wait to give their orders at the counter. The menu is limited to tacos, Mexican-style sandwiches, empanadas, and quesadillas. It's hard to go wrong here, but I recommend the tacos, which come three to an order. Try the grilled halibut or yam tacos, both of which are topped with a delicious avocado sauce. Add a couple of sides— cranberry slaw, pineapple-jicama salsa, creamy chile potatoes—for a filling and inexpensive meal. They also serve pretty good margaritas here. In addition, the restaurant rents kayaks for $10 to $15 per hour.

1303 NE Boat St. © 206/545-8570. Reservations not accepted. Main courses $3.75–$5.50. AE, DISC, MC, V. Mon–Sat 11am–4pm and 5–10pm, Sun noon–6pm.

Himalayan Sherpa Restaurant ⭐ *Finds* HIMALAYAN   If you've ever been to Nepal, you may not remember the food with the fondest of memories. But should you be struck with pangs of nostalgia for that trek you once took, you might be interested to know that you can relive your fonder Himalayan culinary memories in Seattle's University District. The food here is both surprisingly authentic and far superior to most of the Nepali food served in budget restaurants in Nepal. For the full experience, opt for the Nepalese fixed menu or the Himalayan Sherpa combo. With a minimum of four people and an hour's notice, the restaurant can also prepare a traditional Tibetan hot-pot *(gyakok)* dinner for you.

4214 University Way NE. © 206/633-2100. www.himalayansherpa.com. Reservations recommended. Main courses $7–$15. AE, DC, DISC, MC, V. Daily 10am–10pm.

Red Mill Burgers ⭐ AMERICAN   Located just a little north of the Woodland Park Zoo, this retro burger joint is tiny and always hoppin' because everyone knows they do one of the best burgers in Seattle. Try the verde burger, made with Anaheim peppers for just the right amount of fire. Don't miss the onion rings. And don't come dressed in your finest attire—burgers here are definitely multi-napkin affairs. There's a second Red Mill Burgers at 1613 W. Dravus St. (© 206/ 284-6363).

312 N. 67th St. © 206/783-6362. Burgers $2.89–$5.25. No credit cards. Tues–Sat 11am–9pm, Sun noon–8pm.

74th St. Ale House ⚛ AMERICAN   This neighborhood pub, designed to resemble pubs in England, not only serves a good variety of locally brewed ales, but it also has some of the best pub fare in the city. The burger, made with lean ground beef and served on a hunk of French baguette covered with grilled onions and red bell peppers, is one of the best burgers in the city. The gumbo is another winner; it's a rich, dark stew that's perfect for a cold, rainy night. Located about a mile north of the Woodland Park Zoo, this is a great spot for lunch before or after visiting the zoo. *Note:* Because it is a tavern, children are not allowed.

7401 Greenwood Ave. N. ⓒ 206/784-2955. www.seattlealehouses.com. Main courses $7–$10. DISC, MC, V. Sun–Wed 11:30am–10pm, Thurs–Sat 11:30am–11pm.

11 West Seattle

EXPENSIVE

Salty's on Alki Beach ⚛⚛ SEAFOOD   Although the prices here are almost as out of line as those at the Space Needle, and the service is unpredictable, this restaurant has *the* waterfront view in Seattle, and the food is usually pretty good. Because the restaurant is set on the northeast side of the Alki Peninsula, it faces downtown Seattle on the far side of Elliott Bay. Come at sunset for dinner and watch the setting sun sparkle off skyscraper windows as the lights of the city twinkle on. On sunny summer days, lunch on one of the two decks is a sublimely Seattle experience. Don't be discouraged by the ugly industrial/port area you drive through to get here; Salty's marks the start of Alki Beach, the closest Seattle comes to a Southern California beach scene. Just watch for the giant rusted salmon sculptures swimming amid rebar kelp beds and the remains of an old bridge (hey, Seattle even recycles when it comes to art).

1936 Harbor Ave. SW. ⓒ 206/937-1600. www.saltys.com. Reservations recommended. Main courses $20–$40. AE, DC, DISC, MC, V. Mon–Thurs 11am–2:30pm and 5–10pm, Fri 11am–2:30pm and 5–11pm, Sat 11:30am–3pm and 4–11pm, Sun 9am–2pm and 4–10pm.

INEXPENSIVE

Alki Homestead Restaurant ⚛ AMERICAN   This restaurant, just half a block off Alki Beach, is such a throwback that it's even housed in an old log house. But if it's good, old-fashioned home cooking you crave, this place is worth searching out. Although the menu has other dishes, the fried chicken family dinner is the meal to order here. The log house is set behind neatly trimmed lawns shaded by trees as old as the house. Inside the various dining rooms, you'll eat seated at tables draped with lace tablecloths and set with pink napkins.

2717 61st Ave. SW. ⓒ 206/935-5678. Reservations recommended. Main courses $9.25–$14.50. AE, DISC, MC, V. Wed–Sat 5–10pm, Sun 3–8:30pm.

12 The Eastside (Including Bellevue & Kirkland)

By far the most celebrated restaurant on the Eastside is the **Herbfarm,** a much-lauded restaurant serving herb-driven Northwest cuisine. The restaurant's nine-course dinners are legendary in the Northwest. For information on this restaurant, which in 2001 moved into a new building in Woodinville, see the review on p. 220, in chapter 11, "Side Trips from Seattle."

EXPENSIVE

Third Floor Fish Cafe ⚛⚛ SEAFOOD   Take the elevator up to the third floor of this downtown Kirkland restaurant for fabulous views of Lake Washington and seafood cooked with an expert touch. The atmosphere is very clubby and the clientele tends to be well off and well dressed. It's the superb seafood that pulls them in; you might start with Dungeness crab spring rolls or Northwest ceviche made with marinated salmon, tuna, and halibut. As at so many other restaurants around town, seared ahi tuna is currently very popular, here served with a peppercorn crust and whatever seasonal sides strike the fancy of the chef. Seared scallops have also become quite popular in Seattle; here they might be served with black-truffle-infused risotto, roasted fennel, and leek cream. There's also an extensive, well-chosen wine list, and five- and seven-course tasting menus are available nightly.

205 Lake St. S., Kirkland. ✆ 425/822-3553. www.fishcafe.com. Reservations recommended. Main courses $24–$36; tasting menus $50–$70. AE, DC, DISC, MC, V. Daily 5pm–closing. Lounge 4pm–closing.

Yarrow Bay Grill ★★ NORTHWEST   The combination of Northwest cuisine and a view across Lake Washington to Seattle has made this restaurant, in the upscale Carillon Point retail, office, and condo development, a favorite of Eastside diners (we've heard even Bill Gates eats here). The setting is decidedly nouveau riche and about as close as you get to a Southern California setting in the Northwest. The menu is not so long that you can't make a decision, but long enough to provide some serious options. The Thai-style crab cake appetizers with a sweet mustard sauce are favorites of ours, as is the peanut-chile dusted calamari. Entrees are usually equally divided between seafood and meats, with at least one vegetarian dish on the menu daily. Keep in mind that the menu is short and changes daily. Nearly every table has a view, and there is a great deck for good weather.

1270 Carillon Point, Kirkland. ✆ 425/889-9052. www.ybgrill.com. Reservations recommended. Main courses $17–$39. AE, DC, DISC, MC, V. Mon–Fri 5:30–9:30pm, Sat 5:30–9:30pm, Sun 10am–2:30pm (brunch), open until 10pm nightly in summer.

MODERATE

Beach Cafe ★★ INTERNATIONAL   Affiliated with the Yarrow Bay Grill, which is located just upstairs, this casual waterfront cafe is the Eastside's best bet for an economical and creative meal with a view. In summer, the patio dining area just can't be beat. The menu circles the globe, bringing a very satisfying mélange of flavors to Bellevue diners. Because the menu changes daily, you never know what you might find when you drop by.

1270 Carillon Point, Kirkland. ✆ 425/889-0303. www.ybbeachcafe.com. Reservations recommended. Main courses $13–$24. AE, DC, DISC, MC, V. Mon–Thurs 11am–10pm, Fri–Sat 11am–11pm, Sun 11am–9pm.

13 Coffee, Tea, Bakeries & Pastry Shops

CAFES, COFFEE BARS & TEA SHOPS

Unless you've been on Mars for the past decade, you're likely aware that Seattle has become the espresso capital of America. Seattleites are positively rabid about coffee, which isn't just a hot drink or a caffeine fix anymore, but rather a way of life. You'll never be more than about a block from your next cup. There are espresso carts on the sidewalks, drive-through espresso windows, espresso bars, gas station espresso counters, espresso milkshakes, espresso chocolates, even eggnog lattes at Christmas.

Starbucks, the ruling king of coffee, is seemingly everywhere you turn in Seattle. They sell some 36 types and blends of coffee beans. **SBC,** also known as Seattle's Best Coffee, doesn't have as many shops as Starbucks, but it does have a very devoted clientele. Close on the heels of Starbucks and SBC is the **Tully's** chain, which seems to have opened an espresso bar on every corner that doesn't already have a Starbucks or an SBC. However, serious espresso junkies swear by **Torrefazione** and **Caffe Ladro.** If you see one of either of these chains, check it out and see what you think.

Coffee bars and cafes are as popular as bars and pubs as places to hang out and visit with friends. Among our favorite Seattle cafes are the following (organized by neighborhood):

DOWNTOWN

Ancient Grounds, 1220 First Ave. (© **206/749-0747**), is hands down the coolest and most unusual espresso bar in Seattle. This coffeehouse doubles as an art gallery specializing in antique Mexican, Japanese, and Northwest Coast Indian masks and ethnic artifacts from around the world. There are also cases full of colorful minerals and equally colorful insects in glass boxes. It's all very dark and Victorian.

PIONEER SQUARE & THE INTERNATIONAL DISTRICT

The Pioneer Square location of **Torrefazione** ★★, 320 Occidental Ave. S. (© **206/624-5847**), with its hand-painted Italian crockery, has a very old-world feel. The foam on the lattes here is absolutely perfect. It has great pastries, too. Other Torrefaziones can be found at 622 Olive Way (© **206/624-1429**), 1310 Fourth Ave. (© **206/583-8970**); and in Fremont at 701 N. 34th St. (© **206/545-2721**).

Zeitgeist Art/Coffee ★, 171 S. Jackson St. (© **206/583-0497**), with its big windows and local artwork, is popular with the Pioneer Square art crowd.

PIKE PLACE MARKET

Seattle is legendary as a city of coffeeholics, and Starbucks is the main reason. This company has coffeehouses all over town (and all over the world), but the original **Starbucks,** 1912 Pike Place (© **206/448-8762**), is in Pike Place Market. In fact, this is the only chain store allowed in the market. Although you won't find any tables or chairs here, Starbucks fans shouldn't miss an opportunity to get their coffee at the source.

THE SEATTLE CENTER & QUEEN ANNE AREAS

Caffe Ladro Espresso Bar & Bakery ★★, 2205 Queen Anne Ave. N. (© **206/282-5313**), in the heart of the pleasant Upper Queen Anne area, has the feel of a cozy neighborhood coffeehouse. There's another Caffe Ladro in the MarQueen Hotel building in Lower Queen Anne at 600 Queen Anne Ave. N. (© **206/282-1549**). Other Caffe Ladros can be found downtown at 801 Pine St. (© **206/405-1950**) and in the Fremont neighborhood at 452 36th St. N. (© **206/675-0854**).

Uptown Espresso, 525 Queen Anne Ave. N. (© **206/285-3757**), with its crystal chandelier, gilt-framed classical painting, and opera music on the stereo, has a very theatrical, European feel. Good baked goodies, too. There's another Uptown in Belltown at 2504 Fourth Ave.

Over the past few years, Caffe Vita has become known as one of Seattle's finest coffee roasters. In the Lower Queen Anne neighborhood, you can sample these superb coffees at their coffeehouse—**Caffe Vita,** 813 Fifth Ave. N. (© **206/285-9662**).

If you've tired of double tall raspberry mochas and are desperately seeking a new coffee experience, make a trip to Upper Queen Anne's **El Diablo Coffee Co.,** 1811 Queen Anne. Ave. N. (© **206/285-0693**), a Latin-style coffeehouse.

The Cubano, made with two shots of espresso and caramelized sugar, and the *café con leche* (a Cubano with steamed milk) are both devilishly good drinks. *Viva la revolución!*

CAPITOL HILL & EAST SEATTLE

Bauhaus Coffee & Books *ⓕ*, 301 E. Pine St. (© 206/625-1600), on the downtown edge of Capitol Hill, is a great place to hang out and soak up the neighborhood atmosphere. There are always lots of interesting 30-something types hanging out reading or carrying on heated discussions.

Over the past few years, **Caffe Vita,** 1005 E. Pike St. (© **206/709-4440**), has developed a devoted following of espresso fanatics who swear by the perfectly roasted coffee beans and lovingly crafted lattes served here.

If coffee isn't your thing, don't despair. Up on Capitol Hill, you can sip teas and snack on Asian-inspired foods at the **Blue Willow Tea Company,** 1024 E. Pike St. (© **206/325-9889**).

NORTH SEATTLE

Café Allegro, 4214 University Way NE (© **206/633-3030**), located down an alley around the corner from University Way in the U District, is Seattle's oldest cafe and a favored hangout of University of Washington students. Keep looking; you'll find it.

Still Life in Fremont Coffeehouse *ⓕ*, 709 N. 35th St. (© **206/547-9850**), in the eclectic Fremont neighborhood, harks back to hippie hangouts of old. It's big and always crowded, offering good vegetarian meals and great weekend breakfasts, too. There's also **Still Life on the Ave Cafe,** 1405 NE 50th St. (© **206/ 729-3542**), in the University District.

Teahouse Kuan Yin, 1911 N. 45th St. (© **206/632-2055**), in the Wallingford neighborhood, is one of Seattle's favorite coffee alternatives. This Asian-inspired tea shop not only serves an amazing variety of teas, but also sells all manner of tea paraphernalia.

BAKERIES & PASTRY SHOPS

PIONEER SQUARE & THE INTERNATIONAL DISTRICT

Grand Central Baking Company *ⓕ*, 214 First Ave. S. (© **206/622-3644**), in Pioneer Square's Grand Central Arcade, is responsible for awakening Seattle to the pleasures of rustic European-style breads. This bakery not only turns out great bread, but it also does good pastries and sandwiches.

Although the name is none too appealing, **Cow Chips,** 102A First Ave. S. (© **206/292-9808**), bakes the best chocolate chip cookies in the city, and the cookies come in different sizes depending on the size of your cookie craving.

PIKE PLACE MARKET

The Crumpet Shop *ⓕ*, 1503 First Ave. (© **206/682-1598**), in Pike Place Market, specializes in its British namesake pastries but also does scones. It's almost a requirement that you accompany your crumpet or scone with a pot of tea.

Le Panier, 1902 Pike Place (© **206/441-3669**), located in the heart of Pike Place Market, is a great place to get a croissant and a latte and watch the market action.

With a wall of glass cases full of baked goods and a window facing onto one of the busiest spots in Pike Place Market, **Three Girls Bakery,** 1514 Pike Place, Stall no. 1 (© **206/622-1045**), is a favorite place to grab a few pastries or other goodies to go. It also has a counter in back if you prefer to sit down.

BELLTOWN

Macrina ★★, 2408 First Ave. (© 206/448-4032), a neighborhood bakery/cafe in Belltown, serves some of the best baked goodies in the city and is a cozy place for a quick, cheap breakfast or lunch. In the morning, the smell of baking bread wafts down First Avenue and draws in many a passerby.

Tom Douglas's three Seattle restaurants—Dahlia Lounge, Palace Kitchen, and Etta's—are all immensely popular, and there was such a demand for the breads and pastries served at these restaurants that Douglas opened his own **Dahlia Bakery,** 2001 Fourth Ave. (© 206/441-4540), where you can even get Douglas's fabled coconut cream pie to go.

CAPITOL HILL & EAST SEATTLE

Basically, **Dilettante Chocolates** ★★, 416 Broadway E. (© 206/329-6463), is a chocolate restaurant that happens to be Seattle's leading proponent of cocoa as the next drink to take the country by storm. If you don't order something with chocolate here, you're missing the point.

If you've been on your feet at Volunteer Park for a while and need a snack, try the **North Hill Bakery,** 518 15th Ave. E. (© 206/206/325-9007), just a few blocks east of the park. There's always a good selection of baked goods in the cases.

NORTH SEATTLE

Let's say you've spent the morning or afternoon at the zoo and you're suddenly struck with a craving for a fresh apple tart or an almond croissant. What's a person to do? Make tracks to **Boulangerie** ★, 2200 N. 45th St. (© 206/634-2211), a Wallingford neighborhood French pastry shop, that's what.

14 Quick Bites

If you're just looking for something quick and cheap and don't want to resort to McDonald's or Burger King, consider grabbing a wrap. It can be just about anything in a tortilla and has become the food of choice in Seattle these days. Keep your eyes out for a **World Wraps** (of which there are many all around the city).

For variety, it's hard to beat the food court on the top floor of **Westlake Center** shopping mall, 400 Pine St. If you're downtown at lunch and just want a gourmet sandwich and pasta salad that you can grab out of a case, stop by **Briazz Cafe,** 1400 Fifth Ave. (© 206/343-3099).

MARKET MUNCHING

Few Seattle activities are more fun than munching your way through Pike Place Market. The market has dozens of fast-food vendors, and it is nearly impossible to resist the interesting array of finger foods and quick bites. Here are some of our favorite places:

If you're planning a picnic, **DeLaurenti** ★★, at 1435 First Ave. near the market's brass pig (© 206/622-0141), is the perfect spot to get your paté, bread, and wine.

If you're a fan of the stinking rose, don't miss the **Garlic Garden** (© 425/277-1985; www.lebanesebreeze.com), located just around the corner from *Rachel* (the pig statue). The Lebanese Breeze garlic dip/spread is so good they'll only let you have one free sample. Buy a container to spread on some bread from Le Panier.

Michou, 1904 Pike Place (© 206/448-4758), has cases full of delicious French-inspired gourmet foods to go and is located right next door to Le Panier, our favorite French bakery.

Picnicking on Capitol Hill

Volunteer Park is a great spot for a picnic. Before heading to the park, drop by **La Tienda Cádiz**, 350 15th Ave. E. (© **206/267-0570**), for some excellent Mediterranean gourmet-to-go. This casual spot also has plenty of tables if you'd rather eat here.

Piroshky, Piroshky, 1908 Pike Place (© **206/441-6068**), lays it all out in its name. The sweet or savory Russian filled rolls are the perfect finger food.

The Spanish Table, 1427 Western Ave. (© **206/682-2827**), is a specialty food shop on one of the lower levels of Pike Place Market. Besides shopping for paella pans, you can also get simple Spanish-style sandwiches, great soups, Spanish cheeses, and other light meal items. This quiet corner of the market is a great place to get away from the crowds and try some food you might never have encountered before.

Three Girls Bakery, 1514 Pike Place, stall no. 1 (© **206/622-1045**), has not only the bread-and-pastry window on the sidewalk, but a lunch counter as well.

World Class Chili 🌶, inside the market's south arcade at 1411 First Ave. (© **206/623-3678**), really lives up to its name. If you're a chili connoisseur, don't pass it by.

To give direction to a tour of Pike Place Market, why not spend the morning or afternoon shopping for interesting picnic items, then head up to the north end of the waterfront to Myrtle Edwards Park? Or, since a picnic of foods from Pike Place Market should be as special as the food shopping experience, consider heading a bit farther afield, perhaps to Discovery Point, Seattle's waterfront urban wilderness (take Western Ave. north along Elliott Bay to Magnolia and follow the signs). Another good place for a picnic is in Volunteer Park, high atop Capitol Hill. Alternatively, you could have your picnic aboard a ferry headed to Bainbridge Island (a 30-min. trip) or to Bremerton (a 1-hr. trip).

7

Exploring Seattle

I hope you've got a good pair of walking shoes and a lot of stamina (a double latte helps), because Seattle is a walking town. The city's two biggest attractions—the waterfront and Pike Place Market—are the sorts of places where you'll spend hours on your feet. When your feet are beat, you can relax on a tour boat and enjoy the views of the city from the waters of Puget Sound, or you can take a 2-minute rest on the monorail, which links downtown Seattle with Seattle Center, home of the Space Needle. If your energy level sags, don't worry; there's always an espresso bar nearby.

By the way, that monorail ride will now take you right through the middle of Paul Allen's Experience Music Project, the Frank Gehry–designed rock music museum also located in Seattle Center. Paul Allen, who made his millions as one of the co-founders of Microsoft, is busily changing the face of the south end of downtown as well. Here he has renovated Union Station and developed the area adjacent to the city's brand-new stadium, which was built for the Seattle Seahawks football team, whose owner is . . . you guessed it: Paul Allen. The new stadium is adjacent to the Seattle Mariners Safeco Field, which debuted in 1999 as one of the few stadiums in the country with a retractable roof.

Despite Seattle's many downtown diversions, however, the city's natural surroundings are still its primary attraction. You can easily cover all of Seattle's museums and major sights in 2 or 3 days, and with the help of the itineraries below, you should have a good idea of what not to miss. These itineraries will provide a good overview of the history, natural resources, and cultural diversity that have made Seattle the city it is today.

Once you've seen what's to see indoors, you can begin exploring the city's outdoor life. A car is not entirely necessary for exploring this city, but it can be helpful, and if you want to head farther afield—say to Mount Rainier, the San Juans, or the Olympic Peninsula—a car is a must.

SUGGESTED ITINERARIES

If You Have 1 Day

Start your day at **Pike Place Market,** Seattle's sprawling historic market complex. In the market, you can buy fresh salmon and Dungeness crabs packed to go, peruse the offerings of produce and flower vendors, buy art and crafts directly from the makers, and explore the dark depths of the market for unusual shops.

After you've had your fill of the market, head down the Pike Hill Climb to the Seattle waterfront. Directly across the street from the foot of the Hill Climb is Pier 59, site of the **Seattle Aquarium,** where you can learn about the sea life of the region and, next door at the IMAXDome, catch an IMAX film about the eruption of Mount St. Helens.

If you walk south from the aquarium to Pier 55, you can set sail on a 1-hour **harbor tour cruise.** A variety of other boat excursions are also available along the waterfront. You'll pass numerous overpriced seafood restaurants (most with good views and some with good food), as well as quite a few fish-and-chips counters.

When you pass the Washington State Ferries Colman Dock terminal, head away from the waterfront and into the historic **Pioneer Square** area. If you have an appreciation for bad jokes and history, the **Seattle Underground Tour** (see "Good Times in Bad Taste" on p. 115) will provide a little fun and give you a good idea of Seattle's early history.

After exploring Pioneer Square aboveground, head up James Street to the bus tunnel entrance and catch a free bus north to the Westlake Center station. In Westlake Center, an upscale shopping center, you can catch the monorail to Seattle Center, where, if you're a rock music fan, you can explore the **Experience Music Project** and ride the elevator to the top of the **Space Needle,** a great place to finish a long day's exploration.

If You Have 2 Days
If you have 2 days, your schedule can be more leisurely than the rather hectic 1-day itinerary above. On your first day, spend a bit more time in Pike Place Market before heading down to the waterfront. After exploring the aquarium, consider doing the **Tillicum Village Tour,** which includes a boat excursion to Blake Island State Park, where you'll be fed a salmon dinner and entertained with traditional Northwest Coast Native American masked dances.

Start your second day in Pioneer Square and take the Seattle Underground Tour. Then wander over to the nearby **International District (Chinatown)** and have lunch (House of Hong is one of our favorite spots; see chapter 6, "Where to Dine in Seattle"). After lunch, take the free bus through the bus tunnel to the **Seattle Art Museum.** After exploring the museum, continue north to Westlake Center and take the monorail to Seattle Center, where you can check out the **Experience Music Project** or head to the top of the **Space Needle.**

If You Have 3 Days
Start off by following the 2-day strategy outlined above. On your third day, do something very Seattle. Rent a sea kayak on Lake Union, go in-line skating in Green Lake Park, or rent a bike and ride the Burke-Gilman Trail. Wander around the funky **Fremont** neighborhood and maybe go to the **Woodland Park Zoo** or the **Burke Museum,** depending on your interests.

If You Have 4 Days or More
On your fourth and fifth days, plan to take a trip or two outside the city to Mount Rainier, Olympic National Park, Snoqualmie Falls, Bainbridge Island, the San Juan Islands, or Mount St. Helens. All these trips can be turned into overnighters or longer (see chapter 11, "Side Trips from Seattle," for details on these destinations).

1 On the Waterfront

The Seattle waterfront, which lies along Alaskan Way between Yesler Way in the south and Bay Street and Myrtle Edwards Park in the north, is the city's most popular attraction. Yes, it's very touristy, with tacky gift shops, saltwater taffy, T-shirts galore, and lots of overpriced restaurants, but it's also home to the Seattle

Seattle Attractions: The Waterfront, Downtown, First Hill, Belltown, Pike Place Market, Pioneer Square & the International District

Argosy Cruises **13**
Bank of America Tower **2**
Frye Art Museum **1**
IMAXDome Theater **16**
Klondike Gold Rush
   National Historical Park **7**
Occidental Park **6**
Odyssey–The Maritime
   Discovery Center **19**
Pike Place Market **18**
Russian Cobra **10**
Safeco Field **9**
Seahawks Stadium **8**
The Seattle Aquarium **17**
Seattle Art Museum **14**
Smith Tower **4**
Soundbridge Seattle Symphony
   Music Discovery Center **15**
Tillicum Village Tours **5**
The Underground Tour **5**
Washington State Ferries **11**
Wing Luke Asian Museum **3**
Ye Olde Curiosity Shop **12**

Aquarium, the IMAXDome Theater, Odyssey–The Maritime Discovery Center, and Ye Olde Curiosity Shop (king of the tacky gift shops). Ferries to Bainbridge Island and Bremerton, as well as several different boat tours, also operate from the waterfront. This is the best place to hire a horse-drawn carriage for a spin around downtown.

You'll find the Washington State Ferries terminal at **Pier 52,** which is at the south end of the waterfront near Pioneer Square. (A ferry ride makes for a cheap cruise.) At **Pier 55,** you'll find excursion boats offering harbor cruises and trips to Tillicum Village on Blake Island. At **Pier 56,** cruise boats leave for trips through the Chittenden (Ballard) Locks to Lake Union. See section 7, "Organized Tours," later in this chapter, for details. At Pier 57, you'll find both the Bay Pavilion, which has a vintage carousel and a video arcade to keep the kids busy, and **Pier 57 Parasail** (© **206/622-5757**), which will strap a parasail on your back, hook you to a long rope, and then tow you around Elliott Bay. The view from above the water is almost as good as the view from the Space Needle, and, because you take off and land from the back of the boat, you won't even get wet. Rides are $49 for one person and $89 for a tandem ride.

At **Pier 59,** you'll find the Seattle Aquarium (see below for details), the IMAX-Dome Theater (see below), and a small waterfront park. Continuing up the waterfront, you'll find **Pier 66,** the Bell Street Pier, which has a rooftop park. This is also the site of Odyssey–The Maritime Discovery Center (see below), which is dedicated to the history of shipping and fishing in Puget Sound, and Anthony's, one of the best seafood restaurants on the waterfront (see chapter 6 for a full review). At **Pier 67,** you'll find the Edgewater hotel, a great place to take in the sunset over a drink or dinner (see chapter 5, "Where to Stay in Seattle," for details).

Next door, at **Pier 69,** you'll come to the dock for the ferries that ply the waters between Seattle and Victoria, British Columbia, and at **Pier 70,** you'll find the *Spirit of Puget Sound* cruise ship. Just north of this pier is grassy Myrtle Edwards Park, a nice finale to a very pleasant waterfront. This park has a popular bicycling and skating trail, and is the northern terminus for the Waterfront Streetcar, which can take you back to your starting point.

(Value **Saving Money on Sightseeing**

If you're a see-it-all, do-it-all kind of person, you'll definitely want to buy a **CityPass** (© **707/256-0490;** www.citypass.com), which gets you into the Space Needle, Pacific Science Center, Seattle Aquarium, Woodland Park Zoo, and Museum of Flight, and also lets you take a boat tour of the harbor with Argosy Cruises at a savings of 50% if you visit all five attractions

he passes, good for 9 days from date of first use,
21.50 for children ages 4 to 13. Purchase your
ticipating attractions.

pick up a copy of the "Seattle's Favorite Attrac-
ludes coupons good for discounts at numerous
at the **Seattle–King County Convention and Vis-**
r, Washington State Convention & Trade Center,
lleria Level, at the corner of Eighth Avenue and
340; www.seeseattle.org).

IMAXDome Theater ⚡ The IMAXDome is a movie theater with a 180° screen that fills your peripheral vision and puts you right in the middle of the action. This huge wraparound theater is adjacent to the Seattle Aquarium, and for many years now has featured a film about the eruption of Mount St. Helens. Various other special features are screened throughout the year.

Pier 59, 1483 Alaskan Way. ✆ **206/622-1868** or 206/622-1869 for ticket reservations. www.seattleimax dome.com. Admission $7 adults, $6.50 seniors, $6 youth, free under 5 (IMAXDome–Aquarium combination tickets available). Screenings daily beginning at 10am. Closed Christmas. Bus: 10, 12, 15 or 18; then walk through Pike Place Market to the waterfront. Waterfront Streetcar: To Pike Place Market stop.

Odyssey–The Maritime Discovery Center   Sort of an interactive promotion for modern fishing and shipping, this facility at the north end of the Seattle waterfront is aimed primarily at kids and has more than 40 hands-on exhibits highlighting Seattle's modern working waterfront and its links to the sea. Exhibits include a kid-size fishing boat, a virtual kayak trip through the Puget Sound, and a live radar center that allows you to track the movement of vessels in Elliott Bay. In another exhibit, you get to use a simulated crane to practice loading a scale model of a cargo ship.

Pier 66 (Bell St. Pier), 2205 Alaskan Way. ✆ **206/374-4000**. www.ody.org. Admission $6.75 adults, $4.50 seniors and students, free for children under 5. Tues–Sat 10am–5pm, Sun noon–5pm. Closed day before Thanksgiving, Thanksgiving, Dec 24–25, Jan 1. Bus: 15 or 18; then walk through Pike Place Market to the waterfront. Waterfront Trolley: Bell St. Station.

Russian Cobra   This Cold War–era Russian submarine is the latest attraction on the Seattle waterfront and is berthed just south of Washington State Ferries' Colman Dock at the south end of the waterfront. The long black submarine is an ominous sight on this touristy stretch of Seattle shoreline. This sub, code-named Cobra, was built in 1972 and was in service for 20 years. A visit includes an introductory video that provides a bit of background on Russian submarines. After watching the video, you board the sub for a self-guided tour of the sub's main deck. Although an audio recording explains different parts of the sub as you walk through, there is also usually a former U.S. Navy submariner on hand to answer general questions about submarines. For anyone who lived through the Cold War, it is thrilling just to be inside a sub that was once considered "the enemy."

Pier 48, 101 Alaskan Way. ✆ **206/223-1767**. Admission $10 adults, $8 seniors and children ages 5–14. Mon–Sat 9am–9pm, Sun 9am–5:30pm (shorter hours fall through spring).

The Seattle Aquarium ⚡⚡ Although it's not nearly as large and impressive as either the Monterey Bay Aquarium or the Oregon Coast Aquarium, the Seattle Aquarium is still quite enjoyable and presents well-designed exhibits dealing with the water worlds of the Puget Sound region. The star attractions here are the playful river otters and the sea otters, as well as the giant octopus. There's also an underwater viewing dome, from which you get a fish's-eye view of life beneath the waves, and each September, you can watch salmon return up a fish ladder to spawn. Of course there are also plenty of small tanks that allow you to familiarize yourself with the many fish of the Northwest, a beautiful large coral-reef tank, and several smaller tanks that exhibit fish from distant waters. "Life on the Edge," the aquarium's newest exhibit, focuses on tide-pool life along Washington's Pacific Ocean and Puget Sound shores.

Pier 59, 1483 Alaskan Way. ✆ **206/386-4300**. www.seattleaquarium.org. Admission $9.75 adults, $8.75 seniors, $7 ages 6–18, $5 ages 3–5 (joint Aquarium–IMAXDome tickets also available). Labor Day to Memorial Day daily 9:30am–5pm; Memorial Day to Labor Day daily 9:30am–7pm. Bus: 10, 12, 15 or 18; then walk through Pike Place Market to the waterfront. Waterfront Streetcar: To Pike Place Market stop.

2 Pike Place Market to Pioneer Square

Pike Place Market and the Pioneer Square historic district lie at opposite ends of First Avenue; midway between the two is the Seattle Art Museum.

The **Pioneer Square** area, with its historic buildings, interesting shops, museum, and **Seattle Underground Tour** (see the box titled "Good Times in Bad Taste," below), is well worth a morning or afternoon's exploration. We've outlined a **walking tour** of the area in chapter 8, "Strolling Around Seattle."

Pike Place Market ★★★   Pike Place Market, originally a farmers' market, was founded in 1907 when housewives complained that middlemen were raising the price of produce. The market allowed shoppers to buy directly from producers, and thus save on grocery bills. By the 1960s, however, the market was no longer the popular spot it had been. World War II had deprived it of nearly half its farmers when Japanese Americans were moved to internment camps. The postwar flight to the suburbs almost spelled the end of the market, and the site was being eyed for a major redevelopment project. Fortunately, a grass-roots movement to save the 9-acre market culminated in its being declared a National Historic District.

Today the market is once again bustling, but the 100 or so farmers and fishmongers who set up shop on the premises are only a small part of the attraction. More than 150 local craftspeople and artists can be found here, selling their creations as street performers serenade milling crowds. There are also hundreds of small specialty shops throughout the market, plus dozens of restaurants, including some of the city's best. At the information booth almost directly below the large Pike Place Market sign, you can pick up a free map and guide to the market. Keep an eye out for low-flying fish at the Pike Place Fish stall, and be sure to save some change for Rachel, the market's giant piggy bank, which has raised more than $100,000 over the years.

Victor Steinbrueck Park, at the north end of the market at the intersection of Pike Place, Virginia Street, and Western Avenue, is a popular lounging area for both the homeless and people just looking for a grassy place in which to sit in the sun. In the park, you'll find two 50-foot-tall totem poles.

For a glimpse behind the scenes at the market and to learn all about its history, you can take a 1-hour guided **Market Heritage Tour** (© **206/682-7453**, ext. 653, for information and reservations). Tours are offered Wednesday through Sunday at 11am and 2pm. Tours depart from the market's Heritage Center, 1531 Western Ave. (take the Skybridge to the Market Garage and then take the elevator to the Western Ave. level). The Heritage Center is an open-air building filled with historical exhibits. Tours cost $7 for adults and $5 for seniors and children under age 18.

One-hour tours are also offered by the **Pike Place Market Merchants Association** (© **206/587-0351;** www.seattlepublicmarket.com). The tours, which are offered by reservation and cost $7 for adults and $5 for seniors and children under 12, include a healthy dose of fun and facts plus a bit of fiction. You'll even get to meet some market merchants and learn their stories.

See the section titled "Market Munching" at the very end of chapter 6 for a rundown of some of our favorite market food vendors.

Between Pike and Pine sts. at First Ave. © **206/682-7453.** www.pikeplacemarket.org. Mon–Sat 9am–6pm, Sun 11am–5pm. Closed New Year's Day, Easter, Thanksgiving, Christmas. Bus: 15 or 18. Waterfront Streetcar: To Pike Place Market stop.

Good Times in Bad Taste

If you love bad jokes and are fascinated by the bizarre (or maybe this describes your children), you won't want to miss the Underground Tour and a visit to Ye Olde Curiosity Shop. Together, these two outings should reassure you that, espresso, traffic jams, and Microsoft aside, Seattle really does have a sense of humor.

If you have an appreciation for off-color humor and are curious about the seamier side of Seattle history, **The Underground Tour**, 608 First Ave. (**© 206/682-4646**; www.undergroundtour.com), will likely entertain and enlighten you. The tours lead down below street level in the Pioneer Square area, where you can still find the vestiges of Seattle businesses built before the great fire of 1889. Learn the lowdown dirt on early Seattle, a town where plumbing was problematic and a person could drown in a pothole. (Tours are held daily. The cost is $9 for adults, $7 for seniors and students ages 13–17 or with college ID, $5 for children ages 7–12; children under 6 are discouraged.)

Ye Olde Curiosity Shop, 1001 Alaskan Way, Pier 54 (**© 206/682-5844**), is a cross between a souvenir store and Ripley's Believe It or Not! It's weird! It's tacky! It's always packed! The collection of oddities was started in 1899 by Joe Standley, who developed a more-than-passing interest in strange curios. See Siamese-twin calves, a natural mummy, the Lord's Prayer on a grain of rice, a narwhal tusk, shrunken heads, a 67-pound snail, fleas in dresses—all the stuff that fascinated you as a kid.

Klondike Gold Rush National Historical Park   It isn't in the Klondike (that's in Canada) and it isn't really a park (it's a single room in an old store), but this is a fascinating little museum. "At 3 o'clock this morning the steamship *Portland,* from St. Michaels for Seattle, passed up [Puget] Sound with more than a ton of gold on board and 68 passengers." When the *Seattle Post-Intelligencer* published that sentence on July 17, 1897, it started a stampede. Would-be miners heading for the Klondike goldfields in the 1890s made Seattle their outfitting center and helped turn it into a prosperous city. When they struck it rich up north, they headed back to Seattle, the first U.S. outpost of civilization, and unloaded their gold, making Seattle doubly rich. It seems only fitting that this museum should be here. Another unit of the park is in Skagway, Alaska.

117 S. Main St. © 206/553-7220. www.nps.gov/klse. Free admission. Daily 9am–5pm. Closed Thanksgiving, Christmas, and New Year's Day. Bus: 15, 16, 18, 21, or 22. Waterfront Streetcar: To Occidental Park stop.

Seattle Art Museum ★★   You simply can't miss this downtown art museum. Just look for Jonathon Borofsky's *Hammering Man,* an animated three-story steel sculpture that pounds out a silent beat in front of the museum. Inside you'll find one of the nation's premier collections of Northwest Coast Indian art and artifacts and an equally large collection of African art. Exhibits cover European and American art ranging from ancient Mediterranean works to pieces from the medieval, Renaissance, and baroque periods. A large 18th-century collection and a smaller 19th-century exhibition lead up to a large 20th-century collection that includes a room devoted to Northwest contemporary art. (There's also a smattering of Asian art at this museum, but the city's major collection of Asian art is at the Seattle Asian Art Museum in Volunteer Park; see below for details.) Free guided tours of the different collections are offered.

100 University St. ℂ 206/654-3100 or 206/654-3255. www.seattleartmuseum.org. Admission $7 adults, $5 seniors and students, free under 12. Admission higher for some special exhibitions. Free first Thurs of each month (free for seniors first Fri of each month). Admission ticket also valid at Seattle Asian Art Museum if used within 1 week. Tues–Sun 10am–5pm (Thurs until 9pm). Also open on Martin Luther King Jr. Day, Presidents' Day, Memorial Day, July 4th, and Labor Day. Closed Thanksgiving, Christmas, and New Year's Day (open holiday Mon). Bus: 10, 12, 15, 18 or any bus using the bus tunnel.

Soundbridge Seattle Symphony Music Discovery Center Perhaps you're an accomplished musician but have always longed to conduct an orchestra, or perhaps you've never had much musical talent at all but dream of playing the cello like Yo-Yo Ma. At this fascinating little music exploration center, you can at least see what it feels like to be first chair in the string section of the symphony. Not only is there a listening bar with more than 500 classical recordings, but interactive exhibits let you play a cello, tinkle piano keys, or conduct a virtual orchestra. There's also an exhibit on the science of music.

Benaroya Hall, Second Ave. and Union St. ℂ 206/336-6600. www.soundbridge.org. Admission $7 adults, $5 children ages 5–18, free for children under 3. Tues–Sun 10am–4pm (and prior to Seattle Symphony "Masterpiece" concerts for ticket holders).

3 Seattle Center & Lake Union Attractions

Built in 1962 for the World's Fair, Seattle Center is today not only the site of Seattle's famous Space Needle but also a cultural and entertainment park that doubles as the city's favorite festival grounds. Within Seattle Center's boundaries, you'll find the Experience Music Project (EMP), the Pacific Science Center, the Seattle Children's Museum, the Seattle Children's Theatre, Key Arena (home of the NBA's Seattle Supersonics), the Marion Oliver McCaw Hall (scheduled to open in the summer of 2003), a children's amusement park, a fountain that's a favorite summertime hangout, the Intiman Theatre, and the Bagley Wright Theatre. See p. 129, "Especially for Kids," for further details on Seattle Center attractions that young travelers will enjoy.

The Center for Wooden Boats ⭐ This unusual little museum, located adjacent to the Northwest Seaport/Maritime Heritage Center, is basically a collection of wooden boats of all kinds. Most of the boats are tied up to the docks surrounding the museum's floating boathouse, but some are stored in dry dock (on the dock itself). Dedicated to the preservation of historic wooden boats, the center is unique in that many exhibits can be rented and taken out on the waters of Lake Union. There are both rowboats and sailboats. Rates range from $10 to $46 per hour (call for hours of availability). Individual sailing instruction is also available.

1010 Valley St. (Waterway 4, south end of Lake Union). ℂ 206/382-2628. www.cwb.org. Free admission. May to Labor Day daily 11am–6pm; Labor Day to May Wed–Mon 11am–5pm. Bus: 17.

Experience Music Project (EMP) ⭐⭐ The brainchild of Microsoft co-founder Paul Allen and designed by architect Frank Gehry, who is known for pushing the envelope of architectural design, this rock 'n' roll museum is a massive multicolored blob at the foot of the Space Needle. Originally planned as a memorial to Seattle native Jimi Hendrix, the museum grew to encompass not only Hendrix, but all of the Northwest rock scene (from "Louie Louie" to grunge) and the general history of American popular music.

One museum exhibit focuses on the history of guitars and includes some of the first electric guitars, which date from the early 1930s. The museum even has a sort of rock 'n' roll thrill ride. The "ride" consists of a platform of seats that are bounced around, giving you the sensation of being on a roller coaster. But the most popular exhibits here (after the Jimi Hendrix room) are the interactive rooms. In one you can play guitar, drums, keyboards, or even DJ turntables. In another, you can experience what it's like to be onstage performing in front of adoring fans.

Regularly scheduled concerts are held in the museum's main hall, known as the Sky Church. To help you get the most out of your visit (and at almost $20 for a ticket, you certainly expect plenty), every visitor is issued a Museum Exhibit Guide (MEG), a hand-held electronic player filled with recorded audio clips explaining the various exhibits. Give yourself plenty of time to see this unusual museum.

325 Fifth Ave. N. © 877/EMPLIVE or 206/EMPLIVE. www.emplive.com. Admission $19.95 adults, $15.95 seniors and children ages 13–17, $14.95 children ages 7–12, free for children 6 and under. Memorial Day to Labor Day Sun–Thurs 9am–6pm, Fri–Sat 9am–9pm; Labor Day to Memorial Day Sun–Thurs 10am–5pm, Fri–Sat 10am–9pm. Bus: 1, 2, 3, 4, 13, 15, 16, 18, 24, or 33. Monorail: From Westlake Center at Pine St. and Fourth Ave.

Northwest Seaport/Maritime Heritage Center Although this marine heritage center at the south end of Lake Union is currently little more than a shipyard for the restoration of four historic ships, it has grand plans for the future. If you're a fan of tall ships and the age of sailing, you can pay a visit to the 1897 schooner *Wawona*, which is currently under restoration. Also being restored are a 1904 lightship, an 1889 tugboat, and a 1933 salmon troller. Throughout the year, there are folk music concerts ($10 adults, $7 seniors and children) on the deck of the *Wawona* (call for details), and on the second Friday of each month, there's a free Chantey Sing from 8 to 10pm. Nearby, at Chandler's Cove (901 Fairview N.), you'll find the gift shop and the few small exhibits of the **Puget Sound Maritime Historical Society** (© 206/624-3028).

1002 Valley St. © 206/447-9800. www.nwseaport.org. Admission by donation. Tues–Sat 10am–4pm. Bus: 17.

Pacific Science Center ★★ *Kids* Although its exhibits are aimed primarily at children, the Pacific Science Center is fun for all ages. The main goal of this sprawling complex at Seattle Center is to teach kids about science and to instill a desire to study it. To that end, there are life-sized robotic dinosaurs, a butterfly house and insect village (with giant robotic insects), a Tech Zone where kids can play virtual-reality soccer or play tic-tac-toe with a robot, and dozens of other fun hands-on exhibits addressing the biological sciences, physics, and chemistry. The August Bubble Festival is always a big hit, as is February's Bug Out Week. There's a planetarium for learning about the skies (plus laser shows for the fun of it), and an IMAX theater. Be sure to check the schedule for special exhibits when you're in town.

200 Second Ave. N., Seattle Center. © 206/443-2880. www.pacsci.org. Admission $8 adults, $5.50 ages 3–13 and seniors, free for children under 3. IMAX $6.75–$7.50 adults, $5.75–$6.50 ages 3–13 and seniors, free for children under 3. Laser show $5–$7.50. Various discounted combination tickets available. Mid-June to Labor Day daily 10am–6pm; Labor Day to mid-June Mon–Fri 10am–5pm, Sat–Sun and holidays 10am–6pm. Closed Thanksgiving and Christmas. Bus: 1, 2, 3, 4, 13, 15, 16, 18, 24, or 33. Monorail: To Seattle Center.

Seattle Attractions North: Queen Anne & Seattle Center, Capitol Hill & East Seattle & North Seattle

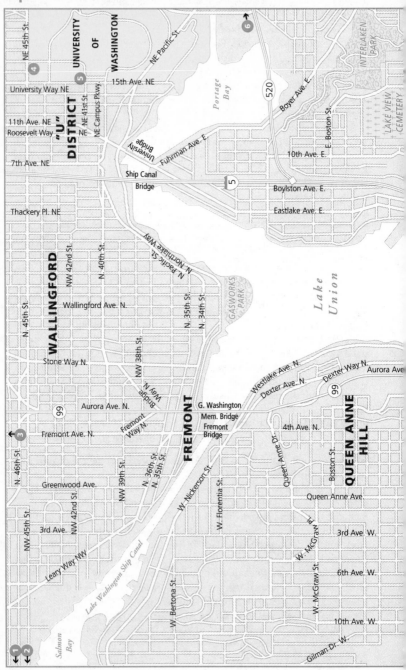

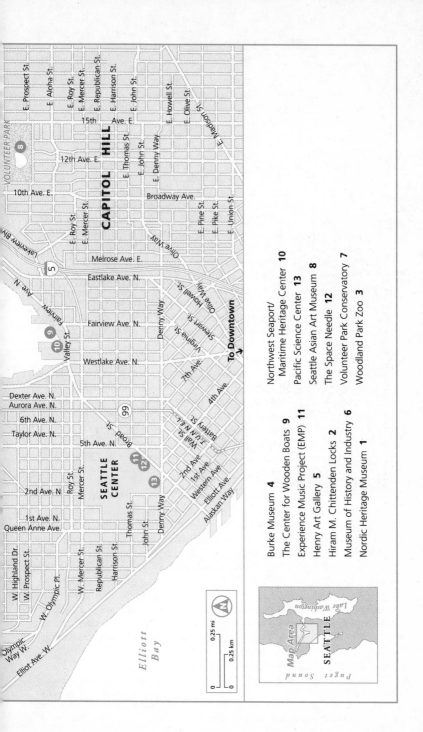

Burke Museum **4**

The Center for Wooden Boats **9**

Experience Music Project (EMP) **11**

Henry Art Gallery **5**

Hiram M. Chittenden Locks **2**

Museum of History and Industry **6**

Nordic Heritage Museum **1**

Northwest Seaport/
Maritime Heritage Center **10**

Pacific Science Center **13**

Seattle Asian Art Museum **8**

The Space Needle **12**

Volunteer Park Conservatory **7**

Woodland Park Zoo **3**

Space Needle Alternatives

If you don't want to deal with the crowds at the Space Needle but still want an elevated downtown view, you have some alternatives. One is the big, black **Bank of America Tower** (© 206/386-5151) at the corner of Fifth Avenue and Columbia Street. At 943 feet, this is the tallest building in Seattle (twice as tall as the Space Needle), more stories (76, to be exact) than any other building west of the Mississippi. Up on the 73rd floor, you'll find an observation deck with views that dwarf those from the Space Needle. Admission is only $5 for adults and $3 for seniors and children. It's open Monday through Friday from 8:30am to 4:30pm.

Not far from the Bank of America Tower, you'll find the **Smith Tower,** 506 Second Ave. (© 206/622-4004; www.chineseroom.com/observation. html). Opened in 1914, this was Seattle's first skyscraper and, for 50 years, was the tallest building west of Chicago. Although Smith Tower has only 42 stories, it still offers excellent views from its 35th-floor observation deck, which surrounds the ornate Chinese Room, a banquet hall with a carved ceiling. A lavish lobby and original manual elevators all make this a fun and historic place to take in the Seattle skyline. April 16 to October 31, the observation deck is open daily from 11am to 6pm; November 1 to April 15, it's open Saturday and Sunday from 11am to 4pm. Admission is $5 for adults, $4 for seniors and students, and $3 for children ages 6 to 12.

If you've ever seen a photo of the Space Needle framed by the high-rises of downtown Seattle, it was probably taken from **Kerry Viewpoint** on Queen Anne Hill. If you want to take your own drop-dead photo of the Seattle skyline from this elevated perspective, head north from Seattle Center on Queen Anne Avenue North and turn left on West Highland Drive. When you reach the park, you'll immediately recognize the view.

Another great panorama is from the water tower in **Volunteer Park** on Capitol Hill at East Prospect Street and 14th Avenue East. See p. 122.

The Space Needle ★★ From a distance it resembles a flying saucer on top of a tripod, and when it was built for the 1962 World's Fair, the 605-foot-tall Space Needle was meant to suggest future architectural trends. Today the Space Needle is the quintessential symbol of Seattle, and at 520 feet above ground level, the observation deck provides superb views of the city and its surroundings. Displays identify more than 60 sites and activities in the Seattle area, and high-powered telescopes let you zoom in on distant sights. You'll also find a pricey restaurant atop the tower (see the review of SkyCity on p. 94). If you don't mind standing in line and paying quite a bit for an elevator ride, make this your first stop in Seattle so that you can orient yourself. There are, however, cheaper alternatives if you just want a view of the city (see the box titled "Space Needle Alternatives," above).

Seattle Center, Fourth Ave. N at Broad St. © **800/937-9582** or 206/905-2100. www.spaceneedle.com. Admission $11 adults, $9 seniors and youths ages 11–17, $5 ages 5–10, free under 5; $16 day pass. No charge if dining in either restaurant. Summer daily 8am–midnight; other months Sun–Thurs 9am–11pm, Fri–Sat 9am–midnight. Valet parking $10 for 4 hr. Bus: 1, 2, 3, 4, 13, 15, 16, 18, 24, or 33. Monorail: From Westlake Center at Pine St. and Fourth Ave.

Seattle Center

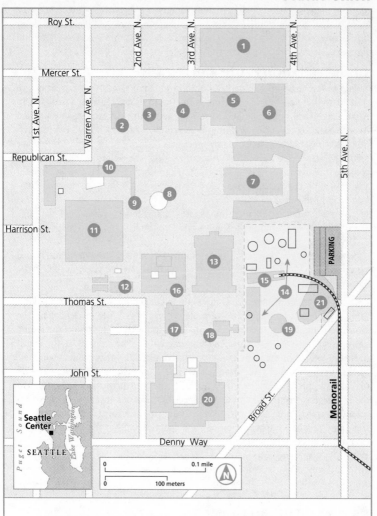

Amusement Park Areas **14**

Bagley Wright Theatre **2**

Center House & Children's Museum **13**

Exhibition Hall **4**

Experience Music Project **21**

Fisher Pavilion **16**

International Fountain **8**

Intiman Playhouse **3**

KeyArena **11**

Marion Oliver McCaw Hall **5**

Memorial Stadium **7**

Mercer Arts Arena **6**

Mercer Street Parking Garage **1**

Monorail Terminal **15**

Mural Amphitheatre **18**

Northwest Craft Center **9**

Northwest Rooms **10**

Pacific Science Center **20**

Seattle Center Pavilions **12**

Seattle Children's Theatre **17**

Space Needle **19**

4 The Neighborhoods

See chapter 8 for walking tours of Pike Place Market, Pioneer Square, and Fremont.

THE INTERNATIONAL DISTRICT

Seattle today boasts of its strategic location on the Pacific Rim, but its ties to Asia are nothing new. This is evident in the International District, Seattle's main Asian neighborhood, which is centered between Fifth Avenue South and 12th Avenue South (between S. Washington St. and S. Lane St.). Called the International District rather than Chinatown because so many Asian nationalities have made the area home, this neighborhood has been the center of the city's Asian communities for more than 100 years. You can learn about the district's history at the Wing Luke Museum (see below), where you can also pick up a walking-tour map of the area.

There are many restaurants, import stores, and food markets, and the huge **Uwajimaya** is all of these rolled up in one (see the listing on p. 163 of chapter 9, "Seattle Shopping," for details).

At the corner of Maynard Avenue South and South King Street, you'll find **Hing Hay Park,** the site of an ornate and colorful pavilion given to the city by Taipei, Taiwan.

Wing Luke Asian Museum   Despite much persecution over the years, Asians, primarily Chinese and Japanese, have played an integral role in developing the Northwest, and today the connection of this region with the far side of the Pacific has opened up both economic and cultural doors. The exhibits at this small museum, located in the heart of Seattle's International District (Chinatown) and named for the first Asian American to hold public office in the Northwest, explore the roles various Asian cultures have played in the settlement and development of the Northwest. Many of the museum's special exhibits are meant to help explain Asian customs to non-Asians. If you're walking around Chinatown, this museum will give you a better appreciation of the neighborhood, but the exhibits tend to have a narrow range of appeal.

407 Seventh Ave. S. ✆ 206/623-5124. www.wingluke.org. Admission $4 adults, $3 students and seniors, $2 ages 5–12, free for children under 5. Free on first Thurs of every month. Tues–Fri 11am–4:30pm, Sat–Sun noon–4pm. Closed New Year's Day, Easter, July 4, Labor Day, Thanksgiving, Christmas eve, and Christmas day. Bus: 7, 14, 36, or any southbound bus using the bus tunnel (get off at the International District station).

FIRST HILL (PILL HILL) & CAPITOL HILL

Seattle is justly proud of its parks, and **Volunteer Park,** on Capitol Hill (drive north on Broadway and watch for signs), is one of the most popular. Here you'll find not only acres of lawns, groves of trees, and huge old rhododendrons, but also an old water tower that provides one of the best panoramas in the city. A winding staircase leads to the top of the water tower, from which you get 360° views. On the observatory level there is also an interesting exhibit about the Olmsted Brothers and the system of parks they designed for Seattle. To find the water tower, park near the Seattle Asian Art Museum if you can, and walk back out of the parking lot to where the road splits. The view from directly in front of the museum isn't bad either.

Frye Art Museum ✿   Located on First Hill not far from downtown Seattle, this museum is primarily an exhibit space for the extensive personal art collection of Charles and Emma Frye, Seattle pioneers who began collecting art in the

1890s. The collection focuses on late-19th-century and early-20th-century representational art by European and American painters, with works by Andrew Wyeth, Thomas Hart Benton, Edward Hopper, Albert Bierstadt, and Pablo Picasso, as well as a large collection of engravings by Winslow Homer. In addition to galleries filled with works from the permanent collection, temporary exhibitions are held throughout the year.

704 Terry Ave. (at Cherry St.). ✆ 206/622-9250. www.fryeart.org. Free admission. Tues–Sat 10am–5pm (Thurs until 8pm), Sun noon–5pm. Closed July 4, Thanksgiving, Christmas, and New Year's Day. Bus: 3, 4, or 12.

Seattle Asian Art Museum ✦   Housed in a renovated Art Deco building, the Asian art collection has an emphasis on Chinese and Japanese art but also includes pieces from Korea, Southeast Asia, South Asia, and the Himalayas. Exhibits of Chinese terra-cotta funerary art, snuff bottles, and Japanese *netsukes* (belt decorations) are among the museum's most notable collections. One room is devoted to Japanese ceramics, while three rooms are devoted to Chinese ceramics. The central hall is devoted to the stone religious sculptures of South Asia (primarily India). There are frequent lectures and concerts.

1400 E. Prospect St., Volunteer Park (14th Ave. E. and E. Prospect St.). ✆ 206/654-3100. www.seattleart museum.org. Admission $3 adults, free 12 and under. Free to all on first Thurs and first Sat of each month (free for seniors on first Fri of each month). Admission ticket plus $4 will get you into the Seattle Art Museum if used within 1 week. Wed–Sun 10am–5pm (Thurs until 9pm); Tues 10am–5pm between Memorial Day and Sept 1. Closed Labor Day, Thanksgiving, Christmas, and New Year's Day. Bus: 10.

Volunteer Park Conservatory ✦   This stately old Victorian conservatory, built in 1912, houses a large collection of tropical and desert plants, including palm trees, orchids, and cacti. There are seasonal floral displays also.

1400 E. Galer St. ✆ 206/684-4743. Free admission. Daily 10am–4pm (Memorial Day to Labor Day daily 10am–7pm). Bus: 10.

NORTH SEATTLE (INCLUDING BALLARD, FREMONT, THE U DISTRICT & MONTLAKE)

The **Fremont District,** which begins at the north end of the Fremont Bridge near the intersection of Fremont Avenue North and North 36th Street, is Seattle's funkiest and most unusual neighborhood. Even livelier, though not nearly as eclectic or artistic, the **University District** (known locally as the U District) has loads of cheap restaurants and the types of shops you would associate with a college-age clientele. But the main attractions for visitors are the two excellent museums on the university campus and the nearby Museum of History and Industry, which is just across the Montlake Bridge from the U District.

Burke Museum ✦   Located in the northwest corner of the University of Washington campus, the Burke Museum features exhibits on the natural and cultural heritage of the Pacific Rim. Permanent exhibits include *Life & Times,* which covers 500 million years of Washington history (and prehistory) with lots of fossils, including a complete mastodon, on display. The second permanent exhibit, *Pacific Voices,* focuses on the many cultures of the Pacific Rim and their connections to Washington state. There is also a smaller temporary exhibit gallery. In front of the museum stand three modern totem poles carved in the style of the 1870s and 1880s.

17th Ave. NE and NE 45th St. ✆ 206/543-5590. www.burkemuseum.org. Admission $6.50 adults, $5 seniors, $3 ages 6–18, free for children under 6. Free the first Thurs of each month. Daily 10am–5pm (Thurs until 8pm). Closed July 4, Thanksgiving, Christmas, and New Year's Day. Bus: 70.

Henry Art Gallery   The focus here is on contemporary art with retrospectives of individual artists, as well as exhibits focusing on specific themes or media. Photography and video are both well represented, and for the most part, the exhibits are the most avant-garde in the Seattle area. Located on the west side of the University of Washington campus, this museum benefits from large, well-lit gallery spaces illuminated by pyramidal and cubic skylights that can be seen near the main museum entrance. There's also a cafe here and a small sculpture court-yard. Parking is often available at the Central Parking Garage at NE 41st Street and 15th Avenue NE. Expect the unexpected and prepare to be challenged in your concept of what constitutes art.

University of Washington, 15th Ave. NE and NE 41st St. ⓒ **206/543-2280**. www.henryart.org. Admission $6 adults, $4.50 seniors, free for students and children under 14. Free Thurs 5–8pm. Tues–Sun 11am–5pm (Thurs until 8pm). Closed July 4, Thanksgiving, Christmas, and New Year's Day. Bus: 70.

Hiram M. Chittenden Locks ⭐   There is something oddly fascinating about locks. No, not the locks on doors, the locks that raise and lower boats. Locks don't provide panoramic views and they aren't nearly as dramatic as waterfalls, but for some strange reason, a lot of people are intrigued by the concept of two side-by-side bodies of water on two different levels. Consequently, the Hiram Chittenden Locks are among the most popular attractions in Seattle. These locks, operated by the Army Corps of Engineers, consist of a large lock and a small lock. The latter accommodates barges, large commercial fishing vessels, and the like, while the small lock stays busy shuttling small private boats (including sea kayaks) between the salt water of Puget Sound and the fresh water of the Lake Washington Ship Canal, which connects to both Lake Union and Lake Washington. It's a slow process locking boats back and forth, but none of the onlookers seem to mind, and people on shore and those on the boats often strike up conversations.

When the gates of the lock are closed, it's possible to continue to the far side of the ship canal to the fish ladders and fish-viewing windows that provide opportunities for salmon viewing during the summer months. The chance to see salmon in a fish ladder is as much of a draw as the locks themselves, and in the past the fish runs have also attracted hungry sea lions, which have become reg-ular salmon-swallowing pests.

Also here at the locks, you can stroll the grounds of the Carl S. English, Jr., Ornamental Gardens, a city park filled with rare and unusual shrubs and trees. See "Public Gardens" below for details.

The locks are located a 10- to 15-minute drive north of downtown. To reach the locks, follow Elliott Avenue north along the waterfront from downtown Seattle; after crossing the Ballard Bridge, drive west on NW Market Street.

Hiram M. Chittenden Locks, 3015 NW 54th St. ⓒ **206/783-7059**. Free admission. Daily 7am–9pm (visitor center daily 10am–6pm). Closed Thanksgiving, Christmas Day, and New Year's Day. Bus: 17.

Museum of History and Industry (MOHAI) ⭐   If the Seattle Underground Tour's vivid description of life before the 1889 fire has you curious about what the city's more respectable citizens were doing back in those days, you can find out here, where re-created storefronts provide glimpses into their lives. Located at the north end of Washington Park Arboretum, this museum explores Seattle's history, with frequently changing exhibits on more obscure aspects of the city's past. While many of the displays will be of interest only to Seattle residents, any-one wishing to gain a better understanding of the history of the city and the Northwest may also enjoy the exhibits here. There's a Boeing mail plane from the 1920s, plus an exhibit on the 1889 fire that leveled the city. This museum also hosts touring exhibitions that address Northwest history. Although not actually in north Seattle, this museum is just across the Montlake Bridge from the University District.

McCurdy Park, 2700 24th Ave. E. ℂ 206/324-1126. www.seattlehistory.org. Admission $5.50 adults, $3 seniors and ages 6–12, $1 ages 2–5, free under 2. Daily 10am–5pm. Closed Thanksgiving and Christmas. From I-5, take Wash. 520 east (exit 168B) to the Montlake exit, go straight through the stoplight to 24th Ave. E., and turn left. Bus: 43.

Nordic Heritage Museum ✩ Housed in a former school building, this small structure is primarily a neighborhood museum that focuses on the experiences of Scandinavian immigrants in Seattle's Ballard neighborhood. But it also mounts exhibits of Scandinavian and Scandinavian-inspired art, and these temporary exhibits are what make this little museum worth seeking out for those who aren't of Scandinavian heritage. The *Dream of America* exhibit on the first floor does an excellent job of explaining why Scandinavians began immigrating to the United States and how they ended up settling in the Ballard neighborhood. Up on the third floor, each of the Nordic countries gets a display room of its own. In mid-July each year, the museum sponsors the Tivoli/Viking Days festival, which includes booths serving Nordic foods.

3014 NW 67th St. ℂ 206/789-5707. www.nordicmuseum.com. Admission $4 adults, $3 seniors, $2 students. Tues–Sat 10am–4pm, Sun noon–4pm. Closed Jan 1, Thanksgiving, Dec 24–25. Bus: 17.

Woodland Park Zoo ✩✩ *Kids* Located in north Seattle, this sprawling zoo has outstanding exhibits focusing on Alaska, tropical Asia, the African savanna, and the tropical rainforest. The brown bear enclosure, one of the zoo's best exhibits, is a very realistic reproduction of an Alaskan stream and hillside. In the savanna, zebras gambol and antelopes and giraffes graze contentedly near a reproduction of an African village. An elephant forest provides plenty of space for the zoo's pachyderms, and the gorilla and orangutan habitats are also very well done. There's even a large walk-through butterfly house ($1 additional fee) during the summer months. Don't miss the giant Komodo lizards from Indonesia. A farm animal area and petting zoo are big hits with the little ones.

601 N. 59th St. ℂ 206/684-4800. www.zoo.org. Admission $9.50 adults, $8.75 seniors and college students, $7 disabled and children ages 6–17, $4.25 ages 3–5, free for children 2 and under. Mar 15–Apr 30 and Sept 15–Oct 14 daily 9:30am–5pm; May 1–Sept 14 daily 9:30am–6pm; Oct 15–Mar 14 daily 9:30am–4pm. Parking $3.50. Bus: 5.

SOUTH SEATTLE

Museum of Flight *Kids* Located right next door to busy Boeing Field, 15 minutes south of downtown Seattle, this museum will have aviation buffs walking on air. Within the six-story glass-and-steel repository are displayed some of history's most famous planes.

To start things off, there's a replica of the Wright brothers' first glider, and from there the collection of planes brings you to the present state of flight. Suspended in the Great Hall are more than 20 planes, including a 1935 DC-3, the first Air Force F-5 supersonic fighter, and the Gossamer Condor, a human-powered airplane; plus there are some 34 other planes on display. You'll also see one of the famous Blackbird spy planes, which were once the world's fastest jets (and you can even sit in the cockpit of one of these babies). A rare World War II Corsair fighter rescued from Lake Washington and restored to its original glory is also on display. Visitors get to board the original Air Force One presidential plane, used by Eisenhower, and can sit in the cockpit of an F/A-18 Hornet fighter. An exhibit on the U.S. space program features an Apollo command module. Of course, you'll also see plenty of Boeing planes, including a reproduction of Boeing's first plane, which was built in 1916. The museum also incorporates part of Boeing's old wooden factory building from its early years.

While any air-and-space museum lets you look at mothballed planes, not many have their own air-traffic control tower and let you watch aircraft taking off and landing at an active airfield. During the summer months, biplane rides are usually offered from in front of the museum.

The **Museum of Flight Restoration Center** (© 425/745-5150) is located north of Seattle at Paine Field, which is near the city of Everett. Here you'll see planes in various stages of restoration. This center is open Tuesday through Thursday from 10am to 5pm. Call for directions. Paine Field is also where you'll find the Boeing Tour Center (see p. 135 for information on tours of the Boeing plant). Together these two make a fascinating half-day outing.

9404 E. Marginal Way S. © 206/764-5720. www.museumofflight.org. Admission $9.50 adults, $8.50 seniors, $5 ages 5–17, free for children under 5. Free first Thurs 5–9pm. Daily 10am–5pm (until 9pm on first Thurs of each month). Closed Thanksgiving and Christmas. Take exit 158 off I-5. Bus: 174.

THE EASTSIDE

Bellevue Art Museum (BAM) ✿ Located on the east side of Lake Washington, Bellevue is one of Seattle's most upscale suburbs and is about a 20- to 30-minute drive from downtown. In recent years the city has become less of a suburb and more of a city in its own right. The Bellevue Art Museum is one of the cultural underpinnings of this new-found Bellevue urbanism, with several large galleries that host shows and installations by regional and national artists. But it goes even further, giving the public ample opportunity to interact with artists. To this end, the museum stages each July the Northwest's largest and most highly regarded art fair. During the rest of the year, it features artists in residence and frequent artist demonstrations. The museum also has several classrooms in which art classes are held throughout the year. Stop by if you happen to be on the Eastside and are an art aficionado.

510 Bellevue Way NE, Bellevue. © 425/519-0770. www.bellevueart.org. Admission $6 adults, $4 seniors and students, free for children under 6. Free for everyone third Thurs of each month. Tues–Sat 10am–5pm (Thurs until 8pm), Sun noon–5pm. Closed New Year's Day, Easter, Memorial Day, July 4th, Labor Day, Thanksgiving, and Christmas. From Seattle, take Wash. 520 east over the Evergreen Point Bridge to I-405 south, then take exit 13A onto NE Fourth St., continue west, and then turn right onto Bellevue Way NE. Alternatively, take I-90 east over Lake Washington to the Bellevue Way exit, and drive north on Bellevue Way for approximately 2 miles.

Rosalie Whyel Museum of Doll Art ✿ If you're a doll collector or happen to be traveling with a small child, this Bellevue museum should definitely be part of your Seattle itinerary. Displays include more than 1,200 dolls from around the world, including 17th-century wooden dolls, 19th-century china dolls, and the original Barbie. Throughout the year, the museum has special exhibits that focus on different types of dolls.

1116 108th Ave. NE. © 425/455-1116. www.dollart.com. Admission $7 adults, $6 seniors, $5 children 5–17, free for children 4 and under. Mon–Sat 10am–5pm, Sun 1–5pm. Closed Jan 1, Easter, July 4, Thanksgiving, and Christmas. From Seattle, take Wash. 520 east over the Evergreen Point Bridge to I-405 south, then take the NE Eighth St. westbound exit and turn right on 108th Ave. NE.

Insider Tip

University of Washington campus parking is expensive on weekdays and Saturday mornings, so try to visit the Burke Museum or Henry Art Gallery on a Saturday afternoon or a Sunday, when parking is free.

5 Parks & Public Gardens

PARKS

Seattle's many parks are what make this such a livable city. In the downtown area, **Myrtle Edwards Park** ⭐, 3130 Alaska Way W. (© **206/684-4075**), at the north end of the waterfront, is an ideal spot for a sunset stroll with views of Puget Sound and the Olympic Mountains. The park includes a 1¼-mile paved pathway.

Freeway Park, at Sixth Avenue and Seneca Street, is one of Seattle's most unusual parks. Built right on top of busy Interstate 5, this green space is more a series of urban plazas, with terraces, waterfalls, and cement planters creating walls of greenery. You'd never know that a roaring freeway lies beneath your feet. Unfortunately, although the park is convenient, the isolated nature of its many nooks and crannies often gives it a deserted and slightly threatening feel.

For serious communing with nature, however, nothing will do but **Discovery Park** ⭐⭐, 3801 W. Government Way (© **206/386-4236**). Occupying a high bluff and sandy point jutting into Puget Sound, this is Seattle's largest and wildest park. You can easily spend a day wandering the trails and beaches here. The park's visitor center is open daily from 8:30am to 5pm. Discovery Park is a 15-minute drive from downtown; to reach the park, follow the waterfront north from downtown Seattle toward the Magnolia neighborhood and watch for signs to the park. When you reach the park, follow signed trails down to the beach and out to the lighthouse at the point. Although the lighthouse is not open to the public, the views from the beach make this a good destination for an hour's walk. The beach and park's bluff-top meadows both make good picnic spots.

Up on Capitol Hill, at East Prospect Street and 14th Avenue East, you'll find **Volunteer Park** ⭐⭐, 1247 15th Ave. E. (© **206/684-4075**), which is surrounded by the elegant mansions of Capitol Hill. It's a popular spot for sunning and playing Frisbee, and it's home to the Seattle Asian Art Museum (p. 123), an amphitheater, a water tower with a superb view of the city, and a conservatory filled with tropical and desert plants (p. 123). With so much variety, you can easily spend a morning or afternoon exploring this park.

On the east side of Seattle, along the shore of Lake Washington, you'll find not only swimming beaches but also **Seward Park** ⭐, 5898 Lake Washington Blvd. (© **206/684-4075**). This large park's waterfront areas may be its biggest attraction, but it also has a dense forest with trails winding through it. Keep an eye out for the bald eagles that nest here. This park is south of the I-90 floating bridge off Lake Washington Boulevard South. From downtown Seattle, follow Madison Street northeast to a right onto Lake Washington Boulevard.

In north Seattle, you'll find several parks worth visiting. These include the unique **Gasworks Park** ⭐, 2101 N. Northlake Way, at Meridian Avenue North (© **206/684-4075**), at the north end of Lake Union. In the middle of its green lawns, this park holds the rusting hulk of an old industrial plant, and the park's small Kite Hill is the city's favorite kite-flying spot. North of here, on Green Lake Way North near the Woodland Park Zoo, you'll find **Green Lake Park** ⭐⭐, 7201 E. Green Lake Dr. N. (© **206/684-4075**), which is a center for exercise buffs who jog, bike, and skate around the park on a 2.8-mile paved path. It's also possible to swim in the lake (there are changing rooms and a beach with summer lifeguards) and picnic on the many grassy areas. For information on renting in-line skates or a bike for riding the path here, see p. 137.

Fish Gotta Swim

It's no secret that salmon in the Puget Sound region have dwindled to dangerously low numbers in recent years. But it's still possible to witness the annual return of salmon in various spots in the sound.

In the autumn, on the waterfront, you can see returning salmon at the **Seattle Aquarium,** which has its own fish ladder. But the very best place to see salmon is at **Hiram M. Chittenden Locks,** 3015 NW 54th St. (© 206/783-7059; see listing above for directions to the locks and hours of operation). Between June and September (July and Aug are the peak months), you can view salmon through underwater observation windows as they leap up the locks' fish ladder. These locks, which are used primarily by small boats, connect Lake Union and Lake Washington with the waters of Puget Sound, and depending on the tides and lake levels, there is a difference of 6 to 26 feet on either side of the locks.

East of Seattle, in downtown Issaquah, salmon can be seen year-round at the **Issaquah Salmon Hatchery,** 125 Sunset Way (© **425/391-9094**). However, it is in October that adult salmon can be seen returning to the hatchery. Each year on the first weekend in October, the city of Issaquah holds a Salmon Days Festival to celebrate the return of the natives.

North of the Ballard neighborhood, you'll find **Golden Gardens** ★★, 8498 Seaview Place NW (© **206/684-4075**), which, with its excellent views of the Olympic Mountains and its somewhat wild feeling, is our favorite Seattle waterfront park. You'll find great views, some small wetlands, and a short trail. But Golden Gardens is best known as one of Seattle's best beaches, and even though the water here is too cold for swimming, the sandy beach is a pleasant spot for a sunset stroll. People often gather here on summer evenings to build fires on the beach. To reach this park, drive north from the waterfront on Elliott Avenue, which becomes 15th Avenue West; after crossing the Ballard Bridge, turn left on Market Street and follow this road for about 2 miles (it will change names to become NW 54th St. and then Seaview Ave. NW).

PUBLIC GARDENS

See also the listing for Volunteer Park Conservatory on p. 123.

Bellevue Botanical Gardens ★   Any avid gardener should be sure to make a trip across one of Seattle's two floating bridges to the city of Bellevue and the Bellevue Botanical Garden. Although this 36-acre garden only opened in 1992, it has matured very quickly to become one of the Northwest's most-talked-about perennial gardens. The summertime displays of flowers, in expansive mixed borders, are absolutely gorgeous. There are also a Japanese garden, a shade border, and a water-wise garden (designed to conserve water).

Wilburton Hill Park, 12001 Main St., Bellevue. © 425/452-2750. www.bellevuebotanical.org. Free admission. Daily 7:30am to dusk; visitor center daily 9am–4pm. Take the NE Eighth St. east exit off I-405.

Carl S. English, Jr. Ornamental Gardens   Located beside the Hiram M. Chittenden Locks in the Ballard neighborhood of north Seattle (a 10-min. drive north of downtown), this park is home to one of Seattle's prettiest little botanical gardens. Although relatively small, the gardens contain more than 500 species of plants.

Hiram M. Chittenden Locks, 3015 NW 54th St. © 206/783-7059. Free admission. Daily 7am–9pm (visitor center daily 10am–6pm).

Japanese Garden   Situated on 3½ acres of land, the Japanese Garden is a perfect little world unto itself, with babbling brooks, a lake rimmed with Japanese irises and filled with colorful koi (Japanese carp), and a cherry orchard (for spring color). A special Tea Garden encloses a Tea House, where, between April and October, on the third Saturday of each month at 1:30pm, you can attend a traditional tea ceremony. Unfortunately, noise from a nearby road can be distracting.

Washington Park Arboretum, 1075 Lake Washington Blvd. E. (north of E. Madison St.). © 206/684-4725. Admission $3 adults, $2 seniors and ages 6–18, free for children under 6. Mar–Nov daily 10am to dusk. Closed Dec–Feb. Bus: 11.

Kubota Garden ⭐   Located in south Seattle, a working-class neighborhood not far from the shores of Lake Washington, this 20-acre Japanese-style garden was the life's work of garden designer Fujitaro Kubota. Today the gardens are a city park, and the mature landscaping and hilly setting make this the most impressive and enjoyable Japanese garden in the Seattle area. Kubota began work on this garden in 1927, and over the years built a necklace of ponds, a traditional stroll garden, and a mountainside garden complete with waterfalls. A tall, arched moon bridge is a highlight. The self-taught Kubota went on to design gardens at Seattle University and at the Bloedel Reserve on Bainbridge Island. Free tours of the gardens are offered between April and October; call for details.

Renton Ave. S. and 55th Ave. S. © 206/725-5060. www.kubota.org. Free admission. Daily dawn to dusk. To reach the gardens from downtown, drive I-5 south to exit 158 (Pacific Hwy. S./E. Marginal Way), turn left toward Martin Luther King Jr. Way and continue uphill on Ryan Way; turn left on 51st Ave. S., right on Renton Ave. S., and right on 55th Ave. S.

Washington Park Arboretum ⭐   Acres of trees and shrubs stretch from the far side of Capitol Hill all the way to the Montlake Cut (a canal connecting Lake Washington to Lake Union). Within the 230-acre arboretum are 5,000 varieties of plants and quiet trails that are pleasant throughout the year but that become most beautiful in spring, when the azaleas, cherry trees, rhododendrons, and dogwoods are all in flower. The north end of the arboretum, a marshland that is home to ducks and herons, is popular with kayakers, canoeists (see p. 138 in "Outdoor Pursuits," below, for places to rent a canoe or kayak), and bird-watchers. A boardwalk with views across Lake Washington meanders along the waterside in this area (though noise from the adjacent freeway detracts considerably from the experience). Free tours are offered Saturday and Sunday at 1pm.

2300 Arboretum Dr. E. © 206/543-8800. http://depts.washington.edu/wpa/general.htm. Free admission. Daily 7am to dusk; Graham Visitors Center daily 10am–4pm. Enter on Lake Washington Blvd. off E. Madison St.; or take Wash. 520 off I-5 north of downtown, take the Montlake Blvd. exit, and go straight through the first intersection. Bus: 11, 43, or 48.

6 Especially for Kids

In addition to the listings below, kids will also enjoy many of the attractions described earlier in this chapter, including the **Pacific Science Center** (p. 117), the **Seattle Aquarium** (p. 113), the **IMAXDome Theater** (p. 113), **Odyssey** (p. 113), and the **Woodland Park Zoo** (p. 125).

Even the surliest teenagers will think you're pretty cool for taking them to the **Experience Music Project** (p. 116).

Adolescent and preadolescent boys seem to unfailingly love **Ye Olde Curiosity Shop** and the **Seattle Underground Tour** (see the "Good Times in Bad Taste" box on p. 115). Younger kids also love the **Museum of Flight** (p. 125).

When the kids need to burn off some energy, see section 5, "Parks & Gardens," above, for descriptions of Seattle's best recreational areas; section 8, "Outdoor Pursuits," later in this chapter, will give you the lowdown on beaches, biking, in-line skating, and more. You can also take the kids to a sporting event; Seattle supports professional football, basketball, and baseball teams. See section 9, "Spectator Sports," later in this chapter.

You might also be able to catch a performance at the **Seattle Children's Theatre** (© 206/441-3322; www.sct.org) in Seattle Center (see below); or at the **Northwest Puppet Center,** 9123 15th Ave. NE (© 206/523-2579; www. nwpuppet.org).

Children's Museum *(Kids)*   Seattle's Children's Museum is located in the basement of the Center House at Seattle Center, which is partly why Seattle Center is such a great place to spend a day with the kids. The museum includes plenty of hands-on cultural exhibits, a child-size neighborhood, a Discovery Bay for toddlers, a mountain wilderness area, a global village, and other special exhibits to keep the little ones busy learning and playing for hours.

305 Harrison St. at Center House in Seattle Center. © 206/441-1768. www.thechildrensmuseum.org. Admission $5.50 per person. Mon–Fri 10am–5pm, Sat–Sun 10am–6pm. Closed Thanksgiving, Christmas, and New Year's Day. Bus: 1, 2, 3, 4, 13, 15, 16, 18, 24, or 33. Monorail: From Westlake Center at the corner of Pine St. and Fourth Ave.

Seattle Center ★ *(Kids)*   If you want to keep the kids entertained all day long, head to Seattle Center. This 74-acre cultural center and amusement park stands on the northern edge of downtown at the end of the monorail line. The most visible building at the center is the **Space Needle** (p. 120), which provides an outstanding panorama of the city from its observation deck. However, of much more interest to children is the **Fun Forest** (© 206/728-1585), with its roller coaster, log flume, merry-go-round, Ferris wheel, arcade games, and minigolf. Seattle Center is also the site of the **Children's Museum** (see above) and **Seattle Children's Theatre** (© 206/441-3322; www.sct.org). This is Seattle's main festival site, and in the summer months hardly a weekend goes by without some special event filling its grounds. On hot summer days, the **International Fountain** is a great place for kids to keep cool (bring a change of clothes).

305 Harrison St. © 206/684-7200. www.seattlecenter.com. Free admission; pay per ride or game (various multiride tickets available). Fun Forest outdoor rides: mid-June to Labor Day Mon–Thurs noon–10 or 11pm; reduced days and hours other months (call for hours); indoor attractions open at 11am year-round. Bus: 1, 2, 3, 4, 13, 15, 16, 18, 24, or 33. Monorail: From Westlake Center at the corner of Pine St. and Fourth Ave.

7 Organized Tours

For information on the **Seattle Underground Tour,** see the box titled "Good Times in Bad Taste" on p. 115.

WALKING TOURS

In addition to the walking tours mentioned here, there are two different Pike Place Market tours offered by market organizations. See the Pike Place Market listing on p. 114 for details.

If you'd like to explore downtown Seattle with a knowledgeable guide, join one of the informative walking tours offered by **See Seattle Walking Tours** (© 425/226-7641; www.see-seattle.com). The tours visit Pike Place Market, the waterfront, the Pioneer Square district, and the International District. Tours cost $20 and can last a half day or a full day, depending on how much stamina you have.

You can also learn a lot about Seattle history and wander through hidden corners of the city on 2-hour tours run by **Duse McLean/Seattle Walking Tour** (© 425/885-3173). These tours start with a ride through the Bus Tunnel to the International District and then make their way back north to Pike Place Market, taking in historic buildings, public art, and scenic vistas. Tours are $15 per person and are offered year-round by reservation.

For an insider's glimpse of life in Seattle's International District, hook up with **Chinatown Discovery Tours** (© 425/885-3085; www.seattlechamber.com/chinatowntour). On these walking tours, which last from 1½ to 3 hours, you'll learn the history of this colorful and historic neighborhood. "A Touch of Chinatown" is a brief introduction to the neighborhood. The "Chinatown by Day" tour includes a six-course lunch. "Nibble Your Way Through Chinatown" provides a sampling of flavors from around the International District. The "Chinatown by Night" tour includes an eight-course banquet. Rates (for four or more on a tour) range from $14.95 to $38.95 per person (slightly higher for fewer than four people).

BUS TOURS

If you'd like an overview of Seattle's main tourist attractions, or if you're pressed for time during your visit, you can pack in a lot of sights on a tour with **Gray Line of Seattle** (© 800/426-7532 or 206/626-5208; www.graylineofseattle.com). Half-day tours are $29 for adults, $14.50 for children; full-day tours are $39 for adults, $19.50 for children. Many other tours, including tours to Mount Rainier National Park and to the Boeing plant in Everett, are also available.

June through mid-October, Gray Line also offers a **Trolley Tour** on a bus made up to look like an old trolley. The tour is really a day pass that allows you to use the trolley, which follows a set route that passes nearly all the major tourist attractions in downtown Seattle. The trolley stops at several places along the waterfront and at Seattle Center, Pike Place Market, the Seattle Art Museum, and Pioneer Square. Tickets are $17 for adults and $9 for children. Because buses in downtown are free and because both the Waterfront Streetcar and the monorail to Seattle Center cost no more than $1.25, the trolley is not a very good deal; but if you don't want to worry about finding the right bus stop, it's worth considering. A $36 family pass allows two adults and up to four children to use the trolley for 2 days. Gray Line also operates open-topped **double decker bus tours** of the city. These tours operate from May 1 to September 30 and cost $21 for adults and $11 for children. Buses depart from Seattle Center and the Seattle Sheraton Hotel and Towers.

A second company, **Double Decker Tours of Seattle** (© 800/403-0024), owned by Greyhound, operates seasonal double-decker buses on a fixed route around the city. There are seven stops where you can get on and off the bus. Basically, this is the same set-up as the Gray Line trolley tour. You buy your ticket ($17 adults, $6 seniors and children 12 and under, $34 family of four), and then you can get on and off the bus as often as you want throughout the day. Buses operate every 30 minutes between 8:30am and 8:30pm from late May to mid-September.

To glimpse a bit more of Seattle on a guided van tour, try the "Explore Seattle Tour" offered by **Customized Tours and Charter Service** (© 800/770-8769 or 206/878-3965: www.customizedtours.net), which charges $35 per person (half-price for children). This tour stops at Pike Place Market, Ballard Locks and Fish Ladder, and the Klondike Gold Rush Historical Park. The company also offers a Boeing plant tour ($40 per person, $30 per child) and a Snoqualmie Falls and wineries tour ($40 per person, four-person minimum except on Wed and Sat).

BOAT TOURS

In addition to the boat tours and cruises mentioned below, you can do your own low-budget cruise simply by hopping on one of the ferries operated by **Washington State Ferries** (© 800/84-FERRY or 888/808-7977 within Washington state, or 206/464-6400; www.wsdot.wa.gov/ferries/). Try the Bainbridge Island or Bremerton ferries out of Seattle for a 1½- to-2½-hour round-trip. There are both car ferries and foot ferries on the Bremerton run; the passenger-only ferries leave from the dock to the south of the car ferry terminal in Seattle. For more information on these ferries, see "Getting Around" in chapter 4, "Getting to Know Seattle."

If you don't have enough vacation time scheduled to fit in an overnight trip to the San Juan Islands, it's still possible to get a feel for these picturesque islands by riding the San Juan Islands ferry from Anacortes to Friday Harbor. These ferries depart from Anacortes, 75 miles north of Seattle. If you get off in Friday Harbor, you can spend a few hours exploring this town before returning to Anacortes. It's also possible to take the first ferry of the day from Anacortes, ride all the way to Sidney, British Columbia, and then catch the next ferry back to Anacortes. However, if you're doing this trip in 1 day, you won't have any time to spend in Victoria. Alternatively, if you have more money to spend (and even less time), boat tours of the San Juan Islands depart from the Seattle waterfront. For information on ferries and boat excursions to the San Juan Islands, see chapter 11.

For a boat excursion that includes a salmon dinner and Northwest Coast Indian masked dances, consider coughing up the cash for the **Tillicum Village Tour** ★★, Pier 55 (© 800/426-1205 or 206/933-8600; www.tillicumvillage. com). Located at Blake Island State Park across Puget Sound from Seattle and only accessible by tour boat or private boat, Tillicum Village was built in conjunction with the 1962 Seattle World's Fair. The "village" is actually just a large

---

Seattle by Duck

Paul Revere would have had a hard time figuring out what to tell his fellow colonists if the British had arrived by Duck. A Duck, if you didn't know, is a World War II vintage amphibious vehicle that can arrive by land or sea, and these odd-looking things are now being used to provide tours of Seattle both on land and water. Duck tours take in the standard Seattle sights but then plunge right into Lake Union for a tour of the Portage Bay waterfront, with its many houseboats and great views. Ninety-minute tours leave from near the Space Needle and cost $22 for adults and $12 for kids. Contact **Seattle Duck Tours** ★ (© 800/817-1116 or 206/441-DUCK; www.seattleducktours.net). Tours leave from a parking lot across from the Space Needle. Because these tours encourage Seattle visitors to get a little daffy while they're in town, they are very popular; reservations are recommended.

---

restaurant and performance hall fashioned after a traditional Northwest Coast longhouse, but with totem poles standing vigil out front, the forest encircling the longhouse, and the waters of Puget Sound stretching out into the distance, Tillicum Village is a beautiful spot. After the dinner and dances, you can strike out on forest trails to explore the island (you can return on a later boat if you want to spend a couple of extra hours hiking). There are even beaches on which to relax. Tours cost $65 for adults, $59 for seniors, $25 for children ages 5 to 12, and are free for children under age 5. Tours are offered daily from May through early October; other months on weekends only. If you can opt for only one tour while in Seattle, this should be it—it's unique and truly Northwestern, the salmon dinner is pretty good, and the traditional masked dances are fascinating (although more for the craftsmanship of the masks than for the dancing itself).

Seattle is a city surrounded by water, and if you'd like to see it from various aquatic perspectives, you can head out with **Argosy Cruises** ★ (© **800/642-7816** or 206/623-4252; www.argosycruises.com). Offerings include a 1-hour harbor cruise (departs from Pier 55; $12.75–$15.25 adults and $6–$7.50 children ages 5–12), a 2½-hour cruise through the Hiram Chittenden Locks to Lake Union (departs from Pier 56; $23–$27 adults and $9–$10 children ages 5–12), and two cruises around Lake Washington (a 2-hr. cruise departs from the AGC Marina at the south end of Lake Union, and a 1½-hr. cruise departs from downtown Kirk-land on the east side of the lake; $20–$24 adults and $8–$9 children ages 5–12). The latter two cruises will take you past the fabled Xanadu built by Bill Gates on the shore of Lake Washington. However, of all these options, we recommend the cruise through the locks; it may be the most expensive outing, but you get good views and the chance to navigate the locks.

Want a meal with your cruise? Try one of Argosy Cruises' lunch or dinner cruises aboard the *Royal Argosy* (lunch cruises: $34 adults, $15 children ages 5–12, $32 seniors; dinner cruises: $67 adults, $25 children ages 5–12, $65 seniors). These cruises get our vote for best dinners afloat. Reservations are recommended for all cruises.

Looking for a quieter way to see Seattle from the water? From May 1 to Octo-ber 15, **Emerald City Charters,** Pier 54 (© **800/831-3274** or 206/624-3931; www.sailingseattle.com), offers 1½- and 2½-hour sailboat cruises. The longer excursions are at sunset. Cruises are $23 to $38 for adults, $20 to $35 for seniors, and $18 to $30 for children under age 12.

For information on ferries and boat excursions to the San Juan Islands, see chapter 11.

VICTORIA EXCURSIONS

Among Seattle's most popular boat tours are day-long excursions to Victoria, British Columbia. These trips are offered by **Victoria Clipper** ★★, Pier 69, 2701 Alaskan Way (© **800/888-2535,** 206/448-5000, or 250/382-8100 in Victoria; www.victoriaclipper.com), and operate several times a day during the summer (once or twice a day in other months). The high-speed catamaran passenger ferry

Seattle Noir

If your tastes run to the macabre, you might be interested in the **Private Eye on Seattle tours** ⭐ ((C) 206/365-3739; www.privateeyetours.com) offered by Windsor Olson. These somewhat bizarre van tours are led by a retired private investigator who shares stories of the interesting and unusual cases he handled over his 40 years as a private eye in the Emerald City. Tours are $20 per person. To balance things out, Olson also offers a tour of some of Seattle's most distinctive churches ($25 per person) and of some of the city's haunted locales ($25 per person).

takes 2 to 3 hours to reach Victoria. If you leave on the earliest ferry, you can spend the better part of the day exploring Victoria and be back in Seattle for a late dinner. Round-trip fares range from $59 (7-day advance purchase) to $125 for adults, $59 (7-day advance purchase) to $115 for seniors, and $49.50 to $62.50 for children ages 1 to 11 (between Oct and mid-May, one child travels free with each adult paying for a 7-day advance-purchase round-trip fare). Some scheduled trips also stop in the San Juan Islands during the summer. Various tour packages are also available, including an add-on tour to Butchart Gardens. Overnight trips can also be arranged.

You can also fly to Victoria from Seattle in a floatplane operated by **Kenmore Air** ((C) 800/543-9595; www.kenmoreair.com). Flights take only 45 minutes, which leaves plenty of time to explore Victoria and still make it back to Seattle in time for dinner. The round-trip fare is $169 per person and includes either a tour of Butchart Gardens, tea at the Empress Hotel, a credit for a treatment at the Empress Hotel Spa, or a discounted whale-watching excursion. You can sometimes even get these flights for half price at **Ticket/Ticket** ((C) 206/324-2744), which has locations in Pike Place Market (First Ave. and Pike St.; open Tues–Sun noon–6pm), on Capitol Hill at the Broadway Market (401 Broadway E.; open Tues–Sat noon–7pm and Sun noon–6pm), and in Bellevue at the Meydendbauer Center (NE Sixth St. and 112th Ave.; open Tues–Sun noon–6pm).

For more information on Victoria, pick up a copy of *Frommer's Vancouver & Victoria.*

SCENIC FLIGHTS & HOT-AIR BALLOON RIDES

Seattle is one of the few cities in the United States where floatplanes are a regular sight in the skies and on the lakes. If you'd like to see what it's like to take off and land from the water, you've got a couple of options. **Seattle Seaplanes** ⭐, 1325 Fairview Ave. E. ((C) 800/637-5553 or 206/329-9638; www.seattleseaplanes.com), which takes off from the southeast corner of Lake Union, offers 20-minute scenic flights over the city for $67.50.

If you'd rather pretend you're back in the days of *The English Patient*, you can go up in a vintage biplane with **Olde Thyme Aviation** ⭐ ((C) 206/730-1412; www.oldethymeaviation.com), which operates from Boeing Field. Flights are offered on sunny weekends, and, if you have a gift certificate, weekday flights can also be arranged (weather permitting). A 20-minute flight along the Seattle waterfront to the Space Needle costs $99 for two people; other flights range in price from $149 to $395 for two people.

Seattle really isn't known as a hot-air ballooning center, but if you'd like to try floating over the Northwest landscape not far outside the city, contact **Over the**

Rainbow (© 206/364-0995; www.letsgoballooning.com), which flies over the wineries of the Woodinville area. Flights are offered both in the morning and in the afternoon and cost $135 to $165 per person.

A RAILWAY EXCURSION

If you're a fan of riding the rails, consider the **Spirit of Washington Dinner Train,** 625 S. Fourth St., Renton (© 800/876-7245 or 425/227-RAIL; www. spiritofwashingtondinnertrain.com). Running from Renton, at the south end of Lake Washington, to the Columbia Winery near Woodinville, at the north end of Lake Washington, this train rolls past views of the lake and Mount Rainier. Along the way, you're fed a filling lunch or dinner. At the turnaround point, you get to tour a winery and taste some wines. Dinner tours range from $60 to $75; lunch tours range from $50 to $65. The higher prices are for seatings in the dome car, which definitely offers finer views.

THE BOEING TOUR ★★

Until Bill Gates and Microsoft came to town, Boeing was the largest employer (by far) in the Seattle area. Although the company announced in 2001 that it was moving its corporate headquarters out of Seattle, Boeing is still a major presence in the city, and it still has something that Microsoft can never claim: the single largest building, by volume, in the world. This building, the company's Everett assembly plant, could easily hold 911 basketball courts, 74 football fields, 2,142 average-size homes, or all of Disneyland (with room left over for covered parking). Tours of the building let you see just how they put together the huge passenger jets that travelers take for granted.

The tours are quite fascinating and well worth the time it takes to get here from downtown Seattle. Guided 1-hour tours of the facility are held Monday through Friday throughout the year. The schedule varies with the time of year, so call ahead for details and directions to the plant. Tours cost $5 for adults and $3 for seniors and children under 16 who meet the height requirement (minimum of 50 in. tall). Tickets for same-day use are sold on a first-come, first-served basis beginning at 8am (8:30am Oct–May); in summer, tickets for any given day's tours usually sell out by noon. To check availability of same-day tickets, call the **Everett Tour Center,** Wash. 526, Everett, WA (© 425/342-8500; www.boeing.com/company offices/aboutus/tours/) between 8:30am and 2pm. It is also possible to make reservations 24 hours or more in advance by calling © 800/464-1476 or 206/544-1264 between noon and 3pm Monday through Friday. However, when making reservations, you'll pay $10 per person regardless of age. Everett is roughly 30 miles north of Seattle (a 30- to 45-min. drive) off I-5.

If you're in town without a car, you can book a tour to the plant through **Customized Tours and Charter Service** (© 800/770-8769 or 206/878-3965), which charges $40 and will pick you up at your Seattle hotel.

8 Outdoor Pursuits

See section 5, "Parks & Public Gardens," earlier in this chapter, for a rundown of great places to play.

BEACHES

Alki (rhymes with *sky*) **Beach** ★, across Elliott Bay from downtown Seattle, is the city's most popular beach and is the nearest approximation you'll find in the Northwest to a Southern California beach scene. The paved path that runs along this 2½-mile-long beach is popular with skaters, walkers, and cyclists; and the road that parallels the beach is lined with shops, restaurants, and beachy houses and apartment buildings. But the views across Puget Sound to the Olympic Mountains confirm that this is indeed the Northwest. Despite the views, this beach lacks the greenery that makes some of the city's other beaches so much more appealing. A water taxi operates between the downtown Seattle waterfront and Alki Beach (see "Getting Around" in chapter 4, "Getting to Know Seattle," for details).

For a more Northwestern beach experience (which usually includes a bit of hiking or walking), head to one of the area's many waterfront parks. **Lincoln Park,** 8011 Fauntleroy Ave. SW, south of Alki Beach in West Seattle, has bluffs and forests backing the beach. Northwest of downtown Seattle in the Magnolia area, you'll find **Discovery Park** ★★, 3801 W. Government Way (© **206/386-4236**), where miles of beaches are the primary destination of most park visitors. To reach Discovery Park, follow Elliott Avenue north along the waterfront from downtown Seattle, then take the Magnolia Bridge west toward the Magnolia neighborhood and follow Grayfield Street to Galer Street to Magnolia Boulevard.

Golden Gardens Park ★★, 8499 Seaview Place NW, which is located north of Ballard and Shilshole Bay, is our favorite Seattle beach park. Although the park isn't very large and is backed by railroad tracks, the views of the Olympic Mountains are magnificent, and on summer evenings people build fires on the beach. Lawns and shade trees make this park ideal for a picnic.

Several parks along the shores of Lake Washington have small stretches of beach, many of which are actually popular with hardy swimmers. **Seward Park** ★, 5898 Lake Washington Blvd., southeast of downtown Seattle, is a good place to hang out by the water and do a little swimming. To reach this park from downtown, take Madison Street east to Lake Washington Boulevard and turn right. Although this isn't the most direct route to Mount Baker Beach or Seward Park, it's the most scenic. Along the way, you'll pass plenty of other small parks.

BIKING

Gregg's Green Lake Cycle, 7007 Woodlawn Ave. NE (© **206/523-1822**); and the **Bicycle Center,** 4529 Sand Point Way NE (© **206/523-8300**), both rent bikes by the hour, day, or week. Rates range from $3 to $7 per hour and $15 to $30 per day. These shops are both convenient to the **Burke-Gilman/Sammamish River Trail** ★★, a 27-mile paved pathway created mostly from an old railway bed. This path is immensely popular and is a great place for a family bike ride or to get in a long, vigorous ride without having to deal with traffic. The Burke-Gilman portion of this trail starts in the Ballard neighborhood of north Seattle, but the most convenient place to start a ride is at **Gasworks Park** on the north shore of Lake Union. From here you can ride north and east, by way of the University of Washington, to **Kenmore Logboom Park** at the north end of Lake Washington. Serious riders can then continue on from Kenmore Logboom Park on the Sammamish River portion of the trail, which leads to the north end of Lake Sammamish and Marymoor Park, which is the site of a velodrome (a bicycle racetrack). This latter half of the trail is our favorite portion of a ride along this trail. This section of the path follows the Sammamish River and passes through several pretty parks. Riding the entire trail out and back is a 54-mile round-trip popular with riders in training for races. Plenty of great picnicking spots can be found along both trails.

The west Seattle bike path along **Alki Beach** is another good place to ride and offers great views of the sound and the Olympics. If you'd like to pedal this pathway, you can rent single-speed bikes at **Alki Crab & Fish Co.,** 1660 Harbor Ave. SW (𝓒 **206/938-0975**), which charges $10 for a 3-hour rental. Because this place has a limited number of bikes, it's a good idea to call ahead and make a reservation. You can then take the water taxi from the downtown waterfront to West Seattle. The water taxi dock is right at Alki Crab & Fish Co.

GOLF

While Seattle isn't a name that springs immediately to mind when folks think of golf, the sport is just as much a passion here as it is all across the country these days. Should you wish to get in a round of golf while you're in town, Seattle has three conveniently located municipal golf courses: **Jackson Park Golf Course,** 1000 NE 135th St. (𝓒 **206/363-4747**); **Jefferson Park Golf Course,** 4101 Beacon Ave. S. (𝓒 **206/762-4513**); and **West Seattle Golf Course,** 4470 35th Ave. SW (𝓒 **206/935-5187**). All three charge very reasonable greens fees of $28 to $30. For information on the Web, check out **www.seattlegolf.com.**

HIKING

Within Seattle itself, there are several large nature parks laced with enough trails to allow for a few good long walks. Among these are **Seward Park,** 5898 Lake Washington Blvd., southeast of downtown; and **Lincoln Park,** 8011 Fauntleroy Ave. SW, south of Alki Beach in West Seattle. However, the city's largest natural park and Seattleites' favorite quick dose of nature is **Discovery Park,** 3801 W. Government Way (𝓒 **206/386-4236**), northwest of downtown at the western tip of the Magnolia neighborhood. This park covers more than 500 acres and has many miles of trails and beaches to hike—not to mention gorgeous views, forest paths, and meadows for lazing in after a long walk. To reach Discovery Park, follow Elliott Avenue north along the waterfront from downtown Seattle, then take the Magnolia Bridge west toward the Magnolia neighborhood and follow Grayfield Street to Galer Street to Magnolia Boulevard.

For more challenging hiking in the real outdoors, head east of Seattle on I-90. Rising abruptly from the floor of the Snoqualmie Valley outside the town of North Bend is **Mount Si** ✦✦, with an exhausting trail to its summit but a payoff of awesome views (take lots of water—it's an 8-mile round-trip hike). From I-90, take the North Bend exit (exit 31), drive into town, turn right at the stoplight onto North Bend Way, continue through town, turn left onto Mount Si Road, and continue 2.1 miles to the trail head.

Farther east on I-90, at **Snoqualmie Pass** and just west of the pass, are several trail heads. Some trails lead to mountain summits, others to glacier-carved lakes, and still others past waterfalls deep in the forest. Because of their proximity to Seattle, these trails can be very crowded, and you will need a Northwest Forest Pass ($5 for a 1-day pass) to leave your car at national forest trail heads (though not at the Mount Si trail head, which is on state land). For more information and to purchase a Northwest Forest Pass, contact the **Snoqualmie Ranger District** (𝓒 **425/888-1421**) in North Bend.

IN-LINE SKATING

The city has dozens of miles of paved paths that are perfect for skating. You can rent in-line skates at **Greg's Green Lake Cycle,** 7007 Woodlawn Ave. NE (𝓒 **206/523-1822**), for $7 to $10 per hour. The trail around **Green Lake** in north Seattle and the **Burke-Gilman/Sammamish River Trail** (see the description under "Biking," above) are both good places for skating and are convenient to Gregg's. Other favorite skating spots to try include the paved path in **Myrtle**

Edwards Park just north of the Seattle waterfront, the paved path along **Lake Washington Boulevard** north of Seward Park, and the **Alki Beach** pathway in West Seattle.

JOGGING

The waterfront, from **Pioneer Square north to Myrtle Edwards Park,** where a paved path parallels the water, is a favorite downtown jogging route. The residential streets of **Capitol Hill,** when combined with roads and sidewalks through **Volunteer Park,** are another good choice. If you happen to be staying in the University District, you can access the 27-mile-long **Burke-Gilman/ Sammamish River Trail** or run the ever-popular trail around **Green Lake.** Out in West Seattle, the **Alki Beach** pathway is also very popular and provides great views of the Olympics.

SEA KAYAKING, CANOEING, ROWING & SAILING

If you'd like to try your hand at **sea kayaking** ✿✿, try the **Northwest Outdoor Center** ✿✿, 2100 Westlake Ave. N. (© **800/683-0637** or 206/281-9694; www.nwoc.com), which is located on the west side of Lake Union. Here you can rent a sea kayak for between $10 and $15 per hour. You can also opt for guided tours lasting from a few hours to several days, and there are plenty of classes available for those who are interested.

Moss Bay Rowing and Kayak Center, 1001 Fairview Ave. N. (© **206/682-2031;** www.mossbay.net), rents sea kayaks (as well as canoes, pedal boats, and sailboats) at the south end of Lake Union near Chandler's Cove. Rates range from $10 per hour for a single to $15 per hour for a double. Because this rental center is a little closer to downtown Seattle, it makes a better choice if you are here without a car.

The **University of Washington Waterfront Activities Center,** on the university campus behind Husky Stadium (© **206/543-9433**), is open to the public and rents canoes and rowboats for $6.50 per hour. With the marshes of the Washington Park Arboretum directly across a narrow channel from the boat launch, this is an ideal place for beginner canoeists to rent a boat.

In this same general area, you can rent kayaks at the **Agua Verde Paddle Club,** 1303 NE Boat St. (© **206/545-8570;** www.aguaverde.com), which is at the foot of Brooklyn Avenue on Portage Bay (the body of water between Lake Union and Lake Washington). Kayaks can be rented from March through October and go for $10 to $15 per hour. Best of all, this place is part of the Agua Verde Café, a great Mexican restaurant! Before or after a paddle, be sure to get an order of tacos. See chapter 6, "Where to Dine in Seattle," for details.

At the **Green Lake Small Craft Center,** 5900 W. Green Lake Way N. (© **206/ 527-0171**), in north Seattle not far from the Woodland Park Zoo, you can rent canoes, paddleboats, and rowboats for a bit of leisurely time on the water. This park also has a paved path around it and is one of Seattle's most popular parks (a great place to join crowds of locals enjoying one of the city's nicest green spaces). Kayaks rent for $10 to $12 per hour, sailboats are $14 per hour, and canoes, rowboats, and paddleboats are $10 per hour.

For information on renting wooden rowboats and sailboats on Lake Union, see the **Center for Wooden Boats** listing on p. 116.

SKIING

One of the reasons Seattleites put up with long, wet winters is because they can go skiing within an hour of the city, and with many slopes set up for night skiing, it's possible to leave work and be on the slopes before dinner, ski for several hours, and be home in time to get a good night's rest. The ski season in the Seattle area generally runs from mid-November to the end of April. Equipment can be rented at the ski area listed below, and at **REI,** 222 Yale Ave. N. (© **206/223-1944**).

CROSS-COUNTRY SKIING In the Snoqualmie Pass area of the Cascade Range, less than 50 miles east of Seattle on I-90, the **Summit Nordic Center** (© **425/434-7669** ext. 4531, or 425/434-6708; www.summitnordic.com), offers rentals, instruction, and many miles of groomed trails.

There are also several sno-parks along I-90 at Snoqualmie Pass. Some have groomed trails; others have trails that are marked but not groomed. When renting skis, be sure to get a **sno-park permit** ($8 for a 1 day pass; $20 season pass). These are required if you want to park at a cross-country ski area. Sno-park permits are available at ski shops.

DOWNHILL SKIING Jointly known as **The Summit at Snoqualmie,** Alpental, Summit West, Summit Central, and Summit East ski areas (© **425/ 434-7669** for information, or 206/236-1600 for the snow report; www.summit-at-snoqualmie.com) are all located at Snoqualmie Pass, less than 50 miles east of Seattle off I-90. Together, these four ski areas offer more than 65 ski runs, rentals, and lessons. Adult all-day lift ticket prices range from $30 to $38 for adults. Call for hours of operation.

TENNIS

Seattle Parks and Recreation operates dozens of outdoor tennis courts all over the city. The most convenient are at **Volunteer Park,** 1247 15th Ave. E. (at E. Prospect St.), and at **Lower Woodland Park,** 5851 W. Green Lake Way N.

If it happens to be raining and you had your heart set on playing tennis, there are indoor public courts at the **Seattle Tennis Center,** 2000 Martin Luther King Jr. Way S. (© **206/684-4764**). Rates here are $16 for singles and $21 for doubles for 1¼ hours. This center also has outdoor courts for $6 for 1½ hours.

9 Spectator Sports

With professional football, baseball, basketball, women's basketball, and ice hockey teams, as well as the various University of Washington Huskies teams, Seattle is definitely a city of sports fans. For those many fans, the sports landscape has been changing dramatically in recent years. In 1999, a stunningly beautiful, state-of-the-art baseball stadium was unveiled in the form of the retractable-roof Safeco Field. In 2000, the venerable and much disparaged Kingdome was demolished to make way for a new football stadium, which opened just in time to kick off the Seattle Seahawks' 2002 season.

Ticketmaster (© **206/622-HITS;** www.ticketmaster.com) sells tickets to almost all sporting events in the Seattle area. You'll find Ticketmaster outlets at area Rite-Aid, Wherehouse, and Tower record and video stores. If they're sold out, try **Pacific Northwest Ticket Service** (© **800/281-0753** or 206/232-0150; www.nwtickets.com).

BASEBALL

Of all of Seattle's major league sports teams, none are more popular than the American League's **Seattle Mariners** (© **800/MY-MARINERS** or 206/346-4000; www.mariners.org). In 2001, egged on by the fans' obsession with Japanese player Ichiro Suzuki, the Mariners won at an astounding clip, tying the 1906 Chicago Cubs for the most regular-season wins in baseball history. The team has a devoted following, so you can expect tickets to be hard to find unless you buy yours well in advance.

The Mariners' retro-style **Safeco Field** ★★★ is indisputably one of the most gorgeous ballparks in the country. It's also one of only a handful of stadiums with a retractable roof (which can open or close in 10–20 min.), allowing the Mariners a real grass playing field without the worry of getting rained out.

Ticket prices range from $6 to $40. Though you may be able to get a single ticket on game day at the Safeco Field box office, that's about all (it would be tough to get two seats together). Mariners' tickets are a hot commodity, so if you want to ensure that you get good seats, order in advance at Mariners Team Stores (see below), or through Ticketmaster (© **206/622-HITS;** www.ticketmaster. com), which has outlets at many Rite-Aid pharmacies, as well as Wherehouse and Tower record stores. Parking is next to impossible in the immediate vicinity of Safeco Field, so plan to leave your car behind.

If you'd like a behind-the-scenes look at the stadium, you can take a **1-hour tour** ($7 adults, $5 seniors, and $3 kids ages 3–12); tickets can be purchased at the Mariners Team Store at Safeco Field, other Mariners Team Stores around the city (there are locations at Fourth and Stewart sts. downtown and in Bellevue Sq.), or through Ticketmaster. Tour times vary, and tours are not offered on days when day games are scheduled.

BASKETBALL

The NBA's **Seattle SuperSonics** (© **800/4NBA-TIX** or 206/283-3865; www. supersonics.com) play in the Key Arena at Seattle Center, and though they always seem to trail behind the Portland Trailblazers, they generally put in a good showing every season. Tickets are $11 to $110 and are available at the arena box office and through Ticketmaster (© **206/628-0888**). Tickets can generally be had even on short notice, except for games against the Lakers and Blazers, which are always well attended.

The University of Washington Huskies women's basketball team has been pretty popular for years, and Seattle also has a pro women's basketball team. The Women's National Basketball Association's (WNBA) **Seattle Storm** (© **206/ 217-WNBA;** www.storm.wnba.com) brings professional women's basketball to Seattle's Key Arena. Ticket prices range from $8 to $44 and are available at the arena box office and through Ticketmaster (© **206/628-0888**).

For information on the women's and men's Huskies basketball games, contact **University of Washington Sports** (© **206/543-2200;** www.gohuskies.com).

FOOTBALL

Although the NFL's **Seattle Seahawks** (© **888/NFL-HAWK** or 206/682-2800; www.seahawks.com) aren't the most highly regarded of Seattle's professional sports teams, the people of Washington State obviously didn't want to see the Seahawks leave town, or they wouldn't have voted to tax themselves in order to build a new stadium. By the time you read this, the Seahawks will have begun playing in their new stadium, which stands on the site of the old Kingdome. Tickets run $20 to $62 and are generally available, depending on how well the team is doing. Games against Oakland, Denver, and a couple of other teams usually sell out as soon as tickets first go on sale in August. Traffic and parking in the vicinity of the new stadium will likely be a nightmare on game days, so take the bus if you can.

Not surprisingly, the **University of Washington Huskies** (© **206/543-2200;** www.gohuskies.com), who play in Husky Stadium on the university campus, have a loyal following. Big games (Nebraska or Washington State) sell out as soon as tickets go on sale in the summer. Other games can sell out in advance, but obstructed-view tickets are usually available on game day. Ticket prices range from $32 to $36 for reserved seats and from $16 to $18 for general admission.

HOCKEY

The Western Hockey League's **Seattle Thunderbirds** (© **206/448-PUCK;** www.seattle-thunderbirds.com) play Major Junior–level ice hockey at the Key Arena in Seattle Center. While Seattle isn't really a hockey town, the Thunderbirds have quite a following. Tickets, which range in price from $8 to $20, are available by calling the above number or Ticketmaster (© **206/628-0888**).

HORSE RACING

The state-of-the-art **Emerald Downs,** 2300 Emerald Downs Dr. (© **888/931-8400** or 253/288-7711; www.emeralddowns.com), is located south of Seattle in the city of Auburn off Wash. 167 (reached from I-405 at the south end of Lake Washington). To get to the racetrack, take the 15th Avenue NW exit. Admission prices range from $4 to $6.50. The season runs from mid-April to mid-September.

MARATHON

The **Seattle Marathon** (© **206/729-3660** or 206/729-3661; www.seattle marathon.org) takes place the Sunday after Thanksgiving. The race starts and ends at Seattle Center and crosses the I-90 floating bridge to Mercer Island.

SOCCER

If you're a soccer fan, you can catch the United Soccer League's **Seattle Sounders** play (© **800/796-KICK** or 206/622-3415; www.seattlesounders.net) at Seattle Center's Memorial Stadium. However, at press time, the team was negotiating to play at the new Seahawks Stadium. Tickets are $8 to $15 and are available through Ticketmaster (© **206/628-0888**).

10 Day Spas

If you prefer pampering to paddling a kayak, facials to fishing, or massages to mountain climbing, then you'll be glad to know that Seattle has plenty of day spas scattered around the metro area. These facilities offer such treatments as massages, facials, seaweed wraps, mud baths, and the like. Seattle day spas include **Aveda,** in the Alexis Hotel, 1015 First Ave. (© **206/628-9605**); **Gene Juarez Salons,** 607 Pine St. (© **206/326-6000;** www.genejuarez.com); **Marketplace Salon and Day Spa,** 2001 First Ave. (© **206/441-5511**); and **Ummelina,** 1525 Fourth Ave. (© **206/624-1370;** www.ummelina.com). A wide variety of treatments are available. Expect to pay $160 to $250 for a half day of pampering and $350 to $450 or more for a full day.

8

Strolling Around Seattle

Downtown Seattle is compact and easily explored on foot (if you don't mind hills). The most popular strolling spot in the city is along the waterfront from Pioneer Square to Pike Place Market. Everything along the waterfront is right there to be seen, so you don't really need us to outline a walking tour of the waterfront for you.

Although you can easily enjoy Pike Place Market simply by getting lost in the market maze for several hours, you might want to consult the walking tour we've outlined here just so you don't miss any of the market's highlights.

Some people make the mistake of dismissing the Pioneer Square area as a neighborhood of winos and street people, but it is much more than that. To help you get the most out of downtown Seattle's only historic neighborhood, we've outlined a walking tour that takes in interesting shops, art galleries, and historic buildings.

The third walking tour will take you through the Fremont District. Home to counterculture types, Fremont is a quirky area filled with tongue-in-cheek art and unusual shops.

WALKING TOUR 1 · PIKE PLACE MARKET

Start:	At the corner of Pike Street and First Avenue.
Finish:	At the corner of Pike Street and First Avenue.
Time:	Approximately 4 hours, including shopping and dining.
Best Times:	Weekends, when crafts vendors set up along Pike Place.
Worst Times:	Weekends, when the market is extremely crowded.

Despite the crowds of tourists and locals, Pike Place Market, a sprawling complex of historic buildings and open-air vendors' stalls, remains Seattle's most fascinating attraction. You'll find aisles lined with fresh produce, cut flowers, and all manner of seafood, as well as unusual little shops tucked away in the many hidden corners of this multilevel maze. Dozens of street performers work here at the market on a regular basis. As you wander around, keep an eye and an ear out for the New Age pianist, the doo-wop group, and the paper-cone man, all of whom are long-time market favorites.

Because Pike Place Market is so large, it is easy to overlook some of its more interesting businesses and its many quirky works of public art. The following walking tour is meant to lead you through the market past the many places we think you wouldn't want to miss. We're sure you'll find lots of other places that will become your own favorites, so don't be afraid to poke into nooks and crannies as you wander through the market. For more information on the market, see "Pike Place Market to Pioneer Square" in chapter 7, "Exploring Seattle."

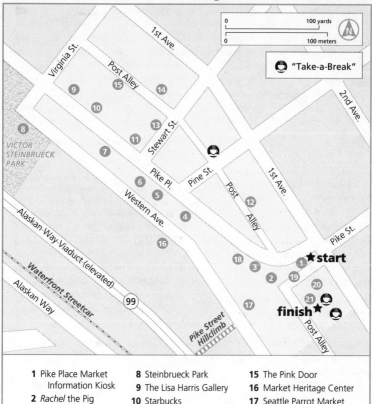

0   100 yards
0   100 meters

🍵 "Take-a-Break"

★ start
finish ★

1 Pike Place Market Information Kiosk
2 *Rachel* the Pig
3 Pike Place Fish
4 Produce stalls
5 Chukar Cherries
6 Mick's Peppourri
7 Crafts vendors
8 Steinbrueck Park
9 The Lisa Harris Gallery
10 Starbucks
11 Le Panier
12 Made in Washington
13 Antiques at Pike Place
14 The Glass Eye Studio
15 The Pink Door
16 Market Heritage Center
17 Seattle Parrot Market
18 The Magic Shop
19 The Garlic Garden
20 DeLaurenti
21 Giant Squid

Start your tour at the corner of Pike Street and First Avenue at the:

❶ Pike Place Market Information Kiosk

This tiny cubicle is one of the most important little buildings in the market. Not only does the kiosk have maps of the market, but it also doubles as the Ticket/Ticket half-price, day-of-show ticket center. Scan the list of tickets available for the day and you can save a bundle on your vacation. This ticket booth even sells half-price tickets for boat tours and floatplane flights to Victoria, Canada.

Directly behind the information kiosk rises the famous Pike Place Market neon sign and clock. Directly below this sign you'll find:

❷ *Rachel* the Pig

This life-size bronze statue of a pig is the unofficial Pike Place Market mascot and also doubles as the market piggy bank. Each year people deposit thousands of dollars into *Rachel*. Hardly any visitor to the market goes home without a shot of some friend or family member sitting on *Rachel*.

It's sometimes difficult to spot *Rachel* because of the crowds that gather here to watch the flying fish at:

❸ Pike Place Fish

The antics of the fishmongers at Pike Place Fish are legendary. No, they don't actually sell flying fish, but if you decide to buy, say, a whole salmon, your fish will go flying through the air (amid much shouting and gesticulating) from the front of the stall to the back, where someone will steak it or fillet it for you and even pack it on dry ice so that you can take it home with you on the plane.

To the right of Pike Place Fish begin the market's main:

❹ Produce stalls

In summer, look for fresh cherries, berries, peaches, and melons. In the fall, it's Washington State apples. Stalls full of colorful cut flowers also line this section of the market.

As you wander through this crowded section of the market, keep an eye out for:

❺ Chukar Cherries

This Washington State candy company specializes in chocolate-covered dried cherries; samples are always available (✆ 206/623-8043).

Also watch for:

❻ Mick's Peppourri

Mick's makes delicious pepper jellies that range from mild to fiery. These jellies go great with cream cheese and crackers or fresh bread from the market. Of course, you can sample the jellies (✆ 206/233-0128).

A little farther along, you'll come to the North Arcade, where you'll find lots of:

❼ Crafts vendors

This is a good place to shop for handmade souvenirs. These craftspeople know their market, so most of the work here is small enough to fit in a suitcase.

On weekends, you'll find more crafts vendors along this side of the street just past the end of the covered market stalls. Across Western Avenue from the last of these outdoor crafts stalls, you'll find:

❽ Steinbrueck Park

Although this small, grassy park is favored by the homeless, it is also home to a pair of impressive totem poles and offers a superb view of Elliott Bay. Watch for the comings and goings of the giant car ferries that link Seattle to Bainbridge Island and Bremerton on the far side of Puget Sound.

From the park, walk back across Western Avenue and Pike Place and head back toward your starting point. You'll now be on the opposite side of Pike Place from the produce vendors' stalls. This stretch of the market has lots of great prepared food stalls, so be sure to do a little grazing. If you've become convinced that Pike Place Market is strictly for tourists, climb the stairs to:

❾ The Lisa Harris Gallery

This art gallery, at 1922 Pike Place (✆ 206/443-3315), always seems to have interesting contemporary artwork, largely done by artists from the Northwest.

A little way up the street you'll find the very first:

❿ Starbucks

That's right, it all started right here in this narrow space, at 1912 Pike Place (✆ 206/448-8762). Unlike today's Starbucks, this espresso bar has no tables or chairs; it's strictly a grab-it-and-go kind of place. Since you've already been on your feet for a while and still have a lot of the market to see, you may want to stop in and order a grande mocha to see you through the rest of your walking tour.

How about a little something tasty to go with that mocha?

⓫ Le Panier

Located at 1902 Pike Place (✆ 206/441-3669), this French-style bakery has good croissants and other pastries to go with your espresso. There are also breads to go with that pepper jelly you bought.

Continue along Pike Place in the same direction for another 2 blocks, passing several more prepared-food stalls, and then turn left into Post Alley. This narrow lane cuts through several blocks of the market, and many shops and restaurants open onto it. For Seattle souvenirs, it's hard to beat:

⑫ Made in Washington

Shortly after you start up Post Alley, you'll come to this store, which has smoked salmon, prepared foods, crafts, books, and plenty of other inexpensive stuff from here in Washington (📞 **206/467-0788**).

TAKE A BREAK
Pike Place Market is full of surprises, not least of which are the many excellent restaurants hidden away in quiet corners of the complex. One of our very favorites is **Café Campagne**, 1600 Post Alley (📞 **206/728-2233**), a classy little French cafe serving delicious lunches. The atmosphere is *très* French. Don't confuse this restaurant with the much more expensive and formal Campagne, which is above the cafe.

Continue up the alley, and at Stewart Street, just downhill on the north side of the street, you'll see:

⑬ Antiques at Pike Place

This large antiques mall, at 92 Stewart St. (📞 **206/441-9643**), has more than 80 dealers. The stalls are packed full of interesting collectibles.

Back on Post Alley, you'll come to:

⑭ The Glass Eye Studio

No, this gallery, at 1902 Post Alley (📞 **206/441-3221**), does not sell artificial eyes as the name might suggest. It is one of the city's more affordable art-glass galleries. Seattle is known throughout the world for its talented glass artists.

Just up the alley from this gallery, you'll spot:

⑮ The Pink Door

This restaurant, at 1919 Post Alley (📞 **206/443-3241**), is one of the market's most famous dinner spots. There's no sign out front, just the pink door. Step through the door, and a flight of stairs leads down to an Italian restaurant and cabaret/bar. The restaurant is

only open for dinner, and the deck is *the* place to eat on summer evenings.

Continue up Post Alley to Virginia Street, turn left, and walk downhill. Once back at Steinbrueck Park, turn left and walk down Western Avenue to the:

⑯ Market Heritage Center

Located at 1531 Western Ave. (📞 **206/682-7453**), this is an open-air exhibit on the history of Pike Place Market. Here you learn all about the various incarnations of the market since its inception. If you'd like to do a guided walking tour similar to this one here, you can contact the Market Foundation at the number above.

Continue down Western Avenue, and in a couple of blocks, you'll see on the opposite side of the street the:

⑰ Seattle Parrot Market

As the name suggests, this pet shop, at 1500 Western Ave. (📞 **206/467-6133**), specializes in exotic birds. The shop is so packed with bird cages that there's hardly room to turn around. Although there is a 50¢ charge to look around the shop, it's well worth it.

This shop is on the Pike Hill Climb, a network of stairways that connect the waterfront with Pike Place Market. If you head up the stairs, you will find the market's Down Under area, which consists of long hallways lined with small shops. Our favorite shop in the Down Under is:

⑱ The Magic Shop

Located on the Down Under's fourth level, this shop sells all kinds of magic tricks and magician's paraphernalia. Kids love this shop, as do aspiring magicians. Directly across the hall from this shop are some unusual coin-operated window displays of giant shoes. Don't miss these shoes!

If you leave the Down Under by way of the Pike Hill Climb, you will find yourself back in the vicinity of *Rachel* the pig and Pike Place Fish. From here, make your way through the crowd of people waiting to see the fish fly and head into the Economy Building. Here, in the walkway leading toward First Avenue, you'll find:

⑲ The Garlic Garden

This stall is famous for its pungent Lebanese Breeze garlic spread. This spread is great on bread (maybe with a little pepper jelly). Just be sure that everyone in your group has some; this stuff may not be pure garlic, but it sure tastes like it (© **206/405-4022**).

Across the hall from the Garlic Garden, you'll find:

⑳ DeLaurenti

This Italian grocery, at 1435 First Ave. (© **206/622-0141**), has a great deli case full of Italian cheeses and meats. It also sells imported pastas and has a great selection of wines and beers. Samples of various olive oils are often available.

If you exit DeLaurenti through the door in the wine shop area, you will find yourself in an atrium from the ceiling of which hangs a:

㉑ Giant Squid

This life-size copper sculpture is one of the market's newest works of art and was done by a local artist. Although you won't see any squids this size in the nearby Seattle Aquarium (on the waterfront), you can see a live giant octopus.

WINDING DOWN
In the same building as the giant squid, you'll find **World Class Chili**, 1411 First Ave. (© **206/623-3678**). If this place is still open by the time you reach this point, don't pass up an opportunity to sample some of the best chili in Seattle. Alternatively, you can head down the block from the giant squid and savor a pint of locally brewed ale at **Pike Pub and Brewery**, 1415 First Ave. (© **206/622-6044**).

<hr />

WALKING TOUR 2   THE PIONEER SQUARE AREA

Start:	Pioneer Place at the corner of Yesler Way and First Avenue.
Finish:	Elliott Bay Book Company.
Time:	Approximately 5 hours, including shopping, dining, and museum stops.
Best Times:	Weekdays, when the neighborhood and the Seattle Underground Tour are not so crowded.
Worst Times:	Weekends, when the area is very crowded, and Mondays, when galleries are closed.

In the late 19th century, Pioneer Square was the heart of downtown Seattle, so when a fire raged through these blocks in 1889, the city was devastated. Residents and merchants quickly began rebuilding and set about to remedy many of the infrastructure problems that had faced Seattle in the years before the fire. Today this small section of the city is all that remains of old Seattle. Because one architect, Elmer Fisher, was responsible for the design of many of the buildings constructed after the fire, the neighborhood has a distinctly uniform architectural style.

While wandering these streets, don't bother looking for a specific site called Pioneer Square; you won't find it. The name actually applies to the whole neighborhood, not a plaza surrounded by four streets, as you would surmise. Do keep your eye out for interesting manhole covers, many of which were cast with maps of Seattle or Northwest Coast Indian designs. Also be aware that this neighborhood, the original Skid Row, still has several missions and homeless shelters—consequently, expect to see a lot of street people in the area.

To get the most out of downtown Seattle's only historic neighborhood, we have outlined a walking tour that takes in shops, art galleries, and historic buildings. Bear in mind that this area was hard hit by the 6.8 earthquake that rocked Seattle on February 28, 2001. At press time, many historic buildings remained unrepaired.

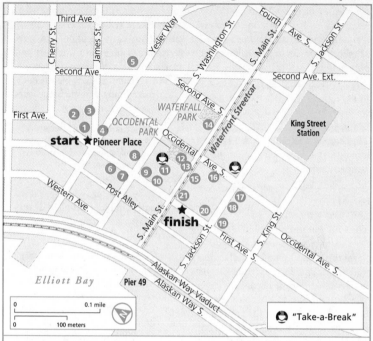

1 Pioneer Place
2 The Underground Tour
3 Pioneer Square Antique Mall
4 Yesler Way
5 Smith Tower
6 Maynard Building
7 Flora & Fauna Books
8 Laguna: A Vintage American Pottery Shop
9 Fireworks Fine Crafts Gallery
10 Grand Central Arcade
11 Michael Maslan Historic Photographs,
        Postcards & Ephemera

12 Occidental Park
13 Seattle Fallen Firefighters' Memorial
14 Waterfall Park
15 Klondike Gold Rush National
        Historical Park
16 Davidson Galleries
17 Foster/White Gallery
18 Stonington Gallery
19 Northwest Fine Woodworking
20 Flurry & Co.
21 Elliott Bay Book Company

Start your tour of this historic neighborhood at the corner of Yesler Way and First Avenue on:

❶ Pioneer Place

The triangular park at the heart of Pioneer Square is the site of a totem pole that's a replacement for one that caught fire in 1938. The original pole had, in 1890, been stolen from a Tlingit village far to the north of Seattle. Legend has it that after the pole burned, the city fathers sent a check for $5,000 requesting a new totem pole. The Tlingit response was, "Thanks for paying for the first one. Send another $5,000 for a replacement." The 1905 cast-iron pergola that was damaged by a truck in early 2001 has now been restored and is back in place on this plaza.

Facing the square are several historic buildings, including the gabled Lowman Building and three buildings noteworthy for their terra-cotta facades. In one of these buildings, at 608 First Ave., you'll find the ticket counter for Seattle's:

❷ Underground Tour

This tour takes a look at the Pioneer Square area from beneath the sidewalks. The tour (☎ **206/682-4646** for information) is a great introduction to the history of the area (if you don't mind off-color jokes) and actually spends quite a bit of time aboveground (duplicating much of the walking tour outlined here).

In the basement of the Pioneer Building, 602 First Ave., one of the architectural standouts on Pioneer Place, you'll find the:

❸ Pioneer Square Antique Mall

This complex (📞 **206/624-1164**) is home to dozens of antiques and collectibles dealers.

Running along the south side of Pioneer Place is:

❹ Yesler Way

This was the original Skid Row. In Seattle's early years, logs were skidded down this road to a lumber mill on the waterfront, and the road came to be known as Skid Road. These days Yesler Way is trying hard to live down its reputation, but, because of the number of missions in this neighborhood, there are still a lot of street people in the area (and they'll most certainly be asking you for change as you wander the streets).

TAKE A BREAK
Merchants Cafe, 109 Yesler Way (📞 **206/624-1515**), is the oldest restaurant in Seattle and a good place for an inexpensive lunch or dinner. If you skipped the Underground Tour, then cross Yesler Way to the corner of Yesler and First Avenue, to the **Starbucks**, where you can pick up a latte to help fuel you through this walking tour. Right next door to Starbucks, you'll find **Cow Chips**, 102A First Ave. S., where you can get one of the best (though messiest) chocolate chip cookies you'll ever taste.

With cookie and coffee in hand, glance up Yesler Way, past a triangular parking deck (a monstrosity that prompted the movement to preserve the rest of this neighborhood), to:

❺ Smith Tower

This structure, at 506 Second Ave. (📞 **206/622-4004**), was the tallest

building west of the Mississippi when it was completed in 1914. The observation floor near the top of this early skyscraper is open to the public and provides a very different perspective on Seattle than the Space Needle does. The ornate lobby and elevator doors are also worth checking out.

Now, walk back down to First Avenue and turn left, away from Pioneer Place. At the next corner, Washington Street, look across First Avenue and admire the:

❻ Maynard Building

This ornate building, which is named for Seattle founding father David "Doc" Maynard, was the site of Seattle's first bank.

If your fingers aren't too messy from eating your Cow Chip cookie, you might want to stop by:

❼ Flora & Fauna Books

Located below street level in the Maynard Building, this specialty bookstore, at 121 First Ave. S. (📞 **206/ 623-4727**), is filled with plant and animal field guides, gardening books, and the like.

Heading up Washington Street away from the water for half a block will bring you to:

❽ Laguna Vintage Pottery

This shop, at 116 S. Washington St. (📞 **206/682-6162**), specializes in mid-century pottery, primarily from California. Fiesta, Bauer, and Weller are all well represented.

From here, head back to First Avenue and turn left. On this block, at 210 First Ave. S., you'll find:

❾ Fireworks Fine Crafts Gallery

This gallery (📞 **206/682-8707**) sells colorful and unusual crafts by Northwest artisans.

Next, at 214 First Ave. S., you'll come to the:

❿ Grand Central Arcade

Inside this small, European-style shopping arcade, with its brick walls and wine cellar–like basement shops and studios, you'll find:

⑪ Michael Maslan Historic Photographs, Postcards & Ephemera

This store (© **206/587-0187**) is crammed full of vintage travel posters, ethnographic photos, and thousands of postcards. Before leaving the Grand Central Arcade, be sure to check out the historic photos in the basement.

TAKE A BREAK
In the arcade you'll also find the **Grand Central Baking Company** (© 206/622-3644), plus some tables and even a fireplace, which together make this a great place to stop for lunch if you didn't already eat. Alternatively, you can grab some food to go and head over to Waterfall Park (see below).

Leaving Grand Central Arcade through the door opposite where you came in will bring you out into:

⑫ Occidental Park

On this shady, cobblestone plaza stand four totem poles carved by Northwest artist Duane Pasco. The tallest is the 35-foot-high *The Sun and Raven,* which tells the story of how Raven brought light into the world. Next to this pole is *Man Riding a Whale.* This type of totem pole was traditionally carved to help villagers during their whale hunts. The other two figures that face each other are symbols of the Bear Clan and the Welcoming Figure.

This shady park serves as a gathering spot for homeless people, so you may not want to linger. However, before leaving the park, be sure to notice the grouping of bronze statues, the:

⑬ Seattle Fallen Firefighters' Memorial

This memorial was inspired by the deaths of four firefighters who died in a 1995 warehouse fire in Chinatown.

The statues are adjacent to South Main Street, and if you walk up this street to the corner of Second Avenue, you will come to:

⑭ Waterfall Park

The roaring waterfall here looks transported straight from the Cascade Range. The park is built on the site of the original United Parcel Service (UPS) offices and makes a wonderful place for a rest or a picnic lunch.

Now, walk back the way you came and, across from Occidental Park at 117 S. Main St., you'll find the:

⑮ Klondike Gold Rush National Historical Park

Not really a "park," this small museum (© **206/553-7220**) is dedicated to the history of the 1897–98 Klondike gold rush, which helped Seattle grow from an obscure town into a booming metropolis.

Around the corner from this small museum is Occidental Mall, where you'll find a couple of art galleries, including:

⑯ Davidson Galleries

You never know what to expect when you walk through the front door here at 313 Occidental Ave. S. (© **206/624-7684**). The gallery sells everything from 16th-century prints to contemporary art by Northwest artists.

TAKE A BREAK
If it's time for another latte, cross the plaza to **Torrefazione,** 320 Occidental Ave. S. (© 206/624-5847), which serves some of the best coffee in Seattle. Be sure to get yours in one of the hand-painted cups.

Diagonally across from Torrefazione, at 123 S. Jackson St., you'll find the:

⑰ Foster/White Gallery

This gallery (© **206/622-2833**) is best known for its art glass. It's the Seattle gallery for famed glass artist Dale Chihuly, and always has several of his works on display.

Right next door, at 119 S. Jackson St., you'll find the:

⑱ Stonington Gallery

This gallery (© 206/405-4040) is one of Seattle's top showcases for contemporary Native American arts and crafts. Here you'll find a good selection of Northwest Coast Indian masks, woodcarvings, prints, and jewelry.

Continue to the corner of First Avenue, where you'll find:

⑲ Northwest Fine Woodworking

This large store at 101 S. Jackson St. (© 206/625-0542) sells exquisite, handcrafted wooden furniture, as well as some smaller pieces. It's well worth a visit.

From here, cross South Jackson Street, where you'll find:

⑳ Flury & Co.

This gallery, at 322 First Ave. S. (© 206/587-0260), specializes in prints by Seattle photographer Edward S. Curtis, who is known for his portraits of Native Americans. There's also an excellent selection of antique Native American art.

From here, head up First Avenue to the corner of Main Street, where you'll find the:

㉑ Elliott Bay Book Company

One of the city's most popular bookstores, the Elliott Bay Book Company stands at 101 S. Main St. (© 206/624-6600). It boasts an extensive selection of books on Seattle and the Northwest. With so much great browsing to be done here, this bookstore makes a great place to end your walking tour of the Pioneer Square area.

WALKING TOUR 3   FUN, FUNKY FREMONT

Start:	South end of Fremont Bridge near Ponti restaurant.
Finish:	Trolleyman Pub at the corner of Phinney Avenue and 34th Street.
Time:	Approximately 2 hours, not including time spent dining.
Best Times:	Sunday, during the Fremont Sunday Market.
Worst Times:	Early morning or evening, when shops are closed.

The Fremont neighborhood definitely marches to the beat of a different drummer than the rest of the city. Styling itself the Republic of Fremont and the center of the universe, this small, tight-knit community is the most eclectic neighborhood in the city. It has taken as its motto "De Libertas Quirkas," which roughly translated means "free to be peculiar." Fremont residents have focused on art as a way to draw the community together, and in so doing, they've created a corner of the city where silliness reigns. At this crossroads business district, you'll find unusual outdoor art, the Fremont Sunday Market (a European-style flea market), several vintage clothing and furniture stores, a couple of brewpubs, and many other unexpected and unusual shops, galleries, and cafes. During the summer, outdoor movies are held on Saturday nights, and in June there's the wacky Solstice Parade, a countercultural promenade with giant puppets, wizards, fairies, face paint, naked bicyclists, and hippies of all ages.

Start your tour by finding a parking spot around the corner from Ponti restaurant at the south end of the:

① Fremont Bridge

This is one of the busiest drawbridges in the United States and spans the Lake Washington Ship Canal. "Welcome to the center of the Universe" reads the sign at the south end of the bridge.

As you approach the north side of the bridge, glance up and in the window of the bridge-tender's tower on the west side of the bridge, where you'll see:

1 Fremont Bridge
2 *Rapunzel*
3 Adobe
4 *Waiting for the Interurban*
5 Portage Bay Goods
6 History House
7 *The Fremont Troll*
8 Frank and Dunya
9 Directional Marker
10 *Lenin*
11 The Fremont Rocket
12 The Edge of Glass Gallery
13 Fremont's Jurassic Park
14 Fremont Sunday Market

☕ "Take-a-Break"

---

❷ *Rapunzel*

This is a neon sculpture of the famous fairy-tale maiden with the prodigious mane. Her neon tresses cascade down the wall of the tower.

On your immediate right, the big modern building crowding up against the bridge is world headquarters for software giant:

❸ Adobe

This is the Adobe of Illustrator and Photoshop fame. Longtime Fremont residents fear that Adobe's presence in the neighborhood could signal the end of Fremont's funky days, and, indeed, in the past few years, this neighborhood has changed considerably and is rapidly losing its appealing funkiness.

As you finally land in the Republic of Fremont, you will see, at the end of the bridge on the opposite side of the street from *Rapunzel*, Seattle's most beloved public sculpture:

❹ *Waiting for the Interurban*

This piece features several people waiting for the trolley that no longer runs between Fremont and downtown Seattle. These statues are frequently dressed up by local residents, with costumes changing regularly.

Cross to the far side of 34th Street and walk east along this street past some of Fremont's interesting shops, including:

⑤ Portage Bay Goods

This store, at 706 N. 34th St. (© **206/ 547-5221**), sells an eclectic array of things that "enrich the soul, support the community, and preserve the environment." Check out the notebooks made from old computer boards.

A few doors down, at 790 N. 34th St., you'll find:

⑥ History House

This neighborhood museum of history (© **206/675-8875**) is complete with modern interactive exhibits and a beautiful, artistic fence out front.

Turn left at History House and head uphill underneath the Aurora Bridge, which towers high above. At the top of the hill, you will see, lurking in the shadows beneath the bridge:

⑦ *The Fremont Troll*

This massive monster is in the process of crushing a real Volkswagen Beetle. No need to run in fear, though, as a wizard seems to have put a spell on the troll and turned it into cement.

Turn left at the troll and walk a block down North 35th Street to the best little cafe in the neighborhood.

TAKE A BREAK
Still Life in Fremont Coffeehouse, 709 N. 35th St. (© **206/547-9850**), is a classic hippie hangout, with a swinging screen door, wood floors, and lots of alternative newspapers on hand at all times. Although oatmeal is a specialty, there are also soups, salads, sandwiches, pastries, and good espresso.

From Still Life in Fremont, it's only a few steps down the hill to the corner of North Fremont Avenue and Fremont Place. Take a left here to reach:

⑧ Frank and Dunya

This shop, at 3418 Fremont Ave. N. (© **206/547-6760**), sells colorful household decor, including switch plates, cups and saucers, mirrors, jewelry, art, rustic furniture, and little shrines. It's all very playful.

Go back up to the corner and cross North Fremont Avenue to the traffic island, where you'll find both the center of the center of the universe and Fremont's:

⑨ Directional marker

This old-fashioned signpost has arrows that point to such important locations as the center of the universe (straight down), the *Fremont Troll, Rapunzel,* Atlantis, and the North Pole.

From the signpost, continue west (away from the intersection) on Fremont Place, and in 1 block (at the corner of N. 36th St.), you will see a larger-than-life statue of:

⑩ *Lenin*

This 20-foot-tall statue in no way reflects the attitudes of the many very capitalistic merchants in the neighborhood.

After communing with Comrade Lenin, cross North 36th Street and walk a block down Evanston Avenue to:

⑪ The Fremont Rocket

Although there is speculation that this rocket was used by the aliens who founded Fremont, the truth is far stranger. You can read the entire history of the rocket on a map board below the rocket. (If you haven't already figured it out, the locals don't want you getting lost in their neighborhood, so they've put up maps all over to help you find your way from one famous Fremont locale to the next.)

From here, head back up to North 36th Street, and continue west for another couple of blocks to:

⑫ The Edge of Glass Gallery

In this showroom at 513 N. 36th St. (© **206/632-7807**), you can often see art-glass artists at work. Even if no one's blowing glass, there are plenty of beautiful pieces of art glass to see.

From here, continue west on North 36th Street and then turn left on Phinney Avenue North, at the foot of which you'll find:

⑬ Fremont's Jurassic Park

Don't worry, no velociraptors here at the corner of North 34th Street and Phinney Avenue North—just a pair of friendly topiary *Apatosauruses* (sort of like brontosaurs) donated to the neighborhood by the Pacific Science Center.

If it happens to be Sunday, you'll see crowds of people and vendors' stalls stretching back toward the Fremont Bridge from Jurassic Park. This is the:

⑭ Fremont Sunday Market

You never know what you might find at this combination flea market and produce market—perhaps some locally made kilts, some organic strawberries, or maybe a rack of vintage Hawaiian shirts.

9

Seattle Shopping

Nordstrom, Eddie Bauer, REI—these names are familiar to shoppers all across the country. They're also the names of stores that got their start here in Seattle, which has long been *the* place to shop in the Northwest. Throw in such regional favorites as Pendleton, Nike, and Filson, and you'll find that Seattle is a great place to shop for clothes and recreational gear and clothing.

As the Northwest's largest city, Seattle has also become home to all the national retail chains you would expect to find in a major metropolitan area. These chains have taken over many of the storefronts of downtown Seattle and have opened flashy stores. The names and merchandise at these stores should be familiar: Banana Republic, Levi Strauss, Ann Taylor, St. John, Louis Vuitton, Coach, Tiffany & Co., Old Navy, FAO Schwarz, Barneys New York. These and many others now have stores in Seattle, so if you forgot to pick up that dress in Chicago or those running shoes in New York, have no fear—you can find them here.

Seattle does, however, have one last bastion of local merchandising, **Pike Place Market.** Whether shopping is your passion or an occasional indulgence, you shouldn't miss this historic market, which is one of Seattle's top tourist attractions. Once the city's main produce market (and quite a few produce stalls remain), this sprawling collection of buildings is today filled with hundreds of unusual shops, including **The Magic Shop** (for magicians and aspiring magicians; ✆ 206/624-4271), **Tenzing Momo** (selling body oils, incense, herbs, and such; ✆ 206/623-9837), **The Rubber Rainbow** (a condom store; ✆ 206/233-9502), **The Women's Hall of Fame** (a feminist bookstore; ✆ 206/622-8427), and **Left Bank Books** (a bookstore for anarchists and their kin; ✆ 206/622-0195). See also the listing for Pike Place Market on p. 163.

After tasting the bounties of the Northwest, it's hard to go back to Safeway, Sanka, and Chicken of the Sea. Sure you can get coffee, wine, and seafood where you live, but do a little food shopping in Seattle and you'll be tapping into the source. Washington State wines, coffee from the original Starbucks, and fish that flies—these are a few of the culinary treats that await you here.

1 The Shopping Scene

Although Seattle is a city of neighborhoods, many of which have great little shops, ground zero of the Seattle shopping scene is the corner of **Pine Street and Fifth Avenue.** Within 2 blocks of this intersection are two major department stores (Nordstrom and The Bon Marché) and two upscale urban shopping malls (Westlake Center and Pacific Place). There's even a sky bridge between Nordstrom and Pacific Place to make shopping that much easier. Fanning out east and south from this intersection are blocks of upscale stores that have begun to take on a very familiar look. Small local shops are rapidly being replaced by national and international boutiques and megastores. Here in this neighborhood you'll now find Ann Taylor, Barneys New York, NIKETOWN, Gap, MaxMara, Banana Republic, and FAO Schwarz. However, you'll still find a few local independents in the neighborhood as well.

The city's main tourist shopping district is the **Pike Place Market** neighborhood. Here you'll find dozens of T-shirt and souvenir shops, as well as import shops and stores appealing to teenagers and 20-somethings. Pike Place Market is a fascinating warren of cubbyholes that pass for shops. While produce isn't usually something you stock up on while on vacation, several market shops sell ethnic cooking supplies that are less perishable than a dozen oysters or a king salmon. You may not find anything here you really need, but it's fun to look (at least that's what millions of Seattle visitors each year seem to think).

Just west of Pike Place Market is the Seattle **waterfront,** where you'll find many more gift and souvenir shops.

South of downtown, in the historic **Pioneer Square area,** is the city's greatest concentration of art galleries, some of which specialize in Native American art. This neighborhood has several antiques stores but is also home to a dozen or more bars and attracts a lot of homeless people.

As the center of both the gay community and the city's youth culture, **Capitol Hill** has the most eclectic selection of shops in Seattle. Beads, imports, CDs, vintage clothing, politically correct merchandise, and gay-oriented goods fill the shops along Broadway. Capitol Hill's main shopping plaza is the Broadway Market, which has lots of small shops.

The **Fremont** neighborhood just north of Lake Union is filled with retro stores selling vintage clothing, mid-century furniture and collectibles, and curious crafts. As of this writing, however, the neighborhood is undergoing a fairly rapid gentrification that is forcing out many of the smaller and more unusual shops.

A couple of miles east of Fremont is the **Wallingford** neighborhood, which is anchored by an old schoolhouse that has been converted into a shopping arcade with interesting crafts, fashions, and gifts.

The **University District,** also in north Seattle, has everything necessary to support a student population and also goes upscale at the University Village shopping center.

2 Shopping A to Z

ANTIQUES & COLLECTIBLES

If antiques are your passion, you won't want to miss the opportunity to spend a day browsing the many antiques stores in the historic farm town of **Snohomish,** located roughly 30 miles north of Seattle. The town has more than 400 antiques dealers and is without a doubt the antiques capital of the Northwest. For more on Snohomish and its wealth of antiques, see chapter 11, "Side Trips from Seattle."

The Crane Gallery   Chinese, Japanese, and Korean antiquities are the focus of this shop in the Queen Anne neighborhood, which prides itself on selling only the best pieces. Imperial Chinese porcelains, bronze statues of Buddhist deities, rosewood furniture, Japanese ceramics, netsukes, snuff bottles, and Chinese archaeological artifacts are just some of the quality antiques you'll find here. Some Southeast Asian and Indian objects are also available. 104 W. Roy St. ✆ **206/298-9425.**

Honeychurch Antiques   For high-quality Asian antiques, including Japanese wood-block prints, textiles, furniture, and ivory and woodcarvings, few Seattle antiques stores can approach Honeychurch Antiques. Regular special exhibits give this shop the feel of a tiny museum. The store's annex, called **Glenn Richards,** 964 Denny Way (© **206/287-1877**), specializes in "entry-level" antiques. 1008 James St. © 206/622-1225.

Jean Williams Antiques   If your taste in antiques runs to 18th- and 19th-century French and English formal or country furniture, this Pioneer Square antiques dealer may have something to add to your collection. 115 S. Jackson St. © **206/622-1110.** www.jeanwilliamsantiques.com.

Laguna A Vintage American Pottery Shop   Twentieth-century art pottery is the specialty of this shop in Pioneer Square. Pieces by such mid-century pottery factories as Fiesta, Roseville, Bauer, Weller, and Franciscan fill the shelves here. This is a great place to look for dinnerware and vintage tiles. 116 S. Washington St. © **206/682-6162.** www.lagunapottery.com.

Michael Maslan Vintage Photographs, Postcards & Ephemera   Located in the Pioneer Square area's Grand Central Arcade, this store is crammed full of vintage travel posters, ethnographic photos, and thousands of postcards. With a focus on social, industrial, and historical images, Michael Maslan's philosophy is to collect (and sell) just about anything "written, printed, or painted" that's old or interesting. 214 First Ave. S. © 206/587-0187.

ANTIQUES MALLS & FLEA MARKETS

Antiques at Pike Place   Located in the Pike Place Market area, this antiques and collectibles mall is one of the finest in Seattle. There are more than 80 dealers, and much of what's available here is fairly small, which means you might be able to fit your find into a suitcase. 92 Stewart St. © **206/441-9643.** www.antiques atpikeplace.com.

Fremont Sunday Market   Crafts, imports, antiques, collectibles, and fresh produce combine to make this Seattle's second favorite public market (after Pike Place Market). The market is open Sunday from 10am to 5pm year-round. N. 34th St. (1 block west of the Fremont Bridge). © **206/781-6776.**

Pioneer Square Antique Mall   This underground antiques mall is in the heart of Pioneer Square right beside the ticket booth for the Seattle Underground tour and contains 65 stalls selling all manner of antiques and collectibles. Look for glass, old jewelry, and small collectibles. 602 First Ave. © **206/624-1164.**

ART GALLERIES

The **Pioneer Square area** has for many years been Seattle's main art gallery district, and although it still has quite a few galleries, many have, in the past few years, moved to other parts of the metropolitan area, including the two wealthy Eastside suburbs of Bellevue and Kirkland. Still, there are enough galleries left around Pioneer Square that anyone interested in art should be sure to wander south of Yesler Way. Some galleries are closed on Mondays.

GENERAL ART GALLERIES

Carolyn Staley   This Pioneer Square area gallery specializes in Japanese prints and has a wide range of prints both old and new. The highlight, however, is the large collection of 19th- and 20th-century wood-block prints. 314 Occidental Ave. S. © **206/621-1888.**

Davidson Galleries   Located in the heart of the Pioneer Square neighborhood, this gallery focuses on three different areas—contemporary paintings and sculptures (often by Northwest artists); contemporary prints by American and

European artists; and antique prints, some of which date from the 1500s. 313 Occidental Ave. S. ✆ **206/624-7684**. www.davidsongalleries.com.

Greg Kucera Gallery   Established in 1983, this showroom in the Pioneer Square area serves as one of Seattle's most reliably cutting-edge galleries. The shows here tend to address political or social issues or movements within the art world. 212 Third Ave. S. ✆ **206/624-0770**. www.gregkucera.com.

Kimzey Miller Gallery   The evocative Northwest landscape paintings of Z. Z. Wei are always a highlight of a visit to this downtown gallery not far from the Seattle Art Museum. Keep an eye out for the sculptural glass-and-steel constructions of David Gignac. 1225 Second Ave. ✆ **206/682-2339**.

Lisa Harris Gallery   Landscapes and figurative works, by both expressionist and realist Northwest and West Coast artists, are specialties of this gallery, which is located on the second floor of a building in Pike Place Market. 1922 Pike Place. ✆ **206/443-3315**. www.lisaharrisgallery.com.

ART GLASS

Foster/White Gallery   If you are enamored of art glass, as we are, be sure to stop by one, two, or all three of the Foster/White galleries in the Seattle area. These galleries represent Dale Chihuly and always have works by this master glass artist. Some of Chihuly's pieces even sell for less than $10,000! Foster/White also represents top-notch Northwest artists in the disciplines of painting, ceramics, and sculpture. 123 S. Jackson St. ✆ **206/622-2833**. www.foster white.com. Also at 1331 Fifth Ave. (✆ 206/583-0100) and in Kirkland at 126 Central Way (✆ **425/822-2305**).

The Glass Eye Studio   The Glass Eye is one of Seattle's oldest art-glass galleries and specializes in colorful hand-blown pieces made from Mount St. Helens ash from the volcano's 1980 eruption. Works by artists from around the country are available, and many pieces are small enough to carry home. 1902 Post Alley, Pike Place Market. ✆ **206/441-3221**. www.glasseye.com.

Glasshouse Studio   Located in the Pioneer Square area and founded in 1972, Glasshouse claims to be the oldest glass-blowing studio in the Northwest. In the studio, you can watch hand-blown art glass being made, and then, in the gallery, you can check out the works of numerous local glass artists. 311 Occidental Ave. S. ✆ **206/682-9939**. www.glasshouse-studio.com.

Phoenix Rising Gallery   The art glass here is more high-end than what you'll find at the nearby Glass Eye Gallery. Artists from around the country are represented, and there is always some highly imaginative decorative work on display. The gallery now sells ceramic pieces and wooden crafts as well. 2030 Western Ave. ✆ **206/728-2332**. www.phoenixrisinggallery.com.

Portfolio Glass   This small, appointment-only gallery specializes almost exclusively in the works of Dale Chihuly and usually has lots of older pieces and small pieces. Consequently, prices here are often lower than those you'll find at the Foster/White Gallery, which is Chihuly's main Seattle gallery. You'll also find Chihuly paintings here. 2100 Western Ave., no. 87. ✆ **206/748-9166**. www.portfolioglass.com.

Vetri   Vetri, which is affiliated with the prestigious William Traver Gallery, showcases innovative work primarily from emerging glass artists and local area studios, but includes works by artists from other countries. It's all high quality and riotously colorful. Prices are relatively affordable. 1404 First Ave. ✆ **206/667-9608**. www.vetriglass.com.

William Traver Gallery   In business for more than 25 years, this is one of the nation's top art-glass galleries and showcases the works of 80 glass artists. Works shown here are on the cutting edge of glass art, so to speak, and will give you a good idea of the broad spectrum of work being created by contemporary glass artists. You'll find the gallery on the second floor. 110 Union St. ☏ **206/587-6501.** www.travergallery.com.

NATIVE AMERICAN ART

Flury & Company   This Pioneer Square gallery specializes in prints by famed Seattle photographer Edward S. Curtis, who is known for his portraits of Native Americans. The gallery also has an excellent selection of antique Native American art and artifacts. 322 First Ave. S. ☏ **206/587-0260.** www.fluryco.com.

The Legacy Ltd.   In business since 1933, The Legacy Ltd. is Seattle's oldest and finest gallery of contemporary and historic Northwest Coast Indian and Alaskan Eskimo art and artifacts. You'll find a large selection of masks, boxes, bowls, baskets, ivory artifacts, jewelry, prints, and books for the serious collector. 1003 First Ave. ☏ **800/729-1562** or 206/624-6350. www.thelegacyltd.com.

Stonington Gallery   This is one of Seattle's top galleries specializing in contemporary Native American arts and crafts. Here you'll find a good selection of Northwest Coast Indian masks, totem poles, mixed-media pieces, prints, carvings, and Northwest Coast–style jewelry. 119 S. Jackson St. ☏ **206/405-4040.** www.stonington gallery.com.

BOOKS

In addition to the stores listed below, you'll find more than a half dozen locations of **Barnes & Noble** around the metro area, including one downtown at 600 Pine St. (☏ **206/264-0156**). There's also a **Borders** at 1501 Fourth Ave. (☏ **206/622-4599**).

Elliott Bay Book Company   With battered wooden floors, a maze of rooms full of books, and frequent readings and in-store appearances by authors, this Pioneer Square bookstore feels as if it has been around forever. It has an excellent selection of books on Seattle and the Northwest, so if you want to learn more about the region or are planning further excursions, stop by. There is also a good little cafe down in the basement. 101 S. Main St. ☏ **206/624-6600.** www.elliott baybook.com.

Flora & Fauna   Gardeners, bird-watchers, and other naturephiles, take note. Down below street level in what passes for the active Seattle underground of the Pioneer Square area, you'll find a store filled with books that'll have you wishing you were in your garden or out in the woods identifying birds and flowers. 121 First Ave. S. ☏ **206/623-4727.**

Peter Miller   Looking for a picture book of Frank Gehry's architectural follies? How about a retrospective on the work of Alvar Aalto? You'll find these and loads of other beautiful and educational books on architecture and design at this specialty bookstore at the edge of trendy Belltown. 1930 First Ave. ☏ **206/441-4114.**

Seattle Mystery Bookshop   If books that keep you wondering whodunit are your passion, don't miss an opportunity to peruse the shelves of this specialty bookstore in the Pioneer Square area. You'll find all your favorite mystery authors, lots of signed copies, and regularly scheduled book signings. 117 Cherry St. ☏ **206/587-5737.** www.seattlemystery.com.

COFFEE & TEA

All over the city, on almost every corner, you'll find espresso bars, cafes, and coffeehouses. And while you can get coffee back home, you might want to stock up on whichever local coffee turns out to be your favorite. If you're a latte junkie, you can even make a pilgrimage to the shop that started it all, the original Starbucks, listed below.

Starbucks   Seattle is well known as a city of coffeeholics, and Starbucks is the main reason. This company has coffeehouses all over town (and all over the world), but this is the original. Although you won't find any tables or chairs here, Starbucks fans shouldn't miss an opportunity to get your coffee at the source. 1912 Pike Place, Pike Place Market. (© 206/448-8762. www.starbucks.com.

Teahouse Kuan Yin   Perhaps you've heard about the health benefits of green tea, or maybe you just want a break from espresso. Whatever your reasons for wanting a cup of tea instead of coffee, you'll find lots of options at this Wallingford tea shop, which serves an amazing variety of teas, from smoky Keemun to flamingo-pink Kashmiri chai and frothy green Japanese tea. All teas are also available in bulk, and there's plenty of tea paraphernalia as well. 1911 N. 45th St. (© 206/632-2055.

Ten Ren Tea Co., Ltd.   Ever wondered what $150-a-pound Chinese tea tastes like? At this International District tea shop, you can find out. Not only do they have dozens of different teas here, they also have a little table in back where you can sample varieties and observe the traditional Chinese tea ceremony. 506 S. King St. (© 206/749-9855.

CRAFTS

The Northwest is a magnet for skilled craftspeople, and shops all around town sell a wide range of high-quality and imaginative crafts. At Pike Place Market, you can see what area craftspeople are creating and meet the artisans themselves.

Crackerjack Contemporary Crafts   With colorful and imaginative crafts by more than 250 artists from around the country, this shop in the eclectic Wallingford Center shopping arcade (an old schoolhouse) is a great place to check for something interesting and unique to bring home from a trip to Seattle. Lots of interesting jewelry. Wallingford Center, 1815 N. 45th St., Ste. 212. (© 206/547-4983.

Fireworks Fine Crafts Gallery   Playful, outrageous, bizarre, beautiful—these are just some of the terms that can be used to describe the eclectic collection of Northwest crafts on sale at this Pioneer Square gallery. Cosmic clocks, wildly creative jewelry, and artistic picture frames are some of the fine and unusual items you'll find here. 210 First Ave. S. (© 206/682-8707. www.fireworks gallery.net. Also at Westlake Center, 400 Pine St. ((© 206/682-6462); Bellevue Sq., NE Eighth St. and Bellevue Way, Bellevue ((© 425/688-0933); and the University Village shopping plaza, 2629 NE University Village Mall ((© 206/527-2858).

Frank and Dunya   Located in the middle of funky Fremont, this store epitomizes the Fremont aesthetic. The art, jewelry, and crafts here tend toward the colorful and the humorous, and just about everything is made by Northwest artists and artisans. 3418 Fremont Ave. N. (© 206/547-6760.

Northwest Fine Woodworking   This store is a showcase for some of the most amazing woodworking you'll ever see. Be sure to stroll through here while you're in the Pioneer Square area even if you aren't in the market for a one-of-a-kind piece of furniture. The warm hues of the exotic woods are soothing, and the designs are beautiful. Furniture, boxes, sculptures, vases, bowls, and much more are created by more than 35 Northwest artisans. 101 S. Jackson St. ✆ 206/625-0542. www.nwfinewoodworking.com. Also in Bellevue at the Bellevue Pedestrian Corridor, 601 108th Ave. NE, Plaza 100 ((✆ 425/462-5382).

Twist This impressively large store is filled with items such as unusual artist-created jewelry, Adirondack chairs made from recycled water skis, twisted glass vases, candlesticks, and ceramics. All are slightly offbeat yet tasteful objets d'art. 1503 Fifth Ave. ✆ 206/315-8080.

DEPARTMENT STORES

The Bon Marché Seattle's "other" department store, established in 1890, is every bit as well stocked as the neighboring Nordstrom department store, and with such competition nearby, The Bon, as it's known, tries every bit as hard to keep its customers happy. Third Ave. and Pine St. ✆ 206/506-6049.

Nordstrom Known for personal service, Nordstrom stores have gained a reputation for being among the premier department stores in the United States. The company originated here in Seattle (opening its first store in 1901), and its customers are devotedly loyal. This is a state-of-the-art store, with all sorts of little boutiques, cafes, and other features to make your shopping excursion an experience.

Best of all, whether it's your first visit or your 50th, the knowledgeable staff will help you in any way they can. Prices may be a bit higher than those at other department stores, but for your money you get the best service available. The store is packed with shoppers during the half-year sale in June and the anniversary sale in July. You'll also find Nordstrom at area shopping malls. 500 Pine St. ✆ 206/628-2111. www.nordstrom.com.

DISCOUNT SHOPPING

Nordstrom Rack *(Value)* This is the Nordstrom overflow shop where you'll find three floors of discontinued lines as well as overstock, all at greatly reduced prices. Women's fashions make up the bulk of the merchandise here, but there is also a floor full of men's clothes and shoes, plus plenty of kids' clothes. 1601 Second Ave. ✆ 206/448-8522.

FASHION

In addition to the stores listed below, you'll find quite a few familiar names in downtown Seattle, including Ann Taylor, Banana Republic, Barneys New York, Eddie Bauer, Gap, and MaxMara.

ACCESSORIES

Byrnie Utz Hats In the same location since 1934 and boasting the largest selection of hats in the Northwest, this cramped hat-wearer's heaven looks as if it hasn't changed in 50 years. There are Borsalino Panama hats, Kangol caps, and, of course, plenty of Stetsons. 310 Union St. ✆ 206/623-0233.

CHILDREN'S CLOTHING

Boston St. Located in the renovated old schoolhouse that is now the Wallingford Center shopping arcade, this store stocks fun play clothes, as well as more dressy fashions, for kids. There's lots of locally made 100% cotton clothing. Prices are moderate to expensive. Wallingford Center, 1815 N. 45th Ave. ✆ 206/634-0580.

MEN'S & WOMEN'S CLOTHING

Eddie Bauer   Eddie Bauer got his start here in Seattle back in 1922, and today the chain is one of the country's foremost purveyors of outdoor fashions—although these days, outdoor fashion is looking quite a bit more urban. 1330 Fifth Ave. ✆ 206/622-2766. www.eddiebauer.com.

NIKETOWN   Around the country, there are currently more than a dozen NIKETOWNs selling all things Nike and only things Nike. If you don't live near one of these high-tech megastores, and you do wear swooshes, then this store should definitely be on your shopping itinerary. 1500 Sixth Ave. ✆ 206/447-6453. www.niketown.com.

Northwest Pendleton   For Northwesterners, and for many other people across the nation, Pendleton is and always will be *the* name in classic wool fashions. This store features tartan plaids and Indian-pattern separates, accessories, shawls, and blankets. 1313 Fourth Ave. ✆ 800/593-6773 or 206/682-4430. www.nwpendleton.com.

WOMEN'S CLOTHING

Alhambra   Alhambra stocks an eclectic collection of women's clothing and jewelry. There are purses from France, shoes from Italy, and fashions from Turkey and the U.S. These add up to an eclectic European look that's a little more refined than what you'll find at Baby and Co. 101 Pine St. ✆ 206/621-9571. www.alhambranet.com.

Baby and Co.   Claiming stores in Seattle and on Mars, this up-to-the-minute store stocks fashions that can be trendy, outrageous, or out of this world. The designs are strictly French, so you aren't likely to find these fashions too many other places in the U.S. Whether you're into earth tones or bright colors, you'll likely find something you can't live without. 1936 First Ave. ✆ 206/448-4077.

Coldwater Creek   This huge store based out of Sandpoint, Idaho, carries both classic and comfortable casual fashions for women and home furnishings of a rustic nature. And wouldn't you know it—a creek runs through the store. 1511 Fifth Ave. (at Pine St.). ✆ 206/903-0830. www.coldwatercreek.com.

Darbury Stenderu   Drapey velvet dresses with big, bold patterns and super-bright colors are the hallmarks of local fashion designer Darbury Stenderu. These fashions are definitely not for everyone, but they sure make a big statement. 2121 First Ave. ✆ 206/448-2625. www.darburystenderu.com.

Margaret O'Leary   Simple and beautiful wool sweaters are the specialty of this little Belltown boutique. The owner is from Ireland, so she knows her knits. But is fleece-obsessed Seattle really ready for hand-knit wool sweaters? 2025 First Ave. ✆ 206/441-6691.

Passport Clothing Company   Soft and easygoing is the current style at this large store near Pike Place Market. Velvet, linen, cotton, rayon, and other natural fibers are the fabrics of choice here. 123 Pine St. ✆ 206/628-9799.

Ragazzi's Flying Shuttle   Fashion becomes art and art becomes fashion at this chic boutique-cum-gallery on Pioneer Square. Hand-woven fabrics and hand-painted silks are the specialties here, but of course such sophisticated fashions require equally unique body decorations in the form of exquisite jewelry creations. Designers and artists from the Northwest and the rest of the nation find an outlet for their creativity at the Flying Shuttle. 607 First Ave. ✆ 206/343-9762.

GIFTS/SOUVENIRS

Pike Place Market is the Grand Central Station of Seattle souvenirs, with stiff competition from Seattle Center and Pioneer Square.

Made in Washington Whether it's salmon, wine, or Northwest crafts, you'll find a selection of Washington State products in this shop. This is an excellent place to pick up gifts for all those friends and family members who didn't get to come to Seattle with you. Pike Place Market (Post Alley at Pine St.). ✆ 206/467-0788. www.madeinwashington.com. Also in downtown's Westlake Center mall (✆ 206/623-9753).

Portage Bay Goods If you'd like to give a gift with a conscience, drop by this unusual store in the Fremont neighborhood. Almost everything here is made from recycled materials. We like the notebooks with covers made from computer boards, but there are lots of fun decorative home accessories as well. 706 N. 34th St. ✆ 206/547-5221. www.portagebaygoods.com.

Ye Olde Curiosity Shop If you can elbow your way into this waterfront institution, you'll find every inch of space, horizontal and vertical, covered with souvenirs and crafts, both tacky and tasteful (but mostly tacky). Surrounding this merchandise are the weird artifacts that have made this one of the most visited shops in Seattle. 1001 Alaskan Way, Pier 54. ✆ 206/682-5844. www.yeolde curiosityshop.com.

HOUSEWARES, HOME FURNISHINGS & GARDEN ACCESSORIES

Kasala Boldly styled contemporary furnishings are this store's main business. While you probably don't want to ship a couch home, they do have lots of easily packed accent pieces (vases, candlesticks, picture frames) that are just as wildly modern as the furniture. 1505 Western Ave. ✆ 800/KASALA1 or 206/623-7795. www. kasala.com. Also in Bellevue at 1014 116th Ave. NE (✆ 866/KASALA2 or 425/453-2823).

Kobo Japanophiles won't want to miss this unusual little Capitol Hill shop and gallery, located in one of the most interesting old buildings in the neighborhood. There are all manner of very tasteful decorative items inspired by the Japanese artistic aesthetic. 814 E. Roy St. ✆ 206/726-0704. www.koboseattle.com.

The Spanish Table If you've decided your life's goal is to prepare the perfect paella, this store will set you on the path to perfection. Paella pans and everything you could ever want for cooking Spanish cuisine fill this Pike Place Market shop. 1427 Western Ave. ✆ 206/682-2827. www.tablespan.com.

Sur La Table Gourmet cooks will not want to miss an opportunity to visit Pike Place Market's Sur La Table, where every imaginable kitchen utensil is available. There are a dozen different kinds of whisks, an equal number of muffin tins, and all manner of cake decorating tools, tableware, napkins, cookbooks— simply everything a cook would need. 84 Pine St. ✆ 206/448-2244.

Lutefisk Anyone?

If you're suddenly struck with an insatiable craving for Scandinavian lutefisk, lingonberries, or lefse bread, then head to Ballard, Seattle's Nordic neighborhood, where you can peruse the deli cases and frozen foods at **Olsen's Scandinavian Foods,** 2248 NW Market St. (✆ 206/783-9798). With flatbread and Danish ham in hand, you can head out to the Ballard Locks (Hiram M. Chittenden Locks) for a picnic.

JEWELRY

Unique artist-crafted jewelry can be found at **Ragazzi's Flying Shuttle** (p. 161) and **Twist** (p. 160).

Fox's Gem Shop   Seattle's premier jeweler, Fox's has been around for 90 years, and always has plenty of a girl's best friends. Colorless or fancy colored diamonds available here are of the finest cut. 1341 Fifth Ave. ✆ 206/623-2528.

MALLS/SHOPPING CENTERS

Bellevue Square   Over in Bellevue, on the east side of Lake Washington, you'll find one of the area's largest shopping malls, with more than 200 stores, including Nordstrom, FAO Schwarz, a Disney Store, Banana Republic, Coach, Eddie Bauer, and Made in Washington. Bellevue Way and NE Eighth Ave., Bellevue. ✆ 425/454-2431.

Broadway Market   Located in trendy Capitol Hill, the Broadway Market is a stylish little shopping center with a decidedly urban neighborhood feel. The mall houses Urban Outfitters and numerous small shops and restaurants with reasonable prices. There's also a movie theater and a convenient public parking garage. 401 Broadway E. ✆ 206/322-1610. www.thebroadwaymarket.com.

City Centre   This upscale downtown shopping center is the Seattle address of such familiar high-end retailers as Barneys New York, FAO Schwarz, and Ann Taylor. There are works of art by Dale Chihuly and other Northwest glass artists on display throughout City Centre, and also a very comfortable lounge where you can rest your feet and escape from the Seattle weather. 1420 Fifth Ave. ✆ 206/624-8800. www.shopcitycentre.com.

Pacific Place   This downtown mall is located adjacent to Nordstrom and contains five levels of upscale shop-o-tainment, including Cartier, Tiffany & Co., bebe, J. Crew, MaxMara, five restaurants, and an 11-screen cinema. A huge skylight fills the interior space with much-appreciated natural light, and an adjoining garage ensures that you'll find a place to park (maybe). 600 Pine St. ✆ 206/405-2655. www.pacificplaceseattle.com.

Westlake Center   Located in the heart of Seattle's main shopping district, this upscale, urban shopping mall has more than 80 specialty shops, including Godiva Chocolatier, Crabtree & Evelyn, Aveda, and Made in Washington. There is an extensive food court. The mall is also the southern terminus for the monorail to Seattle Center. 400 Pine St. ✆ 206/467-3044. www.westlakecenter.com.

MARKETS

Pike Place Market   Pike Place Market is one of Seattle's most famous landmarks and tourist attractions. It shelters not only produce vendors, fishmongers, and butchers, but also artists, craftspeople, and performers. Hundreds of shops and dozens of restaurants (including some of Seattle's best) are tucked away in nooks and crannies on the numerous levels of the market. With so much to see and do, a trip to Pike Place Market can easily turn into an all-day affair. See also the sightseeing listing on p. 114. Pike St. and First Ave. ✆ 206/682-7453. www.pike placemarket.org.

Uwajimaya   Typically, your local neighborhood supermarket has a section of Chinese cooking ingredients; it's probably about 10 feet long, with half that space taken up by various brands of soy sauce. Now imagine your local supermarket with nothing but Asian foods, housewares, produce, and toys. That's

Uwajimaya, Seattle's Asian supermarket in the heart of the International District. A big food court here serves all kinds of Asian food. 600 Fifth Ave. S. ℂ 206/624-6248. www.uwajimaya.com.

MUSICAL INSTRUMENTS

Lark in the Morning Musique Shoppe   At Lark in the Morning, you can find just about any kind of instrument from around the world, from Greek bouzoukis and traditional African drums to didgeridoos and bagpipes. Customers are encouraged to try out the instruments in the store. 1411 First Ave. ℂ 206/623-3440. www.larkinam.com.

PERFUME

Parfumerie Nasreen   Located just inside the lobby of the luxurious Alexis Hotel, this perfume shop is packed with thousands of bottles of perfume from all over the world. You'll find some of the world's most expensive scents here. 1005 First Ave. ℂ 888/286-1825 or 206/682-3459. www.parfumerienasreen.com.

RECREATIONAL GEAR

Filson   This Seattle company has been outfitting people headed outdoors ever since the Alaskan gold rush at the end of the 1890s. You won't find any high-tech fabrics here, just good old-fashioned wool, and plenty of it. Filson's clothes are meant to last a lifetime (and have the prices to prove it), so if you demand only the best, even when it comes to outdoor gear, be sure to check out this Seattle institution. 1555 Fourth Ave. S. ℂ 206/622-3147. www.filson.com.

KAVU World Retail Headquarters   Rock jocks rejoice. Now you can get your favorite rugged outdoor clothes at half price. KAVU is a Seattle-based clothing manufacturer and has its tiny outlet store on a shady street in the Ballard neighborhood. The durable outdoor clothing here is great not just for rock climbers but for everyone. 5423 Ballard Ave. ℂ 206/783-0060. www.kavu.com.

The North Face   The North Face is one of the country's best-known names in the field of outdoor gear, and here in their downtown shop you can choose from a diverse selection. 1023 First Ave. ℂ 206/622-4111. www.thenorthface.com.

Patagonia Seattle   Patagonia has built up a very loyal clientele based on the durability of its outdoor gear and clothing. Sure the prices are high, but these clothes are made to last. Although there are plenty of outdoor designs, the clothes sold here these days are equally at home on city streets. 2100 First Ave. ℂ 206/622-9700. www.patagonia.com.

REI   Recreational Equipment, Incorporated (REI), was founded here in Seattle back in 1938 and today is the nation's largest co-op selling outdoor gear. The company's impressive flagship store is located just off I-5 not far from Lake Union and is a cross between a high-tech warehouse and a mountain lodge. The store is massive and sells almost anything you could ever need for pursuing your favorite outdoor sport. The store also has a 65-foot climbing pinnacle, a rain room for testing rain gear, a mountain-bike trail for test-driving bikes, a footwear test trail, even a play area for kids. With all this under one roof, who needs to go outside? Up on the top floor is a cafe with an outstanding view of downtown. 222 Yale Ave. N. ℂ 206/223-1944. www.rei.com.

SALMON

If you think that the fish at Pike Place Market look great but that you could never get it home on the plane, think again. Any of the seafood vendors in Pike Place Market will pack your fresh salmon or Dungeness crab in an airline-approved container that will keep it fresh for up to 48 hours. Alternatively, you can buy vacuum-packed smoked salmon that will keep for years without refrigeration.

Pike Place Fish   Located behind *Rachel,* Pike Place Market's life-sized bronze pig, this fishmonger is just about the busiest spot in the market most days. What pulls in the crowds are the antics of the workers here. Order a big silvery salmon and you'll have employees shouting out your order and throwing the fish over the counter. Crowds are always gathered around the stall hoping to see some of the famous "flying fish." 86 Pike Place, Pike Place Market. (C) 800/542-7732 or 206/682-7181. www.pikeplacefish.com.

Totem Smokehouse   Northwest Coast Indians relied heavily on salmon for sustenance, and to preserve the fish they used alderwood smoke. The tradition is carried on today to produce smoked salmon, one of the Northwest's most delicious food products. This store, located at street level in Pike Place Market, sells vacuum-packed smoked salmon that will keep without refrigeration until the package is opened. 1906 Pike Place, Pike Place Market. (C) 800/972-5666 or 206/443-1710. www.totemsmokehouse.com.

TOYS

Archie McPhee   You may already be familiar with this temple of the absurd through its mail-order catalog. Now imagine wandering through aisles full of goofy gags. Give yourself plenty of time and take a friend. You'll find Archie's place in the Ballard neighborhood. 2428 NW Market St. (C) 206/297-0240. www.mcphee.com.

Magic Mouse   Adults and children alike have a hard time pulling themselves away from this, the wackiest toy store in downtown Seattle. It's conveniently located in Pioneer Square and has a good selection of European toys. 603 First Ave. (C) 206/682-8097.

Wood Shop Toys   Despite the name, this toy shop doesn't have many wooden toys. But if you're a parent and you need to get your kids to walk another block, here's a place where you can get something for under $5 to entertain them. This shop is also great for fun and inexpensive stocking stuffers. 320 First Ave. S. (C) 206/624-1763.

WINE

Because the relatively dry summers, with warm days and cool nights, provide an ideal climate for growing grapes, the Northwest has become one of the nation's foremost wine-producing regions. After you've sampled Washington or Oregon vintages, you might want to take a few bottles home.

Grand Central Wine Merchants   This Pioneer Square area wine shop is down below street level in a building that was once a bank. This isn't to imply that the wines here will cost you a fortune—sure, the shop stocks some pricey wines from the more renowned regional wineries, but it has plenty of reasonably priced wines as well. 214 First Ave. S. (C) 206/340-5999.

Pike and Western Wine Shop Visit this shop for an excellent selection of Washington and Oregon wines, as well as wines from California, Italy, and France. The extremely knowledgeable staff will be happy to send you home (or out on a picnic) with the very best wine available in Seattle. Free wine tastings are held on Friday afternoons between 3 and 6pm. 1934 Pike Place, Pike Place Market. © 206/441-1307. www.pikeandwestern.com.

Seattle Cellars Wine merchant to the residents of Seattle's Belltown neighborhood, this wine shop sells wines from all over the world, with a substantial selection from Washington and Oregon. If you liked the wine you had last night with dinner, this is a good place to buy a bottle. Prices are reasonable, and wine tastings are held Thursday evenings between 5 and 7pm. 2505 Second Ave. © 206/256-0850.

10

Seattle After Dark

It's true that Seattleites spend much of their free time enjoying the city's natural surroundings, but that doesn't mean they overlook the more cultured evening pursuits. In fact, the winter weather that keeps people indoors, combined with a longtime desire to be the cultural mecca of the Northwest, have fueled a surprisingly active and diverse nightlife scene. The Seattle Opera is ranked one of the top opera companies in the country, and its stagings of Wagner's *Ring* series have achieved near-legendary status. The Seattle Symphony also receives frequent accolades. Likewise, the Seattle Repertory Theatre has won Tony awards for its productions, and a thriving fringe theater scene keeps the city's lovers of avant-garde theater contentedly discoursing in cafes about the latest hysterical or thought-provoking performances. Music lovers will also find a plethora of classical, jazz, and rock offerings.

Much of Seattle's evening entertainment scene is clustered in the Seattle Center Theater District and the Pioneer Square areas. The former hosts theater, opera, and classical music performances; the latter is a nightclub district. Other concentrations of nightclubs can be found in Belltown, where crowds of the young and the hip flock to the neighborhood's many nightclubs, and Capitol Hill, with its ultracool gay scene. Ballard, formerly a Scandinavian enclave in north Seattle, attracts a primarily middle-class, not-too-hip, not-too-old crowd, including lots of college students and techies. It's not the hipster Belltown scene, it's not the Bud-swilling blues scene of Pioneer Square, and it's not the sleek gay scene of Capitol Hill.

While winter is a time to enjoy the performing arts, summer brings an array of outdoor festivals. These take place during daylight hours as much as they do after dark, but you'll find information on all these festivals and performance series in this chapter.

To find out what's going on when you're in town, pick up a free copy of *Seattle Weekly* (www.seattleweekly. com), Seattle's arts-and-entertainment newspaper. You'll find it in bookstores, convenience stores, grocery stores, newsstands, and newspaper boxes around downtown and other neighborhoods. On Friday, the *Seattle Times* includes a section called "Ticket," a guide to the week's arts and entertainment offerings.

1 The Performing Arts

While the Seattle Symphony performs in downtown's Benaroya Hall, the main venues for the performing arts in Seattle are primarily clustered in **Seattle Center,** the special events complex that was built for the 1962 Seattle World's Fair. Here, in the shadow of the Space Needle, you'll find the Marion Oliver McCaw Hall (scheduled to open in summer of 2003), Bagley Wright Theater, Intiman Playhouse, Seattle Children's Theatre, Seattle Center Coliseum, Memorial Stadium, and Experience Music Project's Sky Church performance hall.

OPERA & CLASSICAL MUSIC

The **Seattle Opera** (② 206/389-7676; www.seattleopera.org) is considered one of the finest opera companies in the country and will soon be performing at Seattle Center's new Marion Oliver McCaw Hall (scheduled to open in summer of 2003). It is *the* Wagnerian opera company in the U.S. The stagings of Wagner's four-opera *The Ring of the Nibelungen* are breathtaking spectacles that draw crowds from around the country. However, the *Ring* cycle was staged in 2001 and won't be staged again for a couple more years. In addition to such classical operas as *The Magic Flute* and *The Barber of Seville*, the season usually includes a more contemporary production. Ticket prices range from $35 to $107. Until the new performance hall opens, opera performances are being held in the Mercer Arts Arena at Seattle Center.

The 90-musician **Seattle Symphony** (② 206/215-4747; www.seattle symphony.org), which performs in the acoustically superb Benaroya Hall, offers an amazingly diverse musical season that runs from September to July. With several different musical series, there is a little something for every type of classical music fan. There are evenings of classical, light classical, and pops, plus afternoon concerts, guest artists, and more. Ticket prices range from $11 to $71.

The **Northwest Chamber Orchestra** (② 206/343-0445; www.nwco.org), a perennial favorite with Seattle classical music fans, is a showcase for Northwest performers. The season runs from September to May, and performances are held primarily in Benaroya Hall in downtown Seattle, although there are also concert series at the Seattle Asian Art Museum. Ticket prices range from $14.50 to $35.

THEATER
MAINSTREAM THEATERS

The **Seattle Repertory Theater** (② 877/900-9285 or 206/443-2222; www. seattlerep.org), which performs at the Bagley Wright and Leo K. theaters, Seattle Center, 155 Mercer St., is Seattle's top professional theater and stages the most consistently entertaining productions in the city. The Rep's season runs from September to June, with five plays performed in the main theater and four in the more intimate Leo K. Theatre. Productions range from classics to world premieres. Ticket prices range from $15 to $46. When available, rush tickets are available half an hour before shows for $20.

With a season that runs from March to December, the **Intiman Theatre Company** (② 206/269-1900; www.intiman.org), which performs at the Intiman Playhouse, Seattle Center, 201 Mercer St., fills in the gap left by those months when the Seattle Rep's lights are dark. Ticket prices range from $27 to $42.

Performing in the historic Eagles Building theater adjacent to the Washington State Convention and Trade Center, **A Contemporary Theater (ACT),** 700 Union St. (② 206/292-7676; www.acttheatre.org), offers slightly more adventurous productions than the other major theater companies in Seattle, though it's not nearly as avant-garde as some of the smaller companies. The season runs from the end of May to November (plus *A Christmas Carol* in Dec). Ticket prices usually range from $24.50 to $44.

FRINGE THEATER

Not only does Seattle have a healthy mainstream performing-arts community, it has the sort of fringe theater life once only associated with such cities as New York, Los Angeles, London, and Edinburgh. The city's more avant-garde performance companies frequently grab their share of the limelight with daring, outrageous, and thought-provoking productions.

Seattle's interest in fringe theater finds its greatest expression each September,
when the **Seattle Fringe Theater Festival** (② **206/342-9172;** www.seattle
fringe.org), a showcase for small, self-producing theater companies, takes over
various venues. The festival includes more than 500 performances by theater
groups from around the country.

Even if you don't happen to be in town for Seattle's annual fringe binge, check
the listings in *Seattle Weekly* or the *Seattle Times*' Friday "Ticket" entertainment
guide to see what's going on during your visit. The following venues are some of
Seattle's more reliable places for way-off Broadway productions, performance
art, and spoken word performances:

- **Book-It Repertory Theater** (② **206/325-6500;** www.book-it.org). Works
  by local playwrights, adaptations of literary works. Performances are held at
  various venues around the city.
- **Empty Space Theatre,** 3509 Fremont Ave. N. (② **206/547-7500;** www.
  emptyspace.org). One of Seattle's biggest little theaters, Empty Space stages
  mostly comedies and is popular with a young crowd.
- **Northwest Asian-American Theater,** Theatre Off Jackson, 409 Seventh
  Ave. S. (② **206/340-1049**). Works by Asian-American writers, actors, and
  musicians.
- **Theater Schmeater,** 1500 Summit St. (② **206/324-5801;** www.
  schmeater.org). Lots of weird and sometimes wonderful comedy, including
  ever-popular live late-night stagings of episodes from *The Twilight Zone.*

DANCE
Although it has a well-regarded ballet company and a theater dedicated to contemporary dance and performance art, Seattle is not nearly as devoted to dance
as it is to theater and classical music. That said, hardly a week goes by without
some sort of dance performance being staged somewhere in the city. Touring
companies of all types, the University of Washington Dance Department faculty
and student performances, the UW World Dance Series (see below for details),
and the Northwest New Works Festival (see below) all bring plenty of creative
movement to the stages of Seattle. When you're in town, check *Seattle Weekly* or
the *Seattle Times* for a calendar of upcoming performances.

The **Pacific Northwest Ballet,** Seattle Center Opera House, 301 Mercer St. (© 206/441-2424; www.pnb.org), is Seattle's premier dance company. During the season, which runs from September to June, the company presents a wide range of classics, new works, and (the company's specialty) pieces choreographed by George Balanchine (tickets $16–$110). This company's performance of *The Nutcracker,* with outstanding dancing and sets and costumes by children's book author Maurice Sendak, is the highlight of every season. Until the new Marion Oliver McCaw Hall is completed in the summer of 2003, the Pacific Northwest Ballet will be performing in Seattle Center's Mercer Arts Arena.

Much more adventurous choreography is the domain of **On the Boards,** Behnke Center for Contemporary Performance, 100 W. Roy St. (© 206/217-9888; www.ontheboards.org), which, although it stages a wide variety of performance art, is best known as Seattle's premier modern-dance venue (tickets $7–$24). In addition to dance performances by Northwest artists, there are a variety of productions each year by internationally known performance artists.

MAJOR PERFORMANCE HALLS

With ticket prices for shows and concerts so high these days, it pays to be choosy about what you see, but sometimes *where* you see it is just as important. Benaroya Hall, the Seattle Symphony's downtown home, has such excellent acoustics that a performance here is worth attending just for the sake of hearing how a good symphony hall should sound. Seattle also has two restored historic theaters that are as much a part of a performance as what happens onstage.

Benaroya Hall (© 206/215-4747), on Third Avenue between Union and University streets in downtown Seattle, is the home of the Seattle Symphony. This state-of-the-art performance hall houses two concert halls—the main hall and a smaller recital hall. The concert hall is home to the Watjen concert organ, a magnificent pipe organ. There's also a Starbucks, a cafe, and a symphony store here. But amenities aside, the main hall's excellent acoustics are the big attraction.

The **5th Avenue Theatre,** 1308 Fifth Ave. (© 206/625-1418 for information, or 206/292-ARTS for tickets; www.5thavenuetheatre.org), which first opened its doors in 1926 as a vaudeville house, is a loose re-creation of the imperial throne room in Beijing's Forbidden City. In 1980, the theater underwent a complete renovation that restored this Seattle jewel to its original splendor, and today the astounding interior is as good a reason as any to see a show here. Don't miss an opportunity to attend a performance. Broadway shows are the theater's mainstay (tickets $16–$58).

The **Paramount Theatre,** 911 Pine St. (© 206/682-1414; www.thepara mount.com), one of Seattle's few historic theaters, has been restored to its original beauty and today shines with all the brilliance it did when it first opened. New lighting and sound systems have brought the theater up to contemporary standards. The theater stages everything from rock concerts to Broadway musicals (tickets $7–$127). Tickets are available through Ticketmaster.

PERFORMING ARTS SERIES

When Seattle's own resident performing-arts companies aren't taking to the dozens of stages around the city, various touring companies from around the world are. If you're a fan of Broadway shows, check the calendars at the Paramount Theatre and the 5th Avenue Theatre, both of which regularly serve as Seattle stops for touring shows.

The **UW World Series** (© 206/543-4880), held at Meany Hall on the University of Washington campus, is actually several different series that include a chamber music series, a classical piano series, a dance series, and a world music and theater series. Together these four series keep the Meany Hall stage busy between October and May. Special events are also scheduled (tickets $28–$45).

Seattle loves the theater, and each September the city binges on the fringes with the **Seattle Fringe Theater Festival** (see "Fringe Theater," above). Avant-garde performances are also the specialty of the **Northwest New Works Festival** (© 206/217-9888; www.ontheboards.org), **On the Boards'** annual barrage of contemporary dance and performance art held each spring.

Another series worth checking out is the **Seattle Art Museum's "After Hours."** Every Thursday from 5 to 9pm, the museum hosts live music, frequently jazz, and sets up a bar in its main lobby. Shows are free with museum admission.

Summer is a time of outdoor festivals and performance series in Seattle, and should you be in town during the sunny months, you'll have a wide variety of alfresco performances from which to choose. The city's biggest summer music festivals are the **Northwest Folklife Festival** over Memorial Day weekend and **Bumbershoot** over Labor Day weekend. See the "Seattle Calendar of Events" in chapter 2, "Planning Your Trip to Seattle," for details.

AT&T Wireless Summer Nights at the Pier (© 206/628-0888; www.summer\nights.org) presents a summer's worth of big-name acts at Pier 62/63 on the waterfront. Blues, jazz, rock, and folk acts generally pull in a 30-something to 50-something crowd (tickets $15–$57).

Here on the waterfront, you can also catch some alfresco jazz at the Seattle Aquarium's **Sea Sounds** summer concert series. The concerts are held between June and early October (weather permitting) at the end of the Aquarium's pier (Pier 59). Tickets are $24 to $26. For more information, phone © **206/386-4314** or check out the aquarium's website: www.seattleaquarium.org.

At **Woodland Park Zoo** (© 206/615-0076; www.zoo.org), the Zoo Tunes concert series brings in more big-name performers from the world of jazz, easy listening, blues, and rock (tickets $12–$19).

In Woodinville, on the east side of Lake Washington, Chateau Ste. Michele, 14111 NE 145th St., stages the area's most enjoyable outdoor summer concert series. The **Summer Festival On The Green** (© 425/415-3300 for information, or 206/628-0888 for tickets) is held at the winery's amphitheater, which is surrounded by beautiful estatelike grounds. Chateau Ste. Michele is Washington's largest winery, and plenty of wine is available. Once again the lineup is calculated to appeal to the 30- to 50-something crowd (Bonnie Raitt, Linda Ronstadt, Kenny Loggins, Cowboy Junkies, Gipsy Kings). Ticket prices range from $30 to $100. See chapter 11 for more on Woodinville and Chateau Ste. Michele.

2 The Club & Music Scene

If you have the urge to do a bit of clubbing and bar-hopping, there's no better place to start than **Pioneer Square.** Good times are guaranteed, whether you want to hear a live band, hang out in a good old-fashioned bar, or dance. Keep in mind that this neighborhood tends to attract a very rowdy crowd and can be pretty rough late at night.

Belltown, north of Pike Place Market, is another good place to club-hop. Clubs here are far more trend-conscious than those in the Pioneer Square area. Club-goers tend to be 20- and 30-somethings.

Seattle's other nightlife district is the former Scandinavian neighborhood of **Ballard,** where you'll find more than half a dozen nightlife establishments, including a brewpub, taverns, bars, and live-music clubs.

FOLK, ROCK & REGGAE
PIONEER SQUARE

The Pioneer Square area is Seattle's main live music neighborhood, and the clubs have banded together to make things easy for music fans. The **"Joint Cover"** plan lets you pay one admission to get into seven different clubs. The charge is $5 Sunday through Thursday and $10 on Friday and Saturday ($8, 8–9pm Fri–Sat; occasionally $12 for national-act nights). Participating clubs currently include Larry's Blues Cafe, Doc Maynard's, the Central Saloon, the Bohemian Café, Old Timer's Cafe, Zasu Dance Club, and the New Orleans. Most of these clubs are short on style and hit-or-miss when it comes to music (which makes the joint cover a great way to find out where the good music is on any given night).

The Bohemian Café, Lounge & Backstage   This Pioneer Square club is Seattle's main venue for reggae, with live music several nights a week. Caribbean food is served, and there is an after-hours scene here on Friday and Saturday nights. 111 Yesler Way. ✆ 206/447-1514, reggae hot line 206/447-9868. www.bohemian reggaeclub.com. Joint cover $5–$10.

The Central Saloon   Established in 1892, the Central is the oldest saloon in Seattle. As a Seattle institution, it's a must-stop during a night out in Pioneer Square. You might catch sounds ranging from funk to reggae. 207 First Ave. S. ✆ 206/622-0209. Joint cover $5–$10.

BELLTOWN & ENVIRONS

The Crocodile Cafe   With its rambunctious decor, this Belltown establishment is a combination nightclub, bar, and restaurant. There's live rock Tuesday through Saturday nights. The music calendar here is always eclectic, with everything from rock to folk to jazz, though alternative rock dominates. 2200 Second Ave. ✆ 206/441-5611. www.thecrocodile.com. Cover $5–$20.

EMP   The Experience Music Project, Seattle's humongous lump o' color rock museum, isn't just some morgue for dead rockers. This place is a showcase for real live rockers, too. EMP's main hall, the **Sky Church,** plays host to everything from indie rockers to theater productions with live rock accompaniment. There's also the smaller **Liquid Lounge,** a club with no cover and a wide range of musical sensibilities. One night might be a reggae dance party while another night might feature hip-hop or an acoustic show. 325 Fifth Ave. N. ✆ 206/770-2702. www.emplive.com. Cover: Liquid Lounge free; Sky Church $7–$32.

Showbox   Located across the street from Pike Place Market, this club books a wide variety of local and name rock acts. Definitely *the* downtown rock venue for performers with a national following. 1426 First Ave. ✆ 206/628-3151. www.showbox online.com. Cover $10–$30.

Sit and Spin   It's a club, it's a juice bar, it's a cafe, it's a Laundromat! This Belltown cafe/club is all of these and more. A popular hangout for the city's young scene-makers, Sit and Spin books an eclectic range of music, and has a Wednesday night poetry slam. Decor is 1950s funky. 2219 Fourth Ave. ✆ 206/441-9484. No cover–$8.

CAPITOL HILL

Baltic Room   This swanky Capitol Hill hangout for the beautiful people provides a wide range of entertainment, from happy hour DJs between 5 and 9pm to live or DJ dance music ranging from Britpop to hip-hop and bhangra later in the evening. 1207 Pine St. ✆ 206/625-4444. Cover $3–$10.

Century Ballroom   With a beautiful wooden dance floor and a genuine bandstand, this classic ballroom now plays host to some of the best touring acts to come to town. This is also Seattle's top spot for swing and salsa dancing, each of which tops the bill a couple of nights per week. The crowd here is very diverse, with customers of all ages who come to check out a schedule that might include an evening of Hawaiian slack-key guitar music or an avant-garde electric violin performance. 915 E. Pine St. (C) **206/324-7263**. www.centuryballroom.com. Cover $5–$30.

BALLARD

The Firehouse   An eclectic assortment of musical styles finds its way onto the bandstand of this converted firehouse in Ballard. Now it's just the music that's hot, and that's the way they want to keep it. The crowd is young, and the music generally ranges from techno/trance to hip-hop to the latest local indie rockers. 5429 Russell Ave. NW (C) **206/784-3516**. No cover–$10.

Tractor Tavern   For an ever-eclectic schedule of music for people whose tastes go beyond the latest rap artist, the Tractor Tavern is the place to be. You can catch almost anything from Hawaiian slack-key guitar to rockabilly to singer-songwriters to banjo music to Celtic to folk to zydeco. Sound like your kind of place? 5213 Ballard Ave. NW. (C) **206/789-3599**. www.tractortavern.citysearch.com. No cover–$20.

JAZZ & BLUES

Dimitriou's Jazz Alley   Cool and sophisticated, this Belltown establishment is reminiscent of a New York jazz club and has been around for more than 20 years. Seattle's premier jazz venue, it books only the best performers, including name acts. 2033 Sixth Ave. (C) **206/441-9729**. www.jazzalley.com. Cover $15.50–$30.

New Orleans   If you like your food and your jazz hot, check out the New Orleans in Pioneer Square. Throughout the week, there's Cajun, Dixieland, R&B, jazz, and blues. 114 First Ave. S. (C) **206/622-2563**. Joint cover $5–$10.

The Pampas Room   You can smell the cigar smoke from this club way out on the sidewalk halfway down the block (and the club is down a long flight of stairs from street level). The big-money crowd claims this retro-swank upscale jazz club as its very own on Friday and Saturday nights when there's live jazz and swing dancing. Currently there is salsa dancing (with lessons) on Wednesday nights. 90 Wall St. (C) **206/728-1337**. No cover–$10 (Wed).

Tula's   This is the real thing: a jazz club that's a popular jazz musicians' after-hours hangout and a good place to catch up-and-coming musicians. American and Mediterranean food is served. 2214 Second Ave. (C) **206/443-4221**. www.tulas.com. Cover $5–$15.

COMEDY, CABARET & DINNER THEATER

The Cabaret at Crepe de Paris   Throughout the year, this club stages a wide variety of entertaining programs of music, dance, and humor. Updated torch songs and numbers from classic musicals assure that the shows here will appeal to young and old alike. Reservations are required. Rainier Sq., 1333 Fifth Ave. (C) **206/623-4111**. $45 dinner and show; $18 show only.

Comedy Underground   This club is located in Pioneer Square, where the Seattle Underground tour has proven that too much time beneath the city streets can lead even normal people to tell bad jokes. Currently Monday is open-mike

So Who Needs Cirque du Soleil, Anyway?

Cirque du Soleil may be the coolest circus in the world, but man (and woman) cannot live on cotton candy alone. Circus acts aimed at the upper crust should be accompanied by gourmet cuisine. At least that's the concept behind **Teatro ZinZanni**, 2301 Sixth Ave. (© **206/805-0015; www.zinzanni.com**), a European-style cabaret of the highest order. Staged in a classic *spiegeltent* (mirror tent) imported from Belgium, this evening of comedy, dance, theater, and fine food (catered by Seattle's celeb chef Tom Douglas) offers clowns, acrobats, illusionists, and cabaret singers. In fact there's more entertainment packed into a night at Teatro ZinZanni than anywhere else in Seattle. Don't miss it. Tickets are $89 Sunday through Thursday and $99 Friday and Saturday. Reserve well in advance!

night, in case you want to get onstage and make a fool of yourself or the audience. 222 S. Main St. © **206/628-0303**. www.comedyunderground.com. Cover $4–$12.

Market Theatre   Competitive improvisational comedy at this small back-alley theater in Pike Place Market pits two teams against each other. Suggestions from the audience serve as the inspiration for sketches that can sometimes be hilarious but that just as often fall flat. The young, rowdy crowd never seems to mind one way or the other. 1428 Post Alley. © **206/781-9273**.

The Pink Door   Better known as Pike Place Market's unmarked restaurant, the Pink Door has a hopping after-work bar scene that tends to attract a 30-something crowd. It also doubles as a cabaret featuring Seattle's most eclectic lineup of performers. Lots of fun and not to be missed. 1919 Post Alley. © **206/443-3241**. No cover.

DANCE CLUBS

Club Medusa   Located just a couple of blocks from Pike Place Market, this brand new dance club affects a Roman/Greek ruins decor and, with its bouncer in a suit and tie, is trying hard to attract young scene-makers from the Belltown clubs a few blocks away. This club is open Thursday through Saturday only. 2218 Western Ave. © **206/448-8887**. Cover $15.

Contour   Located a few blocks up First Avenue from Pioneer Square, this modern dance club attracts a more diverse crowd than most Pioneer Square clubs. The music ranges from deep house to trance to drum-and-base, and the partying on Fridays and Saturdays goes on until 8 the next morning. Laser light shows, fire dancers—this joint is one wild party! 807 First Ave. © **206/447-7704**. www.clubcontour.com. Cover $5–$10.

Lico Lounge   With its open-air deck atop a covered parking lot, this second-floor bar provides not only a great spot for a few drinks on a warm summer evening but also a primo people-watching perspective on the busy bar block in Belltown. Lico Lounge is affiliated with Tia Lou's, a street-level Mexican restaurant, so, of course, margaritas are the drink of choice here. There's DJ dance music Wednesday through Saturday; Fridays are Miami night. 2218 First Ave. © **206/733-8226**. No cover–$10 (Fri–Sat after 9:30 or 10pm).

Polly Esther's/Culture Club   If disco, funk, and '80s new wave music are what get your booty shakin', don't miss this club (part of a national chain) across the street from the Experience Music Project. There are two clubs under one roof. As you can imagine, this place tends to attract a clientele that wasn't even born when disco was all the rage. In other words, this is a 20-something pickup joint. 332 Fifth Ave. N. ✆ 206/441-1970. www.pollyesthers.com. Cover $10 (free before 9pm).

3 The Bar Scene

BARS

THE WATERFRONT

Restaurant 67 Bar   If you get any closer to the water, you'll have wet feet. Located inside downtown Seattle's only waterfront hotel, this bar boasts what just might be the best bar view in the city. Watch the ferries come and go, or see the sun set over Puget Sound and the Olympics. In the Edgewater Hotel, Pier 67, 2411 Alaskan Way. ✆ 206/728-7000.

DOWNTOWN

The Bookstore—a Bar   Located just off the lobby of the posh Alexis Hotel, this cozy little bar is—surprise—filled with books. There are plenty of interesting magazines on hand as well, so if you want to sip a single malt and smoke a cigar but don't want to deal with crowds and noise, this is a great option. Very classy. In the Alexis Hotel, 1007 First Ave. ✆ 206/382-1506.

McCormick & Schmick's   The mahogany paneling and sparkling cut glass lend this restaurant bar a touch of class, but otherwise the place could have been the inspiration for *Cheers*. Very popular as an after-work watering hole of Seattle moneymakers, McCormick & Schmick's is best known for its excellent and inexpensive happy-hour snacks. 1103 First Ave. ✆ 206/623-5500.

Oliver's   Maybe you've seen one too many places that claim to make the best martini and you're dubious. Here at Oliver's they've repeatedly put their martinis to the test and come out on top. The atmosphere is classy and the happy hour appetizers are good, but in the end, only you can decide whether or not these martinis are the best in Seattle. In the Mayflower Park Hotel, 405 Olive Way. ✆ 206/623-8700.

BELLTOWN

Axis   This is where it all begins most nights for the black-clad crowds of ultra-hip Seattle scenesters who crowd the sidewalks and bars of Belltown on weekend nights. Get here early enough and maybe you'll even snag one of the coveted sidewalk tables. If you're too late, don't worry: The front walls roll up and there's still the second row. It's a serious singles scene with good food. 2214 First Ave. ✆ 206/441-9600.

Bada Lounge   If Swedish modern, molded plastic, and techno are your scene, this place is for you. With its retro-futurist decor and wall of monitors projecting video wallpaper, this bar is as stylin' as they come here in Seattle. The white-on-white decor is calculated to make people in black look their very best. Don't miss the red-lit chill-out room with its couches and pillows. Early in the evening, this is a pan-Asian restaurant, and later on there's DJ dancing to beat-driven dance tracks. 2230 First Ave. ✆ 206/374-8717.

Toi   Ostensibly an upscale Thai restaurant, this place has become one of the hottest bars in Belltown. There's a bar downstairs in the main dining room, but the real action is in the upstairs bar at the back of the building. Toi packs 'em in late in the evening and is a busy singles scene. 1904 Fourth Ave. ⑦ 206/267-1017.

The Virginia Inn   Although the Virginia Inn is located in oh-so-stylish Bell-town, this bar/restaurant has a decidedly old Seattle feel, due in large part to the fact that this place has been around since 1903. Best of all, this is a nonsmoking bar and it serves French food! 1937 First Ave. ⑦ 206/728-1937.

PIKE PLACE MARKET

Alibi Room   If you've been on your feet all day in Pike Place Market and have had it with the crowds of people, duck down the alley under the market clock and slip through the door of this hideaway. The back-alley setting gives this place an atmospheric speakeasy feel. 85 Pike St. ⑦ 206/623-3180.

PIONEER SQUARE

FX McRory's   Located across the street from Seattle's new football stadium and not far from Safeco Field, this bar attracts upscale sports fans (with the occa-sional Mariners and Seahawks players thrown in for good measure). You'll find Seattle's largest selection of bourbon here. There's also an oyster bar and good food. 419 Occidental Ave. S. ⑦ 206/623-4800. www.fxmcrorys.com.

Marcus's   Seattle's only underground martini and cigar bar, Marcus's is hidden beneath a Taco del Mar just off First Avenue in Pioneer Square. You'll be drinking below street level with the ghosts of Seattle's past and the lounge lizards of today. There's DJ music several nights each week. This is a much mellower alternative to Pioneer Square's rowdy street-level bars. 88 Yesler Way. ⑦ 206/624-3323.

BREWPUBS

Big Time Brewery and Alehouse   Big Time, Seattle's oldest brewpub, is located in the University District and is done up to look like a turn-of-the-century tavern, complete with a 100-year-old back bar and a wooden refrigerator. The pub serves as many as 12 of its own brews at any given time, and some of these can be pretty unusual. 4133 University Way NE. ⑦ 206/545-4509. www.bigtimebrewery.com.

Elysian Brewing Company   Although the brewery at this Capitol Hill brewpub is one of the smallest in the city, the pub itself is quite large and has an industrial feel that says "local brewpub." The stout and strong ales are especially good, and the brewers' creativity here just can't be beat. Hands-down the best brewpub in Seattle. 1221 E. Pike St. ⑦ 206/860-1920. www.elysianbrewing.com.

Hales Ales Brewery and Pub   Located about a mile west of the Fremont Bridge heading toward Ballard, this is a big, lively brewpub. 4301 Leary Way NW. ⑦ 206/782-0737. www.halesales.com.

The Pike Pub and Brewery   Located in an open, central space inside Pike Place Market, this brewpub makes excellent stout and pale ale. There's live instrumental music a couple of nights a week and, with its comfortable couches, the Pike is a great place to get off your feet after a day of exploring the market. 1415 First Ave. ⑦ 206/622-6044.

Pyramid Ale House   Located south of Pioneer Square in a big old warehouse, this pub is part of the brewery that makes Thomas Kemper lagers and Pyramid ales. It's a favorite spot for dinner and drinks before or after baseball games at Safeco Field and football games at the new Seahawks Stadium. There's good pub food, too. 1201 First Ave. S. ⑦ 206/682-3377. www.pyramidbrew.com.

IRISH PUBS

Fadó   This Irish pub is part of a national pub chain but has the feel of an independent. Lots of antiques, old signs, and a dark, cozy feel make it a very comfortable place for a pint. There's live Irish music several nights a week. 801 First Ave. © 206/264-2700. www.fadoirishpub.com.

Kells   At one time the space now occupied by this pub was the embalming room of a mortuary. However, these days the scene is much more lively and has the feel of a casual Dublin pub. They pull a good pint of Guinness and feature live traditional Irish music 7 nights a week. Kells also serves traditional Irish meals. 1916 Post Alley, Pike Place Market. © 206/728-1916. www.kellsirish.com. Cover Fri–Sat only, $5.

The Owl & Thistle Pub   Located right around the corner from Fadó, this is an equally authentic-feeling pub. The Post Alley entrance, with its blue doors, gives this place the ambience of a back-street Dublin pub. There's live music most nights, with the house band playing Irish music on Friday and Saturday nights. 808 Post Alley. © 206/621-7777. www.owlnthistle.com.

T. S. McHugh's   Located in the Lower Queen Anne neighborhood adjacent to Seattle Center and many of Seattle's mainstream theaters, T. S. McHugh's has a very authentic feel. It's a good place to relax after an afternoon spent exploring the Seattle Center. 21 Mercer St. © 206/282-1910.

4 The Gay & Lesbian Scene

Capitol Hill is Seattle's main gay neighborhood, with the greatest concentration of gay and lesbian bars and dance clubs. Look for the readily available *Seattle Gay News* (© 206/324-4297; www.sgn.org), where you'll find ads for many of the city's gay bars and nightclubs.

BARS

C. C. Attle's   Located across the street from Thumpers, this bar is a Seattle landmark on the gay bar scene. It's well known for its cheap, strong cocktails, but it can be something of a regulars' scene. There are a couple of patios and three separate bars. 1501 E. Madison St. © 206/726-0565.

The Cuff Complex   A virtual multiplex of gay entertainment, this place has no less than four separate bars. There's a quiet bar, a dance club, and a patio for those rain-free nights. It's primarily a leather-and-Levis crowd, but you're still welcome even if you forgot to pack your leather pants. 1533 13th Ave. © 206/323-1525. www.thecuff.com.

Man Ray   This retro-futuristic Capitol Hill bar is well known for attracting Seattle's beautiful people, at least the gay ones. High-priced designer martinis are the specialty. In the summer, you can hang out on the patio, but it's all the video monitors that make this such an unusual place. 514 E. Pine St. © 206/568-0750.

R Place Bar and Grill   With three floors of entertainment, you hardly need to go anywhere else for a night on the town. There's a video bar on the ground floor, pool tables and video games on the second floor, and up on the top floor, a sports bar that turns into a dance club on weekends. 619 E. Pine St. © 206/ 322-8828. www.rplaceseattle.com.

Thumpers   Perched high on Capitol Hill, Thumpers is a classy bar/restaurant done up in oak. It's been a favorite of Seattle's gay community for nearly 20 years. The seats by the fireplace are perfect on a cold and rainy night, and for sunny days there are two decks with great views. There's live music several nights each week (maybe even a Judy & Liza show). 1500 E. Madison St. ✆ 206/328-3800.

Wildrose This friendly restaurant/bar is a longtime favorite of the Capitol Hill lesbian community and claims to be the oldest lesbian bar on the West Coast. During the spring and summer, there is an outdoor seating area. 1021 E. Pike St. ✆ 206/324-9210. www.thewildrosebar.com.

DANCE CLUBS

Neighbours This has been the favorite dance club of Capitol Hill's gay community for years, and, as at other clubs, different nights of the week feature different styles of music. You'll find this club's entrance down the alley. 1509 Broadway Ave. ✆ 206/324-5358. www.neighboursonline.com. Cover $1–$5.

Re-Bar Each night there's a different theme, with the DJs spinning everything from world beat to funk and hip-hop. This club isn't exclusively gay, but it's still a favorite of Seattle's gay community. 1114 Howell St. ✆ 206/233-9873. No cover–$6.

Timberline Spirits If the boot-scootin' boogie is your favorite dance, the Timberline is the place to be. There's dancing to C&W music several nights a week. Sundays at 4pm, this place also hosts Seattle's biggest, best, and only gay tea dance. Unfortunately, the building housing this venerable old club has been sold, and the club's lease will expire in May 2003. 2015 Boren Ave. ✆ 206/622-6220. www.timberlinespirits.com. No cover–$5.

5 More Entertainment

MOVIES

Movies come close behind coffee and reading as a Seattle obsession, and you'll find a surprising number of theaters in Seattle showing foreign and independent films. These include **Grand Illusion,** 1403 NE 50th St. at University Way NE (✆ 206/523-3935); **Harvard Exit,** 807 E. Roy St. at Broadway Avenue East (✆ 206/323-8986); the **Egyptian,** 801 E. Pine St. (✆ 206/32-EGYPT); and the **Varsity,** 4329 University Way NE (✆ 206/632-3131).

There's no better place in town to catch a mainstream movie than **Cinerama,** 2100 Fourth Ave. (✆ 206/441-3080), a space-age 1950s wide-screen theater brought up to 21st-century standards of technology.

The **Seattle International Film Festival (SIFF)** (✆ 206/324-9996 or 206/324-9997; www.seattlefilm.com) takes place each May and early June, with around 150 films shown at various theaters. For information, check the website or, at festival time, the local papers.

The **Seattle Art Museum,** 100 University St. (✆ 206/654-3100; www.seattleartmuseum.org), has Thursday-night screenings of classics and foreign films. If you're a movie buff, be sure to check out this series.

At the **Experience Music Project (EMP),** 325 Fifth Ave. N. (✆ 206/770-2702; www.emplive.com), you can catch music-oriented documentary films and silent movies that are shown with live musical accompaniment. Tickets are $7.

The **Paramount Theatre,** 911 Pine St. (✆ 206/682-1414; www.theparamount.com), does Silent Movie Mondays, with classic silent films and musical accompaniment on a Wurlitzer organ. Tickets are $12 ($9 for seniors and students) and are available through Ticketmaster.

In Fremont, the **Fremont Saturday Nite Outdoor Movies** series (✆ 206/781-4230; www.outdoorcinema.com), a summer event, shows modern classics,

B movies (sometimes with live overdubbing by a local improv comedy company), and indie shorts. Films are screened in the parking lot at North 35th Street and Phinney Avenue North. The parking lot opens at 7:30pm, and there is a $5 suggested donation.

AT&T Outdoor Cinema screens movies at the Seattle Center Mural Stage and at the Harbor Steps, First Avenue and Seneca Street. For information on these movies, contact **Lunar Flicks** (© **206/297-6801;** www.lunarflicks.com). Gates open at 6pm, with music at 7pm and movies at dusk.

6 Only in Seattle

While Seattle has plenty to offer in the way of performing arts, some of the city's best after-dark offerings have nothing to do with the music. There's no better way to start the evening (that is, if the day has been sunny or only partly cloudy) than to catch the **sunset from the waterfront.** The Bell Street Pier and Myrtle Edwards Park are two of the best and least commercial vantages for taking in nature's evening light show. Keep in mind that sunset can come as late as 10pm in the middle of summer.

Want the best view of the city lights? Hold off on your elevator ride to the top of the **Space Needle** until after dark. Alternatively, you can hop a ferry and sail off into the night. Now, what could be more romantic?

Well, I suppose a **carriage ride** could be as romantic. Carriages can be found parked and waiting for customers, couples and families alike, on the waterfront.

For a cheap date, nothing beats the **first Thursday art walk.** On the first Thursday of each month, galleries in Pioneer Square stay open until 8 or 9pm. Appetizers and drinks are usually available (and sometimes live music). On those same first Thursdays, the Seattle Art Museum, the Seattle Asian Art Museum, the Frye Art Museum, the Henry Art Gallery, the Burke Museum, and the Museum of Flight stay open late, and most waive their usual admission charges. All of these museums are open late every Thursday, not just the first Thursday of the month, though you'll have to pay on those other nights (except at the Frye, which never charges an admission).

Want to learn to dance? Up on Capitol Hill, the sidewalk along Broadway is inlaid with **brass dance steps.** Spend an evening strolling the strip, and you and your partner can teach yourselves classic dance steps in between noshing on a piroshki and savoring a chocolate torte.

11

Side Trips from Seattle

After you've explored Seattle for a few days, consider heading out of town on a day trip. Within 1 to 1½ hours of the city you can find yourself hiking in a national park, cruising up a fjordlike arm of Puget Sound, exploring the San Juan Islands, or sampling a taste of the grape at some of Washington's top wineries. With the exception of the San Juan Islands, the excursions listed below are all fairly easy day trips that will give you glimpses of the Northwest outside the Emerald City. Another possible excursion is to Mount St. Helens National Volcanic Monument.

For more in-depth coverage of the areas surrounding Seattle, pick up a copy of *Frommer's Washington State* (Wiley Publishing).

1 The San Juan Islands

On a late afternoon on a clear summer day, the sun slants low, suffusing the scene with a golden light. The fresh salt breeze and the low rumble of the ferry's engine lulls you into a dream state. All around you, rising from a shimmering sea, are emerald-green islands that are the tops of glacier-carved mountains flooded at the end of the last ice age. A bald eagle swoops from its perch on a twisted madrone tree. Off the port bow, the knifelike fins of two orca whales slice the water. As the engine slows, you glide toward a narrow wooden dock with a simple sign above it that reads SAN JUAN ISLANDS. With a sigh of contentment, you step out onto the San Juan Islands and into a slower pace of life.

There's something magical about traveling to the San Juans. Some people say it's the light, some say it's the sea air, some say it's the weather (temperatures are always moderate, and rainfall is roughly half what it is in Seattle). Whatever it is that so entrances, the San Juans have become the favorite getaway of urban Washingtonians, and if you make time to visit these idyllic islands, we think you, too, will fall under their spell.

There is, however, one caveat. The San Juans have been discovered. In summer, if you're driving a car, you may encounter waits of several hours to get on ferries. One solution is to leave your car on the mainland and come over either on foot or by bicycle. If you choose to come over on foot, you can rent a car, moped, or bike; take the San Juan or Orcas island shuttle bus; or use taxis to get around. Then again, you can just stay in one place and relax.

Along with crowded ferries come hotels, inns, and campgrounds that can get booked up months in advance and restaurants that can't seat you unless you have a reservation. If it's summer, don't come out here without a room reservation and expect to find a place to stay.

In other seasons, it's a different story. Spring and fall are often clear, and in spring, the islands' gardens and hedgerows of wild roses burst into bloom, making this one of the nicest times of year to visit. Perhaps best of all, in spring and fall room rates are much less than they are in the summer.

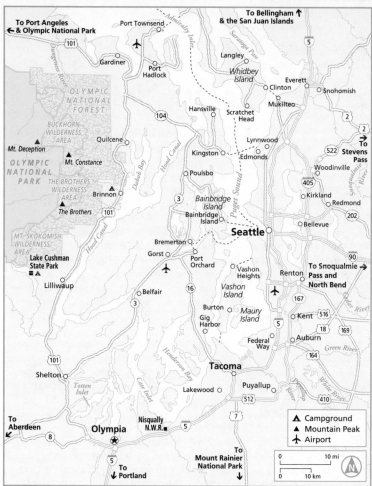

Depending on whom you listen to, there are between 175 and 786 islands in the San Juans. The lower number constitutes those islands large enough to have been named, while the larger number represents all the islands, rocks, and reefs that poke above the water on the lowest possible tide. Of all these islands, only four (San Juan, Orcas, Lopez, and Shaw) are serviced by the Washington State Ferries, and of these, only three (San Juan, Orcas, and Lopez) have anything in the way of tourist accommodations.

VISITOR INFORMATION

Contact the **San Juan Island Chamber of Commerce,** P.O. Box 98, Friday Harbor, WA 98250 (© **360/378-5240;** www.sanjuanisland.org); or the **Orcas Island Chamber of Commerce,** P.O. Box 252, Eastsound, WA 98245 (© **360/ 376-2273;** www.orcasisland.org). For information on Lopez Island, contact the **Lopez Island Chamber of Commerce,** P.O. Box 102, Lopez, WA 98261 (© **360/468-4664;** www.lopezisland.com).

On the Internet, check out the following: www.sanjuanweb.com, www.orca sisle.com, www.thesanjuans.com.

GETTING THERE

If it's summer and you'd like to visit the San Juans without a car, we recommend booking passage through Victoria Clipper (see below), which operates excursion boats from the Seattle waterfront. If you're traveling by car, you'll need to drive north from Seattle to Anacortes and head out to the islands via Washington State Ferries.

Washington State Ferries (© **800/84-FERRY** or 888/808-7977 in Washington, or 206/464-6400; www.wsdot.wa.gov/ferries/) operates ferries between Anacortes and four of the San Juan Islands (Lopez, Shaw, Orcas, and San Juan) and Sidney, British Columbia (on Vancouver Island near Victoria). The fare for a vehicle and driver from Anacortes to Lopez is $17 to $27, to Shaw or Orcas $20 to $31.75, to San Juan $22.50 to $36, and to Sidney $34 to $41. The higher fares reflect a summer surcharge.

The fare for passengers from Anacortes to any of the islands ranges from $6.80 to $9.60 ($12.40 from Anacortes to Sidney). The fare for a vehicle and driver on all westbound interisland ferries is $10.25 to $13, and walk-on passengers and passengers in cars ride free. Except for service from Sidney, fares are not collected on eastbound ferries, nor are walk-on passengers charged for interisland ferry service. If you plan to explore the islands by car, you'll save some money by starting your tour on San Juan Island and making your way back east through the islands.

During the summer you may have to wait several hours to get on a ferry, so arrive early.

To cross into Canada and return to the United States, adult U.S. citizens born in the United States need two pieces of identification, such as a passport, driver's license, birth certificate, voter registration card, or credit card. U.S. citizens who were not born in the United States need a passport or certificate of naturalization. If you are a foreign citizen but a permanent resident of the United States, be sure to carry your A.R.R. card. Foreign citizens who are only visiting the United States must carry a passport when traveling to or from Canada. Children traveling to or from Canada with both parents must have a birth certificate; a child traveling with only one parent should have both a birth certificate and a notarized letter from the other parent giving permission for the child to travel out of the country.

There are also passenger-ferry services from several cities around the region. **Victoria Clipper** (© **800/888-2535** or 206/448-5000; www.victoriaclipper.com) operates excursion boats between Seattle and both Friday Harbor on San Juan Island and Rosario Resort on Orcas Island and also stops in Victoria. The roundtrip fare to Friday Harbor is $59 round-trip; the fare to Rosario Resort is $69 round-trip. Advance-purchase discounts of $10 are available on round-trip tickets.

If you're short on time, you can fly to the San Juans. **Kenmore Air,** 950 Westlake Ave. N. (© **800/543-9595** or 425/486-1257; www.kenmoreair.com), offers floatplane flights that take off from Lake Union (and also from the north end of Lake Washington). Round-trip fares to the San Juans are between $159 and $189 (lower for children). Flights go to Friday Harbor and Roche Harbor on San Juan Island, Rosario Resort and Westsound on Orcas Island, and the Lopez Islander on Lopez Island.

You can also get from Sea-Tac Airport to the San Juan Islands ferry terminal in Anacortes on the **Airporter Shuttle** (© **866/235-5247** or 360/380-8800; www.airporter.com), which charges $31 one-way and $56 round-trip.

The San Juan Islands

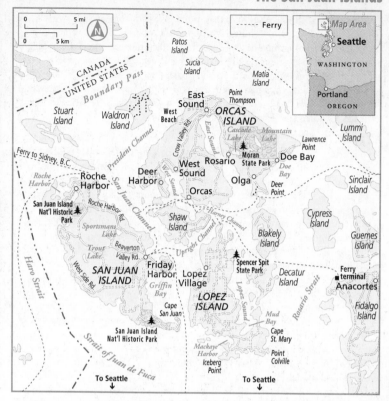

SAN JUAN ISLAND

Although neither the largest nor the prettiest of the islands, San Juan is the most populous and touristy of the San Juan Islands. **Friday Harbor,** where the ferry docks, is the county seat for San Juan County and is the only real town on all of the islands. As such, it is home to numerous shops, restaurants, motels, and bed-and-breakfast inns that cater to tourists. It's also where you'll find the grocery and hardware stores that provide the necessities of island life. With its large, well-protected marina, it's one of the most popular places in the islands for boaters to drop anchor.

GETTING AROUND

Car rentals are available on San Juan Island from **M&W Auto Sales,** 725 Spring St. (© **800/323-6037** or 360/378-2886; www.interisland.net/mandw/), which charges between $30 and $70 per day. Cars can also be rented from **Susie's Mopeds** (© **800/532-0087** or 360/378-5244; www.susiesmopeds.com), which charges $96 per day.

You can also rent scooters and mopeds. They're available in Friday Harbor by the hour or by the day from **Island Scooter Rental,** 85 Front St. (© **360/378-8811;** www.islandscooter.com), or from **Susie's Mopeds** (see above), both located at the top of the ferry lanes. Expect to pay $17 to $23 per hour or $51 to $69 per day for a moped or scooter.

For a cab, call **San Juan Taxi** (© **360/378-3550**).

San Juan Transit (© **800/887-8387,** or 360/378-8887 on San Juan; www.san juantransit.com) operates a shuttle bus during the summer. This shuttle can be boarded at the ferry terminal and operates frequently throughout the day, stopping at all the major attractions on the island, which makes this a great way to get around if you come out without a car. Day passes are $10 for adults, $9 for seniors, and $5 for kids ages 5 to 12, with discounted 2-day rates available. One-way ($4 adults, $2 kids 5–12) and round-trip ($7 adults, $3 kids 5–12) tickets are available. Children ages 4 and under always ride free.

EXPLORING THE ISLAND

If you arrived by car, you'll first want to find a parking space, which can be difficult in the summer. Once on foot, stroll around town admiring the simple wood-frame shop buildings constructed in the early 20th century. At that time, Friday Harbor was thought of as the southernmost port in Alaska and was a busy harbor. Schooners and steamships hauled the island's fruit, livestock, and lime (for cement) off to more populous markets. Today these pursuits have all died off, but reminders of the island's rural roots linger on, and these memories have fueled the island's new breadwinner: tourism. Many of the town's old buildings now house art galleries and other interesting shops.

One of your first stops should be the tasting room at **Island Wine Company,** Cannery Landing (© **360/378-3229**), which is the only place you can buy wine from San Juan Cellars (which makes its wine with grapes from eastern Washington). You'll find the wine shop on the immediate left as you leave the ferry.

Whale-watching is one of the most popular summer activities in the San Juans. Before you head out, stop by the **Whale Museum** ⚓, 62 First St. N. (© **800/946-7227** or 360/378-4710; www.whale-museum.org). Here you can see whale skeletons and models of whales and learn all about the area's pods of orcas (also known as killer whales). The museum is open daily from 10am to 5pm (shorter hours in winter); admission is $5 for adults, $4 for seniors, and $2 for children 5 to 18 and college students.

Here in Friday Harbor, you'll find the headquarters of the **San Juan Island National Historical Park** ⚓ (© **360/378-2240**; www.nps.gov/sajh), at the corner of Spring and First streets. It's open daily from 8:30am to 5pm in summer (Mon–Fri 8:30am–4:30pm in winter). This park commemorates the San Juan Island Pig War, one of North America's most unusual and least remembered confrontations. Way back in 1859, San Juan Island nearly became the site of a battle between the British and the Americans. The two countries had not yet agreed upon the border between the United States and Canada when a British pig on San Juan Island decided to have dinner in an American garden. Not taking too kindly to this, the owner of the garden shot the pig. The Brits, rather than welcome this succulent addition to their evening's repast, threatened redress. In less time than it takes to smoke a ham, both sides were calling in reinforcements. Luckily, this pig-headedness was defused, and a more serious confrontation was avoided. The park's headquarters is here in Friday Harbor, but the main historic sites are English Camp, at the north end of the island, and American Camp, at the south end of the island. At both camps, you can visit historic buildings that are much as they looked in 1859.

Most of the island's main attractions can be seen on a long loop drive around the perimeter of the island. Start the drive by following Roche Harbor signs north out of Friday Harbor (take Spring St. to Second St. to Tucker Ave.). In about 3 miles, you'll come to **San Juan Vineyards** ⚓, 2000 Roche Harbor Rd. (© **360/**

378-9463; www.sanjuanvineyards.com), which makes wines both from grapes grown off the island and from its own estate-grown Siegrebbe and Madeline Angevine grapes. The tasting room is housed in an old schoolhouse built in 1896 and is open daily 11am to 6pm in summer (call for hours in other months).

A little farther north, you come to **Roche Harbor Resort,** once the site of large limestone quarries that supplied lime to much of the West Coast. Today many of the quarries' old structures are still visible, giving this area a decaying industrial look, but amidst the abandoned machinery stands the historic Hotel de Haro, a simple whitewashed wooden building with verandas across its two floors. Stop and admire the old-fashioned marina and colorful gardens. The deck of the hotel's lounge is one of the best places on the island to linger over a drink. In an old pasture on the edge of the resort property, you'll see the **Westcott Bay Reserve** (© 360/370-5050), a new sculpture park that includes more than 45 works of art set in grassy fields and along the shores of a small pond. Back in the woods near the resort you'll find an unusual **mausoleum** that was erected by the founder of the quarries and the Hotel de Haro.

South of Roche Harbor, on West Valley Road, you'll find **English Camp.** Set amid shady trees and spacious lawns, the camp is the picture of British civility. There's even a formal garden surrounded by a white picket fence. You can look inside the reconstructed buildings and imagine the days when this was one of the most far-flung corners of the British Empire. If you're full of energy, hike up to the top of 650-foot **Mount Young** for a panorama of the island. An easier hike is out to the end of **Bel Point.**

South of English Camp, watch for the Bay Road turnoff. This connects to the Westside Road, which leads down the island's west coast. Along this road, you'll find **San Juan County Park,** a great spot for a picnic. A little farther south you'll come to **Lime Kiln State Park** ★★, the country's first whale-watching park and a great place to spot these gentle giants in summer.

At the far south end of the island is the windswept promontory on which stood the **American Camp** during the Pig War. Here you'll find a visitor center and a few reconstructed buildings. Before the American Camp was built here, this was the site of a Hudson's Bay Company farm. The meadows sweeping down to the sea were once grazed by sheep and cattle, but today you'll see only rabbits browsing amid the high grasses and wildflowers. **Hiking trails** here lead along the bluffs and down to the sea. One trail leads through a dark forest of Douglas firs to **Jackle's Lagoon,** a great spot for bird-watching. Keep your eyes peeled for bald eagles, which are relatively plentiful around here.

SPORTS & OUTDOOR PURSUITS

BIKING ★ Winding country roads are ideal for leisurely trips. If you didn't bring your own wheels, you can rent from **Island Bicycles,** 380 Argyle St., in Friday Harbor (© **360/378-4941**), which charges $6 per hour (2-hr. minimum) and $30 per day.

SEA KAYAKING ★★ Two- to four-hour **sea-kayak tours** ($39–$49) are offered by **San Juan Safaris** (© **800/450-6858** or 360/378-1323; www.sanjuansafaris.com) at Roche Harbor Resort, **Leisure Kayak Adventures** (© **800/836-1402** or 360/378-5992; www.leisurekayak.com), and **Crystal Seas Kayaking** (© **877/SEAS-877** or 360/378-7899; www.crystalseas.com). Most of these companies also offer full-day and overnight trips.

Three- and four-day trips are offered by **San Juan Kayak Expeditions** (© **360/378-4436;** www.sanjuankayak.com), which charges $325 and $420, respectively, for its outings.

WHALE-WATCHING ★★ When it's time to spot some whales, you have two choices. You can take a whale-watching cruise, or you can head over to **Lime Kiln State Park** ★★, where a short trail leads down to a rocky coastline from which orca whales, minke whales, Dall's porpoises, and sea lions can sometimes be seen. The best months to see orcas are June to September, but it's possible to see them throughout the year.

Whale-watching cruises lasting from 4 to 6 hours are offered in the summer by **San Juan Excursions** (© 800/80-WHALE or 360/378-6636; www.watch whales.com), which operates out of Friday Harbor. Cruises are $49 for adults and $35 for children age 4 to 12. Three-hour whale-watching trips from Roche Harbor Resort, on the north side of the island, are offered by **San Juan Safaris** (© **800/450-6858** or 360/378-1323; www.sanjuansafaris.com), which charges $49 for adults and $39 for children 4 through 12.

WHERE TO STAY

Friday Harbor House ★★ With its contemporary yet distinctly Northwest architecture, this luxurious little boutique hotel brings urban sophistication to Friday Harbor. From the hotel's bluff-top location you can see excellent views of the ferry landing, the adjacent marina, and, in the distance, Orcas Island. Guest rooms have fireplaces and double whirlpool tubs, which make this place a great choice for a romantic getaway. As you relax in your tub, you can gaze out at both the view and your own crackling fire. Most rooms have decks or balconies. These are some of the best rooms in the San Juan Islands, and if you enjoy contemporary styling, you'll love this place. The dining room is one of the best on the island and serves Northwest cuisine. At press time, there were plans to add two more suites and four more rooms.

130 West St. (P.O. Box 1385), Friday Harbor, WA 98250. © **360/378-8455.** Fax 360/378-8453. www.friday harborhouse.com. 20 units. Memorial Day to Sept $200–$265 double, $300 suite; Oct to Memorial Day $140–$195 double, $255 suite. Rates include continental breakfast. AE, DISC, MC, V. **Amenities:** Restaurant (Northwest); access to nearby health club; massage; babysitting. *In room:* TV/VCR, fridge, coffeemaker, hair dryer, iron.

Olympic Lights Bed and Breakfast ★★ Located at San Juan's dry southwestern tip, the Olympic Lights is a Victorian farmhouse surrounded by windswept meadows, and if it weren't for the sight of Puget Sound out the window, you could easily mistake the setting for the prairies of the Midwest. There are colorful gardens, an old barn, even some hens to lay the eggs for your breakfast. The ocean breezes, nearby beach, and friendliness of innkeepers Christian and Lea Andrade lend a special feel to this American classic. Our favorite room here is the Ra Room, which is named for the Egyptian sun god and features a big bay window. The view out the windows is enough to settle the most stressed-out soul.

146 Starlight Way, Friday Harbor, WA 98250. © **888/211-6195** or 360/378-3186. Fax 360/378-2097. www. olympiclights.com. 4 units. May–Oct $125–$135 double; Nov–Apr $90 double. Rates include full breakfast. No credit cards. *In room:* No phone.

Roche Harbor Village ★★ (Kids) Located at the north end of the island, Roche Harbor Village is steeped in island history, with the historic Hotel de Haro, established in 1886, serving as the resort's centerpiece. A brick driveway and manicured gardens provide the foreground for the white two-story hotel, which overlooks the marina and has porches running the length of both floors. Although the rooms in the Hotel de Haro are quite basic (all but four have shared bathrooms) and have not been updated in years, the building has loads of atmosphere. The best accommodations here, however, are the four new luxury McMillin suites in a restored home adjacent to the historic hotel. These suites are among the finest rooms on the island. The modern condominiums are good bets for families. The resort's dining room has a view of the marina, and the deck makes a great spot for a sunset cocktail. In addition to amenities listed below, there are whale-watching cruises, sea kayak tours, a marina, and a general store.

248 Reuben Memorial Dr. (P.O. Box 4001), Roche Harbor, WA 98250. ℂ **800/451-8910** or 360/378-2155. Fax 360/378-6809. www.rocheharbor.com. Historic hotel: 20 units (16 with shared bathroom). Modern accommodations: 25 condos, 9 cottages, 4 suites. Mid-May to Sept $79–$99 double with shared bathroom; $139–$299 suite; $129–$299 condo; $155–$229 cottage. Lower rates Oct to mid-May. AE, MC, V. **Amenities:** 3 restaurants (Continental/Northwest, American), lounge; outdoor pool; 2 tennis courts; Jacuzzi; bike and moped rentals; shopping arcade; coin-op laundry. *In room:* Hair dryer, iron.

WHERE TO DINE

In addition to the restaurants listed below, Friday Harbor has several other places where you can get a quick, simple meal. At the **Garden Path Café,** 135 Second St. (ℂ **360/378-6255**), you'll find a good selection of deli salads, soups, and baked goods. Just around the corner is the popular **Felicitations,** 120 Nichols St. (ℂ **360/378-1198**), which is the best bakery on the island.

If you're up near the north end of the island and suddenly find yourself hungry for lunch or a light dinner, try the **Lime Kiln Cafe** (ℂ **360/378-2155**) on the dock at Roche Harbor Resort. This lively little cafe serves filling breakfasts and good chowder and fish-and-chips. Big windows let you gaze out at the boats in the marina.

Duck Soup Inn ✰✰ NORTHWEST/INTERNATIONAL   Four-and-a-half miles north of Friday Harbor is the Duck Soup Inn, a barnlike restaurant beside a pond frequented by—you guessed it—ducks. Inside this quintessentially Northwestern building you'll find lots of exposed wood and a fieldstone fireplace. The menu changes frequently, depending on the availability of fresh produce, but it is always very creative. The chef has a penchant for the flavors of Asia and you might find lamb sirloin rubbed with Indian spices or spicy coconut sea scallops. In spring and fall, you might even find duck soup on the menu!

50 Duck Soup Lane. ℂ 360/378-4878. www.ducksoupinn.com. Reservations highly recommended. Main courses $20–$28. DISC, MC, V. Summer Wed–Sun 5:30–9:30pm; spring and fall Fri–Sat 5:30–9:30pm. Closed Nov to early Apr.

Friday Harbor House Dining Room ✰✰ NORTHWEST   Located in the luxurious Friday Harbor House boutique hotel, this is the most sophisticated restaurant on San Juan Island. Striking contemporary decor sets the tone, but doesn't distract diners from the harbor views out the glass walls. The menu is short and relies heavily on local ingredients, including island-grown greens and Westcott Bay oysters (perhaps prepared with chanterelle mushrooms and Parmesan cheese). The chef draws on diverse inspirations for the dishes served here, which are always attractively presented and carefully prepared. A recent menu included perfectly cooked salmon with coconut-red curry sauce.

130 West St. ℂ 360/378-8455. Reservations highly recommended. Main courses $14–$26. AE, DISC, MC, V. Daily 5:30–9pm.

The Place Bar & Grill ✰✰ NORTHWEST/INTERNATIONAL   Located on the waterfront to the right as you get off the ferry and housed in a small wooden building that was once part of a U.S. Coast Guard station, this aptly named establishment is San Juan Island's finest waterfront restaurant. With lots of local art on the wall, this place aims to attract the upscale Seattle market, and it's right on target. The menu changes regularly, with an emphasis on seafood preparations such as Asian-style crab cakes and Pacific Rim bouillabaisse.

1 Spring St. ℂ 360/378-8707. Reservations highly recommended. Main courses $19–$28. MC, V. Daily 5–9:30 or 10pm (Tues–Sat in winter).

Vinny's ★★ ITALIAN From the name you might guess that this place is some dark dive serving New York–style pizza. Not exactly. Located across the street from the Friday Harbor House and claiming the same good views of the marina, Vinny's is San Juan Island's premier Italian restaurant. This is the sort of place you discover on the first night of your visit and decide to eat at every night until you leave. Local oysters and mussels dominate the appetizer menu, although the calamari with pine nuts, tomatoes, raisins, lemon, and vinaigrette should not be missed. This is seafood country, for sure, but the charbroiled, dry-aged Delmonico steaks are a big hit (try it with Gorgonzola-Parmesan butter), and the menu features plenty of well-prepared standards such as lasagna and penne alla puttanesca.

165 West St. ℂ360/378-1934. Reservations recommended. Main courses $13–$27.50. AE, DISC, MC, V. Daily 5–10pm.

ORCAS ISLAND

Shaped like a horseshoe and named for an 18th-century Mexican viceroy (not for the area's orca whales, as is commonly believed), Orcas Island has long been a popular summer-vacation spot and is the most beautiful of the San Juan Islands. Orcas is a particular favorite of nature lovers, who come to enjoy the views of green rolling pastures, forested mountains, and fjordlike bays. **Eastsound** is the largest town on the island and has several interesting shops and good restaurants. Other, smaller villages include Deer Harbor, West Sound, and Olga.

To rent a car on Orcas Island, contact **M&W Auto Sales** (ℂ **800/323-6037** or 360/378-2886; www.interisland.net/mandw/), which charges $50 to $70 per day. **Rosario Resort** (ℂ **800/562-8820** or 360/376-2222) also rents cars and charges $79 to $89 per day. If you need a cab, call **Orcas Island Taxi** (ℂ **360/ 376-8294**).

Around the island you'll find several interesting pottery shops. A few miles west of Eastsound off Enchanted Forest Road is **Orcas Island Pottery,** 366 Old Pottery Rd. (ℂ **360/376-2813;** www.orcasislandpottery.com), the oldest pottery studio in the Northwest; and, at the end of this same road, on West Beach across from the West Beach Resort, you'll find **The Right Place Pottery Shop** (ℂ **360/ 376-4023**). Between Eastsound and Orcas on Horseshoe Highway is **Crow Valley Pottery,** 2274 Orcas Rd. (ℂ **360/376-4260;** www.crowvalley.com), in an 1866 log cabin. On the east side of the island in the community of Olga, you'll find **Orcas Island Artworks,** Horseshoe Highway (ℂ **360/376-4408**), which is full of beautiful work by island artists.

SPORTS & OUTDOOR PURSUITS

Moran State Park ★★ (ℂ **360/376-2326;** www.parks.wa.gov), which covers 5,252 acres of the island, is the largest park in the San Juans and the main destination for most island visitors. If the weather is clear, you'll find great views from the summit of Mount Constitution, which rises 2,409 feet above Puget Sound. There are also 5 lakes, 32 miles of hiking trails, and an environmental learning center. Fishing, hiking, boating, mountain biking, and camping (campsite reservations through **Washington State Parks** ℂ **888/226-7688;** www.parks.wa.gov/reserve.asp) are all popular park activities. The park is off Horseshoe Highway, approximately 12½ miles from the ferry landing.

BIKING ✿   Although Orcas is considered the most challenging of the San Juan Islands for biking, plenty of cyclists pedal the island's roads. One of the best places to rent bikes here is **Dolphin Bay Bicycles** (© **360/376-4157;** www.rock island.com/~dolphin), located just to the right as you get off the ferry. From here you can explore Orcas Island or take a free ferry to Lopez Island or Shaw Island. Bikes rent for $25 per day, $65 for 3 days, and $90 per week. Guided bike rides are also sometimes available. In Eastsound, you can rent bikes from **Wildlife Cycles,** North Beach Road, Eastsound (© **360/376-4708;** www.wildlife cycles.com). The cost is about $10 to $12 per hour or $30 to $35 per day.

BOAT CHARTERS   If you're interested in heading out on the water in a 33-foot sailboat, contact Capt. Don Palmer at **Amante Sail Tours** (© **360/376-4231**), which charges $35 per person (with a two-person minimum and a maximum of six) for a half-day sail.

HIKING   With 32 miles of hiking trails, **Moran State Park** ✿✿ offers hikes ranging from short, easy strolls alongside lakes to strenuous, all-day outings. South of the community of Olga, on the east arm of the island, you'll also find a ½-mile trail through **Obstruction Pass Park** ✿✿. This trail leads to a quiet little cove that has a few walk-in/paddle-in campsites. The park is at the end of Obstruction Pass Road.

SEA KAYAKING ✿✿   The best way to see the Orcas Island coast is by sea kayak. Located at the Orcas Island ferry landing, **Orcas Outdoors** (© **360/376-4611;** www.orcasoutdoors.com) offers guided sea-kayak tours lasting from 1 hour ($25) to overnight ($220). Three-hour guided tours ($45) are offered by **Shearwater Adventures** (© **360/376-4699;** www.shearwaterkayaks.com). Two-hour paddles ($25) are offered by **Spring Bay Inn** (© **360/376-5531;** www.springbayinn.com), which is located on the east side of the island near the village of Olga. These trips are in an area where bald eagles nest in the summer.

WHALE-WATCHING ✿✿   If you want to see some of the orca whales for which the San Juans are famous, you can take a whale-watching excursion with **Deer Harbor Charters** (© **800/544-5758** or 360/376-5989; www.deerharbor charters.com), which operates out of both Deer Harbor and Rosario Resort and charges $47 for adults and $32 for children; or with **Orcas Island Eclipse Charters** (© **800/376-6566;** www.orcasislandwhales.com), which operates out of the Orcas Island ferry dock and charges $46.50 for adults and $30 for children.

WHERE TO STAY

Orcas Hotel ✿   Located at the Orcas ferry landing, this attractive old Victorian hotel has been welcoming guests since 1904 and is a good choice for anyone coming over without a car. The guest rooms, done in a simple country style, vary in size, but all are carpeted and furnished with antiques, and all are nonsmoking. On the first floor of the three-story building you'll find a quiet lounge, bakery, cafe, and restaurant.

P.O. Box 155, Orcas, WA 98280. © **888/672-2792** or 360/376-4300. Fax 360/376-4399. www.orcashotel.com. 12 units (5 with shared bathroom, 3 with half bathroom). $79–$109 double with shared bathroom, $129–$159 double with half bathroom, $149–$198 double with private bathroom. Rates include continental breakfast. AE, MC, V. **Amenities:** 2 restaurants; lounge; access to nearby health club; massage. *In room:* No phone.

The Resort at Deer Harbor ✿✿   Set on an open hillside above the spectacular Deer Harbor inlet, this casual resort looks across the water to a forested cliff and offers the best views on the island. Add to this a few small islands at the mouth of the inlet and a marina with sailboats bobbing at anchor, and you have the quintessential island setting. Each of the 14 cottages has a hot tub on its porch; of these, 11 are newly renovated and are the most luxurious accommodations here, with double whirlpool tubs in the bathrooms, fireplaces, and separate seating areas. The **Starfish Grill,** the resort's casual and moderately priced bistro, is one of the best restaurants in the San Juans.

P.O. Box 200, Deer Harbor, WA 98243. ℂ **888/376-4480** or 360/376-4420. Fax 360/376-5523. www.deer harbor.com. 26 units. July–Sept $189–$399 suite or cottage; Oct–June $129–$299 suite or cottage. Rates include continental breakfast. AE, DISC, MC, V. **Amenities:** Restaurant (International); outdoor pool. *In room:* TV, coffeemaker.

Rosario Resort & Spa ★★★ *(Kids)*

Rosario is the most luxurious accommodation on Orcas Island and is the only place in the San Juans that can actually claim to be a resort. Although the resort has a wide variety of modern accommodations, the centerpiece remains the 1904 Moran Mansion, an imposing white stucco building on the shore of Cascade Bay. This mansion houses the resort's main dining room, lounge, spa, and library. The larger and more luxurious rooms (with fireplaces, good views, and French country decor) are across the marina and up a steep hill from this main building, so if you aren't keen on walking, request a room in one of the buildings directly adjacent to the Moran Mansion.

1400 Rosario Rd., Eastsound, WA 98245. ℂ **800/562-8820** or 360/376-2222. Fax 360/376-2289. www. rosarioresort.com. 127 units. June to mid-Oct $229–$399 double, $369–$650 suite; mid-Oct to May $129–$299 double, $269–$550 suite. AE, DC, DISC, MC, V. **Amenities:** 3 restaurants (American, seafood); lounge, poolside bar; 1 indoor and 2 outdoor pools; tennis court; exercise room; spa; Jacuzzi; sauna; watersports equipment rentals; bike rentals; children's center; concierge; car-rental desk; room service; massage; babysitting; coin-op laundry; laundry service. *In room:* A/C, TV, dataport, coffeemaker, hair dryer, iron.

Spring Bay Inn ★★

Just by virtue of being one of the only waterfront B&Bs in the San Juans, this inn would deserve a recommendation. However, innkeepers Sandy Playa and Carl Burger, both retired park rangers, make a stay here both fun and educational, and the setting and inn are great for a romantic getaway. You can soak in the hot tub on the beach and watch the sunset, spot bald eagles from just outside the inn's front door, hike on the nature trails, and best of all, go for a guided sea-kayak tour each morning. Four of the five guest rooms have fireplaces, two have views from their tubs, and two have balconies.

P.O. Box 97, Olga, WA 98279. ℂ **360/376-5531.** Fax 360/376-2193. www.springbayinn.com. 5 units. $220–$260 double (2-night minimum). Rates include continental breakfast, brunch, and daily kayak tour. DISC, MC, V. **Amenities:** Activities desk; Jacuzzi; water-sports equipment; concierge. *In room:* Fridge, hair dryer.

Turtleback Farm Inn ★★

Nowhere on Orcas will you find a more idyllic setting than this bright-green restored farmhouse overlooking 80 acres of farmland at the foot of Turtleback Mountain. Simply furnished with antiques, the guest rooms range from cozy to spacious, and each has its own special view. Our favorite room in the main house is the Meadow View Room, which has a private deck and a claw-foot tub. The four rooms in the orchard house are among the biggest and most luxurious on the island (gas fireplaces, claw-foot tubs, balconies, wood floors, kitchenettes). Days here start with a big farm breakfast served at valley-view tables that are set with bone china, silver, and linen. Finish your day with a nip of sherry by the fire.

1981 Crow Valley Rd., Eastsound, WA 98245. ℂ **800/376-4914** or 360/376-4914. Fax 360/376-5329. www. turtlebackinn.com. 11 units. Main house: May 15–Oct 31 $90–$175 double; Orchard House: June 15–Sept 15 $225 double. Lower rates other months. Rates include full breakfast. 2-night minimum stay June 15–Sept 15, weekends, and holidays. DISC, MC, V. **Amenities:** Access to nearby health club; concierge; massage. *In room:* Hair dryer, iron.

WHERE TO DINE

For baked goods, imported cheeses, and other gourmet foodstuffs, stop by **Rose's Bread and Specialties** (© 360/376-5805), which is also in Eastsound Square. For great cookies, don't miss **Teezer's Cookies** (© 360/376-2913) at the corner of North Beach Road and A Street. In Olga, don't miss the **Olga Store,** Olga Road (© 360/376-5862), which until recently was a little general store but is now a great little cafe and eclectic gift shop. In West Sound, at the corner of Deer Harbor Road and Crow Valley Road, the **West Sound Cafe** (© 360/376-4440), housed in a former general store and with a great view of the water, serves good breakfasts, lunches, and light meals.

Cafe Olga ★ *Finds* INTERNATIONAL   Housed in an old strawberry-packing plant that dates from the days when these islands were known for their fruit, Cafe Olga is the best place on the island for breakfast or lunch. Everything here is homemade, using fresh local produce whenever possible. The blackberry pie is a special treat, especially when accompanied by Lopez Island Creamery ice cream. This building also houses Orcas Island Artworks, a gallery representing more than 70 Orcas Island artists.

Horseshoe Hwy., Olga. © 360/376-5098. Main courses $7–$15. MC, V. Daily 10am–6pm (until 5pm Nov–Dec). Closed Jan–Feb.

Christina's ★★ NORTHWEST   Located on the second floor of an old water-front building in Eastsound, Christina's has a beautiful view down the sound, just right for sunsets. If the weather is pleasant, the deck is *the* place on the island for sunset dinner. The menu here is short, changes regularly, and features innovative cuisine prepared with an emphasis on local ingredients. For the most part, Christina's showcases its creativity in its appetizers rather than in its entrees, so whether you crave the unusual or the familiar, you'll likely be satisfied here. The desserts can be heavenly.

Horseshoe Hwy., Eastsound. © 360/376-4904. www.christinas.net. Reservations highly recommended. Main courses $28–$32. AE, DISC, MC, V. Daily 5:30–9 or 9:30pm. Closed 3 weeks in Nov and all of Jan.

The Inn at Ship Bay ★★ NORTHWEST   About midway between Eastsound and the turnoff for the Rosario Resort, you'll spot the Inn at Ship Bay, an old white house that sits in a field high above the water. (Should you arrive after dark and be tempted to walk over to the water, be aware that the restaurant's front yard ends in a sheer cliff.) Inside, you'll find traditional maritime decor and plenty of windows to let you gaze out to sea. Oysters are a specialty here; you can opt for pan-fried oysters, oyster shooters, and of course, fresh local oysters on the half shell. You can make a meal of oysters alone, but the entree menu includes plenty of other tempting dishes.

326 Olga Rd., Eastsound. © 360/376-5886. www.innatshipbay.com. Reservations recommended. Main courses $17–$25. AE, DC, DISC, MC, V. Tues–Sat 5:30–8:30 or 9pm, Sun brunch 10:30am–3:30pm. Closed Thanksgiving through Feb.

LOPEZ ISLAND

Of the three islands with accommodations, Lopez is the least developed. Although it is less spectacular than Orcas or San Juan, it is flatter, which makes it popular with bicyclists who prefer easy grades over stunning panoramas. Lopez maintains more of its agricultural roots than either Orcas or San Juan, and likewise has fewer activities for tourists. If you just want to get away from it all and hole up with a good book for a few days, Lopez may be the place for you.

Lopez Islanders are particularly friendly—they wave to everyone they pass on the road. The custom has come to be known as the Lopez Wave.

For a taxi on Lopez, call **Lopez Cab** (© 360/468-2227).

Lopez Village is the closest this island has to a town, and here you'll find almost all of the island's restaurants and shops, as well as the **Lopez Island Historical Museum** (© 360/468-2049), where you can learn about the island's history and pick up a map of historic buildings. In July and August the museum is open Wednesday through Sunday from noon to 4pm. In May, June, and September, it's open Friday through Sunday from noon to 4pm.

Lopez Island Vineyards ⭐ (© 360/468-3644), on Fisherman Bay Road between the ferry landing and Lopez Village, was until recently the only winery that actually made wine from fruit grown here in the San Juans. Both their Siegerrebe and Madeleine Angevine are from local grapes, as are their organic fruit wines. They also make wines from grapes grown in the Yakima Valley. In summer, the winery tasting room is open Wednesday through Saturday from noon to 5pm; spring and fall, it's open on Friday and Saturday only.

SPORTS & OUTDOOR ACTIVITIES

Eight county parks and one state park provide plenty of access to the woods and water on Lopez Island. The first park off the ferry is **Odlin County Park** (© 360/468-2496 for information, or 360/378-1842 for reservations), which has a long beach, picnic tables, and a campground. Athletic fields make this more a community sports center than a natural area, so this should be a last resort camping choice.

For a more natural setting for a short, easy hike, check out **Upright Channel Park,** which is on Military Road (about a mile north of Lopez Village in the northwest corner of the island).

A little farther south and over on the east side of the island you'll find **Spencer Spit State Park** ⭐ (© 360/468-2251), which has a campground. Here, the forest meets the sea on a rocky beach that looks across a narrow channel to Frost Island. You can hike the trails through the forest or explore the beach.

South of Lopez Village on Bay Shore Road, you'll find the small **Otis Perkins Park,** which is between Fisherman Bay and the open water and has one of the longest beaches on the island.

Down at the south end of the island, you'll find the tiny **Shark Reef Sanctuary** ⭐⭐, where a short trail leads through the forest to a rocky stretch of coast that is among the prettiest on all the ferry-accessible islands. Small islands offshore create strong currents that swirl past the rocks here. Seals and the occasional whale can be seen just offshore. It's a great spot for a picnic.

BIKING ⭐⭐   Because of its size, lack of traffic, numerous parks, and relatively flat terrain, Lopez is a favorite of cyclists. You can rent bikes for $5 to $20 an hour or $25 to $65 a day from **Lopez Bicycle Works & Kayaks,** 2847 Fisherman Bay Rd. (© 360/468-2847; www.lopezbicycleworks.com), at the marina on Fisherman Bay Road.

SEA KAYAKING ⭐⭐   If you want to explore the island's coastline by kayak, contact **Lopez Island Sea Kayaks** (© 360/468-2847; www.lopezkayaks.com), which is located at the marina on Fisherman Bay Road and is open May through October. Tours cost $75 for a full-day trip with lunch included. Single kayaks can also be rented here for $12 to $25 per hour, or $25 to $50 per half day. Double kayaks rent for $20 to $35 per hour and $40 to $60 per half day.

WHERE TO STAY

Edenwild Inn ✦✦   Located right in Lopez Village, this modern Victorian B&B is a good choice if you've come here to bike or want to use your car as little as possible. Within a block of the inn are all the island's best restaurants. Most of the guest rooms here are quite large, and most have views of the water. All the rooms have interesting antique furnishings, and several have fireplaces. In summer, colorful gardens surround the inn, and guests can breakfast on a large brick patio. The front veranda, overlooking Fisherman Bay, is a great place to relax in the afternoon.

132 Lopez Rd. (P.O. Box 271), Lopez Island, WA 98261. ✆ **800/606-0662** or 360/468-3238. Fax 360/468-4080. www.edenwildinn.com. 8 units. $110–$170 double. Rates include full breakfast. AE, MC, V. *In room:* No phone.

Lopez Farm Cottages and Tent Camping ✦✦ *Value*   Set on 30 acres of pastures, old orchards, and forest between the ferry landing and Lopez Village, these modern cottages are tucked into a grove of cedar trees on the edge of a large lawn (in the middle of which stand three huge boulders). From the outside, the board-and-batten cottages look like old farm buildings, but inside you'll find a combination of Eddie Bauer and Scandinavian design. There are kitchenettes, plush beds with lots of pillows, and, in the bathrooms, showers with double shower heads. If showering together isn't romantic enough for you, there's a hot tub tucked down a garden path. Also on the property is a deluxe tents–only campground.

555 Fisherman Bay Rd., Lopez Island, WA 98261. ✆ **800/440-3556.** www.lopezfarmcottages.com. 4 units. $99–$150 double. Tent sites (available May–Oct) $33 double. Cottage rates include continental breakfast. MC, V. **Amenities:** Jacuzzi. *In room:* Kitchenette, fridge, coffeemaker.

Lopez Islander Resort ✦ *Kids*   Located about a mile south of Lopez Village, the Lopez Islander may not look too impressive from the outside, but it's a very comfortable lodging. All the rooms have great views of Fisherman Bay, and most rooms have balconies. The more expensive rooms have coffeemakers, wet bars, microwaves, and refrigerators. In addition to amenities listed below, the Islander has a full-service marina with kayak rentals.

Fisherman Bay Rd. (P.O. Box 459), Lopez Island, WA 98261. ✆ **800/736-3434** or 360/468-2233. Fax 360/468-3382. www.lopezislander.com. 28 units. July–Sept $79.50–$139.50 double; $199.50–$259.50 suite. Lower rates Oct–June. AE, DISC, MC, V. **Amenities:** Restaurant (American); lounge; outdoor pool; tennis court; exercise room; Jacuzzi; bike rentals; coin-op laundry. *In room:* TV, fridge, coffeemaker, hair dryer, iron.

WHERE TO DINE

When it's time for coffee, you'll find the island's best in Lopez Village at **Caffé Verdi,** Lopez Plaza (✆ **360/468-2257**); and right next door, you'll find divinely decadent pastries and other baked goods at **Holly B's Bakery** (✆ **360/468-2133**). Across the street, in Lopez Island Pharmacy, you'll find the old-fashioned **Lopez Island Soda Fountain** (✆ **360/468-2616**).

Bay Café ✦✦ NORTHWEST/INTERNATIONAL   Housed in an eclectically decorated old waterfront commercial building with a deck that overlooks Fisherman Bay, the Bay Café serves some of the best food in the state. This is the sort of place where diners animatedly discuss what that other flavor is in the savory cheesecake with macadamia-cilantro pesto, where the dipping sauces with the pork satay are unlike anything you've ever tasted before, and where people walk through the door and exclaim, "I want whatever it is that smells so good." The menu, though short, spans the globe and changes frequently. Come with a hearty appetite; meals include soup and salad, and the desserts are absolutely to die for (imagine velvety pumpkin crème caramel decorated with a nasturtium flower and candied ginger). Accompany your meal with a bottle of wine from Lopez Island Vineyards for the quintessential Lopez dinner.

Village Center, Lopez Village. (© **360/468-3700**. Reservations highly recommended. Main courses $17–$30. AE, DISC, MC, V. Daily 5–8:30pm (hours may vary in winter).

Bucky's ⊛ AMERICAN   With a laid-back island feeling and an outside water-front deck, this tiny place is where the locals hang out. The food, though simple, is consistently good—nothing fancy, just delicious. The black-and-blue burger with blue cheese and Cajun spices definitely gets our vote for best burger in the islands. If you feel more like seafood, there are fish tacos and fish-and-chips.

Lopez Village Plaza. (© **360/468-2595**. Reservations taken for parties of 5 or more only. Main courses $5–$15. MC, V. Apr–Sept Sun–Thurs 11:30am–8pm, Fri–Sat 11:30am–8:30pm; usually closed other months.

2 Port Townsend: A Restored Victorian Seaport

Named by English explorer Capt. George Vancouver in 1792, Port Townsend did not attract its first settlers until 1851. By the 1880s the town had become a major shipping port and was expected to grow into one of the most important cities on the West Coast. Port Townsend felt that it was the logical end of the line for the transcontinental railroad that was pushing westward in the 1880s; and, based on the certainty of a railroad connection, real estate speculation and development boomed. Merchants and investors erected mercantile palaces along Water Street and elaborate Victorian homes on the bluff above the wharf district. Unfortunately, the railroad never arrived. Tacoma got the rails, and Port Townsend got the shaft.

With its importance as a shipping port usurped by Seattle and Tacoma, Port Townsend slipped into quiet obscurity. Progress passed it by, and its elegant homes and commercial buildings were left to slowly fade away. In 1976 the waterfront district and bluff-top residential neighborhood were declared a National Historic District, and the town began a slow revival. Today the streets of Port Townsend are once again crowded with people; the waterfront district is filled with boutiques, galleries, and other interesting shops; and many of the Victorian homes atop the bluff have become bed-and-breakfast inns.

ESSENTIALS

VISITOR INFORMATION   Contact the **Port Townsend Chamber of Commerce Visitors Information Center,** 2437 E. Sims Way, Port Townsend, WA 98368 ((© **888/365-6978** or 360/385-2722; www.ptguide.com).

GETTING THERE   Port Townsend is on Wash. 20, off U.S. 101 in the northeast corner of the Olympic Peninsula. The Hood Canal Bridge, which connects the Kitsap Peninsula with the Olympic Peninsula and is on the route from Seattle to Port Townsend, sometimes closes due to high winds; if you want to be certain that it's open, call (© **800/695-7623.**

  Washington State Ferries ((© **800/84-FERRY** or 888/808-7977 within Washington state or 206/464-6400; www.wsdot.wa.gov/ferries) operates a ferry between Port Townsend and Keystone on Whidbey Island. The crossing takes 30 minutes and costs $7 to $8.75 for a vehicle and driver, and $2 per passengers (discounted fares for seniors and youths).

  Between Port Townsend and Friday Harbor, passenger service is available from early May to late September from **P.S. Express** ((© **360/385-5288;**

www.pugetsoundexpress.com), which will also carry bicycles and sea kayaks. One-way fares are $34.50 for adults and $24.50 for children; round-trip fares are $52.50 for adults and $36 for children.

GETTING AROUND   Because parking spaces are hard to come by in downtown Port Townsend on weekends and anytime in the summer, **Jefferson Transit** (© **360/385-4777**; www.jeffersontransit.com), the local public bus service, operates a shuttle into downtown Port Townsend from a park-and-ride lot on the south side of town. Jefferson Transit also operates other buses around Port Townsend. Fares are 50¢ to $1. If you need a taxi, call **Peninsula Taxi** (© **360/385-1872**).

FESTIVALS   As a tourist town, Port Townsend schedules quite a few festivals throughout the year. The last week of March, the town celebrates its Victorian heritage with the **Victorian Festival** (© **888/698-1116**; www.victorianfestival.org). The **Jazz Port Townsend** festival is held toward the end of July. The **Wooden Boat Festival,** the largest of its kind in the United States, is on the first weekend after Labor Day. During the **Kinetic Sculpture Race,** held the first Sunday in October, outrageous human-powered vehicles race on land, on water, and through a mud bog. To see inside some of the town's many restored homes, schedule a visit during the **Historic Homes Tour** on the third weekend in September.

The **Olympic Music Festival** (© **206/527-8839**; www.olympicmusic festival.org), held nearby in an old barn near the town of Quilcene, is the area's most important music festival. This series of weekend concerts takes place between mid-June and mid-September.

EXPLORING THE TOWN

With its abundance of restored Victorian homes and commercial buildings, Port Townsend's most popular activity is simply walking or driving through the historic districts. The town is divided into the waterfront commercial district and the residential Uptown Port Townsend, which is atop a bluff that rises precipitously only 2 blocks from the water. Uptown Port Townsend developed in part so that proper Victorian ladies would not have to associate with the riffraff that frequented the waterfront. At the Port Townsend Visitor Information Center you can pick up a guide that lists the town's many historic homes and commercial buildings.

Water Street is the town's main commercial district. It is lined for several blocks with 100-year-old restored brick buildings, many of which have ornate facades. Within these buildings are dozens of interesting shops and boutiques, several restaurants, and a handful of hotels and inns. To learn a little more about the history of this part of town and to gain a different perspective, walk out on **Union Wharf,** at the foot of Taylor Street. Here you'll find interpretive plaques covering topics ranging from sea grass to waterfront history.

Before exploring the town, stop by the **Jefferson County Historical Museum and Library,** 540 Water St. (© **360/385-1003**; www.jchsmuseum.org), where you can learn about the history of the area. Among the collections here are regional Native American artifacts and antiques from the Victorian era. It's open Monday through Saturday from 11am to 4pm and Sunday 1 to 4pm (Jan–Feb open Sat–Sun only). Admission is $2 for adults and $1 for children under 12.

The town's noted Victorian homes are in Uptown Port Townsend, atop the bluff that rises behind the waterfront's commercial buildings. Here you'll find stately homes, views, and the city's favorite park. To reach Uptown, either drive up Washington Street (1 block over from Water St.) or walk up the stairs at the end of Taylor Street, which start behind the Haller Fountain.

At the top of the stairs are both an 1890 bell tower that once summoned volunteer firemen, and the **Rothschild House,** Taylor and Franklin streets (© 360/379-8076; www.jchsmuseum.org), a Washington State Parks Heritage Site. Built in 1868, this Greek Revival–style house is one of the oldest buildings in town and displays a sober architecture compared to other area homes. The gardens contain a wide variety of roses, peonies, and lilacs. It's open May through September, daily from 10am to 5pm. Admission is $2 for adults and $1 for children.

But the most fascinating Uptown home open to the public is the **Ann Starrett Mansion,** 744 Clay St. (© 360/385-3205), Port Townsend's most astoundingly ornate Queen Anne Victorian home. Currently operated as a bed-and-breakfast inn, this mansion is best known for its imposing turret, ceiling frescoes, and unusual spiral staircase. The house is open for guided tours daily from noon to 3pm. Tours cost $2.

Also here in Uptown, at the corner of Garfield and Jackson streets, you'll find **Chetzemoka Park,** which was established in 1904 and is named for a local S'Klallum Indian chief. The park perches on a bluff overlooking Admiralty Inlet and has access to a pleasant little beach. However, it is the rose garden, arbor, and waterfall garden that attract most visitors.

Shopping is just about the most popular activity in Port Townsend's old town, and of the many stores in the historic district, several stand out. **Earthenworks Gallery,** 702 Water St. (© 360/385-0328), showcases colorful ceramics, glass, jewelry, and other American-made crafts; **Ancestral Spirits Gallery,** 701 Water St. (© 360/385-0078), is a large space with a great selection of Northwest Native American prints, masks, and carvings; and **Artisans on Taylor,** a small boutique at 236 Taylor (© 360/379-8098), specializes in blown glass and pottery by local craftspeople. Women enamored of Port Townsend's Victorian styling will want to visit the **Palace Emporium,** 1002 Water St. (© 360/385-5899), a dress shop specializing in modern Victorian fashions.

FORT WORDEN STATE PARK

Fort Worden State Park, once a military installation that guarded the mouth of Puget Sound, is north of the historic district and can be reached by turning onto Kearney Street at the south end of town, or onto Monroe Street at the north end of town, and following the signs. Built at the turn of the century, the fort is now a 360-acre state park where a wide array of attractions and activities assure that it's busy for much of the year. Many of the fort's old wooden buildings have been restored and put to new uses.

At the **Fort Worden Commanding Officer's House** (© 360/344-4400; www.olympus.net/ftworden), you can see what life was like for a Victorian-era officer and his family. The home has been fully restored and is filled with period antiques. In summer, it's open daily from 10am to 5pm, and in spring and fall, it's open weekends from 1 to 4pm; admission is $1, free for children under 5.

Here at the park you can also learn about life below the waters of Puget Sound at the **Port Townsend Marine Science Center,** 532 Battery Way (© 360/385-5582; www.ptmsc.org). In summer, the center is open Wednesday through Monday from 11am to 5pm, and fall through spring, it's open Friday through Monday from noon to 4pm. Admission is $3 for adults and $2 for students and children.

For many people, however, the main reason to visit the park is to hang out on the beach or at one of the picnic areas. Scuba divers also frequent the park, which has an underwater park just offshore. In spring, the Rhododendron Garden puts on a colorful floral display. Throughout the year, there is a wide variety of concerts and other performances at the **Centrum** (© **800/733-3608** or 360/385-5320; www.centrum.org). Also within the park are campgrounds, a restaurant, and restored officers' quarters that can be rented as vacation homes.

PORT TOWNSEND FROM THE WATER (& AIR)

If you'd like to explore the town from the water, you've got several options. Three-hour sailboat tours ($65) are offered by **Brisa Charters** (© **877/41-BRISA** or 360/385-2309; www.olympus.net/brisa_charters/) and **Bryony Charters** (© **360/481-0605;** www.sailbryony.com). This latter company only operates between April and October. In the spring and fall, **Port Townsend Marine Science Center** (© **360/385-5582;** www.ptmsc.org) operates educational boat tours ($45) to nearby Protection Island, a wildlife refuge that is home to more than 70% of Puget Sound's nesting seabirds. May through September, cruises ($52.50 per adult) through the San Juan Islands are offered by **Puget Sound Express,** 431 Water St. (© **360/385-5288;** www.pugetsoundexpress.com), which also offers passenger ferry service to Friday Harbor. During the summer you're almost certain to see orca whales on these trips. If you'd like to try your hand at paddling a sea kayak around the area's waters, contact **Kayak Port Townsend,** 435 Water St. (© **800/853-2252** or 360/385-6240; www.kayak pt.com), which offers 2-hour ($30), half-day ($40), and full-day tours ($76), and also rents sea kayaks.

AREA WINERIES

While in town, you might want to check out Port Townsend's two wineries, both located south of town. **Sorensen Cellars,** 274 S. Otto St. (© **360/379-6416;** www.sorensencellars.com), is open March through September, Friday through Sunday from noon to 5pm (or by appointment). To find this winery, turn east off Wash. 20 onto Frederick Street and then south on Otto Street. **Fair Winds Winery,** 1984 Hastings Ave. W. (© **360/385-6899;** www.fairwinds winery.com), is open Friday through Monday from 11am to 5pm. Be sure to try the unusual Aligoté white wine. This is the only winery in the state producing this French-style wine. To find the winery, drive south from Port Townsend on Wash. 20 and turn west on Jacob Miller Road.

WHERE TO STAY

Ann Starrett Mansion ★★   Built in 1889 for $6,000 as a wedding present for Ann Starrett, this Victorian jewel box is by far the most elegant and ornate bed-and-breakfast in Port Townsend (and the entire state for that matter). The rose and teal-green mansion is a museum of the Victorian era: A three-story turret towers over the front door, and every room is exquisitely furnished with period antiques. In fact, if you aren't staying here, you can still have a look during one of the afternoon house tours ($2). Breakfast is an extravaganza that can last all morning and will certainly make you consider skipping lunch. Have no doubt; this B&B is all about being pampered amid Victorian elegance.

744 Clay St., Port Townsend, WA 98368. © 800/321-0644 or 360/385-3205. Fax 360/385-2976. www.starrett mansion.com. 11 units. $105–$225 double. Rates include full breakfast. AE, DISC, MC, V. *In room:* No phone.

F. W. Hastings House/Old Consulate Inn ★★   Though not quite as elaborate as the Starrett Mansion, the Old Consulate Inn is another example of the Victorian excess so wonderfully appealing today. The attention to detail and quality craftsmanship both in the construction and the restoration of this elegant mansion are evident wherever you look. Despite its heritage, however, the Old Consulate avoids being a museum; it's a comfortable, yet elegant, place to stay. If you're here for a special occasion, consider splurging on one of the turret suites. Of the other rooms, our favorite is the Parkside. For entertainment, you'll find a grand piano, a billiards table, and a VCR, as well as stunning views out most of the windows. A multicourse breakfast is meant to be lingered over, so don't make any early morning appointments. Afternoon tea, evening cordials, and a hot tub add to the experience.

313 Walker St., Port Townsend, WA 98368. © 800/300-6753 or 360/385-6753. Fax 360/385-2097. www. oldconsulateinn.com. 8 units. $99–$160 double; $175.50–$210 suite. Rates include full breakfast. MC, V. **Amenities:** Jacuzzi. *In room:* Hair dryer, no phone.

Manresa Castle ★★ *Value*   Built in 1892 by a wealthy baker, this reproduction of a medieval castle later became a Jesuit retreat and school. Today traditional elegance pervades Manresa Castle, and of all the hotels and B&Bs in Port Townsend, this castle offers the most historic elegance for the money. The guest rooms have a genuine, vintage appeal that manages to avoid the contrived feeling that so often sneaks into the room decor of B&Bs. The best deal in the hotel is the tower suite during the off season. For $135 a night you get a huge room with sweeping views from its circular seating area. An elegant lounge and dining room further add to the Grand Hotel feel of this unusual accommodation.

Seventh and Sheridan sts. (P.O. Box 564), Port Townsend, WA 98368. © 800/732-1281 or 360/385-5750. Fax 360/385-5883. www.manresacastle.com. 40 units. Summer, $85–$100 double; $105–$175 suite. Lower rates mid-Oct to Apr. Rates include continental breakfast. DISC, MC, V. **Amenities:** Restaurant (Continental/International); lounge. *In room:* TV.

WHERE TO DINE

One place on nearly everyone's itinerary during a visit to Port Townsend is **Elevated Ice Cream,** 627 Water St. (© **360/385-1156**), which is open daily and scoops up the best ice cream in town. For espresso, drop by **Tyler Street Coffee House,** 215 Tyler St. (© **360/379-4185**). For tea instead of coffee, check out **Wild Sage,** 227 Adams St. (© **360/379-1222**). For pastries, light meals, and good coffee, try **Bread & Roses Bakery,** 230 Quincy St. (© **360/385-1044**).

The Belmont ★ NORTHWEST   With so much water around, the most surprising thing about dining in Port Townsend is that there are so few waterfront restaurants. This, the best of them, is also the oldest waterfront restaurant and hotel in town, dating back to 1889. While the interior doesn't really conjure up the 1890s, the view out the back, especially from the small deck, is great. The menu delves into interesting flavor combinations and draws on a lot of influences (chicken with a pistachio and raspberry-bacon vinaigrette; grilled prawns with a citrus Grand Marnier sauce and cranberries; baby-back pork ribs baked in ale, brown sugar, and barbecue sauce).

925 Water St. © 360/385-3007. www.the-belmont.com. Reservations recommended. Main courses $9–$25. AE, DC, DISC, MC, V. Daily 11:30am–8:30 or 9pm (shorter hours in winter).

The Fountain Café ★ *Finds* ECLECTIC   Housed in a narrow clapboard building, this funky little place is smaller and even more casual than the Silverwater Café, below. Eclectic furnishings decorate the room and there are a few stools at the counter. The menu changes seasonally, but you can rest assured that the simple fare here will be utterly fresh and that the menu will include plenty of shellfish and pasta. The Greek pasta is a mainstay that's hard to beat. The wide range of flavors here assures that everyone will find something to his or her liking. This is a local and counterculture favorite.

920 Washington St. ✆ **360/385-1364**. Reservations not accepted. Main courses $6.50–$15. MC, V. Mon–Thurs 11am–3pm and 5–9pm, Fri 11am–3pm and 5–9:30pm, Sat 8am–3pm and 5–9:30pm, Sun 8am–3pm and 5–9pm.

Khu Larb Thai ⚘ THAI Located half a block off busy Water Street, Khu Larb seems a world removed from Port Townsend's sometimes-overdone Victorian decor. Thai easy-listening music plays on the stereo, and the pungent fragrance of Thai spices wafts through the dining room. One taste of any dish on the menu and you'll be convinced that this is great Thai food. The *tom kha gai*, a sour-and-spicy soup with a coconut-milk base, is particularly memorable. The curry dishes made with mussels are also good bets.

225 Adams St. ✆ **360/385-5023**. Reservations not accepted. Main courses $7.50–$9. MC, V. Sun–Thurs 11am–9pm, Fri–Sat 11am–10pm.

Lonny's Restaurant ⚘⚘ ITALIAN/NORTHWEST Located across the street from the Boat Haven marina south of downtown Port Townsend, this romantic, low-key place is a welcome alternative to the touristy restaurants downtown. The menu is fairly long and always features plenty of daily specials. Whether you come for lunch or dinner, be sure to start with the oyster stew, which is made with pancetta and fennel. At both lunch and dinner, you'll find a wide variety of interesting pasta dishes from which to choose, but the rigatoni Gorgonzola is our favorite. Traditional Spanish paella is another tasty dish. Local oysters, mussels, and clams show up frequently on the fresh sheet and are hard to resist. Interesting wines are usually available by the glass.

2330 Washington St. ✆ **360/385-0700**. www.lonnys.com. Reservations recommended. Main courses $7.50–$11 at lunch, $12–$22 at dinner. AE, DISC, MC, V. Mon–Fri 11:30am–2pm and 5–9pm, Sat–Sun 5–9pm (no lunch served in summer, no dinner served Tues Oct–June).

Silverwater Café ⚘⚘ *(Value)* NORTHWEST Works by local artists, lots of plants, and New Age music on the stereo set the tone for this casually chic restaurant. Though the menu focuses on Northwest dishes, it includes preparations from around the world. You can start your meal with an artichoke-and-Parmesan paté and then move on to ahi tuna with lavender pepper, prawns with cilantro-ginger-lime butter, or smoked chicken with brandy and apples. The oysters in a blue cheese sauce are a favorite of ours. If you're a vegetarian, you'll find a half-dozen options.

237 Taylor St. ✆ **360/385-6448**. www.silverwatercafe.com. Reservations accepted only for 6 or more. Main courses $5.50–$9.50 at lunch, $10–$18 at dinner. MC, V. Daily 11:30am–10pm (shorter hours in winter).

3 Olympic National Park & Environs

The Olympic Peninsula, located in the extreme northwestern corner of Washington and home to Olympic National Park, is a rugged and remote region that was one of the last places in the continental United States to be explored. For decades its nearly impenetrable rain-soaked forests and steep, glacier-carved mountains effectively restricted settlement of the peninsula's coastal regions.

Though much of the Olympic Peninsula was designated a National Forest Preserve in 1897, and in 1909 became a national monument, it was not until 1938 that the heart of the peninsula—the jagged, snowcapped Olympic Mountains—became Olympic National Park. This region was originally preserved in order to protect the area's rapidly dwindling herds of Roosevelt elk, which are named for Pres. Theodore Roosevelt (who was responsible for the area becoming a national monument). At the time, these elk herds were being decimated by commercial hunters.

Today, however, Olympic National Park, which is roughly the size of Rhode Island, is far more than an elk reserve. It is recognized as one of the world's most important wild ecosystems. The park is unique in the contiguous United States for its temperate rainforests, which are found in the west-facing valleys of the Hoh, Queets, Bogachiel, Clearwater, and Quinault rivers. In these valleys, rainfall can exceed 150 inches per year, trees (Sitka spruce, western red cedar, Douglas fir, and western hemlock) grow nearly 300 feet tall, and mosses enshroud the limbs of big-leaf maples.

Within a few short miles of the park's rainforests, the Olympic Mountains rise to the 7,965-foot peak of Mount Olympus and an alpine zone where no trees grow at all. Together, elevation and heavy snowfall (the rain of lower elevations is replaced by snow at higher elevations) combine to form 60 glaciers within the park. It is these glaciers that have carved the Olympic Mountains into the jagged peaks that mesmerize visitors and beckon to hikers and climbers. Rugged and spectacular sections of the coast have also been preserved as part of the national park, and the offshore waters are designated the Olympic Coast National Marine Sanctuary.

With fewer than a dozen roads, none of which leads more than a few miles into the park, Olympic National Park is for the most part inaccessible to the casual visitor. Only two roads penetrate the high country, and only one of these is paved. Likewise, only two paved roads lead into the park's famed rainforests. Although a long stretch of beach within the national park is paralleled by U.S. 101, the park's most spectacular beaches can only be reached on foot.

The park may be inaccessible to cars, but it is a wonderland for hikers and back-packers. Its rugged beaches, rainforest valleys, alpine meadows, and mountaintop glaciers offer an amazing variety of hiking and backpacking opportunities. For alpine hikes, there are the trail heads at Hurricane Ridge and Deer Park. To experience the rainforest in all its drippy glory, you can take to the trails of the Bogachiel, Hoh, Queets, and Quinault valleys. Of these rainforest trails, the Hoh Valley has the more accessible (and consequently more popular) trails, including the trail head for the multiday hike to the summit of Mount Olympus. Favorite coastal hikes include the stretch of coast between La Push and Oil City and from Rialto Beach north to Lake Ozette and onward to Shi Shi Beach.

VISITOR INFORMATION

For more information on the national park, contact the **Olympic National Park,** 600 E. Park Ave., Port Angeles, WA 98362-6798 (© **360/565-3131** or 360/565-3130; www.nps.gov/olym). For more information on Port Angeles and the rest of the northern Olympic Peninsula, contact the **North Olympic Peninsula Visitor and Convention Bureau,** 338 W. First St. (P.O. Box 670), Port Angeles, WA 98362 (© **800/942-4042** or 360/452-8552; www.olympicpeninsula.org); or the **Port Angeles Visitors Center,** 121 E. Railroad Ave., Port Angeles, WA 98362 (© **877/456-8372** or 360/452-2363; www.cityofpa.com). Park admission is $10 per vehicle and $5 per pedestrian or cyclist.

GETTING THERE

U.S. 101 circles Olympic National Park, with main park entrances south of Port Angeles, at Lake Crescent, and at the Hoh River south of Forks.

Horizon Air (© 800/547-9308; www.horizonair.com) flies between Seattle–Tacoma International Airport and Port Angeles. Rental cars are available in Port Angeles from Budget Rent-A-Car.

Two **ferries,** one for foot passengers only and the other for vehicles and foot passengers, connect Port Angeles and Victoria, British Columbia. The ferry terminal for both ferries is at the corner of Laurel Street and Railroad Avenue. **Victoria Express** (© 800/633-1589; www.victoriaexpress.com) is the faster of the two ferries (1 hr. between Victoria and Port Angeles) and carries foot passengers only. This ferry runs only between Memorial Day weekend and the end of September. One-way fares are $12.50 for adults, $7.50 for children 5 to 11, and free for children under 5. The **Black Ball Transport** (© 360/457-4491 or 250/386-2202 in Victoria; www.cohoferry.com) ferry operates year-round except 2 weeks in late January or early February and carries vehicles as well as walk-on passengers. The crossing takes slightly more than 1½ hours. The one-way fares are $8 for adults, $4 for children 5 to 11; $31 for a car, van, camper, or motor home and driver. *Note:* Black Ball Transport does not accept personal checks or credit/charge cards.

EXPLORING THE PARK'S NORTH SIDE

The northern portions of Olympic National Park are the most accessible and most heavily visited areas of the park. It is here, south of Port Angeles, that the only two roads leading into the high country of the national park are found. Of

 Lose the Crowds: Hiking Olympic Peninsula East

South of Port Townsend, U.S. 101 follows the west shore of Hood Canal. Off this highway are several dead-end roads that lead to trail heads in Olympic National Forest. These trail heads are the starting points for many of the best day hikes on the Olympic Peninsula and lead into several different wilderness areas, as well as into Olympic National Park. Many of these hikes lead to the summits of mountains with astounding views across the Olympic Mountains and Puget Sound. Because this part of the peninsula is off the regular tourist route, these trails are far less crowded than trails at Hurricane Ridge or the Hoh Valley.

Two miles south of Quilcene, you'll find Penny Creek/Big Quilcene River Road, which leads to the trail heads for both **Marmot Pass** and **Mount Townsend**—two of the best day-hike destinations on the peninsula. Both of these trails are between 10- and 11-mile round-trip hikes. Up the Dosewallips River Road west of Brinnon, you'll find the trail head for the very popular 4-mile round-trip hike to **Lake Constance.** Up the Hamma Hamma River Road, just north of Eldon, is the trail head for the hike to the beautiful **Lena Lakes** area. West of Hoodsport are popular **Lake Cushman** and the trail heads for the 2-mile round-trip hike along the scenic **Staircase Trail,** the 4½ -mile round-trip hike to the summit of **Mount Ellinor,** and the 16-mile round-trip hike to the **Flapjack Lakes,** which are a very popular overnight destination. For information contact **Quilcene Ranger Station,** 295142 U.S. 101 S. (P.O. Box 280), Quilcene, WA 98376 (© 360/765-2200).

these, the Hurricane Ridge area is the more easily reached. The Deer Park area is at the end of a harrowing gravel road and thus is little visited. West of Port Angeles and within the national park lie two large lakes, Lake Crescent and Lake Ozette, that attract boaters and anglers. Also in this region are two hot springs—the developed Sol Duc Resort and the natural Olympic Hot Springs.

Outside the park boundaries, along the northern coast of the peninsula, are several campgrounds, and a couple of small sportfishing ports, Sekiu and Neah Bay, that are also popular with scuba divers. Neah Bay, which is on the Makah Indian Reservation, is the site of one of the most interesting culture and history museums in the state. This reservation encompasses Cape Flattery, the north-westernmost point in the contiguous United States. Along the coastline between Port Angeles and Neah Bay are several spots popular with sea kayakers.

Port Angeles, primarily a lumber-shipping port, is the largest town on the north Olympic Peninsula and serves both as a base for people exploring the national park and as a port for ferries crossing the Strait of Juan de Fuca to Victoria, British Columbia. It is here that you will find the region's greatest concentration of lodgings and restaurants.

Port Angeles is also home to the national park headquarters, and it's here that you'll find the **Olympic National Park Visitor Center,** 3002 Mount Angeles Rd. (© **360/565-3130**). In addition to having lots of information, maps, and books about the park, the center has exhibits on the park's flora and fauna, old-growth forests, and whaling by local Native Americans. It's open daily from 8:30am to 5:30pm in summer (shorter hours fall through spring). This visitor center is on the south edge of town.

HURRICANE RIDGE

From the main visitor center, continue another 17 miles up Mount Angeles Road to Hurricane Ridge, which on clear days offers the most breathtaking views in the park. In summer the surrounding subalpine meadows are carpeted with wildflowers. Several hiking trails lead into the park from here, and several day hikes are possible (the 3-mile **Hurricane Hill Trail** and the 1-mile **Meadow Loop Trail** are the most scenic). At the **Hurricane Lodge** visitor center (© **360/565-3130**), you can learn about the area's fragile alpine environment. In winter, Hurricane Ridge is a popular cross-country skiing area and also has two rope tows and a Poma lift for downhill skiing. However, because the ski area is so small and the conditions so unpredictable, this ski area is used almost exclusively by local families. For more information, contact **Hurricane Ridge Public Development Authority** (© **360/ 457-4519** or 360/565-3131 for road conditions; www.hurricaneridge.net). The Hurricane Ridge Visitor Center has exhibits on alpine plants and wildlife. In summer, you're likely to see deer grazing in the meadows and marmots, relatives of squirrels, lounging on rocks or nibbling on flowers.

DEER PARK

A few miles east of Port Angeles, another road heads south into the park to an area called **Deer Park.** This narrow, winding gravel road is a real test of nerves and consequently is not nearly as popular as the road to Hurricane Ridge. However, the scenery once you reach the end of the road is just as breathtaking as that from Hurricane Ridge. As the name implies, deer are common in this area. To reach this area, turn south at the Deer Park movie theater.

OLYMPIC HOT SPRINGS

West of Port Angeles a few miles, up the Elwha River, you'll find the short trail (actually an abandoned road) that leads to **Olympic Hot Springs.** These natural hot pools are in a forest setting and are extremely popular and often crowded, especially on weekends. For more developed hot springs soaking, head to Sol Duc Resort, west of Lake Crescent.

LAKE CRESCENT

West of Port Angeles on U.S. 101 lies **Lake Crescent,** a glacier-carved lake surrounded by steep forested mountains that give the lake the feel of a fjord. This is one of the most beautiful lakes in the state and has long been a popular destination. Near the east end of the lake, you'll find the **Storm King Ranger Station** (© **360/928-3380**), which is usually open in the summer and at other seasons when a ranger is in the station; and the 1-mile trail to 90-foot-high **Marymere Falls.** From this trail, you can hike the steep 1.7 miles up **Mount Storm King** to a viewpoint overlooking Lake Crescent (climbing above the viewpoint is not recommended). On the north side of the lake, the **Spruce Railroad Trail** parallels the shore of the lake, crosses a picturesque little bridge, and is one of the only trails in the park open to mountain bikes. As the name implies, this was once the route of the railroad built to haul spruce out of these forests during World War I. Spruce was the ideal wood for building biplanes because of its strength and light weight. By the time the railroad was completed, however, the war was over and the demand for spruce had dwindled.

You can rent various types of small boats during the warmer months at several places on the lake. At **Lake Crescent Lodge** you can rent rowboats, and at the **Fairholm General Store** (© **360/928-3020**), at the lake's west end, kayaks, canoes, rowboats, and motorboats are available between April and October.

SOL DUC HOT SPRINGS

Continuing west from Lake Crescent, watch for the turnoff to **Sol Duc Hot Springs** (© **360/327-3583**). For 14 miles the road follows the Soleduck River, passing the Salmon Cascades along the way. Sol Duc Hot Springs were for centuries considered healing waters by local Indians, and after white settlers arrived in the area, the springs became a popular resort. In addition to the hot swimming pool and soaking tubs, you'll find cabins, a campground, a restaurant, and a snack bar. The springs are open daily from late March to late October; admission is $10 for adults. A 4½-mile loop trail leads from the hot springs to **Sol Duc Falls,** which are among the most photographed falls in the park. Alternatively, you can drive to the end of the Sol Duc Road and make this an easy 1½-mile hike. Along this same road, you can hike the half-mile **Ancient Groves Nature Trail.** Note that Sol Duc Road is one of the roads on which you'll have to pay an Olympic National Park admission fee.

EXPLORING THE PENINSULA'S NORTHWEST CORNER

Continuing west on U.S. 101 from the junction with the road to Sol Duc Hot Springs brings you to the crossroads of Sappho. Heading north at Sappho will bring you to Wash. 112, an alternative route from Port Angeles. It is about 40 miles from this road junction to the northwest tip of the Olympic Peninsula and the town of **Neah Bay** on the Makah Indian Reservation.

Between Clallam Bay and Neah Bay, the road runs right alongside the water, providing opportunities to spot seabirds and marine mammals, including gray, orca, humpback, and pilot whales. Between February and April, keep an eye out for the dozens of bald eagles that gather along this stretch of coast. In Clallam Bay, at the county day-use park, you can hunt for agates and explore tide pools. Near Slip Point Lighthouse, fossil beds are exposed at low tides.

Neah Bay is a busy commercial and sportfishing port, and is also home to the impressive **Makah Museum,** Bayview Avenue (© **360/645-2711;** www.makah.com/museum.htm), which displays artifacts from a Native American village inundated by a mud slide 500 years ago. This is the most perfectly preserved collection of Native American artifacts in the Northwest, and the exhibit includes reproductions of canoes the Makah once used for hunting whales. There's also a longhouse that shows the traditional lifestyle of the Makah people. Between Memorial Day and September 15, the museum is open daily from 10am to 5pm, and between September 16 and Memorial Day, it's open Wednesday through Sunday from 10am to 5pm; admission is $4 for adults, $3 for students and seniors, free for children 5 and under.

CAPE FLATTERY

The Makah Indian Reservation land includes **Cape Flattery,** the northwestern-most point of land in the contiguous United States. Just off the cape lies Tatoosh Island, site of one of the oldest lighthouses in Washington. Cape Flattery is one of the most dramatic stretches of Pacific coastline in the Northwest, and is a popular spot for a bit of hiking and ocean viewing. There is an excellent 1½-mile round-trip trail, complete with boardwalks, stairs, and viewing platforms, that leads out to the cliffs overlooking Tatoosh Island. Keep an eye out for whales and sea otters. Bird-watchers will definitely want to visit Cape Flattery, which is on the Pacific Fly Way. More than 250 species of birds have been spotted here, and in the spring, raptors gather before crossing the Strait of Juan de Fuca. Also be aware that car break-ins are not uncommon here, so take your valuables with you. For directions to the trail head, stop by the Makah Museum. At the museum, you'll also need to purchase a $7 Recreational Use Permit that will allow you to park at the Cape Flattery trail head.

OZETTE LAKE

A turnoff 16 miles east of Neah Bay leads south to **Ozette Lake,** where there are boat ramps, a campground, and, stretching north and south, miles of beaches accessible only on foot. A 3.3-mile trail on a raised boardwalk leads from the Ozette Lake trail head to **Cape Alava,** one of two places claiming to be the westernmost point in the contiguous United States (the other is Cape Blanco, on the Oregon coast). The large rocks just offshore here are known as haystack rocks or seastacks and are common all along the rocky western coast of the Olympic Peninsula, which is characterized by a rugged coastline. Aside from five coastal Indian reservations, almost all this northern coastline is preserved as part of the national park.

A GUIDED TOUR

For an interesting offshore tour to the Olympic Coast National Marine Sanctuary, contact **Puffin Adventures** (© **888/305-2437;** www.puffinadventures.com). These boat tours, which operate between April and September, explore the waters off Cape Flattery and Tatoosh Island, where you can see as many as eight species of pelagic birds, including tufted puffins.

RAINFORESTS & WILD BEACHES: EXPLORING OLYMPIC NATIONAL PARK WEST

The western regions of Olympic National Park can be roughly divided into two sections—the rugged coastal strip and the famous rainforest valleys. Of course, these are the rainiest areas within the park, and many a visitor has called short a

An Olympic Educational Opportunity

Want to get in a bit of learning while you're on vacation? Book a seminar through the **Olympic Park Institute,** 111 Barnes Point Rd., Port Angeles, WA 98363 (© **360/928-3720;** www.yni.org/opi), which is located in the Rosemary Inn on Lake Crescent. The institute offers a wide array of summerfield seminars ranging from painting classes to bird-watching trips to multiday backpacking trips.

vacation here because of rain. Well, what do you expect? It is, after all, a *rainforest.* Come prepared to get wet.

The coastal strip can be divided into three segments. North of La Push, which is on the Quileute Indian Reservation, the 20 miles of shoreline from Rialto Beach to Cape Alava are accessible only on foot. The northern end of this stretch of coast is accessed from Lake Ozette off Wash. 112 in the northwest corner of the peninsula. South of La Push, the park's coastline stretches for 17 miles from Third Beach to the Hoh River mouth and is also accessible only on foot. The third segment of Olympic Park coastline begins at Ruby Beach just south of the Hoh River mouth and the Hoh Indian Reservation and stretches south to South Beach. This stretch of coastline is paralleled by U.S. 101.

Inland of these coastal areas, which are not contiguous with the rest of the park, lie the four rainforest valleys of the Bogachiel, Hoh, Queets, and Quinault rivers. Of these valleys, only the Hoh and Quinault are penetrated by roads, and it is in the Hoh Valley that the rainforests are the primary attraction.

Located just outside the northwest corner of the park, the timber town of Forks serves as the gateway to Olympic National Park's west side. This town was at the heart of the controversy over protecting the northern spotted owl, and is still struggling to recover from the employment bust after the logging boom of the 1980s.

The town of Forks is the largest community in this northwest corner of the Olympic Peninsula and is on U.S. 101, which continues south along the west side of the peninsula to the town of Hoquiam. For more information on the Forks area, contact the **Forks Chamber of Commerce,** 1411 S. Forks Ave. (P.O. Box 1249), Forks, WA 98331 (© **800/44-FORKS** or 360/374-2531; www. forkswa.com).

West of Forks lie miles of pristine beaches and a narrow strip of forest (called the Olympic Coastal Strip) that are part of the national park but that are not connected to the inland, mountainous section. The first place where you can actually drive right to the Pacific Ocean is just west of Forks. At the end of a spur road you come to the Quileute Indian Reservation and the community of **La Push.** Right in town there's a beach at the mouth of the Quillayute River; however, before you reach La Push, you'll see signs for **Third Beach** ⚔⚔ and **Second Beach** ⚔⚔, which are two of the prettiest beaches on the peninsula. Third Beach is a 1½-mile walk and Second Beach is just over half a mile from the trail head. **Rialto Beach** ⚔⚔, just north of La Push, is another beautiful and rugged beach; it's reached from a turnoff east of La Push. From here you can walk north for 24 miles to Cape Alava, although this is also a very popular spot for day hikes. One mile up the beach is a spot called **Hole in the Wall,** where ceaseless wave action has bored a large tunnel through solid rock. On any of these beaches, keep an eye out for bald eagles, seals, and sea lions.

Native American Celebrations

Each year in mid-July, Quileute Days are celebrated in La Push (on the Quileute Indian Reservation) with canoe races, traditional Native American dancing, a salmon bake, and other events. In late August, Makah Days, with similar events, are celebrated in Neah Bay (on the Makah Indian Reservation).

The waters, islands, and rocks offshore from this stretch of coastline are all part of the **Olympic Coast National Marine Sanctuary,** which was designated in 1994 and covers 3,300 square miles. The sanctuary protects habitats for fish, seabirds, and marine mammals. Among the latter are gray, humpback, and orca whales, as well as harbor porpoises, Steller and California sea lions, harbor and elephant seals, and sea otters. For information, contact **Olympic Coast National Marine Sanctuary,** 138 W. First St., Port Angeles, WA 98362 (© **360/ 457-6622**).

HOH RIVER VALLEY

Roughly 8 miles south of Forks is the turnoff for the Hoh River valley. It's 17 miles up this side road to the **Hoh Visitor Center** (© 360/374-6925), campground, and trail heads. This valley receives an average of 140 inches of rain per year (and as much as 190 in.), making it the wettest region in the continental United States. At the visitor center you can learn all about the natural forces that cause this tremendous rainfall. To see the effect of so much rain on the landscape, walk the ¾-mile **Hall of Mosses Trail,** where the trees, primarily Sitka spruce, western red cedar, and western hemlock, tower 200 feet tall. Here you'll see big-leaf maple trees with limbs draped in thick carpets of mosses. If you're up for a longer walk, try the **Spruce Nature Trail.** If you've come with a backpack, there's no better way to see the park and its habitats than by hiking the **Hoh River Trail,** which is 17 miles long and leads to Glacier Meadows and Blue Glacier on the flanks of Mount Olympus. A herd of elk calls the Hoh Valley home and can sometimes be seen along these trails.

Continuing south on U.S. 101, but before crossing the Hoh River, you'll come to a secondary road (Oil City Rd.) that heads west from the Hoh Oxbow campground. From the end of the road it's a hike of less than a mile to a rocky beach at the **mouth of the Hoh River.** You're likely to see sea lions or harbor seals feeding just offshore here, and to the north are several haystack rocks that are nesting sites for numerous seabirds. Primitive camping is permitted on this beach, and from here hikers can continue hiking for 17 miles north along a pristine wilderness of rugged headlands and secluded beaches.

South of the Hoh River off U.S. 101, you can drive to the **world's largest red cedar.** The tree, which stands 178 feet tall and is almost 20 feet in diameter, is about 4 miles off the highway on Nolan Creek Road. Near milepost 170, watch for road N1000 on the east side of U.S. 101 and follow this road to a right fork onto N1100. Then turn right onto road N1112, and right again onto N112.

RUBY BEACH, KALALOCH & QUEETS

U.S. 101 finally reaches the coast at **Ruby Beach.** This beach gets its name from its pink sand, which is comprised of tiny grains of garnet. With its colorful sands, tide pools, sea stacks, and driftwood logs, Ruby Beach is the prettiest of the beaches along this stretch of coast. For another 17 miles or so south of Ruby

Beach, the highway parallels the wave-swept coastline. Along this stretch of highway there are turnoffs for five beaches that have only numbers for names. Beach 6 is a good place to look for whales and sea lions and also to see the effects of erosion on this coast (the trail that used to lead down to the beach has been washed away). At low tide, the northern beaches offer lots of tide pools to be explored. Near the south end of this stretch of road, you'll find Kalaloch Lodge, which has a gas station, and the **Kalaloch Ranger Station** (© **360/962-2283**), which is usually open in the summer and at other seasons when a ranger is in the station.

Shortly beyond Kalaloch the highway turns inland again and passes through the community of **Queets** on the river of the same name. The Queets River valley is another rainy valley, and if you'd like to do a bit of hiking away from the crowds, head up the gravel road to the Queets campground, from which a hiking trail leads up the valley.

QUINAULT LAKE

A long stretch of clear-cuts and tree farms, mostly on the Quinault Indian Reservation, will bring you to **Quinault Lake.** Surrounded by forested mountains, this deep lake is the site of the rustic Lake Quinault Lodge and offers boating and freshwater fishing opportunities, as well as more rainforests to explore on a couple of short trails (there is a total of about 10 miles of trails on the south side of the lake). On the north shore of the lake you'll find one of the peninsula's largest red cedar trees. This is a good area in which to spot Roosevelt elk.

EXPLORING AROUND PORT ANGELES

The **Port Angeles Fine Art Center** ⚐, 1203 E. Lauridsen Blvd. (© **360/457-3532;** www.olympus.net/community/pafac/), hosts changing exhibits of contemporary art. The museum also maintains an unusual sculpture park in the woods surrounding the center. Sculptures within the park are often barely discernible from natural objects and are fascinating. The gallery is open Thursday through Sunday from 11am to 5pm; admission is free. The sculpture park is open daily from dawn to dusk.

If you'd like to get a close-up look at some of the peninsula's aquatic inhabitants, stop by the **Arthur D. Feiro Marine Life Center,** Port Angeles City Pier, 315 N. Lincoln St. (© **360/417-6254;** www.olypen.com/feirolab). In the center's tanks, you may spot a wolf eel or octopus, and there's a touch tank where you can pick up a starfish or sea cucumber. In summer the center is open Tuesday through Sunday from 10am to 6pm; October through Memorial Day, it's open Saturday and Sunday from noon to 4pm. Admission is $2.50 for adults, $1 for seniors and children 6 to 12, and free for children 5 and under.

If you'd like to taste some local wine, stop by **Olympic Cellars Winery,** 255410 U.S. 101 (© **360/452-0160;** www.olympiccellars.com), which has its tasting room in a huge old barn between Sequim and Port Angeles. May through October, the winery is open daily from 11am to 6pm; November through April, it's open Wednesday through Sunday noon to 5:30pm. You can also visit **Black**

Art in the Outback

Also situated in the Forks area are quite a few artists' studios and galleries. You can pick up an **Olympic West Arttrek** guide and map to these studios and galleries at the Forks Chamber of Commerce (see above for address and phone number).

Diamond Winery, 2976 Black Diamond Rd. (© **360/457-0748**), which produces both fruit and grape wines and is open February through December, Thursday through Monday from 10am to 5pm.

OUTDOOR ADVENTURES

BICYCLING If you're interested in exploring the region on a bike, you can rent one at **Sound Bikes & Kayaks,** 120 E. Front St., Port Angeles (© **360/457-1240;** www.soundbikeskayaks.com), which can recommend good rides in the area and also offers bicycle tours. Bikes are $30 per day or $9 per hour.

FISHING The rivers of the Olympic Peninsula are well known for their fighting salmon, steelhead, and trout. In Lakes Crescent and Ozette you can fish for such elusive species as Beardslee and Crescenti trout. No fishing license is necessary to fish for trout on national park rivers and streams or in Lake Crescent or Lake Ozette. However, you will need a state punch card—available wherever fishing licenses are sold—to fish for salmon or steelhead. For more information on freshwater fishing in the park, contact Olympic National Park. Boat rentals are available on Lake Crescent at Fairholm General Store, the Log Cabin Resort, and Lake Crescent Lodge.

If you want to hire a guide to take you out on the rivers to where the big salmon and steelhead are biting, try **Diamond Back Guide Service** (© **360/452-9966;** www.northolympic.com/diamondback/), which charges $225 per day for two people; or **Sol Duc River Lodge Guide Service** (© **866/868-0128** or 360/327-3709; www.solducriverfishing.com), which charges $380 per day for two people, but that rate includes your room, breakfast, and lunch.

If you're more interested in heading out on open water to do a bit of salmon or deep-sea fishing, numerous charter boats operate out of Sekiu and Neah Bay. In the Sekiu/Clallam Bay area, contact **Puffin Adventures** (© **888/305-2437;** www.puffinadventures.com). In Neah Bay, try **King Fisher Charters** (© **888/622-8216;** www.kingfisherenterprises.com). Expect to pay from $100 to $160 per person for a day of fishing.

LLAMA TREKKING If you want to do an overnight trip into the backcountry of the national park but don't want to carry all the gear, consider letting a llama carry your stuff. **Kit's Llamas,** P.O. Box 116, Olalla, WA 98359 (© **253/857-5274;** www.northolympic.com/llamas), offers llama trekking in the Olympic Mountains. Prices, based on a group of six to eight adults, are $35 to $75 per person for day hikes, $75 to $150 per person per day for overnight and multiday trips, with special rates for children. **Deli Llama,** 17045 Llama Lane, Bow, WA 98232 (© **360/757-4212;** www.delillama.com), also does trips of from 4 to 7 days in Olympic National Park ($125–$145 per person per day).

SEA KAYAKING & CANOEING Sea-kayaking trips on nearby Lake Aldwell, at Freshwater Bay, and at Dungeness National Wildlife Refuge are offered by **Olympic Raft & Kayak** (© **888/452-1443** or 360/452-1443; www.raftand kayak.com), which charges between $42 and $99 per person. Sea-kayak rentals are available at **Sound Bikes & Kayaks,** 120 E. Front St., Port Angeles (© **360/457-1240;** www.soundbikeskayaks.com), which charges $12 per hour or $40 per day.

WHALE-WATCHING Puffin Adventures (© **888/305-2437;** www.puffin adventures.com) offers whale-watching and wildlife cruises for $50 per person.

WHITE-WATER RAFTING The steep mountains and plentiful rains of the Olympic Peninsula are the source of some great white-water rafting on the

Elwha and Hoh rivers. Contact **Olympic Raft & Kayak** (© **888/452-1443** or 360/452-1443; www.raftandkayak.com). Rates start at $49 for a 2- to 2½-hour rafting trip.

WHERE TO STAY

In addition to the lodgings listed here, there are numerous campgrounds in or near Olympic National Park. For general information on national park campgrounds, contact **Olympic National Park** (© **360/565-3130**).

The national park's **Heart O' the Hills Campground** (105 campsites), on Hurricane Ridge Road 5 miles south of the Olympic National Park Visitor Center, is the most convenient campground for exploring the Hurricane Ridge area. On Olympic Hot Springs Road up the Elwha River, you'll find **Elwha Campground** (41 campsites) and **Altaire Campground** (30 campsites). The only campground on Lake Crescent is **Fairholm** (87 campsites) at the west end of the lake. The nearby **Sol Duc Campground** (80 campsites), set amid impressive stands of old-growth trees, is adjacent to the Sol Duc Hot Springs. The national park's remote **Ozette Campground** (14 campsites), on the north shore of Lake Ozette, is a good choice for people wanting to day-hike out to the beaches on either side of Cape Alava.

The national park's **Mora Campground** (94 campsites) is on beautiful Rialto Beach at the mouth of the Quillayute River west of Forks. If you want to say you've camped at the wettest campground in the contiguous United States, head for the national park's **Hoh Campground** (89 campsites) in the Hoh River valley. South of the Hoh River, along the only stretch of U.S. 101 right on the beach, you'll find **Kalaloch Campground** (177 campsites), the national park's largest campground.

IN PORT ANGELES

Domaine Madeleine ★★ Located 7 miles east of Port Angeles, this contemporary B&B is set at the back of a small pasture and has a very secluded feel. Big windows take in the views, while inside you'll find lots of Asian antiques and other interesting touches. Combine this with the waterfront setting and you have a fabulous hideaway—you may not even bother exploring the park. All rooms have fireplaces and views of the Strait of Juan de Fuca and the mountains beyond. Some rooms have whirlpool tubs, and some have kitchens or air-conditioning. For added privacy, there is a separate cottage. The guest rooms are in several different buildings surrounded by colorful gardens.

146 Wildflower Lane, Port Angeles, WA 98362. © **888/811-8376** or 360/457-4174. www.domainemadeleine. com. 5 units. $145–$225 double. Rates include full breakfast. 2-night minimum on mid-Apr to mid-Oct and holidays. AE, DISC, MC, V. **Amenities:** Access to nearby health club; massage. *In room:* TV/VCR, dataport, hair dryer, iron.

WEST OF PORT ANGELES

Beyond Port Angeles, accommodations are few and far between, and those places worth recommending tend to be very popular. Try to have room reservations before heading west from Port Angeles.

Lake Crescent Lodge ★★ This historic lodge is located 20 miles west of Port Angeles on the south shore of picturesque Lake Crescent and is the lodging of choice for national park visitors wishing to stay on the north side of the park. Wood paneling, hardwood floors, a stone fireplace, and a sun room make the lobby a popular spot for just sitting and relaxing (especially on rainy days). The guest rooms in this main lodge building are the oldest and have shared bathrooms.

If you'd like more modern accommodations, there are a number of standard motel-style rooms, but these lack the character of the lodge rooms. If you have your family or some friends along, we recommend reserving a cottage. Those with fireplaces are the most comfortable, but the others are nice as well. All but the main lodge rooms have views of either the lake or the mountains. The lodge dining room has a good view across the lake. Early November through mid-April, the lodge is only open on weekends, and only the fireplace and Singer cabins are available. The dining room is not open in winter.

416 Lake Crescent Rd., Port Angeles, WA 98363. ℂ **360/928-3211.** Fax 360/928-3253. www.lakecrescent lodge.com. 52 units (4 with shared bathroom). $43–$83 double without bathroom, $74–$147 double with bathroom; $94–$165 cottage. AE, DISC, MC, V. Pets accepted ($12). **Amenities:** Restaurant (Continental); lounge; water-sports rentals. *In room:* No phone.

Sol Duc Hot Springs Resort ⭐   The Sol Duc Hot Springs have for decades been a popular family vacation spot, with campers, day-trippers, and resort guests spending their days soaking and playing in the hot-water swimming pool. The grounds of the resort are grassy and open, but the forest is kept just at arm's reach. The cabins are done in modern motel style and are comfortable if not spacious. There's a good restaurant here, as well as a poolside deli and grocery store. Three hot spring–fed swimming pools are the focal point, and are open to the public for a small fee.

Sol Duc Rd., U.S. 101 (P.O. Box 2169), Port Angeles, WA 98362. ℂ **360/327-3583.** Fax 360/327-3593. www.northolympic.com/solduc. 32 units. $110–$130 cabin for 2. AE, DISC, MC, V. Closed Nov–Mar. **Amenities:** 2 restaurants (American, deli); outdoor pool; 3 hot springs–fed soaking pools; massage. *In room:* No phone.

IN THE FORKS AREA

The town of Forks has several inexpensive motels and is a good place to look for cheap lodgings if you happen to be out this way without a reservation.

Olympic Suites Inn ⭐   Located just off U.S. 101 at the north end of town and set back in the forest a bit, this modern motel is your best bet in the area if you don't want to stay at a B&B. The motel has the look and feel of an apartment complex, and most of the rooms are suites with full kitchens. The Calawah River and a boat ramp are just downhill from the motel, and some rooms have limited river views. Other rooms look into the forest.

800 Olympic Dr., Forks, WA 98331. ℂ **800/262-3433** or 360/374-5400. Fax 360/374-2528. www.olympic getaways.com/olympicsuites. 32 units. $54–$99 double. AE, DISC, MC, V. **Amenities:** Coin-op laundry. *In room:* TV, fridge, coffeemaker.

ALONG THE PARK'S WEST SIDE, SOUTH OF FORKS

Kalaloch Lodge ⭐⭐   This is the national park's only oceanfront accommodation; the rustic, cedar-shingled lodge and its cluster of cabins perch on a grassy bluff above the thundering Pacific Ocean. Wide sand beaches stretch north and south from the lodge, and at the base of the bluff huge driftwood logs are scattered like so many twigs. The rooms in the old lodge are the least expensive, and the oceanview bluff cabins are the most in demand. The log cabins across the street from the bluff cabins don't have the knockout views. For modern comforts there are motel-like rooms in the Sea Crest House. A casual coffee shop serves breakfast and lunch while a slightly more formal dining room serves rather unmemorable meals. The lodge also has a general store and a gas station. Because the lodge is popular throughout the year, you should make reservations at least 4 months in advance.

157151 U.S. 101, Forks, WA 98331. ℂ **360/962-2271.** Fax 360/962-3391. www.visitkalaloch.com. 64 units. Early June to mid-Oct, $135–$161 double; $244 suite; $174–$258 bluff cabin; $152–$173 log cabin.

Lower rates Sun–Thurs other months. AE, MC, V. Pets accepted in cabins ($12.50 per night). **Amenities:** 2 restaurants (American). *In room:* No phone.

Lake Quinault Lodge ★★ Located on the shore of Lake Quinault in the southwest corner of the park, this imposing grande dame of the Olympic Peninsula wears an ageless tranquility. Huge old firs and cedars shade the rustic lodge, and Adirondack chairs on the deck command a view of the lawn. The accommodations include small rooms in the main lodge, modern rooms with wicker furniture and small balconies, and rooms with fireplaces. The annex rooms are the least attractive, but they do have large bathtubs. The dining room has the most creative menu this side of the peninsula. The lodge offers lawn games and rainforest tours.

345 S. Shore Rd. (P.O. Box 7), Quinault, WA 98575-0007. ✆ **800/562-6672** or 360/288-2900. www.visit lakequinault.com. 92 units. Mid-June to late Sept and winter holidays, $115–$180 double; $250 suite. Late Sept to mid-June $68–$130 double; $195 suite. AE, MC, V. Pets accepted in Boat House building ($10 per night). **Amenities:** Restaurant (Northwest); lounge; indoor swimming pool; sauna; boat rentals; game room; tour desk; massage. *In room:* No phone.

WHERE TO DINE
IN PORT ANGELES
For sandwiches, pastries, and espresso, don't miss **Bonny's Bakery,** 215 S. Lincoln St. (✆ **360/457-3585**), which is housed in an old fire station.

Bella Italia ★ ITALIAN Located in downtown Port Angeles, this restaurant is only a couple of blocks from the ferry terminal for ferries to and from Victoria, which makes it very convenient for many travelers. Dinners start with a basket of delicious bread accompanied by an olive oil, balsamic vinegar, garlic, and herb dipping sauce. Fresh local seafood makes it onto the menu in smoked salmon ravioli, smoked salmon fettuccine, and steamed mussels and clams. There are also some interesting individual pizzas and a good selection of wines, as well as a wine bar, an espresso bar, and plenty of excellent Italian desserts.

118 E. First St. ✆ 360/457-5442. www.bellaitaliapa.com. Main courses $8–$20. AE, DC, DISC, MC, V. Sun–Thurs 4–9pm, Fri–Sat 4–10pm.

C'est Si Bon ★★ FRENCH Located 4 miles south of town just off U.S. 101, C'est Si Bon is painted a striking combination of turquoise, pink, and purple—which gives the restaurant a sort of happy elegance. Inside, the nontraditional paint job gives way to more classic decor: reproductions of European works of art, crystal chandeliers, and old musical instruments used as wall decorations. The restaurant serves deftly prepared Gallic standards such as French onion soup or escargot for starters. Follow that with *coquille Saint Jacques* or a Dungeness crab soufflé, finish with a rich and creamy *mousse au chocolat,* and *voilà!* you have the perfect French meal. Specials feature whatever is fresh.

23 Cedar Park Rd. ✆ 360/452-8888. www.northolympic.com/cestsibon. Reservations recommended. Main courses $22–$33. AE, DISC, MC, V. Tues–Sun 5–11pm.

WEST OF PORT ANGELES
Outside of Port Angeles, the restaurant choices become exceedingly slim. Your best choices are the dining rooms at **Lake Crescent Lodge** (open mid-Apr through early Nov) and the **Log Cabin Resort** (open Apr–Oct), both located on the shores of Lake Crescent. One other dining option on this lake is the **Fairholm General Store & Cafe,** 221121 U.S. 101 (✆ 360/928-3020), which is at the lake's west end and is open between April and October. Although all you'll get here are burgers, sandwiches, and breakfasts, the cafe has a deck with a view of the lake.

Continuing west, you'll find food at the dining room of **Sol Duc Hot Springs Resort** (open Apr–Oct). Way out west, near Ozette Lake, you'll find the **Lost Resort,** Hoko-Ozette Road (© **360/963-2899**), a general store with a deli, espresso, and a tavern serving lots of microbrews (open daily 9am–9pm May–Oct).

In the town of Forks, you'll find several basic diners and family restaurants, but nothing really worth recommending. South of Forks, your best bets are the dining rooms at the **Kalaloch Lodge** and the **Lake Quinault Lodge.** If you happen to be hungry up the Hoh River, don't miss the juicy burgers at the **Hard Rain Cafe,** 5763 Upper Hoh Rd. (© **360/374-9288**).

4 Mount Rainier

Weather forecasting for Seattleites is a simple matter: Either "The Mountain" is out and the weather is good, or it isn't (out or good). "The Mountain" is, of course, Mount Rainier, the 14,410-foot-tall dormant volcano that looms over Seattle on clear days; and though it looks as if it's on the edge of town, it's actually 90 miles southeast of the city.

The mountain and 235,625 acres surrounding it are part of **Mount Rainier National Park,** which was established in 1899 as the fifth U.S. national park. From downtown Seattle, the easiest route to the mountain is via I-5 south to exit 127. Then take Wash. 7 south, which in some 30 miles becomes Wash. 706. The route is well marked. Allow yourself about 2½ hours to reach the park's Paradise area.

EXPLORING THE PARK

You'd be well advised to leave as early in the day as possible, especially if you're heading to the mountain on a summer weekend. Traffic along the route and crowds at the park can be daunting.

Before you leave, contact the park for information: **Mount Rainier National Park,** Tahoma Woods, Star Route, Ashford, WA 98304-9751 (© **360/569-2211,** ext 3314; www.nps.gov/mora). Keep in mind that during the winter only the Henry M. Jackson Memorial Visitor Center at Paradise is open, and then only on weekends and holidays. Park entrances other than the Nisqually entrance are closed by snow throughout the winter.

Mount Rainier National Park admission is $10 per motor vehicle or $5 per person for pedestrians, motorcyclists, and bicyclists.

Just past the **main southwest entrance (Nisqually),** you'll come to Longmire, site of the National Park Inn; the **Longmire Museum** (exhibits on the park's natural and human history); a **hiker information center** that issues backcountry permits; and a **ski-touring center** where you can rent cross-country skis and snowshoes in winter.

The road then climbs to **Paradise** (elevation 5,400 ft.), the aptly named mountainside aerie that affords a breathtaking close-up view of the mountain. Paradise is the park's most popular destination, so expect crowds. During July and August the meadows are ablaze with wildflowers. The circular **Henry M. Jackson Memorial Visitor Center** provides 360° panoramic views, and a short walk away is a spot from which you can look down on Nisqually Glacier. Many miles of other **trails** lead out from Paradise, looping through meadows and up onto snowfields above timberline. It's not unusual to find plenty of snow at Paradise as late as July. In 1972, the area set a world's record for snowfall in 1 year: 93½ feet! This record held until the 1998–99 winter season, during which La Niña climatic conditions produced record-breaking conditions on Mount Baker

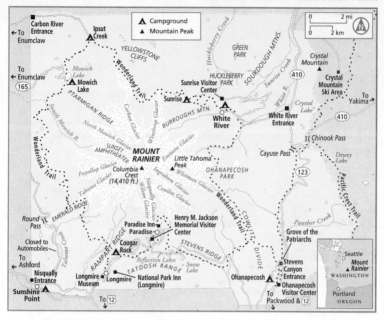

to the north of Mount Rainier. More than 94 feet of snow fell on Mount Baker that season.

In summer, you can continue beyond Paradise to the **Ohanapecosh Visitor Center,** where you can walk through a forest of old-growth trees, some more than 1,000 years old.

Continuing around the mountain, you'll reach the turnoff for **Sunrise.** At 6,400 feet, Sunrise is the highest spot in the park accessible by car, and a beautiful old log lodge serves as the visitor center. From here you can see not only Mount Rainier, seemingly at arm's length, but also Mounts Baker and Adams. Some of the park's most scenic trails begin here at Sunrise. This area is usually less crowded than Paradise.

At both Paradise and Sunrise, hikers can choose from a good variety of outings, from short, flat nature walks to moderately difficult loops to long, steep, out-and-back hikes.

If you want to see a bit of dense forest or hike without crowds, head for the park's **Carbon River entrance** in the northwest corner. Carbon River is formed by the lowest-elevation glacier in the contiguous 48 states. A long day hike in this area provides an opportunity not only to come face to face with the Carbon Glacier but also to enjoy superb alpine scenery. This is the least visited region of the park because it only offers views to those willing to hike several miles uphill. At 3 miles up the main trail, you'll encounter the Carbon Glacier plowing through the middle of the rainforest, and at about 5 miles you reach meadows and in-your-face views of the northwest flank of Mount Rainier. The road into this area is in very bad shape, however, and a high-clearance vehicle is recommended. Be sure to call the park for a road-condition update before heading this way.

If you don't have a car but still want to visit Mount Rainier National Park, book a tour through **Mt. Rainier Tours** (© **888/293-1404** or 206/768-1234;

www.mtrainiertours.com), which charges $64.50 for adults and $49 for children ages 3 to 12 for a 10-hour tour. These tours spend most of that time in transit, but you get to see the mountain up close and even get in a couple of hours of hiking at Paradise.

WHERE TO STAY

Besides the two accommodations listed below, there are several **campgrounds** in Mount Rainier National Park. Two of the park's campgrounds—Cougar and Ohanapecosh—take reservations, and these should be made several months in advance for summer weekends. To make reservations, contact the **National Park Reservation Service** (© 800/365-2267; http://reservations.nps.gov).

National Park Inn ⭐ Located in Longmire, in the southwest corner of the park, this rustic lodge opened in 1920. The inn's front veranda has a view of the mountain, and it is here that guests often gather at sunset on clear days. There's also a lounge with a river-rock fireplace that's the perfect place to relax on a winter's night. Guest rooms vary in size and have rustic furnishings but are definitely not the most memorable part of a stay here. The inn's restaurant manages to have something for everyone, and there are a gift shop and cross-country ski/snowshoe rental shop adjacent to the inn. Because the setting here is not as spectacular as that of the Paradise Inn, this lodge is not nearly as popular, and consequently room reservations are easier to come by. In winter, the National Park Inn is popular with cross-country skiers and snowshoers.

Mount Rainier National Park, Ashford, WA 98304. © 360/569-2275. www.guestservices.com/rainier. 25 units (7 with shared bathroom). $81 double with shared bathroom, $114–$154 double with private bathroom. AE, DC, DISC, MC, V. Free parking. **Amenities:** Restaurant (American); lounge. *In room:* Coffeemaker, hair dryer, no phone.

Paradise Inn ⭐⭐ Built in 1917 high on the flanks of Mount Rainier in an area aptly known as Paradise, this rustic lodge should be your first choice of accommodations in the park (book early). Cedar-shake siding, huge exposed beams, cathedral ceilings, and a gigantic stone fireplace make this the quintessential mountain retreat. Offering breathtaking views of the mountain, the inn is also the starting point for miles of trails that in summer wander through flower-filled meadows. Guest rooms vary in size, but all have rustic hickory furniture. The Sunday brunch in the inn's large dining room is legendary. A snack bar and lounge are dining options.

Mount Rainier National Park, Ashford, WA 98304. © 360/569-2275. www.guestservices.com/rainier. 117 units (33 with shared bathroom). $79 double with shared bathroom, $119–$150 double with private bathroom; $165 suite. AE, DC, DISC, MC, V. Closed early Oct to mid-May. Free parking. **Amenities:** 2 restaurants (American, snack bar); lounge. *In room:* No phone.

5 Ferry Excursions from Seattle

Among Seattle's most popular excursions are ferry trips across Puget Sound to Bainbridge Island (Seattle's quintessential bedroom community) and Bremerton (home of the Naval Shipyards). If your interests run to shopping, small towns, wineries, parks, and gardens, you'll want to head over to Bainbridge Island. If, on the other hand, you're more interested in naval history and antiques and collectibles, you'll want to visit Bremerton. It's also possible to link these two excursions by taking one ferry out and the other ferry back. It's not a long drive between Bainbridge Island and Bremerton (less than 1 hr.), but if you stop often to enjoy the sights, you can certainly have a long day's journey.

BAINBRIDGE ISLAND & POULSBO

Start the trip by taking the **Bainbridge Island ferry** from the Colman Dock ferry terminal at Pier 52 on the Seattle waterfront. For a current sailing schedule, contact **Washington State Ferries** (© 800/84-FERRY or 888/808-7977 in Washington, or 206/464-6400; www.wsdot.wa.gov/ferries/). On board, you can see the Seattle skyline and, on a clear day, Mount Rainier to the southeast and the Olympic Mountains to the west. One-way fares from Seattle to Bainbridge Island (a 35-min. crossing) are $9 ($11.25 mid-May to mid-Oct) for a car and driver, $5.10 for adult car passengers or walk-ons, $2.50 for seniors, and $3.60 for children ages 5 to 18. Car passengers and walk-ons only pay fares on westbound ferries.

Between mid-June and Labor Day weekend, if you'd like to do a little paddling in a sea kayak or canoe, turn left as you get off the ferry and head to Waterfront Park, where you'll find **Bainbridge Island Boat Rentals** (© 206/842-9229), which rents sea kayaks ($20–$30 for 2 hr.) and canoes ($25 for 2 hr.).

With its water views and winding country roads, Bainbridge is a favorite of bicyclists. You can rent from **B. I. Cycle Shop,** 162 Bjune Dr. SE (© 206/842-6413; www.b-i-cycle.com), which is located a block off Winslow Way near the corner of Madison Avenue (in downtown Bainbridge Island/Winslow just a few blocks from the ferry) and charges $5 per hour (2-hr. minimum) or $25 a day for mountain bikes. They can give you a map of the island and outline a good ride for you. This shop also rents bikes right at the ferry landing.

Just up the hill from the Bainbridge Island ferry terminal is the island's main shopping district, where you'll find interesting shops and restaurants. If you'd like to sample some local wines, drop in at the **Bainbridge Island Vineyards and Winery,** 682 Wash. 305 (© 206/842-9463; www.wineryloop.com), which is located half a mile up the hill from the ferry landing and specializes in European-style white wines made from estate-grown grapes. These wines are quite good and are only available here and at a few select restaurants. The winery is open Wednesday through Sunday from noon to 5pm.

Down at the south end of the island, you'll find **Fort Ward State Park** (© 206/842-4041) on the quiet shore of Rich Passage. The park offers picnicking and good bird-watching. Garden enthusiasts will want to call ahead and make a reservation to visit the **Bloedel Reserve** ⋆, 7571 NE Dolphin Dr. (© 206/842-7631), which is 6 miles north of the ferry terminal off Wash. 305 (turn right on Agate Point Rd.). The expansive and elegant grounds are the ideal place for a quiet stroll amid plants from around the world. Admission is $6 for adults and $4 for seniors and children ages 5 to 12. Nearby, at the northern tip of the island, you'll find **Fay Bainbridge State Park** (© 206/842-3931), which offers camping and great views across the sound to the Seattle skyline.

After crossing the Agate Pass Bridge to the mainland of the Kitsap Peninsula, take your first right, and in the village of **Suquamish,** you'll see signs for the grave of Chief Sealth, for whom Seattle was named. Nearby (turn at the Texaco station on the edge of town) you'll find **Old Man House State Park,** which preserves the site of a large Native American longhouse. The Old Man House itself is long gone, but you'll find an informative sign and a small park with picnic tables. From Suquamish, head back to Wash. 305, continue a little farther west, and watch for signs to the **Suquamish Museum,** 15838 Sandy Hook Rd. (© 360/598-3311, ext 422), on the Port Madison Indian Reservation. The museum houses a compelling history of Puget Sound's native people, with lots of historic photos and quotes from tribal elders about growing up in the area. May through

September, the museum is open daily from 10am to 5pm; October through April, it's open Friday through Sunday from 11am to 4pm. Admission is $4 for adults, $3 for seniors, and $2 for children 12 and under.

Continuing north on Wash. 305, you come to the small town of **Poulsbo,** which overlooks fjordlike Liberty Bay. Settled in the late 1880s by Scandinavians, Poulsbo was primarily a fishing, logging, and farming town until it decided to play up its Scandinavian heritage. Shops in the Scandinavian-inspired downtown sell all manner of Viking and Scandinavian souvenirs, but there are also several good art galleries and other interesting shops. Throughout the year there are numerous Scandinavian-theme celebrations. For more information, contact the **Greater Poulsbo Chamber of Commerce,** 19168 Jensen Way NE (P.O. Box 1063), Poulsbo, WA 98370 (*C* **877/768-5726** or 360/779-4848; www.poulsbo.net).

Between downtown and the waterfront, you'll find Liberty Bay Park, and at the south end of Front Street, you'll find the **Poulsbo Marine Science Center,** 18743 Front St. NE (*C* **360/779-5549;** www.poulsbomsc.org), which houses interpretive displays on Puget Sound and is a great place to bring the kids. The center is open daily 11am to 5pm. Admission is $4 for adults, $3 for seniors and teenagers, and $2 for children ages 2 through 12.

If you're interested in seeing Poulsbo from the water, you can rent a sea kayak from **Olympic Outdoor Center,** 18971 Front St. (*C* **360/697-6095;** www.kayak proshop.com), which charges $12 to $17 per hour or $50 to $70 by the day.

If you have time and enjoy visiting historic towns, continue north from Poulsbo on Wash. 3 to **Port Gamble,** which looks like a New England village dropped down in the middle of the Northwest woods. This community was established in 1853 as a company town for the Pope and Talbot lumber mill. Along the town's shady streets are Victorian homes that were restored by Pope and Talbot. Stop by the Port Gamble Country Store, which now houses the **Port Gamble Historical Museum** (*C* **360/297-8074**), a collection of local memorabilia. Admission is $2.50 for adults and $1.50 for seniors and students (children 5 and under are free). From May 1 to October 31, the museum is open daily from 10:30am to 5pm; the rest of the year, it's open by appointment. The same location is home to the **Of Sea and Shore Museum** (*C* **360/297-2426**), which houses an exhibit of seashells from around the world. This museum is open daily from 9am to 5pm, and admission is free.

BREMERTON & ITS NAVAL HISTORY

If your interests run to big ships and naval history, you'll want to ride the ferry from Seattle to Bremerton (see above for information on Washington State Ferries).

Bremerton is home to the Puget Sound Naval Shipyard, where mothballed U.S. Navy ships have included the aircraft carriers USS *Nimitz* and USS *Midway* and the battleships USS *Missouri* and USS *New Jersey.* If you'd like to see the shipyards and mothballed fleet from the water, take a tour with **Kitsap Harbor Tours,** 110 Harrison Ave. (*C* **360/876-1260**). From June through August, tours are offered daily between 11am and 4pm. Tours are $8.50 for adults, $7.50 for seniors, and $5.50 for children ages 5 to 12. This company also offers dinner tours to Tillicum Village (a reproduction Native American longhouse) on Blake Island, which is a state park. The tours, which are offered May through September, include dinner and performances of traditional Native American dances. The cost is $55 for adults, $50 for seniors, $22 for children ages 5 to 12, and free for children 4 and under.

One mothballed destroyer, the USS *Turner Joy,* is now operated by the **Bremerton Historic Ships Association** (© **360/792-2457**) and is open to the public as a memorial to those who have served in the U.S. Navy and who have helped build the navy's ships. The *Turner Joy* is docked about 150 yards east of the Washington State Ferries terminal. From May through September, the ship is open daily from 10am to 5pm; call for hours in other months. Admission is $7 for adults, $6 for seniors and military, and $5 for children ages 5 to 12.

Nearby is the **Bremerton Naval Museum,** 402 Pacific Ave. (© **360/479-7447**), which showcases naval history and the historic contributions of the Puget Sound Naval Shipyard. From Memorial Day to Labor Day, the museum is open Monday through Saturday from 10am to 5pm and Sunday from 1 to 5pm; other months, the museum may be closed on Monday. Admission is by donation.

Heading north from Bremerton on Wash. 3, you'll soon see signs for the **Naval Undersea Museum,** Garnett Way (© **360/396-4148**), which is located 3 miles east of Wash. 3 on Wash. 308 near the town of Keyport. The museum examines all aspects of undersea exploration, with interactive exhibits, models, and displays that include a deep-sea exploration and research craft, a Japanese kamikaze torpedo, and a deep-sea rescue vehicle. The museum is open daily from 10am to 4pm (closed on Tues Oct–May), and admission is free. The reason this museum is here is that the **Bangor Navy Base,** home port for a fleet of Trident nuclear submarines, is nearby. The base is on Hood Canal, a long, narrow arm of Puget Sound.

6 Snoqualmie Falls & the Snoqualmie Valley

One of the reasons so many people put up with Seattle's drawbacks—urban sprawl, congested highways, and high housing prices—is that less than an hour east lie mountains so vast and rugged you can hike for a week without crossing a road. Between the city and this wilderness lie the farmlands of the **Snoqualmie Valley,** the Seattle region's last bit of bucolic countryside. Here you'll find small towns, pastures full of spotted cows, "U-pick" farms, and a few unexpected attractions, including an impressive (and familiar) waterfall and a medieval village. While driving the back roads of the Snoqualmie Valley, keep an eye out for historic markers that include old photos and details of the valley's past.

Snoqualmie Falls ★★, the valley's biggest attraction, plummet 270 feet into a pool of deep blue water. The falls are surrounded by a park owned by Puget Power, which operates a hydroelectric plant inside the rock wall behind the falls. The plant, built in 1898, was the world's first underground electricity-generating facility. Within the park you'll find two overlooks near the lip of the falls and a half-mile trail down to the base of the falls. The river below the falls is popular both for fishing and for white-water kayaking. These falls will be familiar to anyone who remembers the opening sequence of David Lynch's *Twin Peaks,* which was filmed in this area. To reach the falls, take I-90 east from Seattle for 35 to 45 minutes and get off at exit 27. If you're hungry for lunch, try the restaurant at **Salish Lodge,** the hotel at the top of the falls.

Snoqualmie Falls is located just outside the town of **Snoqualmie,** which is where you'll find the restored 1890 railroad depot that houses the **Northwest Railway Museum,** 38625 SE King St. (© **425/888-3030**). The museum, an absolute must for anyone with a child who is familiar with Thomas the Tank Engine, operates the **Snoqualmie Valley Railroad** on weekends April through October. The 65- to 75-minute railway excursions, using steam or diesel trains, run between here and the town of **North Bend.** Fares are $8 for adults, $7 for seniors, and $5 for children ages 3 to 12. Be sure to call ahead for a current schedule. The museum displays railroad memorabilia and has a large display of rolling stock. It's a big hit with kids—and it's free!

Outside of North Bend rises **Mount Si,** one of the most frequently hiked mountains in the state. This mountain, carved by glaciers long ago, presents a dramatic face to the valley, and if you're the least bit athletic, it is hard to resist the temptation to hike to the top. For more information see "Hiking" in chapter 7, "Exploring Seattle."

Between North Bend and the town of **Carnation,** you'll pass several "U-pick" farms, where you can pick your own berries during the summer or pumpkins in the fall.

The Snoqualmie Valley is also the site of **Camlann Medieval Village,** 10320 Kelly Rd. NE (© **425/788-8624;** www.camlann.com), which is located north of Carnation off Wash. 203. On weekends between mid-July and late August, this reproduction medieval village is home to knights and squires and assorted other costumed merrymakers. There are crafts stalls, food booths, and—the highlight each day—jousting matches. Medieval clothing is available for rent if you forgot to pack yours. Throughout the year, there is a wide variety of banquets and seasonal festivals, and the village's Bors Hede restaurant is open Tuesday through Sunday for traditional dinners. Fair admission is $9 for adults, $5 for seniors and children ages 12 and under. Admission to both the fair and a banquet is $39.

On the way to or from Snoqualmie Falls, you may want to pull off I-90 in the town of **Issaquah** (15 miles east of Seattle) for a bit of shopping, wine tasting, and candy sampling. Take exit 17 and, at the bottom of the exit ramp, turn right and then immediately left onto NE Gilman Boulevard. Just a short distance up the road, you'll come to **Hedges Cellars,** 195 NE Gilman Blvd. (© **425/391-6056;** www.hedgescellars.com), which is known for its excellent Cabernet/Merlot blends. The tasting room is open Monday through Saturday from 11am to 5pm. Next door to the winery, you'll find **Boehms Candy Kitchen,** 255 NE Gilman Blvd. (© **425/392-6652**). Housed in a reproduction of a Swiss chalet, the candy shop specializes in chocolate confections, including truffles, chocolate turtles, pecan rolls, and cream-filled chocolates. From Boehms, drive back the way you came (staying on Gilman Blvd. through the intersection that leads to the freeway), and you will come to **Gilman Village,** 317 NW Gilman Blvd. (© **425/392-6802;** www.gilmanvillage.com), an unusual collection of historic buildings that were moved to this site and turned into a shopping center full of interesting little shops.

Also here in Issaquah is the **Issaquah Salmon Hatchery,** 125 Sunset Way (© **425/391-9094**), where throughout the year you can see the different stages of rearing salmon from egg to adult, and in October adult salmon can be seen returning to the hatchery. Each year on the first weekend in October, the city of Issaquah holds a Salmon Days Festival to celebrate the return of the natives.

Here in Issaquah, at the **Cougar Mountain Zoological Park,** 19525 SE 54th St. (© **425/391-5508;** www.cougarmountainzoo.org), you can also see wild animal species that aren't native to Washington. This small zoo focuses on just a few different species, but it has the largest herd of Siberian reindeer in the country. You'll also see large macaws, lemurs, cheetahs, cranes, and, of course, cougars. March through October, the zoo is open Wednesday through Sunday from 10am to 5pm; in November and February, it's open Saturday and Sunday from 10am to 3pm. December and January, it's not open on a regular basis.

Admission is $8.50 for adults, $7 for seniors, $6 for ages 4 to 15, $4.50 for ages 2 and 3, and free for children under age 2.

WHERE TO STAY

Salish Lodge and Spa ✿✿✿   Set at the top of 270-foot Snoqualmie Falls and only 35 minutes east of Seattle on I-90, Salish Lodge is a popular weekend getaway spot for Seattle residents. With its country lodge atmosphere, the Salish aims for casual comfort and hits the mark, though the emphasis is clearly on luxury. Guest rooms, which are designed for romantic weekend getaways, have fireplaces and whirlpool baths, feather beds, and down comforters. To make this an even more attractive getaway, there's a full-service spa. The lodge's country breakfast is a legendary feast that will likely keep you full right through to dinner. By the way, if you were a fan of the TV show *Twin Peaks*, you'll immediately recognize this hotel.

6501 Railroad Ave. SE (P.O. Box 1109), Snoqualmie, WA 98065. ✆ **800/826-6124,** 800/2-SALISH, or 425/888-2556. www.salishlodge.com. 91 units. $199–$389 double; $499–$999 suite (all rates plus $15 resort fee). AE, DISC, MC, V. Valet parking $5. **Amenities:** 2 restaurants (Northwest, Mediterranean); lounge with view of the falls; exercise room; full-service spa with Jacuzzis and saunas; complimentary mountain bikes; activities desk; room service; massage; laundry service; dry cleaning. *In room:* A/C, TV, dataport, minibar, coffeemaker, hair dryer, iron.

7 The Woodinville Wine Country

The state of Washington is the fastest-growing wine region in the country and today produces more wine than any other state except California. Although the main wine country lies hundreds of miles to the east in central and eastern Washington, a small winery region is but a 30-minute drive north of Seattle outside the town of Woodinville. In the Woodinville area, five wineries are open to the public on a regular basis (several others are open only by appointment or not open to the public at all). Five wineries is just about the perfect number for an afternoon of wine tasting, and the proximity to Seattle makes this an excellent day's outing. Woodinville is also home to the Northwest's top restaurant and a gorgeous modern lodge that together with the wineries make this a great place for a romantic getaway.

To reach this miniature wine country, head north on I-5, take the NE 124th Street exit, and drive east to 132nd Avenue NE. Turn left here and continue north to NE 143rd Place/NE 145th Street. Turn right and drive down the hill. At the bottom of the hill, you will be facing the first of the area's wineries.

The **Columbia Winery,** 14030 NE 145th St., Woodinville (✆ **800/488-2347** or 425/488-2776; www.columbiawinery.com), has Washington's largest wine-tasting bar and produces a wide range of good wines (open daily 10am–7pm). This winery tends to be crowded on weekends, so try to arrive early.

Directly across NE 145th Street from the Columbia Winery, you'll find the largest and most famous of the wineries in the area, **Chateau Ste. Michelle** ✿, 14111 NE 145th St., Woodinville (✆ **425/488-1133;** www.ste-michelle.com). Open daily 10am to 4:30pm, this is by far the most beautiful winery in the Northwest, located in a grand mansion on a historic 1912 estate. It's also the largest winery in the state, and is known for its consistent quality. If you take a free tour of the winery, you can sample several of the winery's less expensive wines. For a $5 tasting fee, you can sample some older reserve wines. Because this winery is so big and produces so many different wines, you never know what you might find being poured in the tasting room. An amphitheater on the grounds stages big-name music performances throughout the summer.

If you drive north from Chateau Ste. Michelle, NE 145th Street becomes Woodinville-Redmond Road (Wash. 202) and you soon come to **Silver Lake Winery,** 15029 Woodinville-Redmond Rd. NE, Woodinville (© **425/486-1900;** www.silverlakewinery.com). This winery crafts good reds but can be hit-or-miss. It's open April through December daily noon to 5pm, and January through March Wednesday to Sunday noon to 5pm. Next up the road heading north is a hidden gem, the small **Facelli Winery,** 16120 Woodinville-Redmond NE (© **425/ 488-1020;** www.facelliwinery.com), which is open Saturday and Sunday noon to 4pm and produces some excellent red wines. Continue a little farther to get to **DiStefano Winery,** 12280 Woodinville Dr. NE (© **425/487-1648;** www. distefanowinery.com), which is best known for it full-bodied red wines but also produces some memorable whites. The tasting room is open Saturday and Sunday from noon to 5pm.

Just because this is wine country doesn't mean you can't get a good pint of beer in the area. The large **Redhook Ale Brewery,** 14300 NE 145th St., Woodinville (© **425/483-3232**), next door to Columbia Winery, is one of Washington's top breweries. Tours are available and there's a pub as well. In the summer, outdoor movies are shown here some nights.

If you're up this way on a Saturday between April and October, be sure to stop by the **Woodinville Farmers Market** (© **425/485-1042;** www.woodfarmers market.com) in downtown Woodinville (a few miles north of the wineries). The market is open 9am to 4pm.

WHERE TO STAY

Willows Lodge ★★★ *(Finds)*   From the moment you turn in to the lodge's parking lot, you'll recognize this as someplace special. Located on the banks of the Sammamish River (actually little more than a shallow canal) about 30 minutes north of Seattle and adjacent to the much-celebrated Herbfarm restaurant (see below), this lodge is a beautiful blend of rustic and contemporary. A huge fire-darkened tree stump is set like a sculpture outside the front door, and the landscaping has a distinctly Northwest feel.

Inside, the abundance of polished woods (some salvaged from an old building in Portland) gives the lodge something of a Japanese aesthetic. It's all very soothing and tranquil, an ideal retreat from which to visit the nearby wineries. In the guest rooms, you'll find beds with lamb's wool mattress pads, European linens, and down duvets; slate tables made from salvaged pool tables; and all kinds of high-tech amenities (including digital shower thermostats).

14580 NE 145th St., Woodinville, WA 98072. © **877/424-3930** or 425/424-3900. Fax 425/424-2585. www. willowslodge.com. 88 units. $260–$320 double; $375–$750 suite. Rates include continental breakfast. AE, DC, DISC, MC, V. Pets accepted ($200 refundable deposit). **Amenities:** Restaurant (Northwest); lounge; exercise room; full-service spa; Jacuzzi; sauna; bike rentals; room service; massage; laundry service; dry cleaning. *In room:* A/C, TV, dataport, minibar, fridge, coffeemaker, hair dryer, iron, safe.

WHERE TO DINE

If you aren't out this way specifically to have dinner at the Herbfarm and just want a decent meal while you tour the area, try the **Forecaster's Public House** at the Redhook Ale Brewery, 14300 NE 145th St., Woodinville (© **425/483-3232**). Other good area choices include the dining rooms at the Salish Lodge and Willows Lodge (see above).

The Herbfarm Restaurant ★★★ NORTHWEST   The Herbfarm, the most highly acclaimed restaurant in the Northwest, is known across the nation for its extraordinarily lavish meals. The menu changes throughout the year, with themes to match the seasons. Wild gathered vegetables, Northwest seafood and meats, organic vegetables, wild mushrooms and, of course, the generous use of fresh herbs from the Herbfarm gardens are the ingredients from which the restaurant's chef, Jerry Traunfeld, creates his culinary extravaganzas. Dinners are paired with complementary Northwest wines (and occasionally something particularly remarkable from Europe).

So what's dinner here like? Well to start with, the restaurant is housed in a reproduction country inn beside a contemporary Northwest-style lodge. Highlights of a recent spring forager's dinner included a paddlefish caviar tart; nettle, green garlic, and lovage soup; fiddlehead ferns and black morel served with an unusual risotto; Douglas fir sorbet; coriander-crusted loin of lamb; cured foie gras; and, for dessert, maple-blossom crème brûlée and sweet cicely–and-currant ice cream. Sure it's expensive, but if you're a foodie, you need to do something like this at least once in your life.

The Herbfarm's dinners are so incredibly popular that reservations are taken only a couple of times each year, so you'll have to plan far in advance if you want to be sure of an Herbfarm experience. You can try calling on short notice, however; cancellations often open up tables.

14590 NE 145th St., Woodinville. ✆ 206/784-2222. www.theherbfarm.com. Reservations required. Fixed-price 9-course dinner $149–$179 per person with 5 or 6 matched wines ($50 per-person deposit required). AE, MC, V. Seatings Thurs–Sat at 7pm, Sun 4:30pm.

8 Kirkland: Art Galleries on Lake Washington

The city of **Kirkland,** located on the northeast shores of Lake Washington, is one of Seattle's Eastside bedroom communities, but it is also the Seattle area's main art gallery district. Not only are galleries packed into downtown Kirkland, but the city is full of public art—more than 40 sculptures have been installed in parks and on sidewalks in the downtown Kirkland area. A string of parks stretches south from downtown Kirkland along Lake Washington's Moss Bay waterfront. In summer, the green lawns of the parks and the cool waters of the lake are magnets for swimmers and sunbathers. Even if you forgot your bathing suit, you can stroll along the waterfront and stop in at interesting shops and any of more than a dozen art galleries. There are also several decent restaurants in the area. For restaurant recommendations, see "The Eastside (Including Bellevue & Kirkland)" in chapter 6, "Where to Dine in Seattle."

To reach Kirkland, take Wash. 520 or I-90 (both of which cross Lake Washington on floating bridges) to I-405 north to the NE 85th Street exit, and drive west.

Several of the Kirkland art galleries are affiliated with galleries in Seattle's Pioneer Square area, so don't be surprised if you run across works by some of the same artists you saw in Seattle galleries. Among our favorite Kirkland galleries are **Foster/White Gallery,** 126 Central Way (✆ **425/822-2305;** www.fosterwhite.com); **Patricia Rovzar Gallery,** 118 Central Way (✆ **425/889-4627;** www.rovzargallery.com); **Thomas R. Riley Galleries,** 16 Central Way (✆ **425/576-0762;** www.rileygalleries.com); and **Atelier 31,** 122 Central Way (✆ **425/576-1477;** www.atelier31.com). Also here in town, you can visit the **Kirkland Arts Center,** 620 Market St. (✆ **425/822-7161;** www.kirklandartscenter.org).

If you want to see the area from a different perspective, take a boat tour around Lake Washington with **Argosy Cruises** ⚓ (✆ **800/642-7816** or 206/623-4252; www.argosycruises.com). This company's 1½-hour cruise leaves from downtown Kirkland and will take you past the fabled Xanadu built by Microsoft's Bill Gates on the shores of Lake Washington. Cruises cost $20.25 to $24 adults and $8 to $9 for children ages 5 to 12.

9 Snohomish: Antiques Capital of the Northwest

If antiques are your passion, you won't want to miss the opportunity to spend a day shopping the many antiques stores in the historic farm town of Snohomish. Located roughly 30 miles north of Seattle off I-5, Snohomish was established in 1859 on the banks of the Snohomish River and was the county seat until 1897. When the county government was moved to Everett, Snohomish lost its regional importance and development slowed considerably. Today, an abundance of turn-of-the-century buildings are the legacy of the town's early economic growth. By the 1960s these old homes had begun attracting people interested in restoring them to their original condition, and soon antiques shops began proliferating in the historic downtown area. Today the town has more than 450 antiques dealers and is without a doubt the antiques capital of the Northwest. Surrounding the town's commercial core are neighborhoods full of restored Victorian homes. Each year on the third Sunday in September, you can get a peek inside some of the town's most elegant homes on the annual **Historical Society Home Tour.** To find out more, and to pick up a guide to the town's antiques stores and its historic homes, contact the **Snohomish Chamber of Commerce,** Firehouse Center, 127 Ave. A, Snohomish (© **360/568-2526;** www.cityofsnohomish.com).

While in town, you may want to visit the **Blackman House Museum,** 118 Ave. B (© **360/568-5235**), housed in an 1879 Queen Anne Victorian that has been restored and filled with period furnishings. The museum is open Thursday to Sunday from noon to 4pm, and admission is by donation. For another glimpse into the town's past, head over to **Old Snohomish Village,** a collection of restored cabins and other old buildings at Second Street and Pine Avenue. Each of the buildings is furnished with period antiques. Staffed by volunteers, the Old Snohomish Village is open Thursday through Sunday from noon to 4pm, and admission is by donation.

10 Mount St. Helens National Volcanic Monument

Once it was regarded as the most perfect of the Cascade peaks, a snow-covered cone rising above lush forests, but on May 18, 1980, all that changed. On that day, a massive volcanic eruption blew out the entire north side of Mount St. Helens, laying waste to a vast area and darkening the skies of the Northwest with billowing clouds of ash. Although today the volcano is quiet and life has returned to the once devastated landscape, this volcano and much of the land surrounding it has been designated the Mount St. Helens National Volcanic Monument.

The monument is located roughly 90 miles north of Portland off I-5 (take the Castle Rock exit). Admission to one monument visitor center (or Ape Cave) is $3 ($1 for children 5–15) and to two or more visitor centers (and Ape Cave), is $6 ($2 for children 5–15). If you just want to park at one of the monument's trail heads and go for a hike, all you need is a valid Northwest Forest Pass, which costs $5 per day. If it's winter, you'll need a SnoPark Permit ($8 per day). For more information, contact **Mount St. Helens National Volcanic Monument** (© **360/247-3900;** www.fs.fed.us/gpnf/mshnvm).

Mount St. Helens National Volcanic Monument

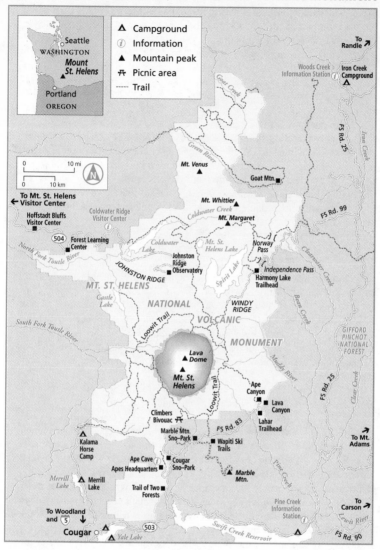

The best place to start an exploration of the monument is the **Mount St. Helens Visitor Center** (© 360/274-2100), which is located at Silver Lake, 5 miles east of Castle Rock on Wash. 504. The visitor center houses extensive exhibits on the eruption and its effects on the region. It's open daily from 9am to 5pm. Before reaching the center, you can stop and watch a 25-minute, 70mm film about the eruption at the **Mount St. Helens Cinedome Theater** (© 877/ ERUPTION or 360/274-9844), which is located at exit 49 off I-5 (tickets $6 adults, $5 seniors and children).

Continuing east from the visitor center, you'll come to the **Hoffstadt Bluffs Visitor Center** (© 360/274-7750; www.mt-st-helens.com) at milepost 27 (open daily 9am–8pm in summer; shorter hours in winter), which has a snack bar and is the takeoff site for 20-minute helicopter flights over Mount St. Helens ($99 with a three-person minimum). A few miles farther, just past milepost 33, is the **Forest Learning Center** (© 360/414-3439), open mid-May through September daily 10am to 6pm and in October daily 10am to 5pm. This is primarily a promotional center for the timber industry but, in a theater designed to resemble an ash-covered landscape, you can watch a short, fascinating video about the eruption. Outside either of these centers you can usually see numerous elk on the floor of the Toutle River valley far below.

The **Coldwater Ridge Visitor Center** (© 360/274-2114), which is at milepost 47 on Wash. 504, only 8 miles from the crater, is the second of the national monument's official visitor centers. This center features interpretive displays on the events leading up to the eruption and the subsequent slow regeneration of life around the volcano. You'll also find a picnic area, interpretive trail, restaurant, and boat launch at Coldwater Lake. The visitor center is open daily from 10am to 6pm.

Of the many visitor centers, none offers a more awe-inspiring view than that from the **Johnston Ridge Observatory** (© 360/274-2140), 10 miles past the Coldwater Ridge Visitor Center. Built into the mountainside and designed to blend into the landscape, this observatory houses the equipment that is still used to monitor activity within Mount St. Helens. The observatory is open daily from 10am to 6pm. If you're up for a bit of hiking, the single best trail on this side of the monument is the Boundary Ridge Trail, which heads east from the Johnston Ridge Observatory, with a jaw-dropping view of the blast zone the entire way. This trail leads for many miles across the monument, so you can hike as much or as little as you want. There is a good turnaround point about 1 mile out from the observatory.

For a different perspective on the devastation wrought by Mount St. Helens's eruption, drive around to the mountain's east side and take the road up to Windy Ridge. Although it takes a couple of hours longer to get to this side of the mountain, you will be rewarded by equally amazing views, better hiking opportunities, and smaller crowds. To reach the east side of the mountain, take U.S. 12 east from exit 68 off I-5. In Randle, head south on Local Route 25. The **Woods Creek Information Station,** on Route 25 just before the junction with Route 26, has information on this part of the monument. South of Woods Creek, watch for Route 99, the road to the **Windy Ridge Viewpoint.** This road crosses many miles of blown-down trees that were felled by a single blast, a reminder of the awesome power of nature. More than 2 decades after the eruption, life is slowly returning to the devastated forest. At the **Windy Ridge Viewpoint,** visitors get one of the best close-up views of the crater. A staircase of 439 stairs climbs 220 feet up the hill above the parking area for even better views. Below Windy Ridge lies Spirit Lake, once one of the most popular summer vacation spots in the Washington Cascades. Today the lake is desolate and lifeless. The 1-mile Harmony Trail leads down to the shore of Spirit Lake and is a very worthwhile hike. Just keep in mind that it is a 600-foot climb back up to the trail head parking lot.

If you are an experienced hiker in good physical condition, consider climbing to the top of Mount St. Helens. From the trail head on the south side of the mountain, the hike takes 8 to 10 hours and can require an ice ax. Permits ($15) are required April through October, and because the climb is very popular, it is advisable to make a reservation (© 360/247-3961). Reservations are taken beginning on February 1, and summer weekends book up fast. However, if you don't have a reservation, you can try your luck by stopping by **Jack's Restaurant and Store** on Wash. 503, 5 miles west of the town of Cougar. Each evening at 6pm this store has a lottery of climbing permits for the next day. Between November 1 and March 31, permits are free and no reservation is necessary, but expect lots of snow.

On the south side of the monument, you can explore the **Ape Cave,** a lava tube that was formed 1,900 years ago when lava poured from the volcano. When the lava finally stopped flowing, it left a 2-mile-long cave that is the longest continuous lava tube in the Western Hemisphere. At Ape Headquarters (open late June through early Sept), you can join a regular ranger-led exploration of the cave or rent a lantern to explore the cave on your own.

Hikers who aren't doing the climb to the summit will find many other hiking trails within the monument, some in blast zones and some in forests that were left undamaged by the eruption. Ask at any visitor center for trail information.

Appendix:
Seattle in Depth

Want to learn more about Seattle? Spend a little time thumbing through this appendix and you'll get to know the city quite a bit better. Although Seattle is not very old even by American standards, it has had an interesting history that has led it to be among the nation's most livable (and visitable) cities.

1 Seattle Past & Present

A LOOK AT SEATTLE'S PAST

Seattle got a late start in U.S. history. Although explorers had visited the region as early as the late 1700s, the first settlers didn't arrive until 1851. Capt. George Vancouver of the British Royal Navy—who lent his name to both Vancouver, British Columbia, and Vancouver, Washington—had explored Puget Sound as early as 1792. However, there was little to attract anyone permanently to this remote region. Unlike Oregon to the south, Washington had little rich farmland, only acres and acres of forest. It was this seemingly endless supply of wood that finally enticed the first settlers.

The region's first settlement was on Alki Point, in the area now known as West Seattle. Because this location was exposed to storms, within a few years the settlers moved across Elliott Bay to a more protected spot, the present downtown Seattle. The new location for the village was a tiny island surrounded by mud flats. Although some early settlers wanted to name the town New York—even then Seattle had grand aspirations—the name Seattle was chosen as a tribute to Chief Sealth, a local Native American who had befriended the newcomers.

In the middle of town, on the waterfront, Henry Yesler built the first steam-powered lumber mill on Puget Sound. It stood at the foot of what is now Yesler Way, which for many years

Dateline

- **1792** Capt. George Vancouver of the British Royal Navy explores Puget Sound.
- **1841** Lt. Charles Wilkes surveys Puget Sound and names it Elliott Bay.
- **1851** The first white settlers arrive in what will become West Seattle's Alki Point.
- **1852** These same settlers move to the east side of Elliott Bay from Alki Point, which is subject to storms.
- **1853** Washington Territory is formed.
- **1864** The transcontinental telegraph reaches Seattle, connecting it with the rest of the country.
- **1866** Chief Sealth, for whom Seattle is named, dies and is buried across Puget Sound at Suquamish.
- **1875** Regular steamship service begins between Seattle and San Francisco.
- **1889** The Great Seattle Fire levels most of downtown.
- **1893** The railroad reaches Seattle.
- **1897** The steamer *Portland* arrives from Alaska carrying more than a ton of gold, thus starting the Yukon gold rush.
- **1907** Pike Place Market is founded.
- **1916** William Boeing launches his first airplane from Lake Union, beginning an industry that will become Seattle's lifeblood.
- **1940** The Mercer Island Floating Bridge opens.
- **1962** The Century 21 exposition is held in Seattle, and the Space Needle is erected.
- **1971** Starbucks Coffee is founded in Seattle.

was referred to as Skid Road, a reference to the way logs were skidded down to the sawmill from the slopes behind town. Over the years Skid Road developed a reputation for its bars and brothels. Some say that after an East Coast journalist incorrectly referred to it as Skid Row in his newspaper, the name stuck and was subsequently applied to derelict neighborhoods all over the country. To this day, despite attempts to revamp the neighborhood, Yesler Way continues to attract the sort of visitors you would expect (due in part to the presence in the neighbor-

■ 1999 Safeco Field, the Seattle Mariners' retractable-roof baseball stadium, opens for business. Riots erupt during meeting of World Trade Organization (WTO).

■ 2000 The Kingdome is demolished to make way for a new football stadium. Experience Music Project opens at Seattle Center.

■ 2001 Riots break out during annual Fat Tuesday celebration. An earthquake damages numerous historic buildings in Pioneer Square area. The Mariners enjoy a record-setting season.

■ 2002 The new Seahawks Stadium is completed on the site of the old Kingdome.

hood of missions and homeless shelters), but it is also in the center of the Pioneer Square Historic District, one of Seattle's main tourist destinations.

By 1889 the city had more than 25,000 inhabitants and was well on its way to becoming the most important city in the Northwest. On June 6 of that year, however, 25 blocks in the center of town burned to the ground. By that time the city, which had spread out to low-lying land reclaimed from the mud flats, had begun experiencing problems with mud and sewage disposal. The fire gave citizens the opportunity they needed to rebuild their town. The solution to the drainage and sewage problems was to regrade the steep slopes to the east of the town and raise the streets above their previous levels. Because the regrading lagged behind the rebuilding, the ground floors of many new buildings eventually wound up below street level. When the new roads and sidewalks were constructed at the level of what had previously been the second floor of most buildings, the old ground-floor stores and businesses moved up into the light of day and the spaces below the sidewalk were left to businesses of shady character. Today sections of this Seattle underground can be toured (see the box titled "Good Times in Bad Taste" in chapter 7, "Exploring Seattle," for details).

Among the most amazing engineering feats that took place after the fire were the regradings of certain cityscapes. Although Seattle once had eight hills, there are now only six—nothing is left of either Denny Hill or Jackson Street Hill. Hydraulic mining techniques, using high-powered water jets to dig into the hillsides, leveled both of these hills. Today the Jackson Street Hill is the flat area to the west of the International District, and Denny Hill, now known as the Denny Regrade, is a flat neighborhood just south of Seattle Center.

Eight years later another event changed the city almost as much as the fire. On July 17, 1897, the steamship *Portland* arrived in Seattle from Alaska carrying a ton of gold from the recently discovered Klondike gold fields. Within the year Seattle's population swelled with prospectors heading north. Few of them ever struck it rich, but they all stopped in Seattle to purchase supplies and equipment, thus lining the pockets of Seattle merchants and spreading far and wide the name of this obscure Northwest city. When the prospectors came south again with their hard-earned gold, much of it never left Seattle, sidetracked by beer halls and brothels.

In 1916, not many years after the Wright brothers made their first flight, Seattle residents William Boeing and Clyde Esterveld launched their first airplane, a floatplane, from the waters of Lake Union. Their intention was to operate an airmail service to Canada. Their enterprise eventually became the Boeing Company, which has since grown to become one of the two largest employers in the area. Unfortunately, until recently Seattle's fortunes were so inextricably bound to those of Boeing that hard times for the aircraft manufacturer meant hard times for the whole city. In recent years, however, industry in the Seattle region has become much more diversified, and the 2001 announcement by Boeing that they would move their headquarters away from Seattle barely caused a stir. Leading the region in its new role as high-tech development center is software giant Microsoft, the presence of which has attracted many other computer-related companies, such as Adobe and Amazon.

The single most recognizable structure on the Seattle skyline is, of course, the Space Needle. Built in 1962 for Century 21, the Seattle World's Fair, the Space Needle was at the time a very futuristic observation tower. Situated just north of downtown in the Seattle Center complex that was the site of the World's Fair, the Space Needle provides stupendous views of the city and all its surrounding natural beauty. Today, the design looks far less 21st century than it once did, and over the 40 years since the Space Needle was erected, the skyline it overlooks has changed radically. At the beginning of the 21st century, the Seattle skyline has become more and more dominated by towering skyscrapers, symbols of Seattle's ever-growing importance as a gateway to the Pacific Rim.

The 1962 World's Fair was far more than a fanciful vision of the future—it was truly prophetic for Seattle. The emergence of this city as a Pacific Rim trading center is a step toward a bright future. The Seattle area has witnessed extraordinary growth in recent years, with the migration of thousands of people in search of jobs, a higher quality of life, and a mild climate. To keep pace with its sudden prominence on the Pacific Rim, Seattle has also been rushing to transform itself from a sleepy Northwest city into a cosmopolitan metropolis. New restaurants, theaters, and museums have been cropping up around the city as new residents demand more cultural attractions.

The bursting of the dot.com bubble, however, hit the city fairly hard, with a lot less disposable income changing hands than only a few years ago. Fewer people seem to be eating out, which is hurting the many high-end restaurants around town. The flip side is that right now it's easy to get last-minute dinner reservations, and many downtown hotels are offering discounted rates even in summer.

SEATTLE TODAY

Seattle is a city in the midst of profound change. The rapid urbanization and upscaling of this once sleepy city can be seen on the bags that downtown shoppers carry. Where once the names were Pendleton, Eddie Bauer, and REI (all Northwest companies), today they are just as likely to be Banana Republic, Pottery Barn, Williams-Sonoma, and even Cartier and Tiffany. Where a decade ago, the downtown area was left to the winos and barflies at night, today people are working and living in the city center. All along First Avenue and Alaskan Way, high-rise water-view condominiums are changing the city's skyline. No longer is the city just a conglomeration of quaint neighborhoods. Today the downtown is an active and vital urban center.

The Sixth Avenue and Pine Street shopping district and the Belltown neighborhood are where the change is most evident, but it isn't limited to these areas. North Seattle's Fremont neighborhood, long a bastion of artistic and hippie aesthetics, is now home to software giant Adobe. Amazon.com claims a hilltop location in South Seattle. The Ballard neighborhood, long a middle-class Scandinavian neighborhood, has taken on a much more contemporary feel and has become one of the city's main nightlife districts.

Seattle proper is a fairly youthful city and nowhere is that more apparent than on the streets of Belltown after the sun goes down. The city's high-tech industry has spawned an entire generation of cellphone-toting hipsters who don their very best basic black outfits whenever they head out for a night on the town. By day, many of these same young Seattleites can be seen driving around with mountain bikes and sea kayaks on the roofs of their Subaru Outbacks. So, when you pack for your visit to Seattle, be sure to pack lots of black clothes, a colorful rain jacket, hiking boots, and high heels.

Positioning itself as a major metropolis has meant thinking big, and to this end, Seattle has been busy adding (and subtracting) large, sometimes controversial structures to its ever-changing cityscape. In 2000, Microsoft cofounder Paul Allen opened his Experience Music Project, a museum of rock and roll that started out as a simple memorial to hometown rocker Jimi Hendrix. The museum building, designed by visionary architect Frank Gehry, is meant to conjure up images of a melted electric guitar and is one of the most bizarre-looking buildings on the planet.

Also in 2000, and also by the hand of Paul Allen, Seattle's venerable and much-disparaged Kingdome came crashing down in a cloud of dust as demolition experts imploded the massive cement structure to make way for a new football stadium for the Seattle Seahawks, the NFL team that happens to be owned by Paul Allen. Allen has also been behind the redevelopment of land that once surrounded the Kingdome, including a renovation of old Union Station.

Not all of the changes around the city are big ones. Upscale restaurants have continued to proliferate in Seattle, though at a slower pace this past year. Belltown is the nexus of this explosion of dining opportunities. Walk along First and Second avenues just north of Pike Place Market and you'll find interesting and pricey restaurants on every block.

However, recent years have not been all good times and grande espressos here in Latte Land. The World Trade Organization riots in 1999 focused the world's attention on Seattle, casting the city in a less-than-flattering light. In 2001, riots broke out again, this time during the city's annual Fat Tuesday celebrations (similar to Mardi Gras). The city was then rocked by a powerful earthquake that left many historic Pioneer Square buildings severely damaged. With the crash of the dot.com economy, Seattle has been particularly hard hit, but so far Microsoft and most of Seattle's largest tech companies have managed to weather the storm.

Traffic congestion continues to be one of the hottest issues in Seattle. A proposed light-rail system, which many people thought was a done deal, may have been derailed in 2002 when the city of Tukwila, south of Seattle, decided it didn't like the routing that the light rail would take within Tukwila's city limits. Likewise, a voter-approved extension of Seattle's famous monorail seems to be stuck in the station as pro-monorail and anti-monorail factions battle over whether or not such a mass transit system would be a blessing or a boondoggle. Until these transit turf wars come to an end, you can expect Seattle traffic to continue getting worse. At least Seattleites know enough to take public transit to sporting events, but that's only because parking near a game can be such a nightmare.

Although for several years now the Seattle Mariners have hogged the sport's limelight here in the Emerald City, 2002 marked a turning point for the NFL's Seattle Seahawks football team. After years of waiting, the team's new stadium was finally completed in 2002. Now if only the new stadium can help turn the Seahawks into a championship team.

Index

See also Accommodations and Restaurant indexes, below.

ACCOMMODATIONS

RESTAURANTS

FROMMER'S® COMPLETE TRAVEL GUIDES

Alaska
Alaska Cruises & Ports of Call
Amsterdam
Argentina & Chile
Arizona
Atlanta
Australia
Austria
Bahamas
Barcelona, Madrid & Seville
Beijing
Belgium, Holland & Luxembourg
Bermuda
Boston
Brazil
British Columbia & the Canadian
    Rockies
Budapest & the Best of Hungary
California
Canada
Cancún, Cozumel & the Yucatán
Cape Cod, Nantucket & Martha's
    Vineyard
Caribbean
Caribbean Cruises & Ports of Call
Caribbean Ports of Call
Carolinas & Georgia
Chicago
China
Colorado
Costa Rica
Denmark
Denver, Boulder & Colorado
    Springs
England
Europe
European Cruises & Ports of Call
Florida

France
Germany
Great Britain
Greece
Greek Islands
Hawaii
Hong Kong
Honolulu, Waikiki & Oahu
Ireland
Israel
Italy
Jamaica
Japan
Las Vegas
London
Los Angeles
Maryland & Delaware
Maui
Mexico
Montana & Wyoming
Montréal & Québec City
Munich & the Bavarian Alps
Nashville & Memphis
Nepal
New England
New Mexico
New Orleans
New York City
New Zealand
Northern Italy
Nova Scotia, New Brunswick &
    Prince Edward Island
Oregon
Paris
Philadelphia & the Amish Country
Portugal
Prague & the Best of the Czech
    Republic

Provence & the Riviera
Puerto Rico
Rome
San Antonio & Austin
San Diego
San Francisco
Santa Fe, Taos & Albuquerque
Scandinavia
Scotland
Seattle & Portland
Shanghai
Singapore & Malaysia
South Africa
South America
South Florida
South Pacific
Southeast Asia
Spain
Sweden
Switzerland
Texas
Thailand
Tokyo
Toronto
Tuscany & Umbria
USA
Utah
Vancouver & Victoria
Vermont, New Hampshire &
    Maine
Vienna & the Danube Valley
Virgin Islands
Virginia
Walt Disney World® & Orlando
Washington, D.C.
Washington State

FROMMER'S® DOLLAR-A-DAY GUIDES

Australia from $50 a Day
California from $70 a Day
Caribbean from $70 a Day
England from $75 a Day
Europe from $70 a Day

Florida from $70 a Day
Hawaii from $80 a Day
Ireland from $60 a Day
Italy from $70 a Day
London from $85 a Day

New York from $90 a Day
Paris from $80 a Day
San Francisco from $70 a Day
Washington, D.C. from $80 a Day

FROMMER'S® PORTABLE GUIDES

Acapulco, Ixtapa & Zihuatanejo
Amsterdam
Aruba
Australia's Great Barrier Reef
Bahamas
Berlin
Big Island of Hawaii
Boston
California Wine Country
Cancún
Charleston & Savannah
Chicago
Disneyland®
Dublin
Florence

Frankfurt
Hong Kong
Houston
Las Vegas
London
Los Angeles
Los Cabos & Baja
Maine Coast
Maui
Miami
New Orleans
New York City
Paris
Phoenix & Scottsdale

Portland
Puerto Rico
Puerto Vallarta, Manzanillo &
    Guadalajara
Rio de Janeiro
San Diego
San Francisco
Seattle
Sydney
Tampa & St. Petersburg
Vancouver
Venice
Virgin Islands
Washington, D.C.

FROMMER'S® NATIONAL PARK GUIDES

Banff & Jasper
Family Vacations in the National
    Parks
Grand Canyon

National Parks of the American
    West
Rocky Mountain

Yellowstone & Grand Teton
Yosemite & Sequoia/ Kings Canyon
Zion & Bryce Canyon

FROMMER'S® MEMORABLE WALKS

Chicago
London

New York
Paris

San Francisco
Washington, D.C.

FROMMER'S® GREAT OUTDOOR GUIDES

Arizona & New Mexico
New England

Northern California
Southern New England

Vermont & New Hampshire

SUZY GERSHMAN'S BORN TO SHOP GUIDES

Born to Shop: France
Born to Shop: Hong Kong,
   Shanghai & Beijing

Born to Shop: Italy
Born to Shop: London

Born to Shop: New York
Born to Shop: Paris

FROMMER'S® IRREVERENT GUIDES

Amsterdam
Boston
Chicago
Las Vegas
London

Los Angeles
Manhattan
New Orleans
Paris
Rome

San Francisco
Seattle & Portland
Vancouver
Walt Disney World®
Washington, D.C.

FROMMER'S® BEST-LOVED DRIVING TOURS

Britain
California
Florida
France

Germany
Ireland
Italy
New England

Northern Italy
Scotland
Spain
Tuscany & Umbria

HANGING OUT™ GUIDES

Hanging Out in England
Hanging Out in Europe

Hanging Out in France
Hanging Out in Ireland

Hanging Out in Italy
Hanging Out in Spain

THE UNOFFICIAL GUIDES®

Bed & Breakfasts and Country
   Inns in:
   California
   Great Lakes States
   Mid-Atlantic
   New England
   Northwest
   Rockies
   Southeast
   Southwest
Best RV & Tent Campgrounds in:
   California & the West
   Florida & the Southeast
   Great Lakes States
   Mid-Atlantic
   Northeast
   Northwest & Central Plains

   Southwest & South Central
      Plains
   U.S.A.
Beyond Disney
Branson, Missouri
California with Kids
Chicago
Cruises
Disneyland®
Florida with Kids
Golf Vacations in the Eastern U.S.
Great Smoky & Blue Ridge Region
Inside Disney
Hawaii
Las Vegas
London

Mid-Atlantic with Kids
Mini Las Vegas
Mini-Mickey
New England and New York with
   Kids
New Orleans
New York City
Paris
San Francisco
Skiing in the West
Southeast with Kids
Walt Disney World®
Walt Disney World® for Grown-ups
Walt Disney World® with Kids
Washington, D.C.
World's Best Diving Vacations

SPECIAL-INTEREST TITLES

Frommer's Adventure Guide to Australia &
   New Zealand
Frommer's Adventure Guide to Central America
Frommer's Adventure Guide to India & Pakistan
Frommer's Adventure Guide to South America
Frommer's Adventure Guide to Southeast Asia
Frommer's Adventure Guide to Southern Africa
Frommer's Britain's Best Bed & Breakfasts and
   Country Inns
Frommer's Caribbean Hideaways
Frommer's Exploring America by RV
Frommer's Fly Safe, Fly Smart
Frommer's France's Best Bed & Breakfasts and
   Country Inns
Frommer's Gay & Lesbian Europe

Frommer's Italy's Best Bed & Breakfasts and
   Country Inns
Frommer's New York City with Kids
Frommer's Ottawa with Kids
Frommer's Road Atlas Britain
Frommer's Road Atlas Europe
Frommer's Road Atlas France
Frommer's Toronto with Kids
Frommer's Vancouver with Kids
Frommer's Washington, D.C., with Kids
Israel Past & Present
The New York Times' Guide to Unforgettable
   Weekends
Places Rated Almanac
Retirement Places Rated

You Need
A Vacation.

700 Airlines, 50,000 Hotels, 50 Rental Car
Companies, And A Million Ways To Save Money.

Travelocity.com
A Sabre Company
Go Virtually Anywhere.